S. S. Hussey was Professor of English
Language and Medieval Literature at the
University of Lancaster from 1973 to
1990. These essays in his honour, by
friends, colleagues and former pupils,
recognise his scholarship and teaching in
medieval English studies, particularly in
those areas reflected by the title:
Langland, the medieval mystics and
religious literature.

For a full list of essays, see the back of
the jacket.

LANGLAND, THE MYSTICS AND THE MEDIEVAL ENGLISH RELIGIOUS TRADITION

ESSAYS IN HONOUR OF S. S. HUSSEY

Stanley Hussey, April 1989

LANGLAND, THE MYSTICS AND THE MEDIEVAL ENGLISH RELIGIOUS TRADITION

ESSAYS IN HONOUR OF S. S. HUSSEY

Edited by
HELEN PHILLIPS

D. S. BREWER

First published 1990 by D. S. Brewer, Cambridge

D. S. Brewer is an imprint of Boydell & Brewer Ltd
PO Box 9, Woodbridge, Suffolk IP12 3DF
and of Boydell & Brewer Inc.
PO Box 41026, Rochester, NY 14604, USA

ISBN 0 85991 301 5

British Library Cataloguing in Publication Data
Langland the mystics and the medieval English religious tradition.
1. English literature, 1066–1400 – Critical studies
I. Phillips, Helen, *1944–*
820.9001
ISBN 0–85991–301–5

Library of Congress Cataloging-in-Publication Data
Langland, the mystics, and the medieval English religious tradition /
edited by Helen Phillips.
        p.   cm.
Includes bibliographical references.
ISBN 0–85991–301–5 (alk. paper)
1. Christian literature, English (Middle) – History and criticism.
2. Langland, William, 1330?–1400? Piers the Plowman. 3. Mysticism
– England – History. 4. Mysticism in literature. I. Phillips, Helen.
PR275.R4L36   1990
820.9'382'0902–dc20

90–1604
CIP

This publication is printed on acid-free paper

Printed in Great Britain by
St Edmundsbury Press, Bury St Edmunds, Suffolk

CONTENTS

ACKNOWLEDGMENTS

We would like to thank both the contributors to this Festschrift and also those who made the publication financially feasible: the subscribers and the Lancaster University Research Committee, who gave a subvention towards the production costs. Many other people have given their help and time generously, and in particular we are grateful to David Barron, of Lancaster University Library, who compiled the bibliography, to Alison Easton, Joyce Hussey, Marion McClintock, Gwen Phillips, and Patricia Thomson. Without Maureen Jex the whole thing would have been impossible. And we owe heartfelt thanks to Richard Barber and Derek Brewer, of Boydell and Brewer, for all their advice, skill and patience.

Helen Phillips
Raman Selden
Meg Twycross
(Festschrift Committee)

S. S. HUSSEY

Stanley Hussey was born on 14th May, 1925, in Trowbridge, Wiltshire. He was educated at Trowbridge High School. On leaving school in 1943 he joined the RAF, serving in Egypt and Cyprus. After demobilization in 1947 he entered University College, London, to read English. The Honours English degree, which followed the three-subject 'Inter' year that was compulsory for ex-servicemen, normally took three years, but it was possible for students who were willing and able to undertake an exceptionally demanding work-load to complete it in two. This Stan Hussey did, graduating in 1950 with a first class degree. This already typifies one of his enduring characteristics: the gift for taking on gargantuan amounts of work and making it look easy.

This achievement was recognized by an immediate assistantship at UCL. Combining teaching with research during the next few years, he embarked first on the MA dissertation on Langland, to which Derek Pearsall pays tribute in this volume, and then on his Ph. D. thesis, an edition of the second book of Walter Hilton's *The Scale of Perfection*. Fate was kind in giving to him as his teachers at London University distinguished scholars who were particularly congenial to his own intellectual interests; they included Harold Jenkins, Winifred Nowottny, George Kane, and Phyllis Hodgson, who supervised his thesis.

He became Assistant Lecturer (later Lecturer) at Queen Mary College, London, in 1952, which was also the year of his marriage to Joyce Harlow, herself a graduate in English of University College, London. The QMC English department, fairly small in the 1950's, grew rapidly during the next decade, the era of British university expansion. The Department, under Professor J. Isaacs, included Norman Callan, Benno Timmer, Marjorie Thompson, Patricia Thomson, and later, Eric Stanley and Avril Henry. The College was lively and sociable: common room life was pleasant, the Principal, Sir Thomas Creed, and Registrar, Robert Tong, knew all the staff and most of the students, and there are happy memories of college concerts, with the Principal presiding, the Registrar conducting, and Benno Timmer as a fine solo violinist.

Here Stanley Hussey laid the foundations of his considerable skills as a lecturer and teacher. Work on Hilton continued: the editing of Book One, begun by Helen Gardner, passed on to T.P. Dunning and, after his death to A.J. Bliss, and more recently to Michael Sargeant; Stan Hussey continued with the work on Book Two. He was also writing at this time on Hilton's conception of the Mixed Life: appropriately enough, for at QMC he began what has proved to be a career full of unselfish service in many areas of academic administration. He particularly enjoyed working as an examiner for the London Training Colleges, and undertook the daunting role of Secretary to the London University Board of Studies. With so many colleges and affiliated institutions, at home and abroad, the Board's meetings correspondence and minutes were seemingly endless.

Patricia Thomson, who joined QMC the year after Stan Hussey did, remembers him as the first person she met on her first morning there, a tall, lean, young man: 'With typical consideration he showed me round the College, plying me with useful information. He came into College daily in those days and soon became the perfect colleaque and reassuring presence ("Not to worry. I'll be in")'. That hasn't changed: the habit of complete involvement, of attention to detail, the sense that the department, and the University, form a daily community. It contributes much to his success as Head of Department and gives a characteristic mixture of humanity and shrewdness to his role as a university elder statesman.

In 1966 Stanley Hussey became Senior Lecturer at the new University of Lancaster. It was a good moment to move to a 'New University', and Lancaster held particular attractions: the University had designed an unusually flexible, multi-subject degree scheme, and the English Department had been set up expressly with the aim of integrating the studies of literature and language, with an emphasis on modern linguistic approaches. A strong Linguistics Section (later Department) was developing, and under Stan Hussey's leadership the areas of Early English language and medieval literature began to flourish. Among many congenial colleagues was Frank Goodridge, whose translation of *Piers Plowman* has brought so many readers to the poem.

A colleague of those early years has said 'Although Stan was not yet a Head of Department, he was the man who made things happen: that neat writing of his was soon everywhere'. In 1973 he became Professor of English Language and Medieval Literature, and when in the same year the School of English, with its three constituent departments was created, Stanley Hussey, with his commitment to the subject as a whole – language and literature, medieval and modern – was the obvious person to become its first Chairman. Medieval Studies courses, and later the Medieval Studies Centre, developed. On the language side he was particularly successful in designing courses which took into account both the needs and expectations of post–1960s English students, and advances in Linguistics, rather than relying solely on traditional philological approaches.

Writings on Langland, Chaucer and other medieval literature, and on Shakespeare, appeared, all of them showing his characteristic breadth and clarity, amid a perennially heavy teaching load and all the commitments of senior academic life: conferences, examining, committees and administration – commitments made more complicated by several of his virtues, like a naturally democratic style of leadership, a readiness to listen, and a courtesy and concern for everyone in the department from the nervous first year student upwards.

As one of the most prominent and widely respected figures in the academic administration of Lancaster University, his service on University committees is so extensive, over the years, that one can only sum it up be saying that there is virtually no major university body on which he has not served. Three in particular, perhaps, should be singled out. The first is the University Library Committee: New University libraries frequently face particular problems, and as Chairman of the Library Committee in a time of retrenchment he was stalwart and resourceful in his championship of the Library's needs. More happily, on the University Building Committee, he took great pleasure in participating in the design of the new School of Creative Arts, with the Scott Gallery, and Lonsdale Hall building (the continuing strength of Theatre Studies at Lancaster, especially, has owed much to his support). Thirdly, and most importantly, comes his work in the University Development Committee and its successor, the Senate Planning, Academic and Research Committee, Lancaster University's small central planning committee. Here he played a key role during difficult years, forceful and eloquent in his defence of his own and other hardpressed areas in an era of government spending cuts.

The formerly separate departments of medieval and modern English merged in 1987, and the fact that the new Department was a success, and the merger ushered in an era of harmony and intellectual vigour, particularly in the areas of research and graduate-teaching, owed much to Stanley Hussey's personal gifts.

Stan and Joyce Hussey, with their shared love of English literature, their concern for teaching and education, their energy, humour and warmth, have come to hold a very special place in the life of Lancaster University. Their hospitality is delightful (the Hussey household has been dominated by a succession of magisterial cats, and if Tibalt, the present incumbant, reads this he will find that one of the contributions, and one particular footnote within it, have particular relevance to him).

Walter Hilton wrote of those whose responsibilities hold them for many years 'bounden to temporal administration': 'they left full often their own rest in contemplation, when they had full liefer have been still thereat . . . and intermeddled them with worldly business in helping of their subjects, and soothly that was charity'. As Stanley Hussey retires from the *vita activa* to one a little more *contemplativa*, his friends, colleagues and pupils offer greetings on his sixty-fifth birthday and every good wish for the years ahead, with respect, affection and gratitude.

S. S. HUSSEY: PUBLICATIONS
(excluding reviews)

'Langland, Hilton and the Three Lives', *Review of English Studies*, New Series 7 (1956), pp. 132–50

'How many Herods in the Middle English Drama?', *Neophilologus* 48 (1964), pp. 252–9

'The Text of *The Scale of Perfection*, Book II', *Neuphilologische Mitteilungen* 65 (1964), pp. 75–92

'Langland's Reading of Alliterative Poetry', *Modern Language Review* 60 (1965), pp. 163–70

'*Sir Gawain* and Romance Writing', *Studia Neophilologica* 40 (1968), pp. 161–74

(ed.) *Piers Plowman: Essays in Criticism* (London 1969)

'Chaucer: The Minor Poems and the Prose', in *The Middle Ages*, vol. 1 of *The Sphere History of English Literature* ed. Whitney F. Bolton (London 1970)

Chaucer: An Introduction (London 1971)

'The Difficult Fifth Book of *Troilus and Criseyde*', *Modern Language Review* 67 (1972), pp. 721–9

'Latin and English in *The Scale of Perfection*', *Mediaeval Studies* 35 (1973), pp. 456–76

'Walter Hilton: Traditionalist?', in Marion Glasscoe, ed., *The Medieval Mystical Tradition in England: Exeter Symposium IV* (Exeter 1980), pp. 1–16.

The Literary Language of Shakespeare (London 1982)

'Chaucer and Character', in *The Medieval Studies Conference, Aachen 1983: Language and Literature* (Frankfurt 1984)

'Chaucer', in Whitney F. Bolton, ed., *The New History of Literature*, vol. 1 (New York 1986) pp. 169–266

'Shakespeare and the English Language', in I. C. B. Dear, ed., *Oxford English* (Oxford 1986), pp. 527–34

'The Audience for the Middle English Mystics', in Michael G. Sargent, ed., *De Cella in Seculum: Religious and Secular Life and Devotion in Late Medieval England* (Cambridge 1989), pp. 109–22

Piers Plowman *Forty Years On*

Derek Pearsall

It is not necessary for me to indulge in fulsome praise of the work that Stan Hussey
has done in and for *Piers Plowman* studies, nor, in particular, to exert myself on
behalf of the M.A.thesis, 'Eighty Years of *Piers Plowman* Scholarship: A Study of
Critical Methods', that the young S.S. Hussey presented to the University of
London in 1952. I have, for the latter, something better than my own words – the
praise of an expert and impartial witness in the person of Anne Middleton (1986),
who has called it 'a most informative and thorough London University
M.A.thesis, unequalled in the published literature' (p.2420). Not quite forty years
has passed since the thesis was presented, at least not as I write, but the interval
seems an appropriate one to signal in offering a tribute to an early work by the
scholar whom we now celebrate, and a modest sequel.

At the time when Hussey wrote, *Piers Plowman* was still a poem under siege,
though the relief forces, in the persons of Kane (1948) and Donaldson (1949),
were at hand. The argument that J.M. Manly had unleashed concerning the
authorship of the poem had raged for nearly fifty years, having found a receptive
audience among those who were much more willing to read a poem of 2500 than
one of 7500 lines and who had always been convinced that the A-text *Visio* was
the only part worth reading anyway. If the rest of the poem, and the other
versions, were now by several other people, then that was a very satisfactory state
of affairs. R.W. Chambers had to fight a running battle to protect the author he
was trying to edit from being divided into five, and the carnage, especially when
T.A. Knott was around, was often terrible.

There was little that could be done with the poem, it seemed, while it was so
embattled, but a number of writers, such as H.W. Wells, Nevill Coghill and
Father T.P. Dunning, tried to set aside the authorship debate and see the poem as
a poem. There were attempts to evolve an explanation of the structure of the
poem, at least of the B-text (C was generally abandoned as being beyond hope),
and in particular to see the *Vita de Dowel, Dobet and Dobest* as something more
than a series of confused and rambling digressions. The schemes that were evolved
were premature, and the emphasis they placed on the interpretation of the three
Lives proved unrewarding (it was Hussey himself who in 1956 turned the tide,
pointing out that the interpretation of Dobest as the 'Mixed' Life had no basis in

the poem, and that a rigid scheme of the Lives was not part of the poem's purpose), but the belief of these early writers in the *intelligibility* of the poem was of vital importance.

Nevertheless, they all remained haunted by the spectre of multiple authorship, and the definitive text that everyone hoped would resolve the problem once and for all seemed as remote as ever. The Second World War found the materials for the Chambers and Grattan edition stored underground in Wales; Grattan was in poor health; Chambers died. But George Kane announced his presence on the scene in 1948 with a characteristically magisterial essay on the problems and methods of editing the B-text, and he subsequently took over the general editorship of the London project to edit all three versions. His critical edition of A appeared in 1960, the text accompanied by a full corpus of variants from all relevant manuscripts and incorporating extensive emendation of a radical kind, the rationale for which is explained in the Introduction. This Introduction (pp.1–172), a work of textual scholarship of fundamental and far-reaching importance, offers the arguments for Kane's conclusion that 'recension is not a practicable method' (p.115) for the editor of a vernacular poem so subject to scribal corruption and interference and therefore to convergent variation, or coincidental error. He rejects the arguments of Knott and Fowler (who had published an edition of A in 1952) for the genealogical method and proposes instead that each variant must be considered on its merits, and on the basis of an intimate knowledge of the poet's way of writing and a systematic understanding of the types of error characteristically introduced by scribes. His statement of method marks an epoch in the history of the theory and practice of textual criticism, and not only in relation to *Piers Plowman*. His text of A is widely accepted as authoritative.

The publication in 1961 of a book on *Piers Plowman* by Fowler, who persisted in maintaining that A, B and C were by different authors, prompted Kane to reopen the question of multiple authorship, and in his definitive study of the subject in 1965 he effectively closed the book on it as far as most disinterested enquirers were concerned. It was a necessary clearing of the ground in preparation for B and C, for which E.Talbot Donaldson and George H. Russell had by now been recruited. B appeared in 1975, edited by Kane and Donaldson, the latter having recanted his earlier belief (of 1955) in the possibility that the manuscripts might bear witness to the existence of more than three authorial versions of the poem. Such a belief, of course, would strike at the heart of the project. The edition of B, like that of A, is accompanied by a full corpus of variants, and the Introduction (pp. 1–224) contains a very extensive description of editorial method. As in A, recension is rejected, and each variant is considered on its merits. The situation with B is complicated, however, by the corrupt nature of the scribal archetype of all extant copies, and by the fact that C, which might be thought to be a source of good readings in passages that correspond closely with B (and is indeed so used in the edition, with the so-far unpublished edition of C by Russell as source), was itself done from a poor copy of B. In these circumstances,

2

the editors resort to a more than usually radical practice of textual reconstruction, some elements in which have not met with universal favour, such as their assumptions about the regularity of Langland's alliterative practice, and their use of these assumptions as a means for detecting inauthentic readings. All the material for criticising their editorial methods is made available, of course, by the editors in what is by any account a monumental work of scholarship.

The edition of C by Russell is still awaited, but the years since 1975 have seen the publication of Schmidt's edition of B (1978), which many have found more acceptable or more comfortable than Kane-Donaldson because of its restraint in the practice of conjectural emendation, and of Pearsall's edition of C (1978). Both of these are essentially students' editions, with extensive annotation and glossing, and they are important in having encouraged teachers to work with one of the longer versions of the poem, and not to rely on the old-established students' edition of the B *Visio* by Skeat nor the edition of the same portion of text by Bennett (1972).

There has also been increasing speculation about the possibility, suggested earlier by Donaldson, that the manuscripts may bear witness to the existence of more than the three versions of the poem for the exclusive integrity of which Kane has argued so vehemently. In particular, the publication of an edition of 'The Z Version' of the poem by Rigg and Brewer (1983), supposedly a text of an authorial version of *Piers Plowman* that preceded A, has persuaded a number of scholars of the possibility of keeping an open mind on the matter. There has also been some questioning, in a brilliant essay by Patterson (1985), of the assumptions made by Kane and Donaldson (and indeed by anyone proposing a critical edition of a Middle English vernacular text extant in multiple copies) concerning the inspired nature of poetic composition, concerning the idea of poetic meaning as somehow graspable, through intuition, as something beyond mere words, and concerning the notion of the literary text as transhistorically stable and permanent. More recently a series of essays by Hoyt Duggan, especially that of 1987, has established what appear to be new 'rules' for alliterative metre, including a structure for the b-verse which may affect some of the editorial decisions of the Athlone Press editors.

Kane's principal ally in this great editorial project, to turn now to critical work on the poem, was the late and deeply lamented Talbot Donaldson, who himself produced in 1949 the first major book-length study of one of the longer versions of the poem, a book that would still stand at the head of most teachers' lists of the critical works they would wish their students to know well. Donaldson gave full scope, in his incomparably witty way, to the diversity and creativity of Langland's poetic processes, and, though still to some extent preoccupied with the authorship question, showed a power of relating close reading of key passages to an argument about the meaning of the poem as a whole that has been an inspiring model for later scholars. A writer like Lawlor (1962), working under the stimulus of Donaldson and of the New Criticism, has seen the traditional structural problems of the

3

poem – the abrupt transitions, digressions and non-sequiturs – in a new way, as a representation of the experience of the dreamer in his quest for truth. It is not the answers that are important, but the answers as painfully arrived at by the dreamer: his recognition of the truth that lies within and that must be constantly sought (in *doing* well) is both the theme of the poem and its method. The excellent short study of the poem by Elizabeth Salter (1962) stresses in a somewhat comparable way the improvisatory and suggestive nature of the poem, and the role of the dreamer as the means through which the reader is drawn to participate in the activity of the quest. She writes perhaps better than anyone else on the poetry of the poem, and also on the relation of the theme of the quest for Truth in Langland to the visionary writing of contemporary English mystics like Julian of Norwich and Walter Hilton. Elizabeth Kirk (1972) has a similar concern with the poem's difficultness as a measure of its truthfulness to the experience of spiritual quest and exploration. She insists on the sequence of events in the poem, the unfolding of its processes in the experience of the reader, as the essential key to understanding its structure.

The handling of the dream and the dreamer, the question of the *persona* of the dreamer, the relation of the dreamer's experience to Langland's own life, have all come to be recognised as key issues. Kane himself delivered an important lecture on the subject (1965); Bowers (1986) has related the problems of the dreamer Will to urgent contemporary theological debate about the defective nature of human will; and modern techniques of analysing the 'construction of the subject' and of demonstrating the contradictions within apparently coherent representations of subjectivity have been interestingly put to use in a recent essay by Lawton (1987).

The structural difficulties of Langland's poem, and especially the enigmatic nature of his allegory, in its dizzying movement betwen the literal and the metaphorical, have also remained a preoccupation of those trying to understand *Piers Plowman*. Muscatine, in a characteristically suggestive short commentary on the poem (1972), sees its disorderly procedures as perhaps an imitation of the experience of exploration and discovery, of a prolonged spiritual struggle on Langland's part, but more significantly as suggestive of instability and imminent collapse in society at large, and in this an enactment of the social, intellectual and spiritual crisis of the late fourteenth century. Muscatine's history is sketchy, but his ideas have been extremely influential, and other writers such as Cantarow, in a little-quoted essay (1972), and Aers (1980) have tried to relate the breakdown of allegory in the poem to a deliberate attempt by Langland to problematise a form of writing that he sees as essentially conservative in its ideological inclination. The sense of internal conflict and incoherence within the poem thus becomes a part of its meaning and of Langland's struggle to break away from powerful and persuasive modes of thought that threaten the honesty of his vision.

The recognition of the political in the apparently formalistic is an important sign of health and maturity in modern Langland studies, though other writers have preferred to read the problems of the poem in more exclusively epistemological ways. Carruthers (1973) sees it as a poem about the problems of knowing truly: allegory breaks down because it is inherently inadequate to its role of revealing religious truth; words slip and slide, not because of Langland's struggle to express himself but because of their inherent powerlessness to communicate that truth. The poem ends in the ruin of language, and the demonstration of the incompatibility of divine truth and human language. Martin (1979) sees the poem, more simply, as a series of deliberately engineered structural collapses, and an attack on the fixed habits of thought encouraged by allegory. There is a more subtle awareness of the working of Langland's allegory in Griffiths (1985), who shows the personifications of the poem moving uneasily but suggestively between the represented world and the world of discourse, to the latter of which they always seem ready to revert. This might be called a structuralist view of Langland's allegory: there is a post-structuralist view, too, in Finke (1987), who has applied to *Piers Plowman* De Man's idea of allegory as a self-cancelling trope, one that continually proclaims its own incapacity to assume referentiality. The recession of the possibility of interpretation is a familiar feature of such approaches, and it is interesting that Finke refuses the final 'No' by treating the acknowledgement of the unreadability of the text as the required leap of faith.

But this discussion of those works that perhaps I myself have found most interesting (and of course I have to confine myself for the most part to book-length studies) has so far neglected what most readers will regard as the major school of modern Langland criticism. I refer to those writers – and they are legion – who believe that the poem has a completed coherence of design, and that careful enquiry into its background in intellectual, scriptural and patristic tradition will gradually reveal and elucidate that design. Langland is a learned and careful scholar, as well as an inspired poet, and firmly within the academic intellectual tradition of the medieval church. The stabilisation of the text of the poem and the laying of the ghost of multiple authorship have both encouraged this view of the poem as a structural masterpiece and as an expression of the central orthodoxies of the medieval Christian faith.

There have been many varieties of approach within the framework of these broad overarching assumptions. The least persuasive is that of Robertson and Huppé (1951), who assume that the Latin scriptural quotations are the key to the allegorical meaning of the poem. Their method is to work from the quotations to the larger biblical context from which they are drawn, from there to patristic commentary, and from the commentary back to the allegorical meaning of the poem, which now stands revealed, not unexpectedly, as entirely traditional in its teaching of Christian doctrine. Where there are no scriptural quotations, the authors deduce their implied existence from allusions to key words and images that appear in biblical concordances. The defects of such a rigid system of analysis may seem obvious, but the method has been employed with almost equal lack of subtlety by Goldsmith (1981). Smith (1966) chooses his ground more carefully and gives welcome emphasis to the poetic reworking of traditional materials. The strength of the tradition is still evident in the more recent and important work of Alford (e.g. 1977) and Allen (e.g. 1982). Both see *Piers Plowman* as the product of a scholar's work on commentaries and biblical concordances and not as an attempt to 'express' any personal vision: the poem is itself generated as a commentary on a development of an array of themes whose essential logic is defined elsewhere, usually in the Bible; it moves from point to point according to the verbal and thematic associations set up by the assembly of *distinctiones* in concordances. Such methods of analysis work quite convincingly on certain occasions in the poem, but of course this does not make them the universal key to its structure and meaning.

Less rigid and systematic, but still assured of the possibility of some access to hidden but ascertainable meanings in *Piers Plowman*, are studies like those of Frank (1957) and Bloomfield (1961). Frank's book comes closest to bridging the gap between the two schools of modern criticism that I have been trying to describe: he accepts the existence of a grand design behind the poem, as the title of his book indicates, but he accepts too that it is the spectacle of man now blundering and now moving forward within the framework of this plan that gives the poem its unique drama. Bloomfield wants to relate the poem to the monastic tradition of perfection (which he sees as its essential subject-matter) and more specifically to the Joachite tradition of apocalyptic history. His work has been important in drawing the attention of readers to areas of the medieval intellectual tradition that they would perhaps prefer to remain in ignorance of, and it has inspired others to try to improve on the models that Bloomfield provided for Langland's intellectual inheritance, particularly in investigating theological developments more closely contemporary with Langland's own writing career. Bourquin (1978), Coleman (1981) and Adams (e.g. 1988) have tried to fill in the gaps in our knowledge of the theological writing of the fourteenth century, especially that of the *moderni*, and its influence on Langland, and Murtaugh (1978) has tried to suggest ways in which Langland was deliberately, and heroically, setting out to mend the bridge between the human and the divine that contemporary theology seemed to have demolished.

Meanwhile a host of scholars have been patiently engaged in the unravelling of the allusions to patristic and scholastic writing within the poem, doing much to convince even the sceptic that a considerable learning went to its making and needs to be recovered. Essays and notes by R.E. Kaske, T.D. Hill, B.J. Harwood, A.V.C. Schmidt, and many others, and more recently by Gerald Morgan and James Simpson, which it would need an extensive bibliography to list, have assembled an impressive record of the depth of Langland's learning and his skill in using it. Alford (1988) has drawn attention to Langland's extensive knowledge of the language of law, and Schmidt (1987) to his subtle skill in deploying a wide and learned vocabulary.

The greatest need still seems to be a detailed and sophisticated historical

6

contextualisation for Langland's poem, not exclusively from an intellectual and theological point of view and not necessarily, either, from the point of view of historical or cultural materialism. The work of Baldwin (1981) on the political and legal background shows what a wealth of material there is to be deployed in a particular area, though her sense of the relationship between poetry and history seems to lack an awareness of the power of cultural and ideological construction in determining that relationship, as does the simpler and less ambitious study of Stokes (1984). However, the materials for a genuinely historical understanding of Langland's poem are beginning to be assembled, and an awareness of the dimensions of the problem exists. The establishment of *The Yearbook of Langland Studies* in 1987, principally under the direction of John Alford, has created a new forum for serious Langland scholarship, and the publication of *A Companion to Piers Plowman* (1988), also edited by Alford, has provided a plateau from which future summits can be surveyed. The present survey can end by looking back to the base-camp that Stan Hussey set up forty years ago and forward to the book by Anne Middleton that is so eagerly awaited by Langland scholars, and to the pleasure that Stan will take in seeing the ascent to understanding, in which he has played such a faithful part, continue.

Chronological List of Works Cited

1948 Kane, George, '*Piers Plowman*: Problems and Methods of Editing the B-Text', *Modern Language Review*, 43: 1–25.

1949 Donaldson, E.Talbot, *Piers Plowman: The C-Text and its Poet*, Yale Studies in English, 113 (New Haven: Yale University Press).

1951 Robertson, D.W., Jr. and Huppé, Bernard F., *Piers Plowman and Scriptural Tradition* (Princeton University Press).

1952 Knott, Thomas A., and Fowler, David C.(eds.), *Piers the Plowman: A Critical Edition of the A-Version* (Baltimore: The Johns Hopkins Press).

1955 Donaldson, E.Talbot, 'MSS R and F in the B-Tradition of *Piers Plowman*', *Transactions of the Connecticut Academy of Arts and Sciences*, 39: 177–212.

1956 Hussey, S.S., 'Langland, Hilton and the Three Lives', *Review of English Studies*, New Series, 7: 132–50.

1957 Frank, Robert Worth, Jr., *Piers Plowman and the Scheme of Salvation: An Interpretation of Dowel, Dobet, and Dobest*, Yale Studies in English, 136 (New Haven: Yale University Press).

1960 Kane, George (ed.), *Piers Plowman: The A Version* (University of London: The Athlone Press).

1961 Bloomfield, Morton W., *Piers Plowman as a Fourteenth-Century Apocalypse* (New Brunswick, NJ: Rutgers University Press).

1962 Fowler, David C., *Piers the Plowman: Literary Relations of the A and B Texts* (Seattle: University of Washington Press).

1962 Lawlor, John, *Piers Plowman: An Essay in Criticism* (London: Edward Arnold).

1962 Salter, Elizabeth, *Piers Plowman: An Introduction* (Oxford: Basil Blackwell).

1965 Kane, George, 'The Autobiographical Fallacy in Chaucer and Langland Studies', The Chambers Memorial Lecture, 1965 (University College, London: H.K. Lewis).

1965 Kane, George, *Piers Plowman: The Evidence for Authorship* (University of London: The Athlone Press).

1966 Smith, Ben H., *Traditional Imagery of Charity in Piers Plowman*, Studies in English Literature, XXI (The Hague: Mouton).

1972 Bennett, J.A.W. (ed.), *Langland, Piers Plowman: Prologue and Passus I–VII of the B Text*, Clarendon Medieval and Tudor Series (Oxford: Clarendon Press).

1972 Cantarow, Ellen, 'A Wilderness of Opinions Confounded: Allegory and Ideology', *College English*, 34: 215–52.

1972 Kirk, Elizabeth D., *The Dream Thought of Piers Plowman*, Yale Studies in English, 178 (New Haven: Yale University Press).

1972 Muscatine, Charles, *Poetry and Crisis in the Age of Chaucer* (Notre Dame: University of Notre Dame Press).

1973 Carruthers, Mary, *The Search for St.Truth: A Study of Meaning in Piers Plowman* (Evanston: Northwestern University Press).

1975 Kane, George, and Donaldson, E.Talbot (eds.), *Piers Plowman: The B Version* (University of London: The Athlone Press).

1977 Alford, John A., 'The Role of the Quotations in Piers Plowman', *Speculum*, 52: 80–99.

1978 Bourquin, Guy, *'Piers Plowman': Etudes sur la Génèse Littéraire des Trois Versions*, Thèse présentée devant la Faculté des Lettres et des Sciences Humaines de Paris, 1970, 2 vols. (Lille: Université de Lille III).

1978 Murtaugh, Daniel Maher, *Piers Plowman and the Image of God* (Gainesville: University Presses of Florida).

1978 Pearsall, Derek (ed.), *Piers Plowman, by William Langland: An Edition of the C-Text*, York Medieval Texts, second series (London: Edward Arnold, 1978; Berkeley and Los Angeles: University of California Press, 1979).

1978 Schmidt, A.V.C. (ed.), *William Langland, The Vision of Piers Plowman: A Critical Edition of the B-Text*, Everyman's Library (London: J.M. Dent; New York: E.P. Dutton).

1979 Martin, Priscilla, *Piers Plowman: The Field and the Tower* (London and New York: Macmillan).

1980 Aers, David, *Chaucer, Langland and the Creative Imagination* (London: Routledge and Kegan Paul).

1981 Baldwin, Anna P., *The Theme of Government in Piers Plowman*, Piers Plowman Studies I (Cambridge: D.S. Brewer).

1981 Coleman, Janet, *Piers Plowman and the Moderni*, Letture di Pensiero e d'Arte (Rome: Edizioni di Storia e Letteratura).

1981 Goldsmith, Margaret E., *The Figure of Piers Plowman: The Image on the Coin*, Piers Plowman Studies II (Cambridge: D.S. Brewer).

1982 Allen, Judson Boyce, *The Ethical Poetic of the Later Middle Ages: A Decorum of Convenient Distinction* (Toronto: University of Toronto Press).

1983 Rigg, A.G., and Brewer, Charlotte (eds.), *William Langland, Piers Plowman: The Z Version*, Studies and Texts 59 (Toronto: Pontifical Institute of Medieval Studies).

1984 Stokes, Myra, *Justice and Mercy in Piers Plowman: A Reading of the B Text Visio* (London: Croom Helm).

1985 Griffiths, Lavinia, *Personification in Piers Plowman*, Piers Plowman Studies III (Cambridge: D.S. Brewer).

1985 Patterson, Lee, 'The Logic of Textual Criticism and the Way of Genius: The Kane-Donaldson *Piers Plowman* in Historical Perspective', in McGann, Jerome J. (ed.), *Textual Criticism and Literary Interpretation* (Chicago and London: University of Chicago Press), pp.55–91. Reprinted in Patterson, *Negotiating the Past: The Historical Understanding of Medieval Literature* (Madison: University of Wisconsin Press, 1987).

1986 Bowers, John M., *The Crisis of Will in Piers Plowman* (Washington: Catholic University of America Press).

1986 Middleton, Anne, 'XVIII. Piers Plowman', in Hartung, Albert E. (ed.), *A Manual of the Writings in Middle English 1050–1500*, Volume 7 (New Haven: The Connecticut Academy of Arts and Sciences), pp.2211–34, 2419–48.

1987 Duggan, Hoyt N., 'Notes toward a Theory of Langland's Meter', *Yearbook of Langland Studies*, 1: 41–70.

1987 Finke, Laurie A., 'Truth's Treasure: Allegory and Meaning in *Piers Plowman*', in Finke, Laurie A., and Shichtman, Martin B. (eds.), *Medieval Texts and Contemporary Readers* (Ithaca and London: Cornell University Press), pp.51–68.

1987 Lawton, David, 'The Subject of *Piers Plowman*', *Yearbook of Langland Studies*, 1: 1–30.

1987 Schmidt, A.V.C., *The Clerkly Maker: Langland's Poetic Art*, Piers Plowman Studies IV (Cambridge: D.S. Brewer).

1988 Adams, Robert, 'Langland's Theology', in Alford, *Companion* (see below), pp.87–114.

1988 Alford, John A. (ed.), *A Companion to Piers Plowman* (Berkeley, Los Angeles and London: University of California Press).

1988 Alford, John A., *Piers Plowman: A Glossary of Legal Diction*, Piers Plowman Studies V (Cambridge: D.S. Brewer).

The Constraints of Satire in 'Piers Plowman' and 'Mum and the Sothsegger'.

James Simpson

In his *Male Regle*, written in 1405, Thomas Hoccleve pauses to relate how truth-tellers have a difficult and dangerous time of it:

> But whan the sobre, treewe, and weel auysid
> With sad visage his lord enfourmeth pleyn
> How þat his gouernance is despysid
> Among the peple, and seith him as they seyn,
> As man treewe oghte vnto his souereyn
> Conseillynge him amende his gouernance,
> The lordes herte swellith for desdeyn
> And bit him voide blyue with meschance[1]

Hoccleve briefly poses here as the champion of courageous speech in the face of potentially hostile power, and in so doing he draws on a tradition of 'truth-telling' which is well attested in later Middle English.[2]

Or that is how it seems, at any rate, when the stanza is taken out of context. In fact Hoccleve is not so much telling the truth here, as disguising it. This passage in the poem comes in a digression about flattery: Hoccleve has related how he listened to flattering boatmen when he could not be bothered to walk home. His unwillingness to walk, and his willingness to listen to flattery, are examples of his '*male regle*', and, as part of his self-castigation, he digresses on the dangers of flattery, of which the cited stanza forms a part. So the stanza is posed as contributing to a *self*-chastisement. But the whole poem is a begging poem, ultimately, though never directly, addressed to the Sub-Treasurer, Lord Fournival. Hoccleve

I should like to thank the Cambridge medieval seminar, Dr Helen Barr and Professor Paul Strohm for many helpful comments on an earlier draft of this article. Dr Paul Miller very generously sent me a copy of his doctoral thesis, for which I am extremely grateful.

[1] Edited by M.C.Seymour, in *Selections from Hoccleve* (Oxford 1981), ll.273–80.
[2] For this tradition, see Andrew Wawn, 'Truth-telling and the Tradition of *Mum and the Sothsegger*', YES, 13 (1983), 270–87.

11

is indeed correcting his powerful addressee for not having paid him on time, but such correction is made in an oblique way, since it is ostensibly directed not at the Sub-Treasurer, but at Hoccleve himself. It is also true that the poem is in fact deeply flattering to Fournival, implicitly likening him to an earthly God who can restore Hoccleve's health. So the very digression on flattery is designed to disguise the fact that Hoccleve is flattering; at the same time, the very statement about telling the truth is designed to legitimate the fact that Hoccleve does, one way or another, tell the truth (i.e. that he has not been paid). Ultimately we might say that if Hoccleve does tell the truth in this poem, he does so without 'sad visage', and his 'enformacion' cannot be described as 'pleyn'.

This little passage raises important questions about the way we read poetry addressed to powerful readers: should we read the power relations evident in this poem as purely fictional, or do we read the text as being informed by non-fictional constraints? And in what ways do power relations between poet and addressee shape poems?

Perhaps because of a New Critical disposition to read literary works 'as literature' – as autonomous, whole textual entities – critics have not much investigated these questions with regard to many medieval poems. This cannot be because we are unfamiliar with the habits of mind required for reading literature produced out of specific power constraints. When we read literature from contemporary Eastern Europe, for example, the very first question we ask of such writing will concern the strategies it has adopted with regard to the constraints of what can and cannot be said in a given society.

Whatever the reasons for our not posing these questions with much insistence to medieval literature, I would like, in the first two sections of this article, to put such questions to *Piers Plowman* (B-Text, c.1378–9) and *Mum and the Sothsegger* (c.1403–6). In section I I will ask whether we should regard the constraints on satire referred to in these texts as part of a fictional, literary construct alone, or whether such constraints can be related to non-fictional prohibitions on speech and writing. This section will be historical, and I will argue that there were in fact powerful constraints on the writing of satire and theological statement in the period 1378–1406, both from ecclesiastical and royal sources. In the second section I will briefly point to the ways in which these poems are informed by these constraints, but how they nevertheless authorize and generate their own satire by various textual strategies. But if satire is authorised and generated as a discourse in *Piers Plowman*, I want in the third section to show how Langland, characteristically, also deconstructs this. I want to argue that the theological problematic of the poem pushes Langland to reflect on, and deeply to question, the practice of the satirist. Langland's satire, that is, is constrained not only by broadly 'political' constraints, but also by what might be called 'theological' constraints.

I

In the Prologue of *Piers Plowman* the narrator draws attention to his own voice often in order to say that he will *not* speak about various things. He says, for example, of the papal curia, that 'I kan and kan naught of court speke moore' (l.111). This apparent non-sequitur must be deploying different senses of the verb 'connen', and be translated 'therefore I know how to, and am not able to, speak more of the papal court'. Or at the end of the mice and rats fable, he addresses his audience in this way:

> What this metels bymeneth, ye men that ben murye,
> Devyne ye – for I ne dar, by deere God in hevene!
>
> (Prologue, 209–210)[3]

The silences of Chaucer's narrator in the General Prologue to the *Canterbury Tales* seem designed to bring the reader into literary play with an unstable text. Here, instead, the narratorial reticence is the result of fear (or so it is declared, at any rate): he does not *dare* to speak. And if he does not dare to conclude the dream with its meaning, this reticence might be explicable from the action of the fable itself. For the essential burden of this fable, in Langland's hands, is that political action is dangerous. The worldly wise rat who is the spokesman for this position dissuades his fellows from defamation of the king: 'defame we hym nevere. / For bettre is a litel los than a long sorwe' (Prol.190–1).[4]

An unwillingness to conclude, to drive home a point, also characterises Conscience. Reticence to speak the truth from him is all the more surprising because it seems to contradict the very concept he personifies. When he addresses Mede in the presence of the king in Passus III, Conscience gives a biblical example of the dangers of desiring 'mede mesureless', the story of Saul's punishment by God. Conscience concludes, or rather fails to conclude, the story:

> The *culorum* of this cas kepe I noght to shewe;
> On aventure it noyed me, noon ende wol I make,
> For so is this world went with hem that han power
> That whoso seith hem sothest is sonnest yblamed!
>
> (III.280–83)

---

[3] All citations from the B-Text of *Piers Plowman* will be from *The Vision of Piers Plowman*, edited by A.V.C.Schmidt, revised edition (London 1987).

[4] In the hands of Bishop Brunton, the fable is turned to diametrically opposite ends, since the timorous mice are taken to be a negative exemplum. Brunton's sermon was delivered on 18 May, 1376. *The Sermons of Thomas Brinton, Bishop of Rochester (1373–1389)*, edited by Mary Aquinas Devlin, Camden Third Series, vols 85 and 86 (London 1954), vol.86, p.317. See Eleanor H.Kellog, 'Bishop Brunton and the Fable of the Rats', *PMLA*, 50 (1935), 57–67.

Conscience, then, might serve as a model for a speaker in the presence of the powerful: he relates an *exemplum* with obvious application to the behaviour of kings, drawn from the Book of Kings, but fails to drive home its specific relevance, out of fear. This model from within the poem serves also to describe moments in the narrator's address to his fictional audience outside the poem.

There are other passages in *Piers Plowman* which imply a reticence to speak openly.[5] But we might move from these examples to *Mum and the Sothsegger*, where reticence to speak occupies a much higher profile than is the case with Langland's poem. *Mum and the Sothsegger* (which I take to be distinct from the text Skeat called *Richard the Redeless*[6]) begins by stating the necessity for a truth-teller to the king, and the dangers inherent in such a position:

> And yf a burne bolde hym to bable þe sothe
> And [mynne] hym of mischief þat misse-reule asketh,
> He may lose his life and laugh here no more,
> Or y-putte into prisone or y-pyned to deeth
> Or y-[brente] or y-shente or sum sorowe haue,
> That fro scorne oþer scathe scape shal he neure ...
>
> (ll.165–170)[7]

After this introductory declamation of the need for a truth-teller, the narrator is about to declare what the truth is, when the constraint on speaking, Mum, enters dramatically into the poem to silence the narratorial voice. This voice, like Conscience's in Passus IV, then fails to 'make an ende':

> I blussid for his bablyng and a-bode stille
> And knytte þere a knotte and construed no ferther ...
>
> (ll.239–40)[8]

---

[5]   Though it must be said that examples of reticence to speak out of declared political caution are relatively rare in *Piers Plowman*. Of course the motive for reticence is not always clear. Possible further examples (from the B-Text) are III.3; XIII.25; XIII.70–72; XV.547. It might also be mentioned that the King is not presented as an object of satirical attack in the Prologue, but rather as an ideal. Instances of reticence to speak out of moral discretion (or encouragements to exercise such discretion) are much more frequent, and are listed in note 46 below.

[6]   In taking these texts to be separate, I follow the persuasive arguments of Dan Embree, '*Richard the Redeless* and *Mum and the Sothsegger*: A Case of Mistaken Identity', *N&Q* n.s., 22 (1975), 4–12.

[7]   Edited Mabel Day and Robert Steele, EETS OS 199 (London 1936). I accept the emendation 'brente' here, as opposed to the MS reading 'blente', for the reasons given by the editors (p.109). It could also be mentioned that one marginal annotator writes in 'brente' beside this line in the MS. The latest editor of the poem, Dr Helen Barr, has kindly communicated to me that she accepts the emendation to 'brente'.

[8]   Other examples from within the text which express the danger of criticism are as follows: ll.38–57; ll.103–113; ll.125–8; ll.152–4; ll.165–178; ll.250–1; ll.674–700; ll.845–7.

There is *prima-facie* internal evidence, then, that these poems are being written within the constraints of censorship, and that they are negotiating those constraints in their movement forward. But such evidence does not of course answer the question as to whether the constraints referred to from within the poems are purely fictional, or whether they refer to constraints outside the poems. I will now turn to some historical evidence, which suggests that the hypothesis of purely fictional constraints is improbable.

This evidence might be divided into two categories, deriving from ecclesiastical sources on the one hand, and from royal sources on the other. Here I will restrict myself to the simplest form of the evidence, which consists of the legislation passed in the period against saying certain things. I will begin with the ecclesiastical legislation, which is the most detailed.

Ecclesiastical legislation prohibiting certain kinds of statements falls into two unequal categories. On the one hand, there is a small amount of legislation against a collection of heterodox (though non-Wycliffite) theological doctrines, including many Pelagian conclusions, and on the other a large amount of anti-Wycliffite legislation. The Pelagian conclusions are anathematised in a mandate sent by by Archbishop Simon Langham to the Chancellor of Oxford in 1368, and include, for example, the following conclusions labelled as 'errors':

– (number 7) 'Sarazenos, Judaeos, ac Paganos adultos et discretos, qui nunquam habuerunt, habent, vel habebunt actum seu habitum fidei christianae, possibile est de communi lege salvari ...'

– (number 11) 'Aliquis potest ex puris naturalibus mereri vitam eternam'.[9]

(In the examples given here and elsewhere, I am choosing ideas which have possible relevance to *Piers Plowman* in particular. I cite parallel passages from the poem in the notes, without claiming that Langland's statements are identical with the banned positions, though my argument relies on the possibility of statements in the poem being confused with the targets of the legislation). The legislation orders that anyone teaching these doctrines should be avoided, and that such doctrines should not be taught in the University or elsewhere. The penalty for contravention is excommunication.

This legislation appears in a single mandate, and is not repeated. The second set of banned positions in the ecclesiastical legislation is against Wyclif and Lollardy. This receives much more detailed and draconian treatment. The first

---

[9]   – 'That it is possible for adult and rational Muslims, Jews and pagans, who never have had, have, or will have the act or habit of the Christian faith, to be saved by "common" law' (cf. *Piers Plowman* B.XI.155–6; XII.285–95);
– 'that it is possible for someone to merit eternal life through their pure, natural powers' (cf. *Piers Plowman* B.XI.155–6; XII.285–95).
These passages are cited from *Concilia Magnae Britanniae et Hiberniae*, edited by David Wilkins, 4 vols (London 1737) (hereafter 'Wilkins'), vol.3, p.76.

relevant source here is a bull by Gregory XI in 1377, ordering Wyclif to be imprisoned, and a confession to be drawn from him, which should then be sent to the Pope.[10] The intensity of attack on Wyclif is extended to 'heretics' generally in the year after the Peasants' Revolt of 1381. In the *Concilia*, we find a letter from Richard II to Archbishop Courtenay (Sudbury had been killed in the Revolt) commanding that anyone preaching these heretical conclusions, either privately or publicly, should be arrested and imprisoned until they recant.[11] And in the proceedings of the Blackfriars' Council of 1382, we find lists of the banned conclusions, divided into 'heresies' and 'errors'. Under those listed as 'heresies' we find, for example,

— (number 5) '... si homo fuerit debite contritus, omnis confessio exterior est sibi superflua vel inutilis'.

Under the conclusions listed as 'errors', we find the following:

— (number 17) '... quod domini temporales possint ad arbitrium eorum auferre bona temporalia ab ecclesiasticis habitualiter delinquentibus, vel quod populares possint ad eorum arbitrium dominos delinquentes corrigere';

— (number 23) '... quod fratres teneantur per laborem manuum, et non per mendicationem victum suum adquirere'.[12]

Before we leave the specifically ecclesiastical legislation, we should notice its culmination in the extremely repressive and exacting *Constitutions* of Archbishop Arundel drafted in 1407, just beyond the period spanned by the two poems we are considering. The first three of these constitutions concern preaching — no one will preach without licence, and preachers will restrict the subjects of their sermons to the faults of their specific audience: lay faults to the laity, clerical faults to clerical audiences, and not *vice versa*. The next two concern the sacraments of the Church — no one is to question any of the sacraments, and no schoolmaster is to teach boys about the sacraments. Constitutions 6 and 7 concern Wycliffite books: no one is to read any book or tractate by Wyclif, unless such reading has been approved by a committee, and no one is to translate Scripture into English.

---

10 Wilkins, vol.3, p.116.
11 Wilkins, vol.3, p.156
12 — 'if a man were duly contrite, any exterior confession is superfluous or of no use to him' (cf. *Piers Plowman* B.XI.80–82).
— '... that temporal lords should be able, at their own judgement, to take away temporalities from habitually delinquent ecclesiastics, and that the people should be able to correct habitually delinquent lords at their own judgement' (cf. *Piers Plowman* B.XV.560–65);
— '... that friars should be constrained to acquire their food through the labour of their hands, and not through begging' (cf. *Piers Plowman* B.XX.234–41; XX.384–5). (Wilkins, vol.3, pp.157–8.) The list also appears in *Fasciculi Zizaniorum Magistri Johannis Wyclif cum Tritico*, edited by W.W.Shirley, Rolls Series 5 (London 1858), pp.278–82.

Constitution 8 asserts that no one is to affirm anything contrary to morals – not even if such arguments can be defended by a 'certain skilfulness of words or terms'. Excommunication is the penalty, unless the offender should recant within a month. The ninth constitution decrees that no one shall dispute any articles of dogma, and singles out especially articles concerning the veneration of the cross and of images; the veneration of saints; pilgrimages and reliquaries; and swearing in ecclesiastical and secular courts. The tenth and eleventh constitutions are not relevant here.[13]

I will now turn briefly to the royal legislation concerned with the repression of opinions and books. The first statute of the period concerned with the repression of speech comes in 1378, and repeats and refines a statute first devised by Edward I in 1275 concerning false lies spread against the great men of the realm. Whereas, however, the Edwardian statute mentions only 'great men of the realm',[14] the Ricardian statute of 1378 clearly has slander against the King's Council in mind. It specifies those who are not to be slandered as 'Prelates, Dukes, Earls, Barons, and other great men of the realm, and also the Chancellor, Treasurer, Clerk of the Privy Seal ... and ... other great officers of the realm'.[15] The penalty for these 'devisors of false news, and of horrible and false lies' is that they be imprisoned until they find the person who first spread these lies. The statute is repeated, though reinforced, in 1388, where it is said that the reporter of false speech against the great men of the realm be imprisoned and punished by the advice of the King's Council when he cannot find the first mover of the news.[16]

The other strand of royal legislation in the period is the anti-heretical legislation. In his bull of 1377, Gregory XI directed Sudbury to inform Edward III of the danger Wyclif posed to the political stability of the kingdom. Despite some powerful secular support for Wyclif and his early followers, the royal legislation against Lollardy implies the view expressed by Gregory – that Lollardy is a threat as much to the state as to the church.[17] In the year after the Peasants' Revolt, the statute of 1382 declares that 'there be divers evil persons within the realm, going from county to county and from town to town ... under the dissimulation of great holiness', who preach in many places, speading 'heresies and notorious errors, to

---

[13] Wilkins, vol.3, pp.314–19. See Anne Hudson, *The Premature Reformation: Wycliffite Texts and Lollard History* (Oxford 1988), pp.82–103 for the Oxford context of Arundel's *Constitutions*.
[14] *Statutes of the Realm*, Anno 3 Ed.I (1275), c.34, vol.I, p.35.
[15] *Statutes of the Realm*, Anno 2 Ric.II (1378), Stat.1, c.5, vol.II, p.9.
[16] *Statutes of the Realm*, Anno 12 Ric.II (1388), c.11, vol.II, p.59. It might be mentioned in passing that Passus IV of the B-Text is closely modelled on the judicial procedures of the King's Council, as Anna Baldwin has shown, in *The Theme of Government in Piers Plowman*, Piers Plowman Studies I (Cambridge 1981), pp.40–50.
[17] For the association of Lollardy with rebellion more generally, see M.E.Aston, 'Lollardy and Sedition, 1381–1431', *Past and Present*, 17 (1960), 1–44.

the great emblemishing of the Christian Faith and the destruction of the laws ...'
It is directed to imprison all such preachers and those who maintain them.[18]

But the most draconian legislation in the period against Lollardy in the *Statutes*
is the statute of 1401, the *De Haeretico Comburendo*. The statute begins by relating
that 'divers false and perverse People of a certain new sect ... do perversely and
maliciously ... under the colour of dissembled holiness, preach and teach these
days openly and privily divers new doctrines and wicked heretical and erroneous
opinions'. It then goes on to direct that 'this wicked sect, preachings, doctrines
and opinions should from hensforth be utterly destroyed'. The practical execution
of this direction consists in the prohibition of unlicensed preaching, as well as in
the prohibition of preaching, holding views, teaching, or having any book made
contrary to the Catholic faith. All books containing such doctrines are to be
delivered to the diocesan within forty days of the publication of the statute; every
person who offends, or who fails to deliver such books, or who is suspected of
offending, will be arrested and imprisoned. If they do not abjure in prison, they
will be sentenced by a secular court, whose officials, after sentence, will receive
the heretics, and 'them before the people in an high place do to be burnt; that
such punishment may strike fear to the minds of other ...'[19]

Clearly this brief survey of ecclesiastical and royal legislation in the period
could be extended by considering its specific occasions and targets, and by reference to actual cases of its enactment. But even within the more limited scope of
this article, we are in a position to summarise by saying that royal and ecclesiastical legislation against slanderous rumour and heresy, as spoken or written, certainly did exist in the period spanning the two texts under consideration. We can
go further and say that the 30 or so years from 1378 witnessed the increasing
intensity of such legislation. *Piers Plowman* B stands, that is, on the borders of a
period of active repression.

This conclusion suggests, though does not prove, that the fictional references
within our two texts to the constraints of satire are not only fictional. Whether or
not these poems were really saying anything dangerous can only be tested within
the terms of the legislation I have just outlined. I will conclude this section with
brief arguments about whether or not Langland and the *Mum* author are actually
saying anything dangerous within the terms of the legislation cited above.

To treat Langland first: with regard to the two sets of ecclesiastical legislation
(the Pelagian and the Wycliffite sets of opinions), we can say that semi-Pelagianism and Wycliffism derive from quite different, and opposed theological camps. It
is a mark of Langland's peculiarity as a poet that he incurs the charge of proposing,
or at least overlapping with, *both* sets of ideas. Langland's central theological
position can be described as semi-Pelagian, as Robert Adams has amply demon-

---

[18] *Statutes of the Realm*, Anno 5 Ric.II (1382), Stat.2, c.5, vol.II, pp.25–6.
[19] *Statutes of the Realm*, Anno 2 Hen.IV (1400–1401), c.15, vol.II, pp.125–8.

strated.[20] As to his overlap with Lollardy, this is a complex question, which has been treated authoritatively, with the conclusion that despite holding many positions similar to those of the Lollards, Langland cannot be said to show 'clear sympathy with specifically and unequivocally Wycliffite positions'.[21] Here I am not concerned with the question as a whole, so much as the more specific question as to whether or not Langland contravenes the legislation against Lollardy. In answering this question we are not concerned as to whether a view once stated in the poem is elsewhere contradicted, or as to whether views expressed in the poem are those of Langland or of *personae* distinct from the author: the *Constitutions* legislate against any statement against the Catholic faith or against morality, 'even if [such statements] might be defended by a certain sophistication of words or terms'. This particular article of legislation cites the authority of Hugh of St Victor: 'Very often what is well said is not well understood'.[22]

Many views expressed in the poem are legislated against: views on the salvation of the heathen (cf. XII.285–95); on fraternal mendicancy (cf. XX.234–241; XX.384–5); on the corruption of the papacy and its claims to authority (cf. XIX.445–451); on disendowment (cf. XV.562–565); and on confession (XI.80–82) are all isolated by the legislation as being heterodox. Beyond these specific points of doctrinal statement, Langland's poem also offends the legislation of the period under consideration in addressing its matter in a context which is not specifically clerical or academic: the criticism of the clergy addressed to a mixed audience contravenes Arundel's *Constitutions* (the third), as does the discussion, outside an academic context, of confession (the fourth and fifth).[23] But such views are being expressed, as I have mentioned, on the verge of their being formally

---

[20] Robert Adams, 'Piers's Pardon and Langland's Semi-Pelagianism', *Traditio*, 39 (1983), 367–418.

[21] The citation is drawn from Anne Hudson, *The Premature Reformation*, p.408. The question of Langland's overlap with Lollardy is treated in the same work on pp.398–408. See also the important article by Pamela Gradon, 'Langland and the Ideology of Dissent', *PBA*, 66 (1980), 179–205; and D.A.Lawton, 'Lollardy and the *Piers Plowman* Tradition', *MLR*, 76 (1981), 780–93, who argues that, instead of Langland having Lollard sympathies, it was rather the case that 'Lollards had Langlandian sympathies' (p.793). I agree with the essential argument of these articles, that Langland is a reformer, but not a Lollard; the only point where I feel the articles of Gradon and Hudson are too tentative is in the treatment of Piers as a papal figure in B.XIX.183–91; Hudson does not discuss this point, while Gradon argues that we should not 'identify Piers with the poor priests or indeed with the priesthood' (p.199). I argue the possible connection with Wycliffite thought here in *Piers Plowman: An Introduction to the B-Text* (Longman, forthcoming), ch.7. For a more sceptical view of the relation of *Piers Plowman* with quasi-Lollard reformism, see Christina von Nolcken, '*Piers Plowman*, the Wycliffites and *Pierce the Plowman's Crede*', *YLS*, 2 (1988), 71–102.

[22] '... etiamsi quadam verborum aut terminorum curiositate defendi possint: nam teste beato Hugone, de sacramentis, "Saepius quod bene dicitur, non bene intelligitur" ' (Wilkins, vol.3, p.317).

[23] This last point is made by Hudson, *The Premature Reformation*, p.408.

legislated against as dangerous. As Anne Hudson has recently argued, Langland's poem is a work 'whose impact became more unorthodox as time passed'. She surmises that had Archbishop Arundel read the poem after the promulgation of the *Constitutions* in 1409, he 'would surely have had to adjudge the poem heretical'.[24]

Was *Mum and the Sothsegger* illegal? Here we would be concerned with the royal legislation against slanderous rumour, since the poem contains nothing which could be read as formally Lollard.[25] It seems to me that the kind of thing being said in *Mum* is dangerous only in a relative way – that is, dangerous according to circumstances. Some of the complaints which emerge from the bag of 'priuy poesy' at the end of the poem are extremely common complaints in the period, and themselves attested in royal statutes (e.g. the complaint against liveried maintenance, which was statuted in 1390[26]). The really dangerous complaint in the poem, against the Council of Henry IV, is implicit in the whole opening sequence of the poem. From the way it is suppressed by Mum as soon as it is about to become explicit (at l.232), we may suppose that it is dangerous. But statements of this kind, too, can be made in the period by by no means revolutionary figures.[27] Attacking the King's Council is certainly a dangerous activity, especially after the two statutes of 1378 and 1388 forbidding such attack, and especially in the unsteady early years of Henry's reign.[28] The poem seems to me to represent the voice of parliamentary, rather than popular, objection to Henry's Council, as expressed in the Commons petitions to the parliament of 1404, for example.[29]

---

[24] Hudson, *The Premature Reformation*, p.408.

[25] D.A.Lawton, in his article 'Lollardy and the *Piers Plowman* Tradition', argues that *Mum and the Sothsegger* does have Lollard sympathies (pp.788–92). He acknowledges that his case is far from conclusive. It seems to me that any argument that the poem does have Lollard sympathies must account for the way in which the overt satirical emphases of the poem are much more broadly political and secular than would be the case with a Lollard tract.

[26] Anno 13 Ric.II (1389–90), Stat.3, vol.II, pp.74–5.

[27] Thomas Brunton is an example. See the sermon cited in note 4 above.

[28] For letters from Henry in 1402 against spreaders of false rumour to the effect that Richard II was still alive, and against criticism of his governance, see Thomas Rymer, *Foedera, Conventiones, Literae, et cuiscunque generis Acta Publica inter Reges Angliae*, 10 vols (London 1740–45), Vol.4, Part I, p.27.

[29] For parliamentary opposition to Henry IV in the early years of his reign, see *Rolls of Parliament*, 5 vols, Vol.3. That the poem represents the voice of parliamentary, rather than popular complaint, is also suggested by the attack on popular rumour in the poem, ll.1388–1488. The attack here on those who spread rumous 'atte nale' (l.1390) parallels complaints made by Henry in his letter of 1402 to the Bishop of Exeter, where he says that malicious complaints about his governance are made 'in tabernis' (*Foedera*, Vol.4, Part I, p.27). In *Mum*, this ill-informed popular rumour is specifically distinguished from parliamentary complaint, 'of knightz þat cometh for þe shires, / That þe king clepith to cunseil with oþer' (ll.1460–61). Reference should also be made to ll.1118–1140, in which the poet encourages knights of the shires to speak up, 'yn place þat is proprid to parle for þe royaulme' l.1132).

The kinds of statements it makes might be dangerous according to circumstance, but not absolutely dangerous, like Lollard opinions, or opinions questioning Henry's legitimacy.

II

Everything that has been said so far might seem to have more to do with literary history than with literary criticism. I would agree with that, but go on to argue that literary history of this kind has immediate implications for literary criticism. For when we come to define the form of these poems, we must, I think, account for their formal properties as a way of negotiating the constraints which both surround and inhabit them. In this second section I will look particularly to *Mum and the Sothsegger*, and point to some of the formal strategies adopted by the poet to generate and justify his role as satirist.

A characteristic objection made to Lollards in both legislation against them, and in accounts of their trials, is that they reply with 'subtle cavilations', that they adopt cunning verbal strategies to camouflage their real position when under examination.[30] It is perhaps this which prompts Arundel to prohibit any conclusions to be affirmed contrary to good morals, 'even if they might be defended by a certain sophistication of words or terms'.[31] If this was characteristic of the verbal strategies of the Lollards under pressure, the author of *Mum*, on the contrary, says that he favours the stance of the plain speaker, who 'can not speke in termes ne in tyme nother,/ But bablith fourth bustusely as barn vn-y-lerid' (ll.49–50). This topos of the plain, low style speaker might itself suggest the poet's sophistication, since it is drawn from the prescriptions of *scholia* and *accessus* concerned with satire.[32] And when we look to the poem, I think we can see that what is really interesting in it are the sophisticated textual strategies the poet adopts whereby he can get into a position to reveal abuses. These strategies are all designed to convey the impression that the narrator adopts the role of satirist despite himself, that he is not seeking the authority of the truth-teller for himself, that he is not himself the source of his own authority.

The poem as we have it misses both its beginning and its end; the text we have opens with a declaration of the need for a truth-teller in the King's Council, who will not be afraid of the evident dangers confronting him. The narrator is about to enter into specific details of the failures of Henry's counsellors, when, as I said

---

30 See Anne Hudson, *The Premature Reformation*, pp.219–24.
31 Wilkins, vol.3, p.317.
32 For the stylistic roughness and low rhetorical register of satirical writing (as recommended by the *scholia* on and *accessus* to classical satirists, see Paul Miller, *The Mediaeval Literary Theory of Satire and its Relevance to the Works of Gower, Langland, and Chaucer* (unpublished Ph.D., The Queen's University of Belfast, 1982), pp.118–20, 165–7.

earlier, he is constrained mid-sentence by Mum: 'Nomore of this matiere' (l.232). The opening thus dramatically reveals that problems of censorship are logically prior to the statement of specific political grievances. The essential action of the poem from this moment forwards deals, as we might expect, with the question of censorship, either external or self imposed. The narrator's response is not to reject outright Mum's advice to keep quiet; instead, he argues the 'reasons of bothe two sides,/ The pro and þe contra as clergie askith' (ll.299–300). But being unable to come to a decision, he deferentially consults a series of institutions on the matter. The first institutions he consults are clerical and ecclesiastical: he goes to the faculties of Arts and Theology in the universities; to the friars; to the monks; and then to the secular clergy attached to the cathedrals. He is no nearer an answer, and Mum counsels him to leave his enquiry, since everyone thinks he is mad, and he is courting danger. The narrator asserts that he received a divine inspiration to continue. He goes to the parish clergy, and is disappointed there too; his disappointment provokes him to attack the clergy's avarice and its resultant cowardice, when he is again restrained by Mum, who warns the narrator that attacking the clergy is especially dangerous (a point repeated in many polemical works of the period, like *Jack Upland* and *Pierce Plowman's Crede*[33]). Mum insists on the narrator's naivety, by conceding that it is indeed immoral, and even illegal, for the clergy *not* to warn the great of imminent dangers: '*qui tacet consentire videtur*'; despite his statement of this truth, Mum says that he will not openly declare it, and dissuades the narrator from any further dealings with the clergy. The narrator now broaches a further set of institutions, those of secular power (the court, and the town mayors), where again he finds only mummers. Exhausted from his search, he lies down, and in an *oraculum*-dream he is instructed by the authority figure that he should follow the truth which is in his own heart; when the narrator wakes up, says the *oraculum*-figure, he should write a book and *conclude*; he should, unlike Conscience in *Piers Plowman*, 'make an ende':

> ... let no feynt herte
> Abate þy blessid bisynes of þy boke-making
> Til hit be complete to clapsyng, caste aweye doutes
> And lete þe sentence be sothe, and sue to þende

(ll.1280–1283).

The dreamer wakes, and, after a short defence of the truth of some dreams, he procedes to open a bag containing many a 'pryue poyse' written in different kinds of books. The narrator summarises the contents of these texts, which are all directed against particular abuses.

---

[33] *Jack Upland, Friar Daw's Reply and Upland's Rejoinder*, edited by P.L.Heyworth (Oxford 1968), p.55, ll.31–3; p.63, ll.214–19; p.65, ll.244–50. *Pierce the Ploughman's Crede*, edited by W.W.Skeat, EETS OS 30 (London 1867), ll.520–45; ll.647–70.

In what ways, then, can this poem be said to be intimately shaped by the constraints on satire which surround and inhabit it? I will make two observations here. Firstly, the strategy of the poem is not to claim authority for itself, but instead to defer to the authority of institutions whose formal responsibility it is to reveal abuses. The movement of the poem is generated out of the fact that these institutions provide inadequate answers. This inadequacy is of different kinds. In the case of the universities, for example, the inadequacy is to do with the fact that what they study is simply irrelevant to contemporary abuses. It is not within the scope of the Liberal Arts to resolve the question; Theology, who might be expected to contain the question of truth-telling within his scope, is of no more use; he says that he has never heard of such a case as the one moved by the narrator:

> Hit is sum noyous nycete of þe newe iette,
> For the texte truly telleth vs nomore
> But how þat goode gouuernance graciousely endith.

> (ll.375–377)

So Theology does embrace political questions, but the frame of his consideration is too limited; for the question posed by the narrator is logically prior to the declaration that 'good governance ends well'. This maxim about good kingship may well be true, but the narrator's problem is how to tell the king that he is not governing well. So here we have the new text, *Mum and the Sothsegger*, being generated out of the insufficiency of authoritative institutions and texts. The inadequacy of the monasteries is of a different kind; for here the narrator is not even admitted because of his poverty. The very approach to the monks, that is, negates the possibility of dialogue.

This, it seems to me, is the poem's essential strategy: apparent deference is shown to sets of authoritative institutions, whose very existence should render a truth-teller, and his poem, unnecessary. But the inadequacy of their responses generates the need for a discourse without institutional backing, the satirical discourse of the poem itself. This is also, it might be added, the strategy of *Pierce Plowman's Crede*, and, I think, the essential strategy which both these poets learn from *Piers Plowman*. In all these poems, poetry is revealed as a discourse by no means independent of institutional discourses; but the poetic text is nevertheless registered as taking its occasion from the inadequacies of those institutions and their authoritative texts – those 'bookes ynowe' which Imaginatif says should satisfy Will in Passus XII of *Piers Plowman*.[34]

---

[34] *Mum and the Sothsegger* and *Pierce the Plowman's Crede* proceed by showing an apparent deference to institutions which the poems are ultimately designed to attack. It would seem that the authors of these poems are indebted to Langland for this satirical strategy (though of course it appears earlier in the satirical tradition, as in, for example, Jean de Hautville's *Architrenius*). But Langland's use of the strategy is much more complex and subtle: Will's deference to institutions is not merely a ploy whereby he can attack them; often an

But this is not to argue that the poems simply claim personal authority for the occasion of new texts, and here I broach my second point. In this poem the authority for speaking out comes not from the poet's own self, but rather through other voices – here notably through the safe conduct the narrator says he received from heaven (ll.584–591), and through the oraculum-figure, whose own authority is distanced through the device of the dream (another distancing technique the Mum author learns from Langland[35]). But most interestingly, perhaps, the authority here comes from Mum himself. Mum stands as an apparent binary opposite to truth-telling; but in fact Mum tells a good deal of truth. This is especially true of his third intervention, concerning the duty of prelates to restrain the anger of kings, and to warn of impending disasters. It is in this intervention that he states the canon law concerning bishops who fail to correct sin, and also suggests that this is proverbial wisdom in any case:

> ... in cuntrey hit is a comune speche
> And is y-write in Latyne, lerne hit who-so wil:
> The reson is "qui tacet consentire videtur".
>
> (ll.743–5)[36]

This device is cunning, since it produces the strongest legal arguments in defence of truth-telling from the voice of Mum. At the same time, it implies that those who are silent are not silent through ignorance. The very existence of someone questioning silence engages the silent against their own interests, and reveals their bad faith.

III

In considering the ways in which poems might be informed by the constraints of satire, I have focussed on Mum and the Sothsegger mainly because, for the two poems under consideration, it presents the situation I am describing in much simpler form. We can see, nevertheless, that the Mum author clearly draws on the same strategies in Piers Plowman; for there, too, Langland authorises his own narrative voice through the failure of different sources of institutional and textual

institution's limitations might be revealed, but a definite value attached to that institution all the same (e.g. Study and Clergy).

[35] It may well be the case that the choice of the dream-form across the whole of Piers Plowman is designed to allow a certain prudent distance between the author and his poem; the most explicit instance of the narrator distancing himself from his dream is B.VII.144–201.

[36] The canon law relevant to bishops blaming when necessary is stated in Corpus Iuris Canonici, ed. Aemilius Friedberg, 2 vols (Leipzig 1879), prima pars, dist. 83, vol.1, col.293–4.

authority. But if *Piers Plowman* is the model for generating the voice and authority of the satirist, it is also true that Langland undoes that in his poem. In this final section, I want to consider how and why Langland should 'deconstruct' the authority of the satirist he so powerfully establishes.

In the inner dream of Passus XI, Will meets the figure Lewtee immediately after he has been betrayed by the friars. He asks Lewtee whether or not he should dare to make known his dream, and thereby denounce the friars. Lewtee replies in a way similar to the *oraculum*-figure in *Mum and the Sothsegger* and, it might be added, to Cacciaguida in Dante's *Paradiso*, who orders Dante 'make manifest your vision' (*Par.* XVII.128). Lewtee unhesitatingly encourages Will to publish his dream. To Will's remark that his detractors will adduce the text 'Judge not, that you may not be judged', Lewtee replies in this way:

> 'And whereof serveth lawe', quod Lewtee, 'if no lif undertoke it –
> Falsnesse ne faiterie? For somwhat the Apostle seide
> *Non oderis fratrem.*
> And in the Sauter also seith David the prophete
> *Existimasti inique quod ero tui similis &c.*
> It is *licitum* for lewed men to [l]egge the sothe
> If hem liketh and lest – ech a lawe it graunteth ...
> Thyng that al the world woot, wherfore sholdestow spare
> To reden it in retorik to arate dedly synne?
> Ac be neveremoore the firste the defaute to blame;
> Though thow se yvel, seye it noght first – be sory it nere amended.
> No thyng that is pryve, publice thow it nevere;
> Neither for love laude it noght, ne lakke it for envye:
> *Parum lauda; vitupera parcius'.*

$$\text{(XI.91–106a)}$$

This is a powerful and largely well informed speech. Lewtee begins by citing first New and then Old Testament authority for public blaming. The first citation ('*Non oderis fratrem ...*') continues '... *tuum in corde tuo, sed publice argue eum*', and is in fact drawn from an Old Testament source, Leviticus 19.17. The second quotation, which is from the Psalms, ends with an affirmation of unequivocal blaming: '*Arguam te, et statuam contra faciem tuam*' (Psalm 49.21). From these biblical defences, Lewtee asserts a legal defence (from both Canon and Civil law) for public truth-telling. He then draws our attention to the fact that there are also standard ethico-literary constraints on (and defences for) the writing of satire. These are drawn from coherent commentary traditions embodied in *scholia* and *accessus* to satirists from the ninth century.[37] As stated here, these constraints from

---

[37] For these commentary traditions, see Miller, *The Mediaeval Literary Theory of Satire*; the sections of this thesis dealing with the commentary traditions are summarised in Paul Miller, 'John Gower, Satiric Poet', in *Gower's 'Confessio Amantis': Responses and Reassessments*, ed. A.J.Minnis (Woodbridge 1983), pp.79–105.

the literary tradition are as follows: speak only with a common voice – what 'al the world woot', and not from merely personal, original provocation;[38] do not attack individuals (what is 'pryve');[39] and do not be vituperative, by speaking out of ill-will, or 'envye'.[40]

But perhaps the strongest authority for the speech, in the context of Langland's poem, is its speaker, Lewtee. The word 'lewtee', derived from Latin *legalitas*, is the closest Latin based word in Langland's lexis to the key Germanic word 'truthe', and is used by Langland as an apparent synonym for 'truthe'.[41] Both words contain senses of both justice and faith keeping ('legality' and 'loyalty').[42] 'Truthe' is clearly a fundamental concept in the poem, and one which entails certain standards of legal justice and social faithfulness, but also certain standards of *speech*. Holy Church's praise of 'truthe' in Passus I focusses first on true speech: whoever is 'trewe of his tonge and telleth noon oother', she says, is divine (I.88–91). So much of Langland's poetry is determined by this injunction, devoted as it is to the elucidation and declaration of what is true. So here in Passus XI, Lewtee's affirmation of the legality of truth-telling is simply making explicit what is implicit in the name 'Lewtee' already, and simply reaffirming profound themes in the poem. It is unsurprising that critics should take it that this speech 'may express the poet's own view of the legitimate scope of satiric and polemical poetry', as A. V. C. Schmidt says.[43]

I think this view is exactly right as far as it goes. But any statement of Langland's 'view' on just about anything must be prepared to take into account the way in which apparently stable positions are often questioned. If Lewtee does affirm the justice of satirical poetry in Passus XI, the words of Clergy in Passus X might make us wary about accepting them without qualification. Clergy's definition of the Dowel triad ends with a description of Dobest, which is no sooner made than it is qualified:

---

[38] Miller, *Mediaeval Literary Theory of Satire*, points out that satirists could either claim personal authority for their voice, or else adopt one of several disclaimers, one of which is the invocation of 'written authority or the authority of common opinion to justify his censure' (p.219). On p.300 he cites Gower's *Vox Clamantis*, where Gower makes this disclaimer: 'Quod dicunt alii scribam, quia nolo quod vlli / Sumant istud opus de nouitate mea' (III. Prol.27–28).

[39] Miller, *Mediaeval Literary Theory of Satire*, p.142; p.235. He cites (p.298) Gower's *Vox Clamantis* for this tradition: 'Non ego personas culpabo, set increpo culpas, / Quas in personis cernimus esse reas' (III. Prol.9–10).

[40] Miller, *Mediaeval Literary Theory of Satire*, pp.108–9; pp.138–9; pp.180–1. Miller cites *Mum and the Sothsegger*, 72–95 in this connection (p.206), where, for example, the narrator says that it is not his 'cunseil to clatre what me knoweth / In sclaundre ne scathe ne scorne of þy brother' (ll.72–3).

[41] See, for example, B.XI.153–6.

[42] For the senses of 'justice' and 'loyalty' contained in both 'lewtee' and 'truthe', see John A.Alford, *Piers Plowman, A Glossary of Legal Diction* (Cambridge 1988), under 'leaute', senses II and III, and under 'treuthe', senses I and III.

[43] Schmidt, *The Vision of Piers Plowman*, p.334.

Thanne is Dobest to be boold to blame the gilty,
Sythenes thow seest thiself as in soule clene;
Ac blame thow nevere body and thow be blameworthy ...
God in the Gospel grymly repreveth
Alle that lakketh any lif and lakkes han hemselve.

(X.256–260)

This passage, coming from Clergy, is directed at priests: if they first correct
themselves, then 'burel clerkes' will be 'abasshed' to attack them (X.281–288).
Will himself might be one of the 'burel clerkes' given to attacking the clergy
(Lewtee implies that he is 'lewed' (XI.96)), but Clergy's strictures for correctors
who should first correct themselves is a two-edged sword, applying equally well to
Will as to priests. Langland's consideration of the justice of satire is not restricted
to questions of verbal 'truthe' alone; he also places the question of verbal 'truthe'
in the larger problematic of his poem, concerning theological 'truthe'. Lewtee's
affirmation of the justice of satire sounds, as I have said, very much like the
justification by the *oraculum*-figure in *Mum and the Sothsegger*; but the *Mum* author
is concerned with only one sense of 'truthe' – that of speaking the truth. Langland, on the contrary, is primarily concerned with theological 'truthe', or justice,
from which social and verbal truth should derive. But if this is the case, then
Passus XI is precisely the moment in the third vision (Passus VIII–XII) when the
crisis of untempered theological 'truthe' is most evident. From the moment that
Truthe sends his austere pardon which is no pardon in Passus VII, Will has
interrogated different parts of his own reason, and the educational institutions and
texts which train the reason, concerning the nature of Do-well. His problem is
that man is simply unable to meet the standards of God's absolute justice by his
own, unaided efforts. But all the figures interrogated by Will (Thoght, Wit, Study,
Clergy and Scripture) merely repeat the idea, with different emphases, that Do-
well consists of obeying the law. This does not advance Will, since his premise is
that men *cannot* obey God's absolute law, the law of Truthe.

It is, interestingly, immediately after the speech by Lewtee that Scripture
precipitates this crisis of theological 'truthe' in the poem: she agrees with Lewtee
about the justice of satire, but goes straight on to relate a parable about the
unremitting justice of God, the parable of the feast to which many are called but
few chosen. Will might have been justified by Lewtee's defence of satire, but he
does not feel justified after Scripture's parable. Instead he trembles in 'tene' before
the apparently unremitting justice implied by this text (just as Piers had pulled the
unremitting 'pardon' apart in 'tene'), and questions himself as to whether or not
he is chosen. I do not have space here to analyse this speech in detail, but it is, it
seems to me, the turning point of the poem: in this confrontation with the naked
text of Scripture, Will makes the recognition that sinners will be damned unless
'Contricion wol come and crye by his lyve/ Mercy for hise mysdedes with mouthe
or with herte' (XI.135–6). This is the first time in the third vision that God's

27

mercy has been invoked, and the first time any affirmation is made that God's absolute law might be tempered by a covenant of statuted law, whereby sinners might 'Do well' through repentance.[44]

I am arguing, then, that this is the point of the poem which marks the movement forward to an understanding of God's mercy. A theology dominated by a sense of God's 'truthe' alone is an oppressive and imprisoning theology. Will can now move beyond the bounds of the God 'Truthe' to an understanding of the God of mercy. But if the crisis provoked by theological 'truthe' is reached and in part resolved here, then what implications does this have for Langland's sense of the 'truthe', or 'lewtee' of poetry? Such satire is premissed on a purely judgemental posture to the world. One might argue that such a judgemental attitude is inconsistent with the theology of mercy that the poem now begins to approach.

Does the development of Langland's theological argument here have implications for his practice as a satirical poet, for a poetry premissed on strict justice? I think it does, and that Langland reflects on his practice as a satirical poet in the light of the new theological themes being broached in the poem. The very juxtaposition of Lewtee, discussing satire, and Scripture, discussing theology, suggests that the two topics are intimately connected for Langland. And the next speaker in the poem after Scripture, Trajan, suggests how the theological development of the poem might influence the literary question of satire. Trajan serves as the archetype of one saved through God's merciful acceptance of his 'pure truthe'. The initial emphasis of Trajan's speech is that law without love is useless; he enjoins his audience to merciful acceptance of each other's faults, given the inevitability of sin:

> Forthi lakke no lif oother, though he moore Latyn knowe,
> Ne undernyme noght foule, for is noon withoute defaute.
>
> (XI.213–4)

The knowledge that 'noon is withoute defaute' had earlier provoked despair in Will; here instead it provokes humility and patience.

Trajan's emphasis on patience is given divine resonance in the inner vision as a whole, since the final accent of this vision is on the suffrance, or patience (in its Latin sense) of God. Will has a vision of Middle Earth, in which he sees all creatures following a divinely ordered pattern of Reason, except man. He complains to Reason about this, to which Reason replies:

---

[44] I argue in more detail that this speech is the turning point of the poem in my forthcoming book, *Piers Plowman: An Introduction to the B-Text* (Longman), ch.4.

28

> '... Recche thee nevere
> Why I suffre or noght suffre – thiself hast noght to doone.
> ...
> Who suffreth moore than God?' quod he; 'no gome, as I leeve'
>
> (XI.375–379)

There is a profound double meaning in this last use of 'suffreth', since God 'allows', or 'permits', and 'suffers' as a result. The whole theological thrust of Langland's poem has been to permit man a certain dignity in his ability to repay God what he owes for the debt of sin; a necessary concomitant of that dignity is that God allow man the choice of whether or not to sin. So God 'suffreth' – allows, and suffers. In *Mum and the Sothsegger*, it is precisely the habit of 'suffrance' which is characteristic of those who are silent from cowardice.[45] But at this point in *Piers Plowman*, we can see that 'suffrance', or patience, as both a divine and a human quality, is a profound response to the human condition. And such a theological perception has immediate implications for Will as a speaker – instead of satirising, he too should 'suffer'.[46]

The implications of this theological theme of patience for satire are suggested in the recurrence of the '*Nolite iudicare*' citation in the following passus, once by Imaginatyf (his defence of clergy refers to the words Christ wrote in the sand, '*Nolite iudicare ...*' (XII.89a)), and once by Patience, who says that the poor perform the commandment '*Nolite iudicare quemquam*' (XIV.286–290a). But they are enacted fully in the fourth vision, where Patience (unsuccessfully) restrains Will from attacking the doctor of divinity,[47] and where Patience himself provides a model of 'patient' but potent address to the powerful. I do not have space to pursue that now, and neither is this the occasion to demonstrate how satire is reinstated in the poem in Passus XV, in the speech of Anima, where the reintegrated individual soul (capable of both loving *and* judging) addresses the church in outspoken, radical satire.[48] We can, however, summarise the this third section

---

[45] Thus, for example, *Mum and the Sothsegger*, l.273; l.760; l.813.

[46] For my understanding of the importance of 'suffrance' in *Piers Plowman*, I am indebted to the article of A.V.C.Schmidt, 'The Inner Dreams in *Piers Plowman*', *Medium Aevum*, 55 (1986), 24–40. The awareness that 'suffrance' might be both a positive and a negative quality may account for the appearance of the phrase 'vnsittynge suffraunce' in the C- Text, at III.207 and IV.189 (line references from *Piers Plowman, An Edition of the C-text*, by Derek Pearsall (London 1978)). Further examples of reticence to attack out of moral 'suffrance' (or encouragements to practise this reticence) are (from the B-Text): II.48; VI.225; X.256–86; XI.213–14; XI.375–402; XI.420–4; XIII.85–97; XIV.290–90a; XV.249–53.

[47] Though it might be noticed that Langland as a poet, as distinct from Will, does not restrain himself from satire of the Doctor here. The strategy is similar to that of *Pierce the Plowman's Crede*, where the narrator remarks on how the friars go against the Gospel by blaming each other (ll.133–145). He thus presents himself as not blaming (just as Langland presents the ideal figure Patience as not blaming), where the poem clearly *is* satirical.

[48] I argue the reasons why satire is reinstated in the poem in Passus XV in *Piers Plowman: An Introduction to the B-Text*, ch.6.

by saying that the crisis of theological 'truthe' in the poem provokes a revaluation of a poetry founded on 'truthe' alone.

In conclusion to the three sections of this article, we might say that there certainly were specific political and ecclesiastical constraints on writing and speaking between the late 1370s and the first decade of the fifteenth century; both *Piers Plowman* and *Mum and the Sothsegger* are intimately shaped by negotiating these constraints, but nevertheless authorise their own satire. But if Langland does authorise his satire, it is equally true that he profoundly questions this authorisation. In the writing of satire for Langland, there are both political and theological constraints.

Langland's Clergial Lunatic

David Burnley

As part of a vision of social and political organization in the Prologue to the B-text of *Piers Plowman* a lunatic addresses a king 'clergially', kneeling and recommending justice to him with the promise of a heavenly reward.[1] This theme is immediately taken up by an angel who, speaking in Latin, rehearses the commonplace of the transience of earthly glory and advises that just severity be moderated by *pietas*, so that royal rule shall be in the image of the rule of God. A 'goliardeis of wordes' also contributes to this scene, interpreting the etymology of *rex* to imply a duty to rule (*regere*), and this is understood by the community to mean that the king's word has the force of law. This scene is followed at once by the fable of belling the cat.

This entire scene has attracted much critical attention, but the constitutional allegory has fared less satisfactorily than the rat fable.[2] Skeat interpreted the lunatic as Langland himself, and Owst, taking the possibility of contemporary reference to extremes, added that the angel might be Bishop Brunton of Rochester, whilst the 'goliardeis' would be Peter de la Mare, Speaker of the House of Commons.[3] Such identifications, which belong to the same world as Manly's new light on Chaucer's pilgrims, have come to seem naive to modern readers. Robert-

---

1   *The Vision of Piers Plowman. A Complete Edition of the B-Text*, edited by A.V.C.Schmidt (London 1978), Prol., 123–7. Quotation of the C-text is from *Piers Plowman by William Langland. An Edition of the C-text*, edited by Derek Pearsall (London 1978).
2   Among those who comment on it are: J.J.Jusserand, *Piers Plowman, A Contribution to the History of English Mysticism*, revised and enlarged, translated by M.E.R. (London 1894); J.A.W.Bennett, 'The Date of the B-text of Piers Plowman', *MÆ* 12 (1943), 55–64; E.T. Donaldson, *'Piers Plowman': the C-text and its Poet* (New Haven 1949), pp.85–120; P.M.Kean, 'Love, Law, and Lewte in *Piers Plowman*', *RES* NS 15 (1964), 241–61; Elizabeth M.Orsten, 'The Ambiguities in Langland's Rat Parliament', *MS* 23 (1961), 216–39; Anna Baldwin, *The Theme of Government in Piers Plowman* (Woodbridge 1981), pp.12–16.
3   *The Vision of William Concerning Piers the Plowman*, edited by W.W.Skeat, 2 vols (Oxford 1886), Vol.2, p.15; G.R.Owst, *Literature and Pulpit in Medieval England*, Second Edition (Oxford 1961), pp.578–88. See also Jusserand, who associates the rat spokesman with Peter de la Mare.

son and Huppé are more sophisticated.[4] The lunatic functions for them as a device of satire, discrediting the pretensions of a too-worldly ruler. Yet satire requires a target, or it is pointless, and their acceptance that the lunatic is Will implies that they too believe that the scene is intended to have particular relevance. To my mind, however, the relevance of the scene to contemporary figures and events is improbable: it is too generalized in reference, too abstract in expression. It states broad political principles which are not specifically applicable until the commencement of the fable of the rats. It is, more arguably, the theory in whose context the narrative of belling the cat operates. If such a view is justified, the equation of the lunatic with Langland or with Will is inappropriate. The lunatic and the angel too must be figures of much greater imprecision and abstraction. Who or what then is the lunatic, and why does he speak 'clergially'?

A step towards answering the first of these questions may be taken by observing that in the C-text the lunatic is replaced by the personification, Kynde Wit, who in the B-text is the joint author, along with the king and the Commons, of 'lawe and leaute'. In discarding the lunatic, the the status of his words is changed. What originally could be taken as merely a pious commentary becomes, in the mouth of Kynde Wit, an allegory of the foundations of legislative responsibility. The speech itself now becomes the act of creation, but although nominally addressed to the King and Commons, it remains imperfectly adapted to its purpose, since the singular form of the pronoun is still used throughout. The lunatic, then, is intimately associated with Kynde Wit, and although no other lunatics are to be found in the B-text, and in fact they do not appear in force until the C-text, some investigation of what Langland meant by Kynde Wit may help to illuminate his conception of this isolated lunatic.

It is apparent from the immediate context that Kynde Wit is a mode of knowing more fundamental than either academic learning or craft skills, for it is that natural understanding upon which both are based.[5] As worldly and immediate perception, it can provide the data upon which reason and conscience may operate, but is itself amoral, lying behind both worldly astuteness and pagan, and therefore unenlightened, learning. Although Kynde Wit also speaks 'clergially' in the C-text, he is quite distinct from Clergie.[6] The latter is an important independent personification, and to Langland clearly implies Christian learning, indeed more narrowly the study of Scripture, beside which pagan learning, arising from mere experience, is but worldly folly:

---

[4] D.W.Robertson, Jr and Bernard F.Huppé, *Piers Plowman and Scriptural Tradition* (Princeton 1951), p.29.
[5] Gerald Morgan, in 'The Meaning of Kind Wit, Conscience, and Reason in the First Vision of *Piers Plowman*', MP 84 (1987), 351–8, associates Kind Wit with *intelligentia*, the basis of both speculative and practical reasoning.
[6] Britton J.Harwood, ' "Clergye" and the Action of the Third Vision in Piers Plowman', MP 70 (1973), 279–90.

'Forthi I conseille alle creatures no clergie to dispise,
Ne sette short by hir science, whatso thei don hemselve.
Take we hir wordes at worth, for hire witnesses be trewe,
And medle we noght muche with hem to meven any wrathe,
Lest cheste cha[f]en us to choppe ech man other:
Nolite tangere christos meos &c.
'For clergie is kepere under Crist of hevene;
[Com] ther nevere no knyght but clergie hym made.
Ac kynde wit cometh of alle kynnes sightes —
Of briddes and of beestes, [of blisse and of sorwe],
Of tastes of truthe and [oft] of deceites.
'[Olde] lyveris toforn us useden to marke
The selkouthes that thei seighen, hir sones for to teche,
And helden it an heigh science hir wittes to knowe.
Ac thorugh hir science soothly was nevere no soule ysaved,
Ne broght by hir bokes to blisse ne to joye;
For alle hir kynde knowyng com but of diverse sightes.
'Patriarkes and prophetes repreveden hir science,
And seiden hir wordes ne hir wisdomes was but a folye;
As to the clergie of Crist, counted it but a trufle:
Sapiencia huius mundi stultitia est apud Deum.

(B XII 121–39)

That Kynde Wit should speak 'clergially' is no less out of character than that a lunatic should do so, but the contrast in title is much more striking, and this alone should argue against the supposition that this line is ironic. No doubt is cast upon the content of the speech by its ascription. Rather, the implication seems to be that what is worthy of note is that some relatively unenlightened speaker, out of natural perception, approximates to an utterance which might have been spoken by a clerk. This notion of simple minded folk who nevertheless perceive the truth by direct experience is to be found repeated elsewhere in the C-text (IX 118–38). But the view expressed is both clichéd and limited, requiring expansion by the angel. So is it indeed the content of the speech which justifies the application of the word 'clergially' in the case of both the lunatic of the B-text and his substitute Kynde Wit in the C-text? Or is perhaps that what is referred to is the manner rather than the content of the speech? One peculiarity about the latter is its invariable yet inappropriate use of the pronouns *thee* and *thi* despite a change in context: both texts use this singular form of address to a king, and in the C-text, in possible disregard for grammar, there is some ambiguity whether it is the king himself or a whole company who are addressed by it.

Readers of this essay might be excused for fearing at this point that the writer is about to make insupportable claims concerning the use of *ye* and *thou* by Langland. Certainly, Chaucer's sensitivity to such usage is equalled by that of the

Gawain-poet, but Langland surely belongs to a different world?[7] An initial defence might be that such compartmentalisation is itself unjustifiable. We should not confuse the authors and their worlds with the world they depict in their works, and the styles and phrasing chosen as appropriate to this latter world. The *Gawain*-poet wrote both clerkly and courtly works, and in certain respects his vocabulary suggests that he looked at literature in a way more related to 'textueel' Langland than to Chaucer; yet Langland was a transient Londoner whose phrasing, despite his alliteration, can have more in common with certain of the less elevated *Canterbury Tales* than with *Gawain*. The use of the *ye* and *thou* discrimination is as much a feature of stylistic selection appropriate to a particular text or imagined situation as a reflection of the author's total linguistic competence. This assertion requires a brief digression.

The use of *ye* as a form of address to a single individual developed first in Latin as early as the fifth century and became part of the ceremonious address used in formal letters. The *artes dictamines* preserve the rules.[9] It was adopted first into French and then into English during the thirteenth century but was an artificiality which did not become widely established in English before the latter part of the fourteenth century. From then on, until the mid-seventeenth century, the forms of address among certain users of English were enriched by the option of addressing an individual either as *ye* or *thou* according to well known social and attitudinal prompts. The employment of this option was not evenly spread through society, and it seems to have been a usage which percolated downwards, commencing from the world of courtly manners and important affairs in which it had been adopted from the French and Latin proper to those milieux.[10] Its stylistic

---

[7] N.Nathan, 'Pronouns of Address in the *Friar's Tale*', MLQ 17 (1956), 39–42 and 'Pronouns of Address in the *Canterbury Tales*' MS 21 (1959), 193–201; J.A.Johnson, ' "Ye" and "Thou" among the Canterbury Pilgrims', *Michigan Academician*, 10 (1979), 71–6; C.Wilcockson, ' "Thou" and "Ye" in Chaucer's Clerk's Tale', *Use of English*, 31 (1980) 37–43; Everett C.Johnson, 'The Significance of the Pronoun of Address in *Sir Gawain and the Green Knight*', *Language Quarterly*, 5.iii–iv (1967), 34–6; Allan A.Metcalf, 'Sir Gawain and "You" ', *ChauR*, 5 (1971), 165–78; William W.Evans, Jr, 'The Dramatic Use of the Second-Person Singular Pronoun in *Sir Gawain and the Green Knight*', SN 39 (1967), 38–45.

[8] Conrad van Mure and Guido Faba in L.Rockinger, *Briefsteller und Formelbücher des 11 bis 14 Jahrhunderts*, Quellen und Erörterungen zur Bayerischen und Deutschen Geschichte, 9 (Munich 1863–4; reprinted Aalen 1969), p.435; p.189.

[9] R.O.Stidtson, *The Use of 'Ye' in the Function of 'Thou' in Middle English Literature* (Stanford 1917)

[10] A useful account of the plural form in singular address in French and Latin forms the introduction to Christine A.Maley, *The Pronouns of Address in Modern Standard French*, Romance Monographs, 10 (University, Mississippi 1974), pp.9–40. A rather bizarre late reflection of the clerkish distaste for the pretentiousness of the plural pronoun is found in revolutionary France when in *Le Mercure national* in December 1790 it was proposed that *vous* be abandoned as a term of respect, and a demand was made for general *tutoiement*. K.Nyrop, *Grammaire historique de la langue française*, 6 vols (Copenhagen 1904–30) Vol.5, p.235. Langland would no doubt have agreed with at least this radical gesture.

association was therefore with the mighty, with formality, and with matter of major secular importance. To express this in medieval terms, it is a linguistic nicety which belongs to the world of *courtoisie*. This is emphasized by the clear correlation which exists in the works of Chaucer between address by *sire, lord, dame, madame* and the pronoun *ye*, and perhaps even more significantly by the circumstance that the conjuration *by youre curteisie* never occurs with the singular pronoun, not even on the lips of the rather uncourtly Alisoun in the Miller's tale, who switches from *thou* when she finds urgent need to use this expression.

Address of an individual by the pronoun *ye*, then, belongs to the higher échelons of fourteenth-century English society; or it belongs to those who are forced to deal with them, or wish to be associated with them. It represents identification with and acceptance of the values of the courtly establishment. It does not sit well therefore with a socially critical or sharply satirical viewpoint. It is not of the same spirit as such statements as:

> For in charnel at chirche cherles ben yvel to knowe,
> Or a knyght from a knave there – knowe this in thyn herte.
>
> (B VI 48–9)

In the outlook expressed above, and in the stylistic level adopted throughout the greater part of its length, *Piers Plowman* is a *thou*-text; its author's expressed attitude to fellow man and woman is rather *leeve brother and sister* or even *goode men and wommen* than *sire* and *madame* or *lord* and *lady*. Indeed, on one occasion where it has been noted that Langland seems to perceive some parallel between his own existence and that of the simple beggars he defends in the C-text, it is expressed in terms of their shared lack of respect for status and authority:

> And thaugh a mete with the mayre amiddes þe strete
> A reuerenseth hym ryght nauht, no rather than another.
>
> (C IX 123–4)

Similar behaviour cost Langland himself his local reputation for sanity:

> And some lakked my lif – allowed it fewe –
> And leten me for a lorel and looth to reverencen
> Lordes or ladies or any lif ellis –
> As persons in pelure with pendaunts of silver;
> To sergeaunts ne to swiche seide noght ones,
> 'God loke yow, lordes!' – ne loutede faire,
> That folk helden me a fool; and in that folie I raved.
>
> (B XV 4–10)

Yet Langland in the B-text uses the ye address form on more than thirty occasions to individuals.[11] This number is a conservative estimate arrived at after discarding a relatively large number of cases in didactic and expository passages where the addressee is unclear or when a personification may be understood to stand for a social group and hence demand a plural. Among the remaining examples, variants cited by Kane-Donaldson show only half a dozen cases in which there is reasonable cause to doubt that Langland wrote *ye*. This leaves us with about two dozen examples in which the context compelled him to depart from his normal practice and adopt a studiedly polite form of address. These occur fairly randomly in both Will and Piers's interviews with the various personifications from whom both seek instruction. Courtesy is apparent, for example, in the following words to Hunger 'Yet I preie yow,' quod Piers, '*pur charite*, and ye konne ...' (VI 253) and in the address to Studie as a lady, using the forms *ye* and *madame* (X 148). *Ye* may be used appeasingly or to show respect between the personifications themselves and from Will to Piers. But this usage is also found in a few representations of the ordinary secular world reflecting actual social relationships. Thus Piers as ploughman respectfully addresses a knight with *ye* (VI 24) and receives *thee* in return. Beggars adopt a wheedling tone, employing *ye* and an inappropriate and unasked for *lord* to Piers 'For we have no lymes to laboure with, lord, ygraced be ye!' (VI 124). Less blatantly, a friar seeks alms by the same means (XX 366). But the most concentrated use of *ye* to individuals is in the scene set in the court found in the B-text in passus III and IV. Here Conscience politely addresses the Lady Mede with *ye*. The king is addressed by Reson and by Mede: both use the pronoun *ye* exclusively, and the king emphasizes his position by returning *thou*. In his representation of a venal, worldly court, Langland observes its proprieties of linguistic address. To have addressed a courtly lady or a king with the pronoun *thou* would have been considered ludicrous, madness, the act of a lunatic.

Yet kings *were* routinely addressed as *thou* in the medieval period. Aeneas Silvius, later Pope Pius II, remarks that this is the liberty of poets (*Tibizando poetae scribunt etiam principibus*), a view previously expressed, and indeed practised, by Christine de Pizan.[12] Jean de Meun addressed King Philippe IV by the pronoun *tu* in the prologue to his translation of Boethius. In brief, that speaker who does not accept the formalities imposed by social sophistication, but who earnestly wishes to communicate information vital to the well-being of a kindred

---

[11] The following is a complete list of examples of the use in the B-text of *ye* to a single addressee. A number of examples, where single individuals seem to be viewed primarily as representatives of social types, have been omitted: III 176, 344, 345, 346, 348, 350; IV 187. All preceding examples belong to the court scene. Most of the following seem to indicate Will's humility before various imposing figures: VI 127; X 370, 371, 386, XI 433, 436, XIII 105, 106, 108, 183; XIV 273; XV 22, 40, 460; XVI 53; XIX 15, 23, 322; XX 366. Several examples almost certainly read *ye* in the original, and do so in a majority of MSS, but also admit some variation: IV 146; VI 24, 124, 253; X 148, 386.

[12] Du Cange, *Glossarium*, also lists John of Janua's view that 'unum vosamus falsa; vereque tuamus'. He lists the verbs *tibissare*, *tuisare*, *vobisare*, and *vosare* to describe such activities in Medieval Latin.

soul has licence to adopt the role of clerkish instructor and address a king by the familiar pronoun. This instructor's role is evident in Chaucer's tale of Melibee, where the general tone and status of the world of Melibee and his wife requires mutual address by ye, but occasionally, in making exhortations and quoting the wisdom of the ancients, Prudence switches to thou. She then moves momentarily outside the structure of relationships demanded by conventional politeness to adopt the authority of learned tradition.

In using the ye form of address in the way he does, Langland is exhibiting perfectly understandable attitudes consistent with the views adumbrated in his work. The ambiguity of his usage is quite explicable. Later in the poem ye is employed to indicate decent everyday politeness to an interlocutor who deserves respect: in Langland's opinion this is earned by moral or learned stature rather than social status. But, in those scenes which represent events and types from the everyday world of beggars or the court, the use of ye is perceived as an aspect of faire speche, and so is equated with euphemistic, equivocating, flattering speech, a kind of speech treated with suspicion by most later medieval English authors including Langland himself (II 42; II 230; XV 350; XVI 154).

This attitude to the option of switching to the pronoun ye in singular address was well entrenched in certain circles in the later Middle Ages. Bokenham finds it indicative of St Elizabeth's humility that she would not permit anyone:

> in þe plurere noumbyr speken hyr to
> But oonly in þe syngulere, she hem dede deuyse,
> As sovereyns to subjectys be won to do.[13]

(896–8)

By Bokenham's time the norm of polite address was well established, but in a thirteenth-century sermon, Alexander Neckham too complains of the pretension which causes courtiers to adopt the plural form of address in contradistinction to the practice of Christ in the Gospels. Nor was this view limited to England, and indeed God, the ancients, and Reason were summoned by French and Italian humanists as witnesses to the unnecessary pretension of vos-address. The topic arises repeatedly in letters exchanged between Coluccio Salutati and Jean de Montreuil. Indeed, at the French court in the opening decades of the fifteenth-century, humanist practice and theory lent a certain chic to the traditional clerkly opposition to the use of the plural in address, so that Christine de Pizan confiden-tly seeks to flatter her dedicatees by ascribing to them an awareness of the advantage to their intellectual prestige of being addressed by the singular form.[14] In a letter to the elderly Eustache Deschamps, she describes this form of address as

---

[13] Stidtson, p.20.
[14] Christine de Pizan calls it the 'stille ... des poetes et orateurs'. J.D.Burnley, 'Christine de Pizan and the So-Called Style Clergial', MLR 81 (1986), 1–6.

the *stille clergial*, the form used among the learned.[15] However, since he had himself addressed Chaucer as *tu* in a well-known *balade*, he perhaps needed no explanation. Recognition that this style of address was that of clerks, careless of the pretensions of the world, does not entirely depend upon its characterization as such by Christine de Pizan. It is probably not mere chance that four of the seven occurrences of the pronoun *thow* in Chaucer's Franklin's tale are found in the speech of the Orleans clerk, whose usage contrasts markedly with the courtly *ye* of the other characters. Clerks had for generations resisted the use of *ye* as a symbol of their disdain of materialism and secular status. Although, in the early fifteenth century, this attitude was to become fashionable in a courtly society on the brink of Renaissance values, Langland seems to belong to the older tradition of the renunciation of courtly pretension. His usage is closely paralleled by that in Chaucer's Parson's tale where *ye* occurs only as a sign of respect from a child to its teacher, from Joseph to Potiphar's wife, and in the mouth of the serpent to Eve in the garden. The usage of the lunatic, then, and the simple but just perception of Kynde Wit, his alter ego in the C-text, is unlikely to have been a matter of chance. The undeviating selection of *thou* to a king, found in both B and C-texts, alongside the later ingratiating courtly usage with *ye*, is a conscious and deliberate linguistic choice carrying with it all the implications of learned authority borne by a recognizably clerkly idiom. Langland's lunatic is *clergial* not simply for the validity of what he says, but for the way he says it.

[15] The significance of the word *stille* may be the epistolary one of a formal mode of address found in Signet letters of the early fifteenth century printed in John H.Fisher, Malcolm Richardson, and Jane L.Fisher, *An Anthology of Chancery English* (Knoxville 1984), pp.84 and 128.

Some Aspects of Biblical Imagery
in Piers Plowman[1]

Avril Henry

It has been said that 'Langland's meanings are rarely stratified . . . he generally confines himself to saying one thing at a time',[2] and that his 'was not a pictorial poetry'.[3] On a few occasions neither of these statements is quite true. Sometimes Langland appears to use the images evoked by familiar biblical events in order to say several things at once. These images have a kind of independent life because they are standard narrative and typological scenes, witness their appearance in major typological compendia such as the great Klosterneuburg ambo,[4] *Biblia pauperum* and *Speculum humanae salvationis*,[5] as well as in the smaller English compendium found at the beginning of Eton MS 177, and known as '*Figurae bibliorum*'.[6] Meanings beyond the historical provide a subtext to the main dis-

---

1 References are to the B-text in A.V.C.Schmidt, *William Langland, The Vision of Piers Plowman: A Critical Edition of the B-Text Based on Trinity College Cambridge MS B. 15.17 with Selected Variant Readings, an Introduction, glosses, and a Textual and Literary Commentary* (London 1978).
2 J.F.Goodridge, trans., *William Langland, Piers the Ploughman: Translated into Modern English* (Harmondsworth 1959), p.13.
3 Schmidt, pp. xvii; the editor goes on to observe that Langland's images are often carefully 'half-realised, because they function as part of an imaginative metaphor, rich in suggestion' (p. xviii).
4 See F.Röhrig, *Der Verduner Altar* (Vienna 1955).
5 I am indebted to Dr Kathleen Scott for a list of illustrated English manuscripts of the *Speculum*: London, BL Sloane MSS 346, 3451 and Harley MS 2838; Paris, Bibliothèque nationale, MS fr. 400; New York, Pierpont Morgan Library, MS M. 766; New Haven, Yale University, Beinecke Library, MS 27; Oxford, Bodleian Library, MS Douce f.4, and Corpus Christi College, MS 161; Chicago, Art Institute, MS 23.420.
6 See *Biblia Pauperum: A Facsimile and Edition*, ed. and trans. A.Henry (Aldershot and Ithaca, N.Y., 1987); '*Speculum Humanae Salvationis*': *Texte critique, traduction inédite de Jean Mielot (1448); les sources et l'influence iconographique principalement sur l'art alsacien du XIVe siècle: Avec la reproduction, en 140 planches, du manuscrit de Sélestat, de la série complète des vitraux de Mulhouse, de vitraux de Colmar, de Wissembourg, etc.*, ed. Jules Lutz and Paul Perdrizet, 2 vols (Mulhouse, 1907, 1909); the unhelpfully-named 'Figurae bibliorum' is renamed 'The Eton Roundels' in the author's edition and translation, *The Eton Roundels:*

course. Book's *two brode eighen* might almost symbolise the typological perspective itself, since the two Testaments together, the Old prefiguring the New, provide a kind of spiritual binocular vision deeper than that of either.

A simple example of Langland's confident reliance on his reader's familiarity with a narrative sequence, and, I suspect, with associated narrative images (see below, pp. 53–4), appears in his use of New Testament events.[7] It is obvious that these occur repeatedly, and not always in chronological sequences: they assume the reader's familiarity with the narrative norm. If the reader were not fully familiar with the ancient story, repeated annually in the liturgy of Lent and perpetually present to him in visual representations round him, how confused he would be by Langland's taking us back to the Carrying of the Cross at the beginning of Passus XIX, when we have already seen the Crucifixion (XVIII 36–79) as the culmination of a Passion sequence. (On the other hand, an informed reader would notice that from that very sequence, the Carrying of the Cross was carefully omitted.)

Langland's use of familiar Old Testament imagery is equally careful and imaginative. Where his Old Testament events prefigure aspects of salvation, the contexts and ways in which they do this are varied and interesting. He uses biblical scenes with a freedom and subtlety equal to his verbal adventurousness. This is not to suggest that he often *describes* such pictures. So ubiquitous were they that a reference to the event they depict must have been enough to summon up a picture. As I hope to show, Langland uses various signals to indicate when such references carry a subtext.

Of course, familiar Old Testament scenes are sometimes mentioned in a simple manner. In these cases, no subtext signal is given. For example, Holichurch's answer to the Dreamer's enquiry about the *dongeon – What may it bemeene?* (I.60) is briefly to describe how Wrong caused the Fall, Cain's murder of Abel, and Judas's payment and suicide:

> Adam and Eve he egged to ille,
> Counseilled Kaym to killen his brother,
> Judas he japed with Jewen silver
> And sithen on an eller hanged hym after (65–68)

Eton MS 177 'Figurae Bibliorum' (Aldershot, forthcoming 1990). In Eton MS 177 it is bound up with an early illustrated *Apocalypse* of the same date, with which it may form a designed pair. Closely related to the lost twelfth-century typological series once in Worcester Cathedral Chapter House, it is important as a wholly typological English work in manuscript. Predating Langland, the *Roundels'* imagery and text (c.1260), are echoed in the *Sherborne Missal* (London, British Library, Loan 82, dated 1396–1407); they are thus evidence of the continuing English typological tradition within which Langland worked.

7 The ubiquitousness of the pictorial *Life of Christ* or *Passion* scarcely needs documenting, but see the long article in E.Kirschbaum, ed., *Lexikon der christlichen Ikonographie*, 8 vols (Rome 1968–1976), under 'Leben Jesu'.

These events neatly illustrate the activity of evil from Creation to the time of Christ; they also display the devil's ability to incite, simulate logic, deceive and induce despair. All are common in art. However, the *Fall of Man*[8] and the *Murder of Abel*, though standard types of the *Temptation of Christ* and the *Betrayal* respectively, are not apparently meant to bring to mind these antitypes. The *Payment of Judas* and the *Suicide of Judas* (if the poet intends to summon up pictures at all) do not recall their Old Testament types.[9] No particular complexity of thought or syntax prompts us to interpet these scenes at more than their literal level.

Traditional imagery without typological connotations is also used sometimes as a kind of stabilising framework for a shifting complexity of thought. There is a good example of this when the first account of learned clergy bent on profit, saying Mass and the Office insincerely, counting silver and giving judgement (with a small 'j'), suddenly gives way to the image of Christ in Judgement (Prol. 98–99):

> drede is at the laste
> Lest Crist in Consistorie acorse ful manye!

This is a dramatic, almost disorientating shift to another world and another time, but also to a scene familiar from the tympana of cathedrals, the pages of manuscripts,[10] and elsewhere, such as at the top of the Hereford Mappa Mundi. Judgement scenes may be of the literal kind, where we actually see the dead rise and the good separated from the damned,[11] or be of the *Maiestas* kind, following the fourth chapter of Apocalypse. Often the enthroned Christ is surrounded by the Apostles who are co-assessors in the Judgment in accordance with Jesus's promise to them (Luke xxii.30),[12] and are the forerunners of the cardinals in a papal consistory court. In the *Christ in Majesty* version, the Apostles may or may not be present;

---

[8] The names of events are presented as italicised titles where they are intended to refer not only to action in the poem, but also to traditional medieval images which may be conjured up by the text. This results in some apparent inconsistency, which I hope the reader will tolerate.

[9] The types of the *Payment* are *Joseph Sold to the Ismaelites* and *Joseph Sold to Potiphar* (*Biblia pauperum* sig. r); the *Suicide of Judas* is not in either *Biblia pauperum* or *Speculum humanae salvationis*, but is a common scene in straight narratives, such as the *Holkham Bible Picture Book* (f. 30r).

[10] The manuscripts most likely to include it are, of course, illustrated Apocalypses and Bibles; the scene appears in *Biblia pauperum* sig. .r.

[11] See, for example, Kirschbaum, under 'Weltgericht': the central west portal of Autun, c.1120, and the south portal of Chartres, which is 13th-century.

[12] See, for example, the tympanum at Carennac, where there are two rows of Apostles, one above the other, in a design common in the twelfth century (G.Schiller, *Ikonographie der christlichen Kunst*, Vols 3, 4.1, 4.2 (Gütersloh 1971–80), Vol. 3, fig. 711).

even if they are not, the iconography of the *Judgement* is quoted in the hand gestures of Christ.[13]

Not without reason does this clear picture of Christ in Consistory Court frame the notoriously difficult passage on the Power of the Keys (not least as the scene might include Peter with his keys, as in our own Apocalyptic *Christ in Majesty* on the ceiling of the sanctuary in the tiny Romanesque church of Kempley):

> I parceyued of the power that Peter hadde to kepe –
> To bynden and unbynden, as the Book telleth –
> How he it lefte with love as Oure Lord highte
> Amonges foure vertues, most vertuous of alle vertues
> That cardinals ben called and closynge yates
> There Crist is in kyngdom, to close and to shette,
> And to opene it to hem and hevene blisse shewe.   (Prol. 100–6)

Goodridge translates the last five lines as:

> Peter, by our Lord's command, left it in the hands of Love, *sharing it out among the four greatest virtues*, which are called Cardinal. For these are the hinges on which swing the gates of Christ's kingdom, closing against some, and opening on the bliss of Heaven to others;

(my italics). This translation ignores Langland's quick echo of St Paul's statement that charity is the greatest of the virtues – the theological virtues, not the cardinal ones: 'And now there remain faith, hope and charity, these three; but the greatest of these is charity' (1 Cor. xiii.13.) The echo suggests another, counterpointed meaning, which may be paraphrased as:

> Peter left [the Power of the Keys] in the care of Love – the most powerful of all virtues even when it is in the company of the four virtues called 'cardinals', [which are the means of] closing the gates of the kingdom where Christ is – to close and lock the kingdom, but also to open it to people and show them the joy of heaven.

This interpretation is supported by the sowing of the cardinal virtues in the soul of man: Piers harrows the ground with the Old and New Testaments to cover the seeds so that *love might wexe / Among thise foure vertues, and vices destruye*

---

[13] Schiller, vol. 3, p. 246, col. 2. Among the best-known examples of *Christ in Judgement* are those on the west portal of Autun (c.1120) and on the thirteenth-century south portal of Chartres. Twelfth-century examples of *Christ in Majesty* are in the tympanum of the narthex of Vézelay; the Prior's Door, Ely (1135–39); the South Porch, Malmesbury Abbey. Thirteenth-century examples are on the west front of Wells Cathedral and in the Judgement Porch, Lincoln Cathedral. See also É.Mâle, *L'Art religieux du XIIIe siècle en France: étude sur l'iconographie du moyen âge et sur ses sources d'inspiration*, 6th ed. (Paris 1925), pp.359–93.

(XIX.312). In the compressed Prologue statement we have two simultaneous readings. First, we perceive the Pope – elected by cardinals – giving or withholding access to God, which is why cardinal virtues are 'most vertuous of alle'. Second, we remember that Love is greater than Hope or Faith: it survives even in the next world, indeed is the mode of existence in the next world, where the other two theological virtues are redundant. For this reason also it is greater than even the four cardinal virtues. Thus Love is also 'most vertuous of alle vertues', and so should control the opening and shutting. Syntactically, the phrase *to close and to shette* may refer to the action of the hinges or of Christ in Judgement. Ambiguity identifies Christ, the Pope and cardinals with each other, the Power of the Keys being executed by Love himself. This brings us directly to:

> Ac of the Cardinals at court that kaughte of that name
> And power presumed in hem a Pope to make
> To han the power that Peter hadde, impugnen I nelle –
> For in love and in lettrure the eleccion bilongeth.

The importance of the Power of the Keys held by the Church is followed by the failure of charity that leads to, and results from, papal corruption. In context, *eleccion* may suggest election of a pope and admission of the elect to heaven, as in 'many are called, but few are chosen'. This extreme compression is facilitated by the very familiarity and clarity of the image of *Christ in Judgement*, the blessed on his dexter, the damned on his sinister side.

The same clustering of pictures of exclusion and enthronement, again exploring love, is found at I.84, in Holichurch's answer to the Dreamer's wondering *How I may save my soule*. We are still barely prompted to look beyond literal meaning, but the standard scenes invoked are more subtly used than in the Passus I group discussed above – the *Fall of Man*, the *Murder of Abel*, the *Payment of Judas*, the *Suicide of Judas* – to which they seem to be deliberately related. In a telling parallel to, and contrast with, the seed of Love which came to earth *For hevene myghte nat holden it, so was it hevy of hymself* (I.153),[14] Holichurch recalls the breaking of divine law by Lucifer and the fallen angels, so that:

> noon hevene myghte hem holde
> But fellen out in a fendes liknesse [ful] nyne dayes togideres.

On the other hand, those who obey the Scripture and *enden . . . in truthe*

> Mowe be siker that hire soules shul wende to hevene:
> Ther Treuthe is in Trinitee and troneth hem alle. (I.120–21, 133).

---

[14] The contrast is noted by J.A.W.Bennett, ed., *Langland: Piers Plowman, The Prologue and Passus I–VII of the B text as found in Bodleian MS. Laud Misc. 581* (Oxford 1972), p.113, n.150.

The images implied are the *Fall of the Angels*, the *Gathering of the Blessed Souls*[15] (sometimes shown as *Abraham's Bosom*)[16] and the *Enthronement of the Soul*.[17] Their first function is to span the history of God's creatures: we see the effects of the Fall overcome even as it is mentioned. There is also a neat antithesis, the *Enthronement of the Soul* being set against Lucifer's literal attempt to usurp the throne of God (as he does at the top of the Creation page in the *Holkham Bible Picture Book*,[18] and in the York Creation Play).[19] However, another dimension is added to these pictures by their relation to the first group. The *Fall of the Angels*, the first rebellion, lies behind and partly accounts for the the *Fall of Man*. The first murder, of Abel, is 'replaced' by the stock image of human harmony, the *Gathering of the Blessed*. The fruitless sin and isolation of Judas is contrasted with the *Enthronement of the Soul*, in which the individual is honoured and enstated. Interesting though this pattern is (if it exists), nothing in the movement of verse or ideas prompts us to look beyond the historical meaning of the scenes.[20]

When Old Testament scenes have a typological dimension the poet alerts us, when for example the *Last Judgement*, that formed a framework to the Prologue's meditation on the Power of the Keys, is used again as the Prologue sequence is echoed in the second Waking, that introduces the *Vita*.[21] Will ponders the validity of Truth's Pardon, and of dreams, recalling, very specifically, Daniel's vision of the broken idol, and Joseph's dream of the sun and stars honouring him.[22] Finally he returns to the Power of the Keys (VII.174), observing that it is real, but of less value to the soul than Dowel

> At the dredful dome, whan dede shulle arise
> And comen alle bifore Crist acountes to yelde. (VII.188–89)

---

[15] *Speculum humanae salvationis*, ch. xlii, where it is prefigured by *Solomon in His Glory* (III Kings x), *Assuerus's Feast* (Esther i.1–8) and *Job's Feast* (Job i.4).

[16] As in *Biblia pauperum*, sig. .t., where it is prefigured by *Job's Feast* and *Jacob's Ladder*.

[17] The *Enthronement of the Soul* image may be simple, as in the closing antitype of *Biblia pauperum*, where Christ crowns the soul, or it may be a complex one in which the coronation and enthronement of the Virgin, Church and Soul are conflated (see the last image in *The Eton Roundels*).

[18] *Holkham Bible Picture Book*, f. 2v.

[19] *The York Plays*, ed. R.Beadle, York Medieval Texts, 2nd series (London 1982), p.51.

[20] The *Fall of The Angels* is a type of the *Jews Fall Back from Christ* in *Biblia pauperum*, sig. v; see John xviii 4–6, Matt. xxvi 36). The two other images are familiar antitypes: the *Gathering of the Blessed* is prefigured in *Speculum humanae salvationis*, ch. xlii by *Solomon in His Glory* (III Kings x), *Assuerus's Feast* (Esther i.1–8) and *Job's Feast* (Job i.4). When the gathering of the blessed appears in the form known as *Abraham's Bosom*, where God gathers souls in a napkin, it is prefigured, as in *Biblia pauperum*, sig. .t., by *Job's Feast* and *Jacob's Ladder*.

[21] Schmidt, p. xxv.

[22] Gen. xxxvii.6–9.

The dreams of Daniel and Joseph are more than authentication for revelation – the poet would hardly need to select specific dreams to achieve this. Both offer a sub-text as common types of the life of Christ. *Daniel's Vision of the Lapis Angularis* – the stone cut from the mountain but not by human hand – is itself an explanation of the meaning of Nabuchodonosor's dream of its falling to destroy a statue of Dagon (Dan. ii.34). The stone is interpreted as Christ by Jesus himself (Luke xx.17).[23] *Daniel's Vision* is a very common type of the *Nativity*.[24] The dreamer's meditation at the start of his personal pilgrimage is thus placed in the whole context of Christ's relationship to man, from Incarnation to Judgement.

Exegesis explains Joseph's dream of sun, moon and stars (Gen. xxxvii.9) as a prefiguration of the honouring of Christ,[25] as in the *Bible moralisée*, which presents Christ enthroned, his worshippers round him.[26] This subtext is therefore the very love of God which the Dreamer has been shown is more important than the mechanical obtaining of forgiveness. The next event mentioned by Langland is Joseph's father reacting to his son's interpetation of the dream (VII.163–64):

> Thanne Jacob jugged Josephes swevene:
> '*Beau fitz*', quod his fader, 'for defaute we shullen –
> I myself and my sones – seche thee for nede'.[27]

As noted by Skeat and others, this is not Jacob's reported reaction:[28] he said 'Shall I and thy mother, and thy brethren worship thee upon the earth?' It is Langland who relates the rhetorical question to *nede*, and so to the next image:

---

23 'Whosoever shall fall upon that stone shall be bruised: and upon whomsoever it shall fall, it will grind him to powder'.

24 See, for example, the twelfth century Canterbury typological glass (M. H. Caviness, *The Windows of Christ Church Cathedral, Canterbury*, Corpus Vitrearum Medii Aevi, Great Britain, 2 (London 1981), p.85) and the lost typological Peterborough series (L.F.Sandler, *The Peterborough Psalter in Brussels & Other Fenland Manuscripts*, (London 1974) pp.110, 112), as well as the thirteenth-century *Eton Roundels*, f.3r, and *Biblia pauperum*, sig. b.

25 Ambrose, *PL* XIV 675: *Quis est ille quem parentes et fratres adoraverunt super terram, nisi Christus Jesus, quando eum Joseph et mater cum discipulis adorabant, Deum verum in illo corpore confitentes de quo solo dictum est: 'Laudate eum, sol et luna; laudate eum, omnes stellae et lumen'* (Ps. 148.3)? *Objurgatio autem patris, quid significat, nisi duritiam populi Israel . . .?* See also Augustine, *PL* XXXIII 919, XXXIV 581–82; Claudius of Turin, *PL* L 1012.

26 *Bible Moralisée: MS Bodley 270b*, ed. W.O.Hassall, Medieval Manuscripts in Microform: Major Treasures in the Bodleian Library, 5 (Bicester 1978), f. 22r, C1, C2; the latter reads: *Ioseph qui dormiuit in campo significat christum qui obdormiu[it] in sepulcro. Joseph qui erat in campo cum fratribus suis cum fratres adorabant eum cum suis manipulis significat ihesum christum qui est in campo diuinitatis et boni christiani fratres sui eum adorant in floribus diuinitatis.*

27 Gen. xxxvii.9–10.

28 W.W.Skeat, ed., *The Vision of William Concerning Piers the Plowman in Three Parallel Texts*, 2 vols (London 1886), Vol. 2, p.129, n.311; Schmidt, p.325, suggests that Langland might have read into Gen. xxxvii.11 ('his father considered [the dream] with himself') the implication that Jacob believed it might come true.

> It bifel as hi fader seide, in Pharaoes tyme,
> That Joseph was Justice Egipte to loke:
> It bifel as hi fader seide – his frendes there hym soghte.[29]

This is a quite separate occasion, when Joseph's brothers were driven by famine to seek help in Egypt. *Joseph Reveals Himself to His Brothers* prefigures the *Appearance of Christ to his Disciples* (Luke xxiv 36).[30] The associated text in *Biblia pauperum* means:

> Joseph signifies Christ, who after his Resurrection appeared to the disciples when they were together, and by speaking comforted them, saying: 'Do not be afraid, it is I'.

(Interestingly, one of the four prophecies on the *Biblia pauperum* page is 'Look to the rock from which you were cut' – Is. li.1, interpreted as a reference to Daniel's Vision.)[31] On the *Biblia pauperum* page the second type of the *Appearance of Christ to his Disciples* is the *Return of the Prodigal Son*: the whole page is about comfort and pardon. Surely it is no accident that this pattern of ideas is echoed during our dreamer's pondering of the Pardon torn up by Piers, and how the pardon offered by God *passeth al the pardon of Seint Petres cherche*. The effect these images, at the end of the so-called *Visio*, is to recall the span of Christ's life from birth to Resurrection, with its message of God's forgiveness.

Typological significance is signalled in XIV.64 by a scene's marginal historical relevance. The theme is again the sacrament of Penance: Conscience sends Haukyn to Contrition (XIV.16), and Dowel, Dobet and Dobest are defined in terms of Penance. Patience promises Haukyn the 'waybread' of *Fiat voluntas tua: pacientes vincunt*, comparing him to the Israelites who wandered for forty years and survived with the help of water struck from the rock (64):

> It is founden that fourty wynter folk lyvede withouten tulying,
> And out of the flynt sprong the flood that folk and beestes dronken.

The water, as opposed to the exodus itself, is not obviously relevant to the idea of patience, and the manna might have been more relevant to waybread than water. However, *Moses Strikes the Water from the Rock* is a common type of the *Crucifix-*

---

[29] Gen. xlv.1–7.
[30] *Biblia pauperum*, sig. .m. and *Speculum humanae salvationis*, ch. xxvii, 2991.
[31] *Biblia pauperum*, sig. .m. The Middle English version of *Speculum humanae salvationis* says:

> Jacob sons honoured thaire brothere, processe of tyme fylowing,
> And many Jewes trowed in Crist fro deth after his ryseing.

The Mirour of Mans Saluacioune, a Middle English Translation of 'Speculum Humanae Salvationis': A Critical Edition of the Fifteenth-century Manuscript Illustrated from Der Spiegel der menschen Behältnis, *Speyer: Drach, c.1475*, ed. A.Henry (Aldershot 1986) 149.

ion: 'The rock or stone signifies Christ, who poured out the waters of salvation (that is, the sacraments) from his side when on the cross'.[32] Langland speaks of patient acceptance of God's will, and the subtext presents us with the perfect example of it, Christ's death making the sacrament of Penance available.

Sometimes the typological sense of an image is quite deeply buried. The best known example is also a reference to the Crucifixion, a subtext once again being signalled by highly condensed verse. In the answer to the Dreamer, when concerning Truth he asks *By what craft in my cors it comseth, and where* (I.139), Holichurch replies that it is an innate understanding that the love of God is paramount, and that

> love is triacle of hevene
> May no synne be on hym seene that that spice useth.
> And alle his werkes he wroughte with love as hym liste,
> And lered it Moyses for the leveste thyng and moost lik to hevene.

It has long been noted that, in the light of exegesis of Num. xxi 8–9, *triacle* is a subtle reference to Christ the serpent as remedy for the bite of the serpent of sin, for the remedy for snake-bite is *tyriacon* (*triacle*), made from the powdered skin of a snake.[33] This thesis is supported, and another layer of meaning added to the image, by the fact that *Moses Lifting Up the Serpent* is a pictorial type of the Crucifixion so common that it appears in the *Biblia Pauperum*:

> According to Numbers xxi 4–8, when the Lord wanted to free from serpents the people whom the serpents had bitten, he instructed Moses to make a brass serpent and hang it upon a stake so that whoever looked at it would be rid of serpents. The serpent hung up and stared at by the

---

32 Translated from *Biblia pauperum*, sig. .f.; the interpretation is from Augustine, *PL* XXXV 1513.

33 B.H.Smith, *Traditional Imagery of Charity in 'Piers Plowman'*, Studies in Literature, 21 (The Hague 1966), pp.22–3, cites Hugh of Saint-Cher, *Opera omnia in universum Vetus & Novum Testamentum*, 8 vols (Venice, 1732), Vol. 6, f.297ᵛ; the full quotation is:

Christus dicitur serpens, quia sicut de serpente fit venenum, & de serpente fit tyriaca in veneni remedium, ita facto de veneno serpente id est de diabolo, voluit dominus fieri serpens, ut de eo fieret tyriaca contra venenum diaboli. Et hoc est, quod Exod.7 serpens Moysi devoravit serpentes Magorum. Item serpens aeneus non est vere serpens, nec venenum habet, & ideo significat Christum, qui habuit similitudinem carnis peccatricis, non carnem peccatricem. Habuit quidem veram carnem, sed non vere peccatricem, imo peccatrice similem, ut dicitur Rom.8. Deus filium suum misit in similitudinem carnis peccati, & de peccato damnavit peccatum, id est per tyriacam venenum expulit, & de Christo, qui vocatur peccatum pro similitudine damnavit diabolum, qui peccatum dicitur veritate, & origine, id est valde peccator, & origo peccati.

For the use of *triacle* in the description of herbal remedies, hence *spice*, see also P.M.Kean, 'Langland on the Incarnation' *RES* NS 16 (1965): 349–63. All these are cited by J.A.W.Bennett, *Piers Plowman*, p.112–13. Cf. *Speculum Vitae*, where backbiters are adders against which no *triacle* avails (Bodleian MS poet.a.1, f.260v), and it is said of Christ (f.251vc): *He was þe neddre . wiþ outen venym / As triacle of hele . com of him.*

people signifies Christ on the cross, whom every believing person who wishes to be rid of the serpent (that is, the devil) should gaze upon.[34]

The *it* in *[God] lered it Moyses for the leveste thyng and moost lik to hevene* is thus not only the Love paramount in the first and second commandments (the primary meaning), but also the cross. The idea recurs in the Dreamer's *descensus ad inferna*, where the Four Daughters of God debate the background to Incarnation and Passion, and Mercy explains: *venym fordoth venym* (XVIII.152).

The same group of ideas (poison, the cross, love in the first two Commandments) appears again in XV, applied to clergy in general and the episcopate in particular. Anima observes that the establishment of the Church by Constantine was its downfall (XV.558):

> *Dos ecclesie* this day hath ydronke venym,
> And tho that han Petres power arn apoisoned alle!'[35]

She goes on:

> A medicyne moot therto that may amende prelates;

it is the embracing of patience and the cross:

> Ac we Cristene creatures, that on the cros bileven,
> Arn ferme as in the feith – Goddes forbode ellis! –
> And han clerkes to kepen us therinne, and hem that shul come after us.
> And Jewes lyven in lele lawe – Oure Lord wroot it hymselve
> In stoon, for it stedefast was, and stonde sholde evere –
> *Dilige Deum et proximum*, is parfit Jewen lawe –
> And took it Moyses to teche men, til Messie coome.

Schmidt rightly observes that when the Dreamer wakes from the second inner dream at the end of XVI he must prepare for meeting Jesus himself by 'becoming acquainted with the workings of God's purpose in the Old Testament, which laid the basis for fulfilment in the New. Hence he must meet Abraham, exemplar of the faith on which charity is built'.[36] The allegory is doing even more than this. Not surprisingly, use of typological subtext increases. The effect is always to suggest the New Law as the Old is described – a link not unlike the compressed opening simile in which Abraham-Faith is *As hoor as an hawethorn* (XVI.173) – hawthorn being white, of course, only in Spring.

The first in a sequence of Abraham images occurs three times: *Abraham Sees the*

---

[34] The text cited is from the forty-page blockbook edition of c.1460 (*Biblia Pauperum*, ed. Henry, pp.96, 98), but it is similar in the surviving early manuscripts of c.1330.

[35] In the note on p. 346, Schmidt remarks on the curious grammar, in which the Donation, not the Church, appears to have drunk poison.

[36] Schmidt, p. xxviii.

Three Youths. It appears first in disguised form at XVI.181, where Abraham-Faith seeks the person he once met whose blazon was *Thre leodes in oon lyth.* This event, in which Abraham addresses three young men in the singular, is traditionally interpreted in terms of the Trinity.[37] It prefigures the *Transfiguration,* itself a Trinity-symbol: *Biblia pauperum's* text observes:

> 'he saw three and worshipped one'. The three angels signified the trinity
> of Persons, but in that he worshipped one, he indicated the singleness of
> its Nature.[38]

More importantly, *Abraham Sees the Three Youths* also prefigures the *Annunciation,* as on the Klosterneuberg ambo.[39] This meaning is highly resonant in *Piers Plowman,* where the scene is followed by meditation on the Incarnation (*So God, that gynnyng hadde never, but tho hym good thoughte, / Sente forth his sone as for servaunt that tyme* – XVI.194–95), and on the trinities of divine persons, of states of life (widowhood, marriage and virginity) and of the family (father, mother, child). The unification of three Persons in the Trinity, and of human and divine natures in Jesus, may be deliberately brought together in the mind.

Not until XVI.225 is *Abraham Sees the Three Youths* fully presented, with carefully chosen pronouns, since he saw three and worshipped one:

> I roos up and reverenced hym, and right faire hym grette.
> Thre men, to my sighte, I made wel at ese.

Finally, at XVII.27 the Dreamer recalls the image and its typological meaning (*Abraham seith that he seigh hoolly the Trinite*) when he wonders if the Old Law might be enough, without the New. At one level Langland ironically presents him asking if the Trinity is enough, without the Incarnation.

In an imaginatively audacious conflation of biblical material, The Trinity is apparently at Abraham's very table when God asks him to kill his son. At XVII.231 we have the *Sacrifice of Isaac;* on the primary level this is a test of faith, but it is also the commonest of all prefigurations of the *Crucifixion.* The effect is once again to bring Annunciation and Crucifixion before the imagination together. Such juxtaposition is a medieval commonplace, as in the popular *Annunciation* image in which a shaft of light to the Virgin bears the infant Christ already carrying a tiny cross.[40]

The next image from the life of Abraham is also an example of faith and obedience. At 235 the patriarch says:

---

[37] Ambrose, *PL* XVI 774, Augustine, *PL,* XLII 809.
[38] *Biblia pauperum,* sig. m.
[39] Röhrig, pls 2–3.
[40] As in *Annunciation* pages in *Biblia pauperum* (sig. a), and, for example, the Warwick Hours.

> I circumcised my sone sithen for his sake –
> Myself and my meynee and alle that male weere
> Bledden blood for that Lordes love, and hope to blisse the tyme.

The unnamed son must be Ismael, circumcised with all Abraham's household (Gen. xvii). The *Circumcision of Ismael* is very rare in art. However, the absence of the boy's name, and the immediately preceding reference to the *Sacrifice of Isaac* suggests, as one first reads the passage, the iconographically common *Circumcision of Isaac* (Gen. xxi.4), which prefigures the *Circumcision of Christ*.[41] As the first shedding of Jesus's blood the latter itself foreshadows the Passion.

The Abraham image at XVI.243–46 is a problem:

> And siththe he sent me, to seye I sholde do sacrifise,
> And doon hym worship with breed and with wyn bothe,
> And called me the foot of his feith, his folk for to save,
> And defende hem fro the fend, folk that on me leveden.

Editors have assumed that this describes one event, and that Langland *confused* Melchisedech's offering of bread and wine to Abraham (Gen. xiv.18) with Abraham's sacrifice (Gen. xv.9), both of which are cited in the Canon of the Mass after the consecration of the wine.[42] This seems very unlikely. Abraham was commanded to offer a cow, a goat, a ram, a dove and a pigeon, not bread and wine. Moreover, Abraham is *the foot of [God's] feith* rather in Gen. xvii, at the Covenant of Circumcision, than in Gen. xv. Above all, Langland could hardly have been unaware of one of the commonest types – *Melchisedech Offers Bread And wine* – or unaware of Jesus as a 'priest after the order of Melchisedech' (Ps. 110.4–5, quoted in Heb. v.5–10, vi.20–vii.21).[43] Lastly, the events linked in apparently chronological sequence by *First, sithen, siththe* – *First he fonded me, if I loved bettre / Hym or Ysaak myn heir* (XVI.231: Gen. xxii), *I circumcised my sone sithen for his sake* (XVI.235: Gen. xvi), *And siththe he sente me, to seye I sholde do sacrifise* (XVI.243: Gen. xv) – are in fact described out of order. As ever, Langland uses his source very freely.

Could it be that XVI.243–46 refer in turn to separate events (hence their all beginning with *And*)? In this case the references would be to Abraham's sacrifice (Gen. xv.9), to his *acceptance* of Melchisedech's offerings of bread and wine (Gen. xiv.20), and to the Covenant of Circumcision (Gen. xv). An alternative explanation is that the sacrifice referred to is not Abraham's offering of animals, or

41 See the Klosterneuberg ambo (Röhrig, pls 8, 9).
42 Skeat, vol. 2, p.241; Schmidt, p.348.
43 The eucharistic implications of Melchisedech's offering were explored in the third century, and became a commonplace (Cyprian, *PL* IV 387–88; Augustine, *PL* XLI 500; Jerome, *PL* XXVI 173; Isidore, *PL* LXXXIII 104, etc.). *Melchisedech Offers Bread and Wine* prefiguring the *Last Supper* appears early in typological art, for example, in the mosaics of S. Vitale in Ravenna, as well as in *Biblia pauperum*, sig. s.

Melchisedech's of bread and wine, but *Abraham's Tithe to Melchisedech. Melchisedech Offers Bread and Wine* and *Abraham's Tithe to Melchisedech* occur in one roundel in *The Eton Roundels*,[44] where in a prefiguration of the *Adoration of the Magi* Melchisedech offers chalice and host, and Abraham, who 'gave tithes out of the principal things' (Heb. vii.4) offers loaves. If, following the common interpretation, Langland is seeing Melchisedech as Christ, then Abraham may be said to offer God sacrifice. Since the Bible does not specify the nature of the 'principal things', and at least one designer showed Abraham offering bread, it is not too great a leap of the imagination to have him offering Melchisedech wine as well, particularly as this allows Langland to present Abraham as celebrating a prototype Mass.[45]

The last Abraham image, at XVI.253, is *Abraham's Bosom*. Here it clearly represents Limbo: Abraham and the souls he holds await the Harrowing of Hell (XVIII.260). The main allegory thus takes us firmly back to the historical sequence, ready for the Harrowing of Hell. However, at another level attested by St Augustine,[46] the image foreshadows the gathering of the blessed in heaven.[47] This sense is signalled by verbal echo. At XVII.21 Abraham cries *Lo! Here in my lappe that leeved on that charme* and at XVII.31 the Dreamer wonders why a New Law is necessary since *He kan noght siggen the somme, and some arn in his lappe*, the echo sounding again in Charity's action in XVII.72 when he took up the wounded man and *in his lappe him leide*. Christ, of course, is about to release souls from Limbo, not place them in it, so this last reference is to the gathering of the saved to God. Passus XVI explicitly spans man's spiritual history from Genesis to the Harrowing of Hell, still to be described in the poem's 'present'. Pictorial tradition, however, presents us with a subtext outlining the life of Christ with the *Annunciation* (and possibly the *Magi*), the *Last Supper* and the *Crucifixion*, ending with the *Gathering of the Blessed* in the harmony of heaven.

The Samaritan episode in Passus XVII is informed by the liturgy of, and commentary on, the thirteenth Sunday after Pentecost, with its Collect 'Give unto us the increase of Faith, Hope and Charity'.[48] The Passus opens with a reference to *Moses Receives the Law*, when Hope-Moses seeks the knight who gave the commandment on Sinai.[49] This is surely meant to recall its antitype, *Pentecost*. The *Biblia pauperum* text at this point means:

---

44 Eton MS 177, f. 3v.
45 Goodridge, p.255, n.36, refers to Abraham learning the sacrifice of the Mass; he does not notice the intepretative difficulty.
46 *PL* XLIV 499.
47 *Biblia pauperum*, sig. .t.
48 R.St-Jacques, 'The Liturgical Associations of Langland's Samaritan', *Traditio* 25 (1969): 217–30, cited by Schmidt, p.348.
49 The seal of the cross with which Hope seeks to have the document that begins *Dilige Deum et proximum tuum* ratified is comparable with the 'notarye signe with whiche shulden be signed and marked alle goode testamentes' in the Middle English version of

Moses was given the law, and it was written on stone tablets. In the same way the new law was written on the hearts of the faithful on the day of Pentecost.[50]

The treatment of the Samaritan parable itself may be based on a complete, familiar typological picture, such as appears in the great thirteenth-century Samaritan window at Sens which names the victim *Homo*.[51] Allegorisation of the parable is common. *Glossa Ordinaria* calls the victim Fallen Man, the robbers sins, the priest and Levite the Old Law, the Samaritan Christ, the inn the Church; Bruno says of the victim: *in hoc uno homine omnes homines exspoliati et praedati sunt.*[52]

On at least one occasion, it is not types and antitypes themselves which create a subtext, but a prophecy traditionally associated with them. Repetition is the signal for our particular attention. *Cum sanctus sanctorum veniat cessabit unxio vestra* ('When the Saint of Saints comes, your anointing shall cease'), or a form of it, occurs twice: at XV.598 and XVIII.109.[53] It first appears at the end of Anima's long answer to the question *Wheither clerkes known [Charity]?* (XV.197–611), where it is primarily the standard warning that Christ will replace Jewish priesthood and power.[54] The second occurrence is also a warning to Jews. It immediately follows the account of the Crucifixion, the horror of which will then plunge the dreamer into his *descensus ad inferna*. Faith castigates those who abused the body of Jesus, and prophesies that death will be conquered, and Jews rendered landless:

Deguileville's *Pèlerinage de la vie humaine* (*The Pilgrimage of the Lyfe of the Manhode*, ed. A.Henry, Vol. 1, EETS OS 288 (London 1985), lines 1342–1412). Christ signs his Testament of Peace with a *pax* sign, in which *p* is for *proximus*, *a* is for *anima* and *x* is for *Christus*, signifying the right relation between one's neighbour, one's soul, and God.
[50] *Biblia pauperum*, ed. Henry pp.116, 118.
[51] Cahier and Martin's drawing of the window is reproduced in Mâle, *xiiie siècle*, p.199, fig. 102.
[52] Bruno Signiensis, 'Glossa Ordinaria', *PL* CXIV 286–7, and *PL* CLXV 985, respectively.
[53] The verse refers to the Nativity in *The Eton Roundels*, f. 3r, where it receives its common attribution to Daniel, which is at least as old as the anonymous 12th-century *Tractatus adversus Iudaeum* (*PL* CCXIII 784). A.Watson, *The Early Iconography of the Tree of Jesse* (London 1934), pl. VII, shows the quotation on a scroll carried by Daniel in a sculptured Tree of Jesse in the Cathedral of Arcetri, N. Italy, and refers to it on Daniel's scroll on the west front of Notre-Dame-la-Grande, Poitiers. The verse is not in the Vulgate, being ultimately derived from pre-Vulgate versions of Dan. ix 24. A form of it was used by Tertullian in his *Adversus Iudaeos* VIII 5–6 (CCL II 1357.29–1358.35; *PL* II 651–52), making it a commonplace of anti-Jewish polemic. The immediate source is the 5th-century Quodvultdeus's *Sermo Contra Judaeos, Paganos, et Arianos* attributed in antiquity to St Augustine (*PL* XLII 1124); Watson, p. 163, noted the Tertullian and pseudo-Augustine. The *Ordo Prophetarum*, derived from Quodvultdeus, gives Daniel a form of the verse (K. Young, *The Drama of the Medieval Church*, 2 vols. (Oxford 1933), Vol. 2, pp. 125–27, 140, 147, 158). I gratefully acknowledge Dr Alastair Logan's tracing of the prophecy's pre-Tertullian history, which is detailed in *The Eton Roundels*.
[54] See previous note.

Cum veniat sanctus sanctorum cessabit unxio vestra. Repetition of the phrase alerts us to its typological sense. The last editor of Langland had not traced the exact source of *Cum sanctus sanctorum veniat cessabit unxio vestra.* In fact it is a stock prophecy of the Nativity, familiar in the *lectio* at Mattins in the Christmas season, and common in literature and art. The prophecy's impact in our text is therefore double. The impact is partly conditioned by the immediately preceding sequence of images which begins with the *Entry into Jerusalem* (the Gospel at the Blessing of Palms), and proceeds to Faith's report that Life will fight Death and in three days achieve the *Harrowing of Hell* (XVIII.34). After this forward glance to victory there is a summary of the Passion which Christ will suffer first (the long Palm Sunday Gospel): the summary is given in terms of the *Judgement of Pilate* (XVIII.37), *Crowning with Thorns* (XVIII.47), *Mocking* (XVIII.50), *Nailing to the Cross* (XVIII.51) and *Crucifixion*. At the very moment of this consummation in the cross, the Nativity is recalled (just as the cross had earlier been recalled in the Nativity – see p.49). *Cum sanctus sanctorum veniat cessabit unxio vestra* thus brilliantly anticipates Mercy's explanation of the noise and darkness:

'Have no merveile', quod Mercy, 'murthe it bitokneth.
A maiden that highte Marie, and moder withouten felyng
Of any kynde creature, conceyved thorugh speche
And grace of the Holy Goost; weex greet with childe;
Withouten wem into this world she broghte hym'; (XVIII.127–31)

There is another point to make about this Crucifixion scene. Readers familiar with the current convention of presenting the *Crucifixion* in two distinct stages – as in *Biblia pauperum*, where they appear side by side on one opening – would understand exactly why the corpse rises momentarily from its grave precisely where it does. The two stages show Jesus alive, then dead. In the first stage, Christ is alive until his eyelids close, darkness falls, there is an earthquake, and the dead rise (XVIII.64). The corpse rises to describe the battle of Life and Death (but as the Resurrection has not yet occurred, returns to its resting place almost at once). In the second stage, the divinity of the dead Christ is acknowledged by the centurion, and Longeus 'jousts' with the body (XVIII.79).

The abbreviated Passion just described, which culminated in the Crucifixion, was briefly relieved by a glance forward to victory in the *Harrowing of Hell*. An earlier summary life of Christ, at XVI.90, is constructed in the opposite way, foreknowledge of death tempering the joy of the Incarnation. The summary follows the marvellous moment when Piers has thrown the second prop of the Tree of Charity at the devil, so representing, it seems to me, mankind's readiness to accept his need for Christ. Instantly the *Annunciation* (*And than spak Spiritus Sancti in Gabrielis mouthe*) leads to the *Nativity*. Each is followed immediately by a reference to the coming 'joust' of the *Crucifixion* – the unborn child waits until Jesus should joust with the devil *bi juggement of armes* (XVI.95), and the infant is capable of fighting him *er ful tyme come* (XVI.102). This narrative technique again recalls the infant Christ already carrying his cross (p.49, above).

The second inner dream will end with a selected survey of the whole life of Christ. After the Nativity just described, Piers Plowman becomes identified with Christ almost imperceptibly, when the Ministry is mentioned: *Piers the Plowman parceyved plener tyme, / And lered hym lechecraft.* Brilliantly, Piers-Jesus speaks only when we reach the Jews' objection to the *Raising of Lazarus* (XVI.113), where he refers to his healing of the sick and his feeding of the five thousand.[55] His anger at ingratitude leads immediately, in Langland's narrative logic, to the *Purging of The Temple* (XVI.127). At the *Last Supper* he speaks again, of the coming *Betrayal* and the *Payment of Judas*, warning of the *Crucifixion* and giving a promise of the *Resurrection* (*and deeth fordede, and day of nyght made,* XVI.165).[56] We are left ready to consider the previously-discussed Abraham sequence as a series of types of this life, for as we have seen, the Abraham passage may foreshadow *Annunciation, Magi, Last Supper* and *Crucifixion.*

The possible use of a sub-text of types is balanced by these recurrent selective summaries of the life of Christ, each acting as a reminder of the familiar narrative series, each treated with great imaginative freedom, and each tailored to its immediate context. Another, simpler, one occurs when Repentance's absolution of his penitents recalls major events in the life of Christ relevant to man's release from sin: *Creation* and the *felix culpa* of the *Fall* (V.480–84) lead to the *Nativity* (V.485), *Crucifixion* (V.489), *Harrowing of Hell* (V.493) and *Resurrection* (V.497).

On at least one occasion Old and New Testament scenes are intermingled. In a series of points in the life of Christ which are associated with the light about to pierce the darkness of hell, Book recalls the star of the *Epiphany* and *Nativity.* With the Four Daughters of God we then see the *Harrowing of Hell.* The devils recall the *Raising of Lazarus,* the *Fall of Man,* the *Temptation of Christ,* the *Crucifixion,* the *Fall of the Angels* (XVIII.265–311). They are remembering previous defeats. Langland, however, is also juxtaposing the *Fall of Man* with its antitype the *Temptation of Christ,*[57] and placing the virtue of Jesus represented by the *Temptation* and *Crucifixion* between balancing images of God's creatures' selfish weakness: the Falls of men and angels.

Although we have already witnessed the Crucifixion and Harrowing of Hell, at XIX.5 the blood-covered Piers-Christ takes us back to the *Carrying of the Cross* which, as already mentioned, was omitted from the Passion sequence that immediately preceded the *decensus ad inferna.* Another rapid sequence of images from the life of Christ follows, this time tailored to reveal the fact that Dobest is to be

---

[55] The Ministry is, of course, represented in full-length pictorial lives of Christ, but it is largely omitted from the standard compendia, which concentrate on the Passion.

[56] The antitypes are found in *Biblia pauperum*: the *Raising of Lazarus* at sig. l, the *Purging of Temple* at sig. p, the *Last Supper* at sig. s, the *Betrayal* at sig. .a., the *Payment of Judas* at sig. r, the *Crucifixion* at sigs .e. and .f., the *Resurrection* at sig. .i.

[57] As in *Biblia pauperum,* sig. k.

understood as the life of Christ perpetuated through the Spirit. The question, *but you call him Christ; for what cause, telleth me?* (XVIII.23), is followed by references to the *Crowning with Thorns*, the *Crucifixion* (XVIII.69) and the *Magi* who acknowledged his kingship (XVIII.75). Dowel, Dobet and Dobest are defined in terms of Christ's life: Dowel is shown in the *Marriage at Cana* (XVIII.108); Dobet in the Ministry, *Crucifixion, Burial, Resurrection, Noli me Tangere*, and *Doubting Thomas*; Dobest in the operation of the Holy Spirit in the Power of the Keys after the *Ascension* (XVIII.192), the Power of the Keys being fulfilled at *Judgement*. Once again a series of images ends with a statement of the importance of the Power of the Keys, and Judgement.

Langland's audience would surely not have expected biblical images to say 'one thing at a time', but would have felt it normal to interpret them in many ways at once. For centuries the images had grown in the Church's mind. It is particularly appropriate that this fruitfulness should be evident in a poem whose central figure is a ploughman and sower. As the caption to the Sherborne Missal's picture of Christ as sower says: *Semen est verbum dei Sator autem christus est.*[58]

---

[58] Page 66 (the Missal is paginated, not foliated).

Langland's Easter

Bruce Harbert

There are two ways of approaching the Passion of Christ. One is to focus on the suffering, both physical and mental, that he endured at the Crucifixion. The other is to look beyond the pathos to see divine power mingled with human weakness, the Resurrection in some way already present in the Passion, so that the Passion itself becomes a moment of triumph and glory. This latter, heroic view was the dominant one in the early Middle Ages, exemplified in Venantius Fortunatus' line *regnavit a ligno Deus*, or in the richly jewelled and decorated crosses of the period. From the twelfth century a more pathetic style of representation took over, producing the large corpus of affective writing on the Passion in Middle English or, an extreme manifestation of this tradition, the writhing, tortured Christ of Mathis Grünewald's Isenheim altarpiece. This well-known development should not, however, blind us to the fact that both traditions are present from the earliest times, both survive throughout the period, and both have their roots in the gospels.

As we trace different lines of devotional tradition through the Middle Ages, the role of liturgy in developing and popularising them should not be overlooked. The liturgy, with its reading and preaching of scripture and acting out of the biblical message, was one of the chief means by which people, especially the illiterate, maintained contact with the Bible. Medieval liturgy was richly varied. Although the liturgical texts remained relatively fixed in the West, ceremonial, which (like theatrical production) always implies an interpretation of the text, could develop quite freely. England had the different uses of Sarum, Hereford and York as well as those of the religious orders, and from one church to another customs would differ. Paraliturgical accretions flourished, as we see from the history of liturgical drama. While some churches would be adventurous and advanced, others remained conservative. The age of rigid liturgical uniformity was still in the future. Langland is unusual for his period in the way in which he represents the Passion, having more of the heroic early medieval spirit than most of his contemporaries: the liturgy was one of the sources from which he imbibed this. We shall appreciate his position in religious history more clearly if we understand the development both of the traditions on which he drew and of those that he rejected. For this we need to go back to the beginning, to the Bible.

There can be no doubt that crucifixion was a painful way of dying. The synoptic gospels bring this out by narrating such details as the agony of Jesus in the Garden of Gethsemane, his need for help in carrying his Cross, and the darkness that covers the earth as he dies. After the darkness of the Cross, for Matthew, Mark and Luke, comes the glory of the Resurrection.

John, by contrast, paradoxically represents the Crucifixion as a glorification. 'When I am lifted up from the earth, I will draw all men to myself' (Jn 12,32) says Jesus before his passion, and as his death draws near he remains in control, casting to the ground with a word those who come to arrest him, standing firm before Pilate and accepting the title of king, carrying his Cross without assistance, and dying with the cry 'It is finished', signifying not merely the end of a life but the completion of a task.

The unity of Passion and Resurrection is further shown in John when the risen Christ appears to his disciples still bearing his wounds in his body. John's Passion narrative offers an account not only of what happened there and then, but also of the significance of those happenings for here and now. His gospel looks forward, more than do the synoptics, to the life of Jesus' disciples after his death and Resurrection: 'I am come that they may have life, and have it abundantly' (Jn 10, 10) says Jesus, and the evangelist himself says of his text: 'These things are written that you may believe ... and that believing you may have life ...' (Jn 20, 31).

The Cross itself has little importance in the gospels except as the instrument of Crucifixion. It is to St Paul that we owe the use of the word 'Cross' to stand for the sufferings of Jesus, whose death was in Paul's eyes both a a humiliation (Phil 2, 8) and something to boast about (Gal 6, 14). The archaeology of the first three Christian centuries reveals few representations of the Cross or of the suffering Christ, and most of those that do survive are small. It was not until the early fourth century that the Cross became a common and publicly used Christian symbol. The story of Constantine's vision on the day before he won control of Rome at the battle of the Milvian bridge, in which he saw a Cross of light in the sky with an inscription attached saying 'conquer by this',[1] encouraged an association of the Cross with triumph, and strengthened the sense of Christ, crucified at a point distant in time and space, as potent here and now. Constantine had the Cross incorporated in the insignia of his armies and carried before them into battle, the first of many instances of the use of the Cross as a battle-ensign, a practice which continued throughout the Middle Ages and beyond. Constantine also had crosses erected over the tomb of St Peter and over his palace at Constantinople, and placed in the Roman Forum a statue of himself holding a Cross.[2]

At Jerusalem as at Rome, the Cross was revered as a symbol of triumph. This is a theme in the Catecheses of Cyril of Jerusalem, written before he became bishop

---

[1] Eusebius, Vita Constantini I 28–31, PL 8, 22–3.
[2] T.D.Barnes, Constantine and Eusebius (Harvard 1981) 310 n.61; Eusebius, Vita Constantini III 49; I 40, PL 8, 62, 26–7.

of the city.[3] He takes up Paul's theme of boasting in the Cross, telling his hearers they should not be ashamed of the Cross, because he who was crucified has risen, and is now in heaven. The Cross itself, he says, is a powerful safeguard against enemies and disease. After he became bishop, he wrote a letter to the emperor Constantius telling of a shining Cross that had been seen in 351 in the sky over Golgotha, the place of Christ's crucifixion: such a Cross, he predicted, would be seen again just before the second coming of Christ.[4] Some time in the late fourth century a large metal Cross was erected on Golgotha. In 417 this was adorned with gold and jewels.[5]

Jerusalem also evoked other sentiments. The places where Christ had been had a powerful attraction as a goal of pilgrimage: those who made the journey could, as they stood *there*, mentally transport themselves back to *then*, to the days of Christ's life and death, and imagine the details of what actually took place. Jerome records the reactions of his friend Paula to the experience:

> She threw herself down in adoration before the cross as if she could see the Lord himself hanging from it. And when she entered the tomb, she kissed the stone which the angel had rolled away .... What tears she shed there, what sighs of grief, all Jerusalem knows.[6]

Such personal devotions were incorporated into communal worship during the annual commemoration of Christ's death and Resurrection. The Spanish pilgrim Egeria, who visited Jerusalem in the late fourth century, tells how the Christian community used to assemble on the Mount of Olives on the Sunday before Easter and process into the city in commemoration of Christ's entry into Jerusalem. On the following Thursday the story of Jesus' arrest was read at Gethsemane amidst much weeping and lament from the people. On Good Friday, the more fervent would go to pray before a column reputed to be the one to which Christ was tied when being scourged. Later, in a service lasting three hours, the length of time that Jesus hung on the cross, the story of the Passion and other biblical texts were read near the place of the Crucifixion. Egeria describes the highly-charged scene:

> At each reading and prayer there is so much emotion and lament among all the people as to cause wonder: for there is nobody, greater or lesser, who does not during those three hours on that day bewail more than can be imagined that the Lord suffered those things for us.[7]

The service of readings was preceded by a rite in which the notes of glory and pathos were combined, the veneration of the wood, thought to be that of Christ's

---

[3] *Catechesis* 4. 14; 3.1–3, 40; PG 33, 471, 772–6, 820–1.
[4] *Epistola ad Constantium imperatorem* 3–6, PG 33, 1168–73.
[5] M.Swanton ed., *The Dream of the Rood* (Manchester 1970) 44.
[6] J.Sumption, *Pilgrimage* (London 1975) 91 and n.
[7] The ceremonies of Holy Week are described in *Peregrinatio* 31–37, in *Itinera Hierosolymitana*, ed. P. Geyer, CSEL 39.

Cross, discovered in Jerusalem some time in the middle years of the century. This was brought out in a silver gilt container, and each worshipper would come forward, bow before the relic and kiss it. The bow, like the rich container, expressed respect, while the kiss will have suggested more intimate sentiments. Many who thus approached the cross must have imagined themselves, like Paula, to be approaching Jesus himself.

Jerusalem's status as the birthplace of Christianity gave it influence. A copy of the Golgotha Cross soon appeared at Rome in the mosaic of the church of Santa Pudenziana (between 387 and 417).[8] Pope Hilarius (461–8), who had met Eastern bishops when he went to Ephesus in 449 to represent Pope Leo I, added to the Lateran baptistery a chapel containing a large cross which recalled the Golgotha cross near to the font at Jerusalem.[9] In the reign of Simplicius (468-83) Santo Stefano Rotondo was built on the Celian hill, its round form echoing Constantine's church over the holy sepulchre. Theodore I, a Greek pope born in Jerusalem, added a mosaic representing the cross of Golgotha.[10]

Rome also had a piece of the supposed wood of the Cross. The tradition that Helena, mother of Constantine, discovered the true Cross at Jerusalem and brought a piece of it to Rome, is not found earlier than the end of the fourth century. There is no literary reference to relics of the Cross before Cyril of Jerusalem in about 350.[11] These facts might lead us to conclude that relics of the Cross were unknown in Rome until late in the fourth century, did not archaeological evidence suggest otherwise. Between 326 and 328 Helena's palace, the Sessorian, was adapted to accomodate a basilica with a small chapel behind its apse, modelled closely on the Martyrium, the chapel in Jerusalem on the spot where the Cross was thought to have been found, and where it was kept. Both chapels had two entrances, as if to accommodate a file of pilgrims venerating the wood of the Cross. The *Liber Pontificalis*, begun in the early sixth century, may be telling the truth when it says that Constantine built a basilica in the Sessorian palace, residence of Helena, and placed there a relic of the Cross, enclosed in gold and precious stones.[12] This would mean that as early as the reign of Constantine the Cross at Rome was seen not only as a political and military symbol but as a focus of individual devotion.

The connection of the Sessorian Basilica with Jerusalem was expressed again between 425 and 442 by the erection in the small chapel of a mosaic with an inscription celebrating the glories of Jerusalem. The basilica came to be regarded as 'Jerusalem-in-Rome': now called Santa Croce in Gerusalemme, it is known in

[8]   R.Krautheimer, *Corpus Basilicarum Christianarum Romae* (Rome 1937–77) III 287, 300.
[9]   P.Journel, 'Le culte de la croix dans la liturgie Romaine', *La Maison-Dieu* 75 (1963) 68–91.
[10]   Krautheimer, *Corpus* IV 237.
[11]   Ambrose, *De Obitu Theodosii* 43–48 CSEL 13, 393–7; Rufinus, *Historia Ecclesiastica I* 7–8 PL 21, 475–8. *Catechesis* 4 10 PG 33, 468–9.
[12]   P.Journel, art.cit.

the *Liber Pontificalis* until the eleventh century, and in the ME *Stations of Rome* as late as the fifteenth, simply as 'Jerusalem'.

As time went on, Rome acquired further relics of the Cross. Pope Sergius I (687-701) a Syrian, claimed to have found one, of unknown provenance, abandoned in a corner of Saint Peter's and took it to the Lateran to be venerated on September 14th. This day was already marked at Jerusalem with special veneration of the supposed wood of the Cross, being the dedication festival of the Martyrium. This festival, which came to be known as the Exaltation of the Cross, was rapidly adopted in the West in the eighth century.

The eighth century also saw another liturgical innovation where the search for realism and pathos characteristic of the Jerusalem Holy Week liturgy began to make itself felt in the West.[13] On Good Friday the Pope would make his way in procession from his palace at the Lateran towards 'Jerusalem', that is, the Sessorian basilica, a journey of a little less than a kilometre. As he went, Psalm 118 would be sung which, with its repetitions of the word *via*, drew attention to the fact that a journey was being made. The effect is of a miniature pilgrimage to Jerusalem, As he went, he carried a smoking censer, and behind him walked a deacon carrying a relic of the Cross surrounded with perfumes in its jewelled container. The incense and perfume have been seen as an Eastern touch, but may have been inspired by the custom of anointing Roman military standards with perfume on feast-days: the rite of veneration of the Cross as a whole may have been influenced by the religious ceremonies associated with such standards.[14] The reminiscences of the east are probably due to the series of Greek and Syrian popes in the late seventh and early eighth centuries. The carrying of the relic may have been intended to reenact the journey of Christ carrying his cross with Simon of Cyrene: one interpreter of the rubrics has even suggested that the reliquary was tied to the Pope's back and supported by the deacon.[15] The liturgy at the Sessorian seems to have had a more sober character, more typically Roman than that of the procession, and to have consisted of readings, including the Johannine passion, prayers and veneration of the Cross.

The idea of the Cross as an emblem of military power had also spread north, as is shown by Oswald's use of the Cross at the battle of Heavenfield in 633, or the hymns written by Venantius Fortunatus at Poitiers in the late seventh century which liken the cross to a legionary emblem. Venantius' hymns were written with a devotional rather than a military purpose, and the military language is metaphorical. The Good Friday veneration had been adopted north of the Alps by the

---

[13] M.Andrieu, *Les Ordines Romani du haut moyen âge* III (Louvain 1951) 270–1; B.Capelle, 'Le Vendredi Saint', *La Maison-Dieu* 37 (1954) 93–117.

[14] Livy III 69, 8; Tacitus, *Annals* II 17, 2; Pliny, *Natural History* 13, 23; Tertullian, *Apology* 16.

[15] A.Baumstark, *Comparative Liturgy* (ET London 1958) 140ff., esp. 143.

eighth century, as a sacramentary from northern France attests,[16] but without the elaborate procession of the papal rite. Not all churches can have owned a fragment of the wood brought from Jerusalem, but a Cross of more recent make will have been venerated.

The Good Friday ceremony was to develop as the Middle Ages proceeded, reflecting and influencing the development of attitudes towards the Passion. In the eighth century, the veneration seems to have taken place in silence, but soon chants began to be provided for it. The most widely used fall into four groups, all of which are already present in the tenth-century English *Regularis Concordia*, and still in use today:

(i) An antiphon addressed to the worshippers *Ecce lignum crucis, in quo salus mundi pependit* which, with their response *Venite adoremus*, draws attention to the wood of the Cross as a focus of veneration. Where a relic was not used, the antiphon will have reminded worshippers of the existence of such relics.

(ii) a set of antiphons addressed to Christ, of which the most widely diffused runs *Crucem tuam adoramus, Domine, et sanctam resurrectionem tuam laudamus et glorificamus: ecce enim propter lignum venit gaudium in universo mundo*. This sees the Cross in the light of the Resurrection as a source of joy.

(iii) The hymn *Pange lingua* by Venantius Fortunatus. Composed in the metre of a Roman soldiers' marching-song, it calls the cross a *tropaeum*, the Latin form of the very word Eusebius had used of it in his life of Constantine, and invites its hearers to join in a song of triumph at Christ's victory. A *tropaeum* was a memorial of a victory, made of equipment captured from the defeated army: to call the Cross a *tropaeum* is to imply that it was the devil's weapon, but has become the sign of Christ's triumph. The note of pathos also comes in with mention of the cries of the infant Jesus or the instruments of the passion, and with the suggestion that the Cross bend in sympathy with the suffering Christ. Although for the most part Christ's triumph is represented as already achieved in the Johannine manner, at one point we are invited with the word *En* 'behold' to imagine ourselves present as Christ is tortured, and to feel the contrast between the hard lance and his soft body: *En acetum fel arundo sputa clavi lancea: mite corpus perforatur*. In this complex poem present and past, triumph and pathos are carefully balanced. In liturgical use the stanza of salute to the cross beginning *crux fidelis inter omnes arbor una nobilis* was used as a refrain, and its repetition will have brought into prominence the triumphal aspect of the text.

(iv) The Improperia or reproaches of Christ to his people for illtreating him although he had brought them out of Egypt into the promised land. They are first

---

[16] A.Dumas ed., *Liber Sacramentorum Gellonensis, Corpus Christianorum* CLIX (Turnhout 1981).

recorded in an Antiphonar written around 880 at Saint Denys, which was at that time a centre of Greek influence.[17] They proclaim by implication the divinity of Christ, since the Exodus, recognised as God's work, took place long before Jesus' human life. The divine aspect is further emphasised by the refrain chanted in Latin and Greek after each of the reproaches: 'Holy is God, holy and strong, holy and immortal one, have mercy on us'. There is no sense of divine power at the Crucifixion, however, but rather of Christ by his pleas inviting sympathy with his human suffering.

Each of these chants implies a different understanding of the rite and offers possibilities for further development, not only in the details of the ceremony, but in attitudes to the passion itself. The Improperia in particular, with their focus on Christ's suffering, hold the germ of much that was to come later.

The *Regularis Concordia* itself gives prayers for the priest to say during the veneration.[18] The image they suggest is drawn from the Improperia, of the worshipper confronted directly with Christ, but the tone of the prayers is less pathetic than that of the chant. They begin 'Lord Jesus Christ, I adore you ascending on the Cross . . .', envisaging not the passive Christ of the Improperia but an active, Johannine one. They go on to consider Christ harrowing hell, rising from the dead and coming again in glory, strong images familiar from Old English poetry. Perhaps we see here an insular reaction to a continental novelty.

But the pathetic elements were to win in the long term, as the idea took hold, in what has come to be known as the meditative movement, that the essence of prayer is to transport oneself imaginatively from the here and now to the there and then of Christ's life and death. A leading role in this development was played by the Franciscan order. Francis himself, when assisting at midnight mass one Christmas in the Umbrian town of Greccio, had placed straw, an ox and an ass near the altar to help people imagine themselves in Bethlehem. By such developments the patristic and early medieval idea of liturgy as anamnesis, making the past effective in the present, is lost. Francis himself visited the Holy Land and in the fourteenth century his order was given the Guardianship of the Holy Places. Jerusalem became more and more popular as a goal of pilgrimage, and thus continued to play its role in the transformation of religious attitudes.

For those who could not go to Jerusalem, Jerusalem could come to them in the form of relics such as, in England, the Blood of Hayles or the Rood of Bromholm. Rome became in the popular mind another Jerusalem by virtue of the astounding number of objects of devotion there that, it was claimed, had been brought from the Holy Land. There was money to be made from pilgrims, and financial considerations obviously played a part in these developments.

While these changes were going on, the texts of the Good Friday liturgy remained constant. However, new interpretations of the rite developed, and its

[17] I.-H.Dalmais, 'L'adoration de la croix', *La Maison-Dieu* 45 (1956) 76–86.
[18] K.Young, *The Drama of the Medieval Church* (Oxford 1933) I 119.

original significance was gradually forgotten. The complaint of Christ, one of the earliest forms of which is the Improperia, became a popular theme in devotional literature designed to evoke intense emotional sympathy with his sufferings, rather than the meditation on his triumph that we find in the *Regularis Concordia*. The Franciscan William Herebert (+1333) in his translation of the Improperia, while remaining fairly close to the original, changes past tenses into present so that we imaginatively follow Christ through the stages of his passion: *þou me ledest to rode troe . . . and þou bufetest and scourgest me . . . and þou betest myn heued wyþ roed.* Also, he does not attempt to render the Latin and Greek 'Holy is God' refrain, so that the note of divine power is considerably weakened.[19]

Changes were made to the ceremonial of Good Friday to foster a sense of being present at the death of Christ.[20] In place of the Cross, a crucifix came to be used for the ceremony of veneration, the worshippers kissing its feet. When the veneration was over the crucifix might be washed in wine and water, recalling the blood and water that flowed from the side of the dead Christ. In some places the figure of Christ was removed from the crucifix and washed, in an enactment of the Deposition. The Ordinal of the nuns of Barking specifies that the wounds on the figure of Christ are to be washed.[21] The recollection of the blood and water in so mournful a context contrasts strongly with the interpretation of that episode by the Fathers, who see in it the beginning of the sacramental life of the Church, a source of power.

The mournful note continued in the ceremony that followed, that of the burial of the Cross or crucifix in the Easter sepulchre, which was hung with cloths and had lights burning before it. From the thirteenth century onwards the custom grew, though it was never universally adopted in England, of burying the eucharistic Host in the sepulchre together with the Cross. This is theological nonsense, as some remarks in a thirteenth-century manuscript from Zurich neatly point out:

> It is against all reason that in some churches the Eucharist is customarily placed and enclosed in such a container, which represents the Sepulchre. For there the Eucharist, which is the true and living body of Christ, represents the dead body of Christ, which is profoundly unsuitable and absurd.[22]

Nonetheless, the practice gained ground. Parish records of London churches in the fourteenth to sixteenth centuries regularly record payments made to those

---

[19] Carleton Brown ed. *Religious Lyrics of the Fourteenth Century* 2nd ed. revised by G.V.Smithers (Oxford 1957) 17f.
[20] Solange Corbin, *La déposition liturgique du Christ au Vendredi Saint* (Lisbon 1960) 50–53; E.Bishop, 'Holy Week rites of Sarum, Hereford and Rouen compared', *Liturgica Historica* (Oxford 1918) 276–300.
[21] K.Young, *Drama* I 164.
[22] id. 154.

employed in keeping watch before the sepulchre from Good Friday to Easter morning. The effect must have been that of a wake for the dead Christ.

After his death, according to the First Epistle of Peter (3, 19) and the Apostles' Creed, Christ descended into Hell. Mattins of Holy Saturday[23] recalled the rest of the body of Christ in the tomb with Psalm 4 and its verse 'I will lie down in peace and take my rest' and the journey of his soul to Hell with 'Lift up your gates, you princes, and be lifted up, you everlasting doors, and the King of Glory shall come in' from Psalm 23. The vigil at the sepulchre will, however, have ensured that the repose of the body was uppermost in people's minds.

An even more striking example of the centrality of the dead Christ to the exclusion of all else at this time is provided by John Mirk.[24] Mattins and Lauds of Holy Saturday were followed by a Mass which in earlier centuries had been celebrated in the night between Saturday and Sunday in commemoration of the Resurrection. Although by the fourteenth century this mass had come to be celebrated in the morning its texts remained unchanged, so that it was plainly the first Mass of Easter. In most English churches, anomalously, the cross and host would still be resting in the Sepulchre with lights burning before it. This mass is unusual in having no Office, that is, entrance-chant, because it is preceded by other ceremonies. Mirk explains this detail by saying that the Office is the head of the mass as Christ is the head of the Church, and as he is not yet risen so the mass has no Office. Mirk has no sense whatever of the original link between the Saturday mass and the Resurrection. For him, the Holy Week liturgy is a repetition of the death and Resurrection of Christ, so that it is possible to say on the Saturday 'he is not risen'.

Evidence that devotion to the Resurrection was waning in the later fourteenth century is given by the Ordinal of the nuns of Barking which records how Katherine of Sutton, abbess from 1363 to 1376, changed the hour of her community's dramatic celebrations of Easter morning, which consisted of a liturgical play enacting the Harrowing of Hell, followed by a procession of the Host from the Sepulchre to the altar of the Holy Trinity. These had taken place before Mattins, but Katherine put them after the third responsory within Mattins.[25] We are not told whether attendance improved. Popular piety is not usually so easily manipulated.

The Barking custom was an adaptation and elaboration of the procession prescribed for Easter Day by the Sarum Breviary, in which the Cross was removed from the sepulchre and carried in procession with singing of the antiphon *Christus resurgens*. Some wealthy churches, such as Saint Paul's Cathedral,[26] had a special

[23] *Breviarium ad Usum Sarum* ed. F.Proctor and C.Wordsworth, Vol.1 (Cambridge 1882) 795–801.
[24] T.Erbe ed., *Mirk's Festial* part I EETS ES 96 (1905) 128.
[25] K.Young, *Drama* I 165.
[26] W.S.Simpson, 'Two Inventories of the Cathedral Church of St Paul, London', *Archaeologia* 50 (1887) 514.

Cross for this with a crystal container at its centre for the Host so that both could be carried together, but usually the Host was carried privately back to its usual place and the Cross was the centre of attention. The rubrics direct that it have a banner attached to it, and the inventories of many London churches record 'cross-cloths', some depicting the Resurrection.

In some places it was the custom for the Cross to be venerated on Easter Day. The Sarum Breviary directs that it be carried to an altar on the north side of the church and there venerated by the clergy. Edward III venerated the cross at Windsor at Easter in the second year of his reign, and some two centuries later the young Princess Mary regularly did the same. This was the custom also in the household of the Earl of Northumberland.[27] Margery Kempe was plainly familiar with the practice, for when she found herself unexpectedly in Norway one Easter she discovered that the custom there was for the cross to be raised about noon on Easter Day, but nonetheless 'she had her meditation and her devotion with weeping and sobbing as well as if she had been at home'.[28] The Easter veneration was still known in 1539, though by that time what stood on the north side of Salisbury cathedral was an image of Christ containing the Host. People were observed to be kneeling and kissing this image in the afternoon of Easter Day.[29]

The procession and veneration of the Cross at Easter preserved something of its triumphal associations although, as Margery Kempe's example suggests, it was possible to have sorrowful thoughts even on Easter Day. For those who knew Latin, however, even Good Friday could still retain its more ancient connotations, for the liturgical texts had remained unchanged for centuries, including the reading of the Passion narrative from John.

Langland moved around a good deal during his life, and will have attended many churches, experiencing many different patterns and styles of worship. He was also familiar with the liturgical texts common to all those churches, as his frequent echoes of the liturgy show. And he was a reader of the Fathers, from whom he will have imbibed something of the early medieval spirituality. On the basis of this formation he approaches the Passion of Christ and its relationship with the liturgy in a manner quite unusual for his time.

The sixth dream of *Piers Plowman* (C Passus XX)[30] begins on Palm Sunday and lasts throughout Holy Week until the dreamer awakens to the sound of church bells on Easter morning. He dreams of the Passion, Harrowing of Hell and Resurrection simultaneously with their liturgical commemoration, and the waking world intrudes into his dream as he hears snatches of the liturgy.

---

[27] Society of Antiquaries, *Liber quotidianus congratulatorius guardarobae A.D.1299 et 1300* (London 1787) 365f.; F.Madden ed., *Privy Purse expenses of the Princess Mary* (London 1831) 24, 66, 111; T.Percy ed., *The Earl of Northumberland's Household Book* (London 1770) 335.

[28] S.B.Meech and H.E.Allen ed., *The Book of Margery Kempe* EETS OS 212 (1940) 231.

[29] H.Thurston, *Lent and Holy Week* (London 1904) 469f.

[30] References are to the edition of the C-Text by D.Pearsall (London 1978)

The mass of Palm Sunday was sombre in tone, containing the reading of Matthew's Passion narrative, but was preceded by a triumphal procession commemorating Christ's entry into Jerusalem. The dreamer hears the opening words of the hymn by Theodulf of Orleans, *Gloria laus et honor*, which accompanied this procession, acclamations (*osanna* and *Fili David*) echoing an antiphon that preceded it and another acclamation (*benedictus qui venit in nomine Domini*) from Matthew's account of the entry which was read during the procession. These help set the tone of triumph which pervades the whole passus.

From the Palm Sunday Mass itself Langland takes some elements from Matthew, combining them with others from John to form his account of the Passion (lines 35 to 71). The blend produces a narrative with neither the pathos of the synoptic tradition nor the majesty of the Johannine, but a harsh conciseness that is Langland's own. The cry *Ave, raby*, the account of the dead coming out of their graves after Christ's death and the centurion's confession *vere filius Dei erat iste* are all from Matthew. John provides the cries from the crowd *crucifige* (twice) and *tolle, tolle* and Jesus' last words *consummatum est*, as well as the episodes of the breaking of the legs of the crucified thieves and the piercing of Jesus' side with a spear, this last elaborated with the legend of the blind Longeus being healed by the blood and water that spring out. There is no echo in Langland of the mournful liturgical washing of the figure of Christ with wine and water before its burial. Indeed, the burial of Christ is something that Langland ignores, despite the elaboration of the motif in contemporary liturgy.

The reading of John's Passion was followed in the Good Friday liturgy by a series of prayers for all sorts and conditions of men, among them one *pro perfidis iudeis*[31] which was probably influenced by the anti-semitism of the fourth gospel. Langland is echoing this when he makes Faith after the death of Jesus rail at the *false Iewes*. Again, it is a harsh note that Langland borrows from his liturgical source.

After the prayers came the veneration of the Cross, from which Langland in three places echoes Venantius' hymn *Pange lingua: thritty wynter ypassed* recalls *lustra sex . . . peracta*; *That was tynt thorw tre, tre shal hit wynne* echoes *ipse lignum tunc notauit damna ligni ut solueret*, and *ars ut artem falleret* is quoted directly. Nothing of Venantius' pathos is taken over: all Langland's echoes reinforce the sense of divine purpose being fulfilled in the Passion. There is no allusion to the Improperia of the Good Friday liturgy.

As he moves towards narrating the Harrowing of Hell, Langland begins to echo the office of Holy Saturday, thus showing himself aware of its ancient significance which was fading from memory in his time. Two psalms are echoed: *In pace in idipsum dormiam et requiescam* is not applied, as one might have expected, to the repose of Christ in the tomb, but is used by the character Peace as a prophecy of Christ's turning righteousness into peace. *Ad vesperum demorabitur fletus, et ad*

---

[31]   J. Wickham Legg ed., *The Sarum Missal* (Oxford 1916) 112.

matutinum leticia (Ps 4,9) also strikes a note of joyful anticipation. *Attollite portas* (Ps 23,7) is used, as in the liturgy, with reference to the Harrowing of Hell, demanding the opening of hell's gates for Christ *þe kynge of all glorie* (*rex gloriae* Ps 23,8).

Before the Resurrection there is one last echo of John's Passion narrative. Jesus' cry of thirst from the cross is postponed until he is in hell and transformed into an expression of his will to save all mankind: *me fursteth 3ut, for mannes soule sake / Sicio*. This bold stroke is faithful to John, for whom *Sicio* is not an anguished or involuntary cry, but one uttered 'that the scriptures might be fulfilled', but Langland goes much further than John in making it a manifestation of Christ's power and of his will to save all humanity.

The final liturgical echo in this dream comes from the liturgy of Easter morning itself, the *Te Deum Laudamus* which was sung at the end of Mattins.[32] At Barking the nuns have finished their Easter play and Langland's dreamer is still in bed, having slept for a whole week. Katherine of Sutton would not have been pleased. Had she, however, been able to read of his dream (an impossibility, for *Piers Plowman* existed only in the A-version at the time of her death) and to learn that he shared with her a devotion to the Harrowing of Hell and the Resurrection rare in their time, she would have recognised a kindred spirit.

When he awakens to the sound of bells ringing for Easter mass, the dreamer calls his wife and daughter to go to church with him and kiss the Cross:

> 'Arise, and go reverense godes resureccioun,
> And crepe to þe croes on knees, and kusse hit for a iewel
> And riht follokest a relyk, noon richore on erthe,
> For godes blessed body hit baer for oure bote,
> And hit afereth the fende, for such is þe myhte
> May no grisly goest glyde þer hit shaddeweth!'

Most editors in commenting on these lines refer to the custom of venerating the Cross on Good Friday, but this is inappropriate. The lugubrious form that that rite had assumed in fourteenth-century England was alien to Langland's spirit and finds no echo in his poem. The custom his dreamer follows is the apparently rarer one of veneration on Easter Day. Moreover, it is a cross that he goes to kiss, not a crucifix, and he speaks of it as a *iewel*, something precious rather than shameful, which has power against the fiend and evil spirits. This is a view of the Cross more characteristic of the early Middle Ages, though we also find it in Chaucer, when Constance in the *Man of Law's Tale* prays for the protection of the Cross in Venantian terms *Victorious tree, proteccioun of trewe*.[33]

Although he manages to dress and go to church, the dreamer only stays awake for half the mass, falling asleep at the offertory to see Christ looking like Piers

---

[32] *id*. 112.
[33] C.T. II 456ff.

Plowman, *peynted al blody* and carrying a cross. This image is a conflation of two traditional ones, the risen Christ carrying his cross, and the *imago pietatis*, in which he is spattered with blood and often surrounded by the instruments of the Passion.[34] Pictures of the suffering Christ painted on cloth were often hung before the chancel during Lent, and the statement that Piers stood *bifore þe comune peple* probably indicates that he stood where such an image would have hung. The church of Saint Peter upon Cornhill, an area Langland knew well, possessed in 1552 a *steyned white clothe with a crucifix Mary and John spotted with bloudde with a holy gost ouer his hed.*[35] Such a picture – perhaps this very one – may have suggested Langland's image, but it is surprising to find it evoked in the context of Easter Day. However, Langland is here again being faithful to John, whose Jesus is still wounded after the Resurrection. Langland's Christ is still bloodstained as he is proclaimed knight, king and conqueror: the continuing reality of human suffering is not something from which he is alienated by the Resurrection. Langland like John looks forward to the establishment of the life of the Church and the complexities of its continuance into the here and now, in which Christ is involved by means of the Holy Spirit.

The concrete everyday world is what counts for Langland: that is where salvation is to be found. Those who set out on pilgrimage to seek Saint Truth in the second dream of *Piers Plowman* are firmly encouraged to remain at home. The journey that matters to Langland is the inner journey, into oneself and towards the discovery of the indwelling God. But for all his interiority Langland does not have a privatised spirituality. Not for him the lonely imaginative journey to a distant time and place: he prays in crowds, his piety shaped by a liturgy of anamnesis, of calling divine power into the here and now.

Recent work on the history of eucharistic controversy in England during the Reformation period has shown that a major underlying cause of disagreement was a loss of the idea of anamnesis, of liturgy as making the past effective in the present.[36] Once this idea is lost, liturgy can only be seen either as merely commemorating the events of the past, or as repeating them. These are the views of the relationship between the Passion and the Eucharist attributed by their opponents to (though not necessarily held by) Protestants and Catholics respectively. Controversy on this matter did not break out in academic circles much before the sixteenth century, but the ground was being prepared earlier by developments in popular piety. The name of Mirk has been cited in this context,[37] and what has been written here should serve to show that he was not an isolated figure, but a witness to the devotional temper of his age. He did see the liturgy of Holy Week

[34] See R.Woolf, *The English Religious Lyric in the Middle Ages* (Oxford 1968) 389–91.

[35] H.B.Walters, *London Churches at the Reformation* (London 1939) 580.

[36] Anglican-Roman Catholic International Commission, *Final Report* (London 1982) 14; 17–20.

[37] C.W.Dugmore, *The Mass and the English Reformers* (London, 1958) see index under 'Mirk'; F.Clark, *Eucharistic Sacrifice and the Reformation* (London 1967) 426–9.

as in some way repeating the events of the Passion and Resurrection, and his contemporaries in general tended to see liturgy as an occasion for reliving the past rather than as a mode of encounter with Christ in the present. This attitude can easily lead to a view of the Mass as a repetition of Calvary with Christ slain afresh every day, the doctrine attributed to Catholics by Protestant polemic. Few would now claim that Catholic academic theology justified that taunt, but some popular attitudes that grew up in the later Middle Ages certainly tended towards such a view.

With regard to Langland, it is often asked whether he is a precursor of the sixteenth-century Reformers. Certainly he saw the need for reform in the Church. But in his theological and devotional attitudes he draws on deep and ancient springs which his contemporaries were forgetting. Had more remembered them, that impoverishment of the western religious consciousness which made it too easy for western Christianity to be torn apart might not have come about. Langland cannot be assigned to either the Catholic or the Protestant camp in sixteenth-century terms. Spiritually he is an heir of the first Christian millennium, to whose patterns of thought and feeling Christian theologians are now returning in their attempts to repair the divisions of the second.

The Triumph of Patience in Julian of Norwich and Langland

Anna P. Baldwin

Patience is discredited now as an answer to the problem of pain. Removing the pain seems a much more positive approach. Consequently, Langland's presentation of patience as a response to poverty in the section of *Piers Plowman* known as 'Dowel' has irritated some critics, particularly when it is contrasted with the more politically aware *Visio*.[1] But Langland does see patience as effecting change, transforming the suffering of poverty first into a penance for sin, and then into a price for heaven, and a weapon against sin. Finally patience personified is shown not merely enduring but transforming the human sinfulness which caused the poverty and suffering in the first place. I shall be exploring the extraordinary importance Langland gives to patience in the light of Biblical and Church exegesis, and in comparison with Julian of Norwich's account of the transforming patience of Christ. In so doing I hope to bring together two great interests of Stan Hussey, Langland and the English mystics, whose interpretation he has helped to transform by his own patient research.

(a) Medieval accounts of patience

It is easy enough to find in the Old Testament the belief that suffering is sent by God as a punishment for man's sin, for that is the basis of the Old Covenant (e.g. Deuteronomy 28[2]). Patience under affliction can then be seen as a humble acknowledgement of guilt, and of the right of God to chastise his chosen people

---

[1] See D. Aers, '*Piers Plowman* and problems in the perception of poverty: a culture in transition', *Leeds Studies in English*, NS 14 (1983), 5–25; Derek Pearsall, 'Poverty and poor people in *Piers Plowman*', *Medieval English Studies presented to George Kane*, ed. Kenneth R. Waldron, and S. Wittig (Suffolk 1988), pp. 167–85. Authorial authority for a 'dowel' section has been discredited by R. Adams, 'The Reliability of the Rubrics in the B-text of *Piers Plowman*', *Medium Aevum*, 54 (1985), 208–31, but I use the term for its convenience.
[2] See L. Besserman, *The Legend of Job in the Middle Ages* (Harvard, 1979), p.11 ff.

through sending the apparently random disasters of life. The New Testament Christians saw themselves as the new heirs of God, and so of the Father's chastisement:

> For whom the Lord loveth He chastiseth, and scourgeth every son whom
> he receiveth.   (Hebrews 12:6, see also Rev. 3:19)

The immensely popular *Somme le Roi*, which is translated into Middle English as the *Aȝenbite of Inwyt* and the *Book of Vices and Virtues*, developed the paradox that God shows His special favour to His chosen by punishing them:

> As þe Holy Gost makeþ his knyȝt hardy to a-bide þe turmentes and þe
> sorwes þat beth to come, riȝt also he makeþ hym strong and suffryng to
> suffre hem whan þei comen: and þat . . . þei clepen pacience, þat is
> suffraunce. Bi þis vertue ouercomeþ a man or a womman here enemys,
> þat is þe deuel, þe flesche, and þe world. . . . wiþ-oute pacience þer haþ
> no wiȝt victorie . . .[3]

'Patientes vincunt', which is a quotation from the apocryphal *Testament of Job*, probably originally expressed the Stoic idea that patience gives the philosopher victory over chance and his passions.[4] But the Christian does not believe in chance, since all events are ordained by God, and he does not disallow passion, for Christ suffered despair and even God seems to have felt, if not to have given way to, anger. Instead he must see the patience in transformational terms: God's 'suffraunce' of man's sin allows His mercy to triumph over His anger; and man's suffraunce of God's will transforms him from dross to gold, from bastard into son.[5]

Such an essentially sacramental notion found a place in the penitential handbooks, as a way of transforming unavoidable poverty into a meritorious penance for sin. Duns Scotus and Thomas of Chobham both advise the priest to give the poor the compassionate penance of simply enduring their everyday sufferings with patience, thereby turning them into satisfaction for sin.[6] In the later fourteenth-century the popular priest's handbook, the *Pupilla Oculi*, gives the same advice:

---

[3] *The Book of Vices and Virtues*, ed. W. N. Francis, EETS OS 217 (1842), p. 167; see also *Dan Michel's Ayenbite of Inwyt*, ed. R. Morris, EETS OS 23 (1866), p. 167; *Speculum Christiani*, ed. G. Holmstedt (Oxford 1930), p. 226.

[4] *The Testament of Job*, ed. R. A. Kraft, Society of Biblical Literature (Missoula, Montana 1974) p. 53 (27:10). On Stoic ideas, see J. D. Burnley, *Chaucer's Language and the Philosophers' Tradition* (Cambridge 1979), pp. 64–81.

[5] Heb. 12:8; Job 23:10; R. Hanna III, 'Some commonplaces of medieval patience discussions: an introduction', *The Triumph of Patience*, ed. G. J. Schiffhorst (Florida 1978), pp. 65–87, see p. 76.

[6] Thomas of Chobham, *Summa Confessorum*, ed. F. Broomfield (Louvain 1968), p. 233 (V.2.1a); Duns Scotus, *In IV Sent*. Dist. XV Q.1, referred to by H. C. Lea, *A History of Medieval Confession and Indulgence in the Christian Church* (Philadelphia 1896 repr. 1968), II, 182.

the scourges which God inflicts on men in this life, if a man willingly and patiently accepts them . . . will count as the purgation of his sin.[7]

This productive attitude to poverty has a prominent place in the widely-read *Prikke of Conscience*

> For thurgh nuys and angers sere,
> He makes a man als his preson here,
> Payn to drighe for hys folye
> In þis lif als he es worthy.
> And, if he it thole noght grotchand,
> In-stede of penance it sal hym stand,
> And yhit whil God hym mare do,
> He wil gif hym mede þat-to
> þat his ioy in heven sal heke,
> If he thole angwyse with hert meke.[8]   IV.3538–3547

But as this last quotation indicates, the New Testament promises rewards as well as punishments to God's chosen heirs. Christ laid the foundation for such hopes by promising reward in heaven for all who suffer for His sake (Matthew 5:10, Luke 21:19), and the Epistle of James develops the role of patience in earning such a reward:

> Blessed is the man that endureth temptation (suffert temtationem), for when he is tried, he shall receive the crown of life, which the Lord hath promised to them that love Him.   (Jas. 1:12)

The possibility of translating 'suffert' here as 'suffer', or of translating 'patiuntur persecutionem' in Matthew 5:10 as 'suffer persecution', might suggest to the medieval reader that it was the suffering rather than the endurance which would be rewarded. This implication is supported by the more revolutionary passages of the New Testament, such as James 2:5, or the Magnificat. But as Hanna has demonstrated, St Augustine had insisted that 'not suffering, but a good cause,

---

[7] 'flagella que Deus immittit hominibus in hac vita, si homo voluntarie acceperit illa ad purgationem peccatorum patienter eis utens, assumunt rationem satisfactionis et sunt satisfactoria pro peccatis', *Pupilla Oculi* (Paris 1510) f. 31r (V c. 4, H). N. Gray, in his unpublished Ph.D. thesis, *Piers Plowman in relation to the medieval penitential tradition* (Cambridge 1984), p. 189, n. 57, adds further examples from *Parson's Tale*, 1052–6; Alain of Lille, *Liber Poenitentialis*, Lib. III, cap. xxiv; Robert Courson, *Summa*, Lib. I cap. 5, b; Raymond of Pennafort, *Summa*, Lib. III tit. 34 section 38; J. Myrc, *Instructions for Parish Priests*, ed. E. Peacock, EETS OS 31 (1868), 1637–42; *Speculum Sacerdotale*, ed. E. H. Weatherly, EETS OS 200 (1936) ch. 23 pp. 80–1.
[8] *The Prikke of Conscience* ed. R. Morris (Berlin 1863 repr. AMS, New York 1973) IV. 3538–3547; see also Chaucer, *Parson's Tale*, 1052–6; *Speculum Christiani*, EETS OS 182 (1933), p. 184.

makes a martyr',[9] and in his work *On Patience* he limits the recipients of such biblical promises to those whose sufferings have been accepted patiently as God's will:

> So also the patience of the poor of Christ, who are to be the enriched heirs of Christ, will not perish forever, . . . because in return for what we have patiently endured here, we will there enjoy eternal happiness.[10]

Later authors also attempted to limit the biblical implication that all suffering on earth would be rewarded in heaven. For example the late thirteenth-century *Remedia* text, which Wenzel has recently edited as a source for Chaucer's *Parson's Tale*, distinguishes patience in suffering for the sake of a heavenly reward, from the patience of an earthly mercenary:

> it may seem that the charity of the saints is mercenary because it serves for the sake of created glory [i.e. heavenly reward] and not for the sake of God alone. To this objection you should reply that the charity of the saints places created glory, which consists in the gifts, as an end beneath another end in its reward, and it places God as the ultimate end, to whom alone one should adhere for his own sake.[11]

Throughout this text the patience of Christ is used as an ideal to inspire the sinful reader, who is thereby shown the value of patience 'for God's own sake', rather than as a virtue which only acknowledges punishment or hopes for reward. Christ's suffering was for others' sins, not for his own, and His patience transforms God's anger into grace, and man's sin into faith:

> It was necessary that all these [sufferings] should happen first in the head, for the health of the members . . . It was absolutely necessary that Christ should thus suffer for our sake, so that from the hewn rock . . . the life-giving water should abound for us.[12]

In dividing the sin from the patient sufferer in this way, the writer moves from the retributive context of punishment and reward, which we have so far been discussing, to a much more positive account of patience transforming the world and giving man the victory. The patience of God expresses the love of God for man; the patience of man can transform his own sinfulness into an answering love.

---

[9] Augustine, Epistle 204:4 (*PL* 33:940), translated Hanna *op.cit.* p. 70 and n.13.
[10] Augustine, *De Patientia*, Ch. 29 (PL 40:626), tr. The Fathers of the Church, *St Augustine: Treatises on Various Subjects* (New York 1952), p. 64, referring to Ps. 9:18 (A.V.) Jas. 2:5.
[11] *Summa Virtutum de Remediis Animae*, ed. S. Wenzel, Chaucer Library (Georgia 1984), p. 206.
[12] *Op.cit.* p. 202.

(b) Julian of Norwich

This process is clearly developed in Julian of Norwich's account of the suffering of Christ. In Chapter 60 of the Long Version of her *Revelations*, she compares a mother's endurance of childbearing with Christ's endurance of his Passion:

> The moders service is nerest, redyest and sekirest, for it is most of trueth. This office . . . ne never non don to the full [but] he alone . . . He, al love, beryth us to ioye and to endles lyving . . . Thus he . . . traveled into the full tyme that he wold suffre the sharpist throwes and the grevousest peynes that ever were or ever shall be, and dyed at the last. . . . Yet myte not al this makyn aseth to his mervelous love, and that shewid he in these hey overpassing wordes of love: 'If I myte suffre more, I wold suffre more,'[13]

These words were said during the ninth revelation in Chapter 22 (also found in the Short Version), where the acceptance of pain is also the supreme expression of love:

> It is a ioy, a blis, an endles lekying to me that ever suffrid I passion for the; and if I myht suffre more, I wold suffre more.[14]

Julian is not using the word 'patience', but my quotation earlier from *The Book of Vices and Virtues* indicated that the ability to be 'strong and suffryng to suffre [turmentes and sorwes]' (p.72 above) could be called either patience or 'suffraunce.' Indeed the willingness and generosity of Jesus' suffering in these passages invites direct comparison with the *Remedia* text's (just-quoted) account of the Crucifixion as an act of patience, releasing 'the life-giving water' for mankind. Julian relates this sacramental flow from Christ's body to the mother's patient offering of her own milk:

> The moder may geven her child soken her mylke, but our pretious moder Iesus, he may fedyn us with hymself . . . with the blessid sacrament that is pretious fode of very lif.   (ch.60)[15]

She may be recalling here St Bernard's famous mystical analysis of the *Song of Songs*, which specifically uses the image of the 'breasts finer than wine' (Vulgate *Canticles* 4:10) to express Christ's patience:

---

[13] *Julian of Norwich, A Revelation of Love*, ed. M. Glasscoe (Exeter 1976), p. 73.
[14] *Op.cit.* p. 24; c.p. *Julian of Norwich: Revelations of Love: The Short Version*, ed. F. Beer (Heidelberg 1978), p. 57, Ch. xii.
[15] *Op.cit.* p. 73. The analogy between the water and the blood flowing from Christ's side, and the sacraments of baptism and mass, was commonplace; see e.g. Aquinas, *Summa Theologica*, 3a q. 62 a. 5.

We may take the two breasts of the Bridegroom to mean the two ways in which he shows his essential clemency, namely his Patience in waiting for the sinner, and his Mercy in receiving the penitent.[16]

This is however a little stiff and abstract; Julian makes a much more direct comparison between the mother's gift of herself through her milk, and Jesus' gift of Himself through the sacraments. Her point is that although her own earthly mother was for her the supreme example of a natural gift of love through patience and suffering, Jesus surpasses her both in the love and in the patient endurance of suffering. This is true not only at His Crucifixion, but in His 'suffraunce' of man's sin through all time:

Al that our lord doeth is rythful, and that he suffrith is worshipful; and in these ii is comprehendid good and ille; for al that is good our lord doith; and that is evil our lord suffrith. I sey not that our evil is worshipful, but I sey the suffrance of our lord God is worshipfull, whereby his goodnes shal be know withoute end in his . . . mercy and grace.   (Ch.35)

As she shows both here and in Chapters 27:29, the very purpose of sin is to evoke this 'suffraunce' from Jesus, so that He may express His love by suffering the pain that saves mankind, and so teach mankind its utter dependence upon Him:

And by his suffraunce we fallyn; and in his blisful love with his myte and his wisdom we are kept; and be mercy and grace we arn reysid to many- fold more ioyes.   (Ch.35)[17]

This extraordinary vision of the way that patient suffering transforms sin into love stands at the opposite extreme from the retributive and penitential teaching on patience derived from the Old Testament.

(c) *Piers Plowman*

There are then in the fourteenth century two different ways of teaching patience, both available to and, as I shall show, both used by Langland. One is retributive, treating patience as a means to pay for sin or to buy heaven; the other more idealistic, showing patience to be the virtue which most directly imitates Christ, and which transforms sin and death into love and life.[18] In 'Dowel' Will is seen

---

[16] S. Bernardus, *Sermones in Cantica Canticorum*, ix. 5, tr. C. S. M. V., *Saint Bernard on the Song of Songs* (London 1952), p. 32.

[17] The 'suffraunce' of God is analysed in *Patience* by E. Kirk in 'Who suffreth more than God', *The Triumph of Patience*, see n.5, pp. 88–104.

[18] See *de Remediis* pp. 158–61, tr. in Chaucer's *Parson's Tale*, 660.

progressing from impatience with Clergy and Reason (and with the ways of God as a whole), to an understanding first of the retributive purpose of patience, and then of its power to change humanity.

The particular problem which confronts Will (and in the C-text, Recklessness) throughout the 'Dowel' section of the poem, is the contrast between the 'haves' and the 'have-nots'. Various antitheses are presented to us: between the rich and the poor, the learned and the lewd; the baptized and the unbaptized. An impatience with the apparent injustice of God is Will's predominant failing here, and one need look no further than Chaucer's *Parson's Tale* to find that such questions are characteristic of Ire, the opposite of patience:

> Yet comen ther of Ire manye mo synnes, . . . as he that arretteth upon God, or blameth God of thyng of which he is hymself gilty, or despiseth God and alle his halwes. 579[19]

The silence and restraint of the Lamb of God, dumb before his unjust shearers, is the true type of patience against this and all other 'sins of the tongue' (included by Chaucer and Peraldus with the sins of Ire and so opposed by patience).[20] The first kind of patience that Will must learn, then, is patience of tongue, and this is taught him by Ymaginatif;

> 'Haldestow suffred,' he seyide, 'slepynge tho thow were,'
> Thou sholdest have knowen that Clergie kan, and conceyved
>   moore through Reson
>
> B.XI.411–12

Will had, broadly speaking, attacked Clergy (through Scripture, X.341–472) for not saving the ignorant, and Reason (B.XI.367–373) for not governing men as he did the beasts. Both are essentially attacks upon God for His apparent injustice, in fact for that very 'suffraunce of sin' which Julian had first questioned and then praised. Why, we might ask with the impatient tongues eating and grumbling in Passus X, did God

> Suffre Sathan his seed to bigile   B.X.120, 127?

Langland had promised (113, 117) that Reason and Ymaginatif would answer such questions, and in Passus XI both these characters duly refute Will by the rather flattening argument that if God 'suffreth' sin 'for somme mannes good' (380), Will should also suffer God's inscrutable ways. Although in Passus XII

---

[19] G. Chaucer, *The Works*, ed. F. N. Robinson (Oxford 1957).
[20] G. Peraldus, *Summa virtutum ac vitiorum*, I (Lyons 1668) II, 8, ii, *Parson's Tale*, 562 ff; see K. O. Peterson, *The Sources of the Parson's Tale* (Boston 1901), p. 52 ff; S. Wenzel, 'The sources of Chaucer's Seven Deadly Sins', *Traditio* 30 (1974), 351–378, see p. 364.

Ymaginatif does in fact provide some more satisfactory answers at least to the problem of the salvation of the unbaptized, we may conclude that Will has now learned that there is an obligation on man to copy the suffraunce of God from which he constantly benefits. The urgent questioning of B.XI–XII, which had prompted a whole series of ambiguous and untrustworthy answers, is replaced in Passus XII and XIV by the long reliable speeches of Ymaginatif and Patience. Athough Will still shows impatience of tongue in XIII, it is directed against his neighbour and not against God. We may prefer the poetry of impatience, but there is no doubt that Langland is clearer when Will is quiet.

If Will seemed alone in his anxiety for the ignorant and the unbaptized, he is by no means the only character in 'Dowel' to believe that the sufferings of the poor should be compensated by heavenly reward. It is notable that of those who make this point (Scripture, Will, Recklessness, and Patience himself), none exploit the revolutionary implication of the biblical texts they use, and claim that a reward is due for the suffering alone.[21] All use patience in the traditional retributive ways to justify God's saving 'poverte with pacience' (B.X.339). Thus patient suffering is said to be the penance for the sins which exclude poor and rich alike from heaven (C.XII.175–208, C.XIII.78–81), or to be the purification which fits souls for heaven (B.XI.255–262, C.XIII.20–32), and even to be the payment which balances the account book between man and God:

> I wiste nevere renk that riche was, that whan he rekene sholde
> Whan he dregh to his deeth day, that he ne dredde him soore,
> And that at the rekenyng in arrerage fel, rather than out of dette.
> Ther the poore dar plede, and preve by pure reson
> To have allowaunce of his lord; by the laws he it cleymeth
> Joye, that neuere joye hadde, of rightful jugge he asketh
>
> B.XIV.105–110

The retributive pattern in all these arguments is particularly clear in this last quotation from the speech of Patience to Hawkyn, with its detailed legal terminology ('arerage' – the debt which opens a reeve's account roll; the 'allowance' or *allocatio* of money owed to the reeve by the manor); the poor man's expenditure of joy has been so small that his Lord owes him a balance.[22] Langland is not invent-

---

[21] *The Vision of Piers Plowman: A Critical Edition of the B-text*, ed. A. V. C. Schmidt (London 1978); *Piers Plowman by William Langland: An edition of the C-text*, ed. D. A. Pearsall (London 1978). See in particular statements re Scripture (B.X. 337–40, referring to Jas. 2:5), by Will (B.X. 457–61, or Recklessness in C.XI. 296–8, referring to Augustine's *Confessions* 8:8), by Recklessness (C.XIII. 78–91 referring to Mk. 16:16) and by Patience (B.XIV. 259–60; C.XVI. 100–114) see also Pearsall's note to C.XIII. 79.

[22] For examples of arerage and allowance in reeve-rolls, see H. S. Bennett, *Life on the English Manor* (Cambridge 1937), pp. 191–2, referring to e.g. N. S. B. Gras, *The Economic and Social History of an English Manor* (Harvard 1930), p. 273: 'Indentura allocationis . . . de diversis superoneratis et disoneratis in presenti compoto'; for accounting law see S. F. C. Milsom, *The Historical Foundations of the Common Law* (London 1969), pp. 235–243.

ing this argument; his wording is in fact very close to its appearance in the Domesday section of *The Prikke of Conscience*:

> Men sal alswa yhelde rekkenynges sere
> Of al gudes þat God has gefen þam here,
> Als of gudes of kynde and gudes of graces
> And gudes of hap þat men purchases. . . .
> I drede many in arrirage mon falle
> And til perpetuele prison gang,   V.5894–5914

Indeed the antithesis of 'Dowel', between the haves and the have-nots, could all be seen as oppositions between those who have, and those who do not have, 'gudes of kynde . . . of graces and . . . of hap'. Clearly both authors are endeavouring, by using the language of contract, to prove that there are mutual obligations between God and man, and that eventually God will be utterly just towards those whom he has apparently treated unjustly in this world, and give them mercy and joy. But Langland is also concerned that the poor man would participate in his own salvation by being patient as well as suffering, so that his suffering will act as a penance that purifies his soul and pays for his sins. So it is that Ymaginatif reconciles Will to Clergy by reminding him that Christian men are *not* responsible for their own salvation. The patient sufferings of the poor man can only act as penance if he also performs the sacrament itself:

> Na moore kan a kynde witted man, but clerkes hym teche,
> Come, for al his kynde wit, to Cristendom and be saved –
> Which is the cofre of Cristes tresor, and clerkes kepe the keyes,
>   B.XII.107–109[23]

Thus Will goes to the reconciling feast with Clergy and Reason armed with patience at least against the *flagella dei*, the sufferings of poverty and other ills for which men appear not to be themselves responsible, but which can be turned to their good.

But the tribulation of poverty, however much it may be willed by God, can also be seen from another angle as the result of one's neighbour's greed. It is this point of view which Will now impatiently expresses at the Feast of Clergy. This may seem to introduce a political dimension into the discussion, but it is probable that Langland is simply following the familiar tripartite division which is the basis of so much medieval patience discussion, from Tertullian's onwards. St Gregory put it succinctly and authoritatively:

> For we must bear some things which are from God, some from our ancient adversary the devil, and some from our neighbor. We endure

---

[23] On the treasury of merit, see Lea, *op. cit.* (n. 6), I, 506.

persecution, loss of possessions, and scornful words, from our neighbor; from the devil, temptations; from God, scourgings.[24]

Will now directs his impatience not against God, but against the immediate causers of his poverty – his rich neighbours typified by the Friar:

> 'Ac this Goddes gloton,' quod I, 'with his grete chekes,
> Hath no pite on us povere, he parfourmeth yvele. . .
>
> 'What is Dowel, sire doctour?' quod I, 'is Dobest any penaunce?' . . .
> 'Do non yvel to thyn evencristen – nought by thi power,'
> 'By this day, sire doctour,' quod I, 'then [in Dowel be ye noght]
> For ye han harmed us two in that ye eten the puddyng,'
>
> B.XIII.77–8, 102–6

Although Langland's satiric tone encourages us not to agree too readily with Will, his point is perfectly valid; indeed Gregory had counted as one of the chief occasions for patience against one's neighbour the kind of deprivation of possessions that the rich inflict on the poor.[25] The *Remedia* text uses the example of Christ to prove that this very deprivation offers a spiritual advantage:

> And notice that when a Lamb is shorn yet its wool grows again . . . Thus when man is stripped of his temporal goods, he is renewed on spiritual ones.[26]

The author developes the spiritual advantages of poverty in very much the same way, and using some of the same arguments, as Patience will do in this and the next Passus.

It is precisely at such points that critics find fault with Langland for glibly allowing the rich to fleece the poor for their spiritual advantage.[27] But Patience here is not recommending the questionable inter-dependence of poor and rich, but rather insisting on their independence. What have the friars' puddings to do with Will's penance, after all? In fact Patience professes an independence of the rich which springs from his Stoical indifference to pain. This is clearest in the C-text, where he lists only the four specific 'molestes exteriores' of Gregory's homily on patience (loss of possession, sickness, bodily hurt, and slander), and by showing how little he cares for any for them Patience robs his neighbour of any

---

[24] Tertullian, *De Patientia*, transl. C. Dodgson, *Apostolic and Practical Treatises of Tertullian*, Library of the Fathers (Oxford 1842), pp. 327–48, see pp. 326–41; Gregory the Great, *Hom. in Evang.*, II, 35 (PL 76:1264) transl. Hanna, *op. cit.* p. 72.
[25] Gregory, 'Patientia vero est aliena mala equanimiter perpeti' (PL 76:1261–2) misquoted *de Remediis* p. 158 and by Chaucer, *Parson's Tale*, 658.
[26] *de Remediis*, pp. 174–5, and see pp. 172–83.
[27] See n.1

advantage, material or other, and is (to quote the famous tag from the *Testament of Job*), victorious:

> 'That loueth lely, ' quod he, 'bote litel thyng coueyteth . . .
>> *Patentes vincunt*
> For, by hym þat me made, myhte neuer pouerte,
> Meseyse, ne meschief, ne man with his tonge
> Tene þe eny tyme and þou take pacience'.   C.XV.154–160

Furthermore, Patience claims that his policy of patient endurance will eventually convert others from their sin; by turning the other cheek he will 'wynnen all Fraunce' (155). He does not discount the responsibility of the rich for causing poverty or the consequent need for reform, but he offers patience as the best means of effecting it, through moral example (rather as Mahatma Ghandi used 'passive resistance' to achieve political independence for India). Confronted by patience, he says,

> The kyng and alle þe comune and clergie to þe [will] loute,
> As for here lord and here ledare and liue as thow techest.
>   C.XV.169–70

This is as politically transforming as Reason's promise in the *Visio* that if he is allowed to rule,

> lawe shal ben a laborer and lede afelde donge
> And loue shal lede thi land as the leef lyketh   C.IV.144–5

Patience does not expect to be understood, and more than Reason did earlier, but their words demonstrate the challenging reversals of Christianity. This patience is not the Stoic indifference to injustice; it is a political policy which expects to right injustice by example. The Doctor and Clergy do not accept this kind of Christianity (BXIII.172–187), but Conscience does, and he goes off with Patience to reform the world.

First he must learn the third kind of patience; not that which endures the 'flagella Dei', or that which suffers persecution by one's neighbour, but that directed against the evil in oneself. As Hanna and Rush have shown, it was St Gregory who introduced temptation into medieval patience discussions, for he believed that Christians should aim for a 'spiritual martyrdom' of their inner selves by patiently enduring internal as well as external evils.[28] Patience under temptation accordingly figures in such well-known treatises as Peraldus' *Summa* and the early fourteenth-century *Oculum Sacerdotis*, using such texts as James 1:12 (which I quoted on p.73). It is therefore entirely appropriate that at this stage in

---

[28] A. C. Rush, 'Spiritual martyrdom in Gregory the Great', *Theological Studies* 23 (1962) 569–89; Hanna, *op. cit.* pp. 76–7.

Piers Plowman Patience should confront Hawkyn, the type of sinful man. Conscience teaches him to purify his soul with the sacrament of penance (in which, as we have seen, Patience also has a part), and Patience then teaches him to perfect himself through patient poverty, whose praise takes up the rest of BXIV and CXV, and is the culmination of Langland's patience discussion.

Patience intends to reform Hawkin's sinfulness by an internal and an external transformation. Both are based on the text of the Lord's Prayer: 'Thy will be done':

> But I lokede what liflode it was that Pacience so preisede;
> And thanne was it a pece of the Paternoster – *Fiat voluntas tua*.
> 'Have Haukyn,' quod Pacience, 'and et this whan the hungreth,
> Or whan thow clomsest for cold or clyngest for drye;
> And shul nevere gyves thee greve ne gret lordes wrathe,
> Prison ne peyne – for *pacientes vincunt*'.   B.XIV.48–53

Internally this reliance on God's will removes the desire to acquire material comforts and possessions at the expense of one's neighbours, which is the basis of so much of Hawkyn's sin. It will replace such feelings by Charity, in imitation of Christ, who, as Kirk has pointed out in her commentary in this passage, also used the phrase 'thy will be done' in the Garden of Gethsemane:[29] The C-text makes the point most clearly:

> 'What is parfit pacience?' quod *Activa Vita*
> 'Meeknesse and mylde speche and men of o wil,
> The whiche wil loue lat to oure lordes place
> And þat is charite, chaumpion, chief of all vertues;
> And þat is pore pacient, alle pereles to soffre'.   C.XV.274–8

Love, *caritas*, as in Julian of Norwich, is expressed by the acceptance of all harm as God's will. The apparent injustice of God is accepted, and redefined as mercy and grace directed towards the poor sufferer. Langland even goes so far as to apply the Charter of Christ allegory, usually applied only to the bleeding body of Christ, to the 'crucifixion' of patient poverty, which attracts God's special grace in a patent of pardon:[30]

> Ac the parchemyn of this patente of poverte be moste,
> And of pure pacience and parfit bileve.
> Of pompe and of pride the parchemyn decourreth,
> And principalliche of alle peple, but thei be poore of herte.
>   B.XIV.191–4

---

[29] Kirk, *op. cit.* (n.17), pp. 95, 100–2.
[30] H. C. Spalding, *The Middle English Charters of Christ* (Bryn Mawr 1914).

As Julian of Norwich felt that her womanliness enabled her to understand and even participate in Christ's patient and redeeming suffering, so does Langland's poverty, and that of his readers, give them a part in the Crucifixion.

Langland ends the Passus by showing how patience can also be an external help against sin, by describing the life of patient poverty as one that is almost without the opportunity of sin. Pearsall characterises this as Milton's 'fugitive and cloistered virtue',[31] but he is missing the political and social importance of patient poverty as a means of transforming society. If justice is the crying need of society (as appears from the *Visio*), it might be better to teach all men to desire poverty, rather than try to prevent the unrepentant rich from oppressing the poor. In the C-text Langland seems to be taking a further step down this path to reform by removing the long passages about Hawkyn's sinfulness. Patient poverty is desired by the Activa Vita of the C-text for its own sake, and not primarily as a weapon against his own sin. He voluntarily accepts poverty, a second Piers Plowman, an imitator of Christ. Instead of trying to change the world by eliminating poverty, Langland is using poverty to change the world. Will leaves the 'Dowel' part of the poem, as Julian leaves her visions of the Crucifixion in Chapter 27, no longer impatient against God's 'suffraunce of sin', but convinced that 'Synne is behovabill, but al shal be wel, and al shal be wel, and al maner of thyng shal be wele.'

[31] Pearsall, *op. cit* p. 183, referring to Milton's *Areopagitica*.

The Goodness of God: A Julian Study

Ritamary Bradley

The meaning of the *Showings* of Julian of Norwich is, she assures us, love.[1] But this insight came to her late – for it is after fifteen years that she finally hears the answer to her desire to know what was intended: 'Love was his meaning' (LT 86.102). The meaning of her visions grows out of contemplating goodness, which is the unifying subject. This study will arrange in a linear order what is said on goodness integrally, in meditative language, in the text, noting at times how Julian's teaching relates to what some philosophers have said about the same subject. From this perspective it will be seen that Julian's focus on goodness – in God, in creation, in prayer – encompasses both discursive knowing and mystical awareness, enabling her to come to her teaching on love. But first it will be shown what overall role the notion of goodness holds in the treatise.

Role in the Showings: Julian's first vision, in which all the others were implicitly contained, was addressed to her reason, to teach us to 'adhere wisely to the goodness of God' (LT 6.6). This occasions an entire chapter built on a motif and refrain of divine goodness. Midway in the whole treatise (LT 33.34) she again says explicitly: '. . . The whole revelation was made about goodness, with little mention of evil . . .' A little further on (LT 46.49) Julian roots in goodness her crucial teaching that there is no wrath in God and repeats that goodness is the key to the showings: 'God is that goodness which cannot be angry, for God is nothing but goodness . . . our soul is united to him, unchangeable goodness . . . so completely united to him by his own goodness that there can be nothing at all between God and the soul . . . Towards this understanding the soul was led by love and drawn by power in every showing'. In a review of the whole experience Julian affirms that the memory of the revelation comes back to her with new insights, by God's goodness (LT 51.58). And again: 'For of the same goodness that he showed it, and for the same purpose – by that same goodness he will make it clear to us, when it is his will' (LT 51.56). Likewise, the scribe writes to the same effect: 'Thank our Lord Jesus Christ, who made these revelations for you – and to you – out of his love, mercy, and goodness' (LT 86.103). In her own summation Julian describes

---

[1] References in this paper are to the Long Text of the *Showings* by chapter, from *Julian of Norwich A Revelation of Love*. ed. Marion Glasscoe (Exeter, 1976).

her depth experience of God as the experience of his goodness, in which lay 'the strength and effect of the whole revelation' (LT 83.100). The soul approaches the good through what reason recognizes as desirable, a commonplace in philosophy.[2] But Julian sees goodness in a distinctive and personal way.

Goodness in Creation

The goodness of God is first made known to her in creatures, in what has been made, seen primarily in the hazelnut vision. This goodness of creatures is revealed in their being and in their working – both of which are rightful and last forever. 'Heaven and earth and all that is made is fair and good' (LT 8.9). 'He made all things in the fullness of goodness' (LT 11.14). 'Nature is all good and fair in itself' (LT 63.77). 'He does not despise anything that he has made – all is of his goodness' (LT 6.7). 'All that is of kind (nature), of fairness and goodness, is in humanity in fullness' (LT 62.76) God's goodness in creation is a matter of our intimate experience, for 'he is everything that is good and comfortable to us' (LT 5.5). And most emphatically of all: 'God is all things that are good' (LT 5). This comment is made even more explicit in her summary statement: 'That goodness which is kind – it is God, the ground, the substance, the same thing as kind'[3] (LT 62.76). By this emphasis on the ground of being, the statement becomes even stronger than a similar one by Augustine: 'This good and that good, take away this and that and see good itself if you can; so you will see God who is . . . the good of every good'.[4]

But the working of creatures as well as their being is also from God – an important view for approaching the problem of evil. God's goodness is at work in nature: 'God in his goodness makes the planets and the elements to work according to their nature for the benefit of the blessed and the cursed' (LT 18.21). Human beings are enabled to work through the special assistance of mercy and grace – words which Julian generally uses to designate Christ and the Holy Spirit: 'In kind we have our life and our being; and in mercy and grace we have . . . our fulfilling; these are three properties of one goodness, and where one works, all

---

[2]   See, for example: 'There are basic truths that the Socratic Plato did not lose sight of any more than did the Platonic Aristotle: in human actions the good we project as hou heneka (that for the sake of which) is concretized and defined only by our practical reason . . . Furthermore, every existent thing is 'good' when it fulfills its telos (purpose or goal)'. Hans-Georg Gadamer, The Idea of the Good in Platonic-Aristotelian Philosophy, trans. P.Christopher Smith, (New Haven and London 1986) 177.

[3]   Kind (Kynde) denotes 'nature', 'the ground of nature', or 'humane', varying with the context.

[4]   De Trinitate 8.3 in St Augustine, The Trinity, trans. Stephen McKenna, (Washington, D.C. 1963) 248.

work – in the things that are proper to us' (LT 56.68). 'From these three – kind, mercy, and grace – we receive all our goodness. The first are goods of kind, bestowed on us in our making, wherein we are made fully good; the others are greater goods, which we can receive only in our spirit' (LT 56.68). The first of these greater goods is faith: 'through the kind goodness of God it is grounded in us and we in it, by the working of mercy and grace' (LT 57.69). The other greater goods (such as the sacraments and the virtues) come through the faith: 'No goodness above the faith is kept in this life . . . and by his goodness and his own working we are enabled to remain in the faith' (LT 70.85). 'The same virtues we have received in our substance – those given to us by nature – these, by the goodness of God, through the working of mercy are given to us in grace' (LT 57.69). And 'knowing his goodness', we are sure his promises will be fulfilled (LT 70.85). We are duty bound to cooperate through our own deeds with this enhanced goodness: 'God will make us partners in his good deed' (LT 43.45). Or, as Simone Weil puts it: 'The presence for which God needs the cooperation of the creature is the presence of God, not as Creator but as Spirit'.[5]

It is in the vision of the point that Julian sees creation united to God under the aspect of the doer: 'Then I saw God in a point . . . I saw truly that God does all things, be they ever so little . . .' (LT 11.13). This vision leads Julian to conclude that all God's works are fully good, 'and all his doings are easy and sweet' (LT 11.14). Since the point image reveals God as doer, it is not (as in Augustine) an instant of time (*Confessions*, Book 9, chapter 10). Nor does it designate a center of a circle with radii flowing from it, either with the circumference or the center signifying God.[6] Rather, it is every point constitutive of reality; it is God as the ground of substantial being. Julian does not, like Bonaventure, use this point image to emphasize the distance of divinity from creation but rather the closeness of God to it. Bonaventure holds that 'being itself is the root principle of viewing the essential attributes' (the unity of God), whereas 'the good itself is the principal foundation for contemplating the emanations . . . the diffusion in time in creation is not more than a center or point in relation to the immensity of divine goodness'.[7]

In Julian, the point which signifies God, the doer, is more like light, perhaps

5   Simone Weil, *Gravity and Grace*, ed. Gustave Thibon, (New York 1952) 85.
6   See Roland Maisonneuve, 'Les Abîmes de L'Univers/Les Symbolismes du Point-Centre, Nuit et Lumière', I.R.I.S, Document A 33, p.4: 'The point is, according to a Christian interpretation, the symbol of the Trinity, Father, Son, and Spirit. Because it includes a unifying centre, radii, and circumference, it is a figure of union in the Deity of the three divine Persons: the Father, the Source (the center); the Son, born of the Father and manifested in the cosmos (the radii); and the Holy Spirit, the embrace and the light of Love (the circle). In this symbol, the centre point expresses perfectly what theologians call the Trinitarian circumincession: the twofold flow of love going from the Father to the Son and from the Son to the Father, in the Spirit'. (my translation).
7   *Journey of the Mind to God*, 6.1 and 6.2, in *Light from Light*, ed. L.Dupré and J.A.Wiseman (New York 1988) 138–9.

even like fire, similar to that image in the Pseudo-Dionysius: Fire 'varies and imparts itself to all that is near it . . . it renews by its rousing heat and gives light by its uncovered illuminations . . . manifesting itself by a sort of seeking'.[8]

Reflecting again in the thirteenth showing on God as doer, Julian perceives that God's working 'in every manner of thing is done so goodly, so wisely, so powerfully that it surpasses all' (LT 43.46).[9] But in this showing Julian cannot avoid coming face to face with the problem of evil. All deeds are done by God, and nothing that God does is by hap or chance (LT 11.13). Therefore, she reasons, since God does not do evil, evil is not a deed. Yet how can this be? In part, the answer is simple: those deeds which appear evil to us are not really so, in view of their final outcome. But how explain those other manifestations that are really not good and look to us like deeds? To this objection she replies that, in fact, they are not actually deeds, because a deed proceeds from the inner nature of a thing working towards its everlasting end and fulfillment. All God's deeds are well-done, having two properties: first, they are right and just in themselves, in their nature; and second, they have a superabundant outflowing, a full flowering and fruitfulness. They are complete, even if mercy and grace had not followed.

Her reflections on this question are cut short for a time by more revelations of goodness. Another vision, in the twelfth showing, reveals God's pervasive goodness in all of human life. There the refrain – 'I it am' – drives home the lesson that whatever is really desirable is God and that God is the only object of desire which truly brings peace. The absolute Good will bestow the fullness of joy, when longing will be stilled, replaced by rest.

It was following this powerful experience that the question of sin recurred: 'After this the Lord brought to my mind the longing that I had for him before; and I saw that nothing hindered me but sin' (LT 27.28). Sin is not a real deed, as defined above, because it lasts only 'for a time' (LT 27.29). And the pain it causes 'purifies us and makes us to know ourselves and ask for mercy' (LT 27.29) – that is, we are 'noughted'. Pain turns us towards good again. A contemporary philosopher, Iris Murdoch, referring to the ultimate pain of facing death, says somewhat the same thing, in more modern terms: 'Goodness is connected with the acceptance of real death and real chance and real transience and only against the background of this acceptance, which is psychologically so difficult, can we understand the full

8 *The Divine Names and Mystical Theology*, trans. John D. Jones (Milwaukee 1980) 69. Also: 'The unlimited and abiding center differentiates and limits itself in be-ing beings . . . the divinity is that from out of which . . . beings emerge, that in which . . . beings dwell . . ., and that into which . . . all beings return', p.70.
9 Colledge and Walsh reject the reading in London, British Library, MS Sloane 2 (*goodly*) translating Sloane 1 (*godly*) as 'divinely': '*godly*: in this remarkably Johannine and Trinitarian passage, this can only mean 'divinely'; and so Sloane 2's *goodly* is erroneous'. (*A Book of Showings to the Anchoress Julian of Norwich*, ed. Edmund Colledge and James Walsh (Toronto 1978), II, p.480, n.39). But given the thematic place of goodness, this may not be so.

extent of what virtue is like. The acceptance of death is the acceptance of our own nothingness [equivalent to Julian's noughting] which is an automatic concern with what is not ourselves.'[10]

This is not the end of Julian's reflections on the subject, however. For one thing, she herself will sin. The beginning of sin, on her part, is to 'fall into sloth, into the losing of time', and this is true for all those creatures 'who have given themselves over to the inward beholding of his blessed goodness' (LT 76.92). But bad as this sin is, it is only a falling away from goodness by inattention, not a deliberate foiling of divine purposes. More importantly, there is the question as to why sin was allowed in the total scheme of things. For God does so allow it: 'the properties of goodness, which is God, were contraried; wickedness was allowed to rise contrary to goodness' (LT 59.71–2). Again, the answer of faith is that 'grace went contrary to the wickedness, and turned all to goodness for those to be saved', bringing greater bliss than would otherwise have been (LT 59.72). This is claiming more than what philosophy holds when it is said that God's goodness must bring some good out of evil – not necessarily a greater good.[11] Appropriate to this insight is the literary symbol of the pearl, which is a disease in the oyster but becomes something beautiful and permanent.

Generally philosophers in the Christian tradition teach, as Julian does, that there are no evil beings and that evil has no substance – just as Julian says that though sin is 'all that is not good', 'it has no manner of substance nor share in being' (LT 27.29). But their further explanations differ. Augustine uses the image of a spider as an analogy: wickedness spits out its web and swells with the consumption of vile food.[12] He further says that the beauty of the whole requires that some parts be 'displeasing', as are vipers and reptiles. '. . . to these lower parts of creation the wicked themselves are well fitted and become the better fitted the more they are unlike you'.[13] There is none of this kind of reasoning in Julian. Thomas Aquinas, like the Pseudo-Dionysius before him, says that evil is not desired, except by some goodness attached to it. It is a privation, like blindness in the eye; and much good would not be without evil: for example, the life of a lion would not be preserved unless the ass were killed. 'Neither would avenging justice

[10] Iris Murdoch, *The Sovereignty of Good*, (New York 1971) 103.
[11] See S.T.I, 2,art.3; rep. obj. 1: 'As Augustine says: *Since God is the highest good, He would not allow any evil to exist in His works, unless his omnipotence and goodness were such as to bring good even out of evil*', (Enchiridion 11).
[12] 'I found that I was far distant from you, in a region of total unlikeness, as if I were hearing your voice from on high saying: 'I am the food of grown men. Grow and you shall feed upon me. And you will not, as with the food of the body, change me into yourself, but you will be changed into me.' And I learned that *Thou, for iniquity, chastened man and Thou madest my soul to consume away like a spider*. . . . And I asked, 'What is wickedness?' and found that it is not a substance but a perversity of the will toward lower things – casting away, as it were, its own insides, and swelling with desire for what is outside it'. (*The Confessions of St. Augustine*, VII, 10–16, trans. Rex Warner (New York 1963) 150–153.
[13] *Confessions* VII.16, 153.

89

nor the patience of a sufferer be praised if there were no injustice'.[14] Julian does not speak like this, for she is counselled to take generally – without inquiring about particular persons – how 'all things shall be well' (LT 35.36).

Closer to what Julian does say, when she speaks of evil rising contrary to the good, is a text from the Pseudo-Dionysius. Evil is 'be-ing' contrary to a specific nature, he says; evil for the soul is what is contrary to reason; for the body, what is contrary to nature. As such, it is more than a mere privation.[15] It is somewhat like a paradox, perceived when propositions are mutually incompatible or contradictory. Evil 'is' the 'contrariness between incompatible ways of being, a failure of an analogical relation between beings'.[16] Or, as Simone Weil says, evil is the unreality which takes the goodness from the good: 'the relations between forces give to absence the power to destroy presence'.[17] These philosophic explanations fit in with Julian's thought when she teaches – after having affirmed that evil has no substance – that 'wickedness was allowed to rise contrary to the good' (LT 59.72).

But Julian does not say much about evil, because, as she has explained, the revelation was primarily about good. For this reason, just a few chapters before the end of the treatise (78), she enumerates 'four kinds of goodness' which God does – and which he wants us to be aware of: (1) he is the ground, from whom we have our life and existence, as she had said in chapter 5; (2) he protects us, mightily and mercifully, in the time of sin and when our enemies lie in wait for us; and (3) he sustains us, courteously, when he makes us realize how we have gone amiss. Or, as she had phrased it earlier: 'that same endless goodness that keeps us from perishing while we are in sin makes a covenant of peace with us against our wrath' (LT 49.52); and (4) he waits for us, never changing his demeanour, his will being that we turn and become one with him in love – a high point in the thirteenth revelation, which shows that 'all shall be well'.

Goodness in God

Julian links to the problem of evil what she says specifically of the goodness of God: 'Goodness is that property in God which does good against evil' (LT 59.72). This applies in particular to the evil in ourselves: 'When we are in peace and love, the contrariness now in us is no obstacle: his goodness makes it profitable' (LT 49.53). 'God is the goodness which cannot be wrathful, for he is naught but goodness' (LT 46.49). Or, to put the argument differently, wrath comes from weakness – 'from lack of goodness (or power or wisdom)' (LT 48.51) and obvious-

14 *Summa Theologica*, I,II, 18, art 1; 48, art. 1.
15 *Divine Names*, IV.32.733, 110.
16 Commentary, *The Divine Names*, 85–6.
17 Introduction by Gustave Thibon to *Gravity and Grace*, 125.

ly there is no such weakness in God. Despite her advertence to the teaching of the church and the conclusions of her own reasoning that we deserve pain and wrath, Julian still holds that God is never wrathful: for he is God, namely good (and also life, truth, love and peace) (LT 46.49).

Goodness is directly a name for God, both for the godhead and the unity, and for the persons and the properties attributed to them. Julian seems to refer to the godhead when she speaks of total union: 'Our soul is united to him, unchangeable goodness' (LT 46.49). Again she refers to God substantially in speaking of the divine indwelling: 'The high goodness of the Trinity is our lord, in whom we are enclosed and he in us' (LT 54.65). And in another place similarly: 'Our substance is in our Father God, in our mother, Wisdom, and in the Holy Ghost, God all goodness: our substance is whole in each person of the Blessed Trinity' (LT 58.71).

But frequently she employs goodness as a name for each of the persons, with a fluidity that suggests that she sees the Trinity as a mutual indwelling of persons as well as unchangeable being – as activity and divine stillness. For example, in a later reflection on the twelfth revelation with its repeated phrase, 'I it am', Julian discovers that his meaning was 'the might and goodness of the fatherhood'; yet not exclusively so, for the meaning was also 'the sovereign goodness of all manner of things' (LT 59.72), and specifically this includes 'all the goodness ordained in holy church for us' (LT 60.73).

Then at times goodness is the name of the second person and hence also of Christ Incarnate. After having said, as noted above, that 'goodness is the property in God which does good against evil', she concludes: 'Thus Jesus Christ who does good against evil is our true mother' (LT 59.72).

Chiefly in the parable of the Lord and the Servant the second person, both as God and as man, is divine goodness: 'By the wisdom and goodness in the servant is understood God's son' (LT 51.59). Again, it is by the 'proper goodness' of 'Christ our mother' that we have 'the godly will safe and whole without end' (LT 59.72). Goodness became yet more prominent to Julian after she followed God's instructions to review and reflect on what was signified by the mysterious parable: she then saw in memory the outward form of the servant with 'the nobility and goodness within – his outward appearance and his inward goodness' (LT 51.56). Indeed, after his fall (as Christ and Adam), he was still 'as lovely and good inwardly as when he had stood before the Lord' (LT 51.55).

Along with being the name for God's substance and the proper name for the Father and the Son, goodness is most frequently of all given as the proper name of the Holy Spirit: 'Our life is grounded in our Mother Jesus – in his own wisdom, in the might of the father, and in the sovereign goodness of the Holy Ghost' (LT 63.77). The same divine names are implied in: 'As we have our being in God's might, wisdom, and goodness, so we have our keeping in the same' (LT 49.52). This parallels: 'When we were made we loved him. This is a love created by the substantial goodness of the Holy Ghost' who is, in the Father and the Son, also powerful and wise (LT 53.64).

This fluidity in applying goodness to the divine is not a mark of philosophy. Thomas Aquinas is consistent, if incomplete on the subject. Goodness is properly attributed to the Holy Spirit, he says.[18] And also: '. . . when we say, God is good . . . the meaning is, Whatever good we attribute to creatures pre-exists in God, and in a higher way. Hence it does not follow that God is good because he causes goodness; but rather, on the contrary, He causes goodness in things because He is good' (and he cites Augustine in support of this).[19] In Aquinas the analogy of being means that God is good by being full actuality. Further, God is called good since he is the last end of creatures – that which they are created to desire.[20] But, as the writer of a recent survey of Aquinas' teachings on goodness concedes, 'we shall have to admit plainly . . . that we shall not be at all able to say directly what it is to be good, just as we are unable to say directly what actual being is'.[21] Julian ventures further than Aquinas in trying at times to say what goodness is, at least by poetic suggestion, even though she admits it is beyond our vision in this life. Bonaventure's teaching on the subject differs directly from Julian's on one important point: for Bonaventure being is the primary name of the unity of God, and good the primary name of the Trinity.[22] For Julian goodness is a name for both.

Prayer to God's Goodness

We are now in a better position to see how profound and challenging is Julian's directive to us to center our prayer on the goodness of God. In connection with the first vision, she is moved by a vision of creation (small as a hazelnut) to realize that the only good which will satisfy our desires is God – and we should therefore pray by cleaving to the goodness of God (LT 6.7). In the thirteenth showing she explains that which is required of us in prayer – longing and trust – is so required because 'God's goodness can ask no less of us' (LT 42.45). To pray to God's goodness is more pleasing to him than to go indirectly through any means – such as the saints – but when we do, these intermediaries are also of his goodness (LT 6.6–7).

She surveys a variety of forms of prayer under the perspective of God's goodness. First, in the overview of the book, she refers to prayers of asking or desire and notes at once that God of his goodness fulfills such prayers (LT 1.2). In developing this point she adds that God has ordained from the beginning to give us what

---

[18] ST I,45.6.ad 2.

[19] ST I,13, art. 2, corpus.

[20] De Veritate, 21.

[21] John Fitzgerald, 'Aquinas on Goodness', Downside Review 105 (Jan., 1987) 30.

[22] Light from Light 135. See Chapter 5 of Journey of the Mind to God.

he makes us ask for, so our asking 'is not the cause of God's goodness' (LT 41.43), as is shown where God says, 'I am the ground of thy beseeching' (LT 41.42).

There is prayer which is simply an awareness, both in weal and in woe, and in both there is a 'spiritual understanding that we are kept in the security of love . . . by the goodness of God' (LT 1.1, referring to seventh showing). Augustine's words apply here: '. . . we must remain in this good and cling to it by love, that we may enjoy the presence of that from which we are, in the absence of which we would not be at all'.[23]

In the prayer of 'kind yearning' – (goodness is that which we desire) – strengthened by the touch of the Holy Spirit, we desire only the goodness which is God.[24] ('Of thy goodness give me thyself . . . only in thee is all . . . this prayer touches God's will and goodness' [LT 5.6]). Always in Julian God's goodness reaches out to us, implants in us a desire which then meshes with God's thirst. In dealing with the divine thirst (both on the cross and in some way in the glorified Christ) Julian inserts the idea that what God's goodness longs for is the fulfilment of the good in our natures. So good also means the fullness of being, achieved in the creature.

In the prayer in temptation, 'we are driven by reason and grace to cry to the Lord out loud, rehearsing his passion and his great goodness' (LT 41.43).

But it is finally in the prayer of beholding that Julian unveils the scope of her understanding of goodness. 'God wants us to behold him, and generally to behold him in all his works, for they are fully good' (LT 11.14). This differs, at least in emphasis, from the frequently used image of the ladder, which leads us – not deeper into creation to find God – but away from creation to the truly good.[25] For Julian all comparisons fail to convey how 'homely', how near, how much a part of life God's goodness is: it comes down to the lowest part of our need (LT 6.7). But because we are 'now so blind and foolish, we cannot see him – unless, of his goodness, he shows himself' (LT 10.11). Yet, 'with his grace, we can stand beholding that love for us coming of his goodness . . . willing and longing till we have him in endless joy' (LT 6.7). The interweaving of goodness and love is clear in this prayer: 'In this prayer of beholding, we can only desire to be one with him, centered in his dwelling, enjoying his loving and delighting in his goodness' (LT 43.46). The link is even more explicit in Julian's prayer of beholding following the temptation of the fiend: 'Our Lord is all power . . . all wisdom . . . all goodness and loves me most tenderly' (LT 77.93).

And again, the prayer of beholding bears fruits in our actions: 'When by his grace we behold him, then we follow him and are drawn into him; and his

---

[23] *De Trinitate*, 8.4.6 (250).

[24] This concept parallels Aquinas' idea of intellect and will as appetites for the good. It is reminiscent also of Augustine's prayer: 'Our hearts are restless until they rest in thee'.

[25] Bonaventure praised Francis of Assisi for 'making of all things a ladder by which he could climb up and embrace him who is utterly desirable.' Bonaventure, *The Life of St. Francis*, trans. Cousins, 263. (in *Light from Light*, 134).

goodness fulfills all our needs' (LT 43.46). Murdoch is speaking in these same terms when she writes: 'The image of the Good as a transcendent magnetic centre seems to me the least corruptible and most realistic picture for us to use in our reflections upon the moral life'.[26] Linking this with prayer she claims that 'it does seem that prayer can actually induce a better quality of consciousness and provide an energy for good action which would not otherwise be available'.[27]

Conclusion

Julian draws her thoughts and spiritual insights together in the 83rd chapter, almost at the end of her book. It is there she records that she had in part 'touching, sight and feeling' of 'three properties in one goodness,' to which her reason desired to be united. Elaborating on these three properties of goodness, she discovers in life God's friendly familiarity; in love God's gentle courtesy; and in light an unending understanding of the true nature of things. Out of the third property, light, comes the image which unifies all: the light causes our life (the second property); and it stands for both reason and faith, and for the grace that lovingly leads us to God (LT 83.100). In the end the blindness that Julian had named as hindering our perception of goodness (LT 10.11) will give way and 'suddenly our eye shall be opened and our sight shall be full'. God (or Goodness) is our endless day (LT 83.100). This improves on Plato's image of the Sun as the Good; for the Sun, though by its light it is everywhere, still conveys a suggestion of something 'out there'. The day, on the other hand, has no boundaries, no dimensions, no dualities, it flows into all, as goodness does. It is closer to us than clothing, it is the point that is now known to be everywhere, it is what we have longed for in the night. Julian with her reference to 'touching, sight and feeling' is more earthy and less ecstatic in expression than is Bonaventure, where, drawing on the Pseudo-Dionysius, he says: 'mystical communication' is 'a darkness which is super-resplendent and in which everything shines forth and which fills to overflowing invisible intellects with the splendor of invisible goods that surpass all good'.[28] Also Julian's expression is more embodied, less concerned with intellect apart from perception, free of the suggestion of degrees of the good. The day illumines what was around us invisibly all along.

Mystics through the ages stress that their religious experience is an experience of an interconnectedness of all reality. Under a single perspective Julian communicates this inter-connectedness in a dynamic fashion: in part she touches, sees, and feels God as the ineffable Good. She beholds the outflowing of this

26 *The Sovereignty of Good* 75.
27 *Ibid.*
28 Bonaventure, *The Journey of the Mind to God* 7.5, in *Light from Light* 148.

goodness in creatures and in all deeds, including the transforming of evil into good and the fulfilling of humanity by mercy and grace. By emphasizing goodness rather than love, Julian includes the whole of creation as tending towards God, and gives rootedness to love. And Murdoch offers another reason for making this distinction:

> Will not 'Act lovingly' translate 'Act perfectly', whereas 'Act rationally' will not? It is tempting to say so. However I think that Good and Love should not be identified, and not only because human love is more self-assertive. The concepts, even when the idea of love is purified, still play different roles ... Good is the magnetic centre towards which love naturally moves. False love moves to false good ... When true good is loved, even impurely or by accident, the quality of the love is automatically refined, and when the soul is turned towards Good the highest part of the soul is enlivened. Love is the tension between the imperfect soul and the magnetic perfection which is conceived as lying beyond it.[29]

Faith is integral in such a vision, a connection also tentatively affirmed by Murdoch.[30] Nonetheless, in the midst of the fullest demands of faith as she looks back on her exalted revelations, Julian continues to rejoice in reason: her reason still desired to be united to the one goodness and to cleave to it mightily (LT 83.100). She is the mystic of the Goodness of God.

[29] *The Sovereignty of Good*, 102–3.
[30] 'I can experience the transcendence of the beautiful, but (I think) not the transcendence of the good ... if we speak of good as transcendent we are speaking of something ... which cannot be experienced ... One might be tempted to use the word 'faith' here ...' p.60.

Idols and Images: Pastoral Adaptations of The Scale of Perfection

Vincent Gillespie

I

þan if þu coueite for to come to þis blessid si3t of verrey pees & ben a
trew pilgrym to Ierusalem-ward, þaw3 it be so þat I were neuer þere,
nerþeles as ferforþ as I kan I schal sette þe in þe weye þederward. þe
bygynnynge of þe hi3e wey in þe whilk þu schalt gon is reformyng in faiþ,
grounded mekly in þe feiþ & in þe lawes of Holy Kirke.

In his recent paper on 'The Audience for the Middle English Mystics', Stanley
Hussey used this passage from *Scale* 2.21 to illustrate his discussion of the evolving
audience for mystical writing in the fifteenth century. Pointing to the taste for
Hilton's writings among 'devout, moderately well-off London tradesmen and mer-
chants' and among 'rich and devout women', he concludes: 'I doubt whether these
people saw themselves as mystics; rather they saw in such books a map to Jerusalem.'[1] The demonstrable ebb and flow of devotional texts and manuscripts into
and out of lay hands in the century following Hilton's death is an important part
of the process by which the laity became articulate in the presence of the deity. [2]

The evolving 'devotional literacy' of the laity is discernible not only by the
movement and copying of whole texts, but also by the taste for florilegia, commonplace books and common-profit books.[3] Difficult as it is to track the shift in

---

[1] S.S.Hussey, 'The Audience for the Middle English Mystics', in *De Cella in Saeculum:
Religious and Secular Life and Devotion in Late Medieval England*, ed. M.G.Sargent (Cam-
bridge 1989), pp.109–22, pp.121–2. The quotation is taken from London, British Library,
MS Harley 6579, f.85r. With characteristic kindness and generosity, Stan's help in the
preparation of this paper was invaluable.
[2] The last phrase is Louis B.Wright's in *Middle Class Culture in Elizabethan England*
(Chapel Hill 1935), p.241; see the account and bibliography in V.Gillespie, 'Vernacular
Books of Religion', in *Book Production and Publishing 1375–1475*, ed. D.A.Pearsall and
J.J.Griffiths (Cambridge 1989), pp.317–44.
[3] M.Aston, 'Devotional Literacy', in *Lollards and Reformers: Images and Literacy in Late
Medieval Religion* (London 1984), pp.101–33; V.Gillespie, 'Lukynge in haly bukes: Lectio in
some Late Medieval Spiritual Miscellanies', in *Spätmittelalterliche geistliche Literatur in der*

patterns of textual taste and ownership over the period, it is even more challenging to attempt to quantify the impact of a writer's ideas on the devotional consciousness of a period or of a particular geographical area by tracking the impact, diffusion, dispersal and adaptation of those ideas once they have spread beyond the immediate confines of the original text.

Hilton's teachings are particularly interesting and important in this light. The continuing popularity of *The Scale of Perfection* into the sixteenth century may indicate, as Stan suggests, the appeal of his advice to lay men and women as much as the influence of his powerful friends among the Carthusians, Bridgettines and the royal family.[4] Part of this appeal may lie in the unusual breadth of personal experience which Hilton brought to bear on his letters and treatises of spiritual instruction. He was trained as a canon lawyer and had some experience of ecclesiastical administration in the consistory court of the diocese of Ely before his temporary move into solitude and his eventual arrival at the Augustinian canons.[5] The humane tolerance of the *Epistle on the Mixed Life* and the direct and forceful teaching of the Latin epistles draw on his awareness of the difficulties of leaving the world as well as the problems of living in it. His own order exemplified in their constitutions a kind of monastic mixed life, and it is striking how many of his colleagues and contemporaries at Cambridge and Ely chose to work out their own blend of the two lives by committing themselves to lives of administration and pastoral dedication. The affinity of Thomas Arundel, Hilton's diocesan at Ely, and later Archbishop of York and Canterbury, has recently been shown to have reflected and refracted Hilton's eremitical and mystical aspirations in their own lives and in their own libraries.[6]

Contributing to the recent re-evaluation of the role of the Carthusians in the transmission of contemplative teachings, Jonathan Hughes has stressed the paral-

---

Nationalsprache, 2, Analecta Cartusiana 106 (1984), pp. 1–27; M.Vale, *Piety, Charity and Literacy among the Yorkshire Gentry, 1370–1480*, Borthwick Papers 50 (1976); S.Cavanaugh, A *Study of Books Privately Owned in England 1300–1450*, unpublished Ph.D. thesis (University of Pennsylvania 1980).

[4] Hussey, 'Audience', pp.119–22; M.G.Sargent, 'Walter Hilton's *Scale of Perfection*: The London Manuscript Group Reconsidered', *Medium Ævum* 52 (1983), 189–216, pp.204–8; Gillespie, 'Vernacular Books', pp.319–20 and plate 27 which prints a common profit inscription from Oxford, Bodleian Library, MS Douce 25. For one example of Hilton's works being used in other vernacular compilations, see A.Hudson, 'A Chapter from Walter Hilton in Two Middle English Compilations', *Neophilologus* 58 (1968), 416–21.

[5] For a summary of the state of knowledge about Hilton's biography, see J.P.H.Clark, 'Walter Hilton in Defence of the Religious Life and of the Veneration of Images', *Downside Review* 103 (1985), 1–25, pp.1–3 and notes.

[6] J.Hughes, *Pastors and Visionaries: Religion and Secular Life in Late Medieval Yorkshire* (Woodbridge 1988), pp.176–229. Although errors of detail abound, especially in discussions of the literary evidence, Hughes provides a persuasive and compelling sense of the mood of the York clergy in the late fourteenth and early fifteenth centuries. On Hilton's place in the Arundel affinity, see espec. pp.179–81.

lel importance of 'the secular clergy of North Lincolnshire and Yorkshire who graduated in canon law':

> When these clerks approached the contemplative life, they experienced and expressed the tension they felt over their inability or refusal to turn their backs on their social environment . . . These personal conflicts also gave them insight into the spiritual problems of laymen with whom they had much more in common, and determined the way in which they would adapt eremitic teachings in the course of their pastoral work.[7]

In making such adaptations, either on their own initiative or in collaboration with religious orders, the cool humanity of Hilton's teachings offered a significant pastoral resource.

II

London, British Library, MS Lansdowne 344 is a clear, competent and characteristically well-executed copy of the popular pastoral manual for priests, the *Speculum Christiani*. One of the earliest datable copies of the work, it contains tables for finding the dominical letter, bissextile and golden number for the year 1425.[8] Like many other copies of this clerical and catechetic compendium, the *Speculum* is the only major text in the manuscript. Shortly after the main text copying was completed, another scribe added a detailed table of contents to the *Speculum* and its supplements, listing the internal rubrics and providing folio references. This touch of professionalism, clearly designed to facilitate casual reference to a work whose internal logic is not initially self-evident, reinforces the impression given by the rest of the book that it was used in a working clerical environment. Excluded from this added index, but separating it from the body of the main text, is a short additional work, written by the main scribe of the book.

The pastoral and clerical orientation of this second text is clear from prologue:

> *Si magnum gaudium fit in celo propter conversionem unius peccatoris, certe et indubitanter magna merces debetur illi qui fuerit causa convercionis illius.*

[7] *Pastors and Visionaries*, p.175.
[8] *Speculum Christiani*, ed. G.Holmstedt, EETS OS 182(1933 for 1929); V.Gillespie, 'Doctrina and Predicacio: The Design and Function of Some Pastoral Manuals', *Leeds Studies in English*, New Ser., 11 (1980 for 1979), 36–50; 'The Evolution of the *Speculum Christiani*', in *Latin and Vernacular*, ed. A.J.Minnis (Cambridge 1989), pp.39–60, which expands and updates Holmstedt's list of manuscripts. Lansdowne is Holmstedt's base manuscript; for a description see H. pp.xxxvii–xli. The manuscript is regularly quired in 8's with catchwords for nine of the ten quires. On the date of the *Cibus Anime* and *Speculum Christiani*, see 'Evolution', p.54. There is nothing in these present texts to rule out a date of c.1390–1420 for their compilation.

Augustinus: Magis est iustificare impium quam creare celum et terram. Anima iusti et ymago dei. ʒif þou in goodenesse lastinge be. In heuene þou schalt crounid be. *Speculum boni et mali. Sacerdos. Anima impii et ydolum peccati. The hed. Veni ad confessionem.* Fro þe prest drawe we hym faste. For in to helle he wolde ut caste.[9]

What follows appears to be an amalgamation or juxtaposition of two different texts which adapt and paraphrase aspects of Hilton's teaching on the image of sin and the image of God for the needs of priests with the *cura animarum* and for the tastes and abilities of their laity. The first section uses fourteen rough couplets, the second three passages of prose. The thrust of both texts is to encourage the laity to use penitential self-examination as a positive and constructive aspect of their spiritual lives, while emphasising the forensic responsibilities of the priest.

The *Speculum Boni et Mali* (if that title can be applied to both texts) is similar in style to the *Speculum Christiani* which precedes it in this manuscript. They both use vernacular verse and prose as the focus for pastoral teaching, exemplifying the vernacular by reference to Latin *auctoritates* or proof-texts attributed to Fathers and Doctors of the Church. Both rely heavily on quotations attributed to Augustine, Gregory, Jerome and Bernard and rarely draw on the *moderni*. Indeed the *Speculum Boni et Mali* shares more than a structural similarity with the larger *Speculum*, for its Latin authorities are overwhelmingly drawn from the same source: the catechetic and pastoral summa known as the *Cibus Anime*.[10] The northern affiliations of the *Speculum Christiani* and the *Cibus Anime* have been thoroughly documented.[11] These new texts, sharing their *modus agendi* and *forma tractandi*, almost certainly derive from the same milieu and from the same pastoral outlook. (Editions of both texts are supplied in Appendix 1.) They also survive

[9] f.70r; the *Speculum Boni et Mali* occupies ff.70r–79r. The prologue couplets are not listed in *IMEV*.

[10] See Gillespie, '*Doctrina* and *Predicacio*', 38–43; 'Evolution', pp.39–42; for a detailed account of both texts, see V.Gillespie, *The Literary Form of the Middle English Pastoral Manual, with particular reference to the Speculum Christiani and some related texts*, unpublished D.Phil. thesis (Oxford 1981).

[11] For a summary, see V.Gillespie, '*Cura pastoralis in deserto*', in *De Cella in Saeculum*, ed. Sargent, pp.161–81, pp.179–81. Hughes, *Pastors and Visionaries*, pp.196–7 and 215–6, argues for a York Minster provenance for both the *Cibus Anime* and the *Speculum Christiani*. I am not persuaded that the evidence of circulation of the *Speculum* at York proves that it must have been composed there. Though Hughes' case is seductive, my own sympathies incline towards a collaboration between the Carthusians and the Minster clergy, with the popularity of the text in lay and secular clerical circles tending to eclipse the Carthusian involvement, though that is particularly strong in the *Cibus Anime*. Nevertheless Hughes does clearly demonstrate the taste for eremitic and contemplative writings among Minster priests. Of the three copies of the *Speculum Boni et Mali*, Corpus has the text on the Minster's lady chapel and Royal contains formulae for the return of mandates to the archdeacon of Lincoln diocese in the name of H.M. curate of H[oughton] Conquest (Beds.) as well as other formulae suggesting the book was in use in Lincoln diocese which, of course, extended as far south as Oxford.

together in two other manuscripts, in one of which a third text is appended to the series, offering a description of images of the virgin in the Lady Chapel of York Minster. This copy also includes an extract from the *Speculum Christiani*.[12] On its own, the prose second section of the *Speculum Boni et Mali* was once preserved in the library of the Brigittine house at Syon. An expanded version of this section is also found embedded in a textually idiosyncratic copy of the *Speculum Christiani*.[13] Moreover a shorter version of this prose section circulates in copies of the *Cibus/Speculum*, supported by different Latin authorities, themselves drawn from the *Cibus Anime*.[14] Even the use of material from Hilton fails to distinguish the *Speculum Boni et Mali* from the other works in this curious textual family: the (perhaps originally distinct) third book of the *Cibus Anime* draws extensively on Fishlake's Latin translation of the *Scale of Perfection*.[15] But unlike the contemplative aspirations of that text, this work focusses itself firmly on the process of 'reformation in faith', using Hilton's distinctive image of the occlusion of the image of God in man's soul by the image of sin.

---

[12] Oxford, Corpus Christi College, MS 132, ff.63v–70r. The extract from the *Speculum* is at ff.173v–79v. An edition and study of the Minster Lady Chapel text will appear in *English Manuscript Studies*, 3 (1990). Although the dialect of Lansdowne is not northern, unlike the other two copies of the text, it has been used as the basis of this discussion because of its unique preservation of the prologue and the general quality of its text.

[13] On the lost Syon copy, see M.Bateson, *Catalogue of the Library of Syon Monastery Isleworth* (Cambridge 1898), entry M.24 (p.102), which includes a *formula noviciorum*, 'Walterus hylton in anglicis de vita actiua & contemplatiua cum tabula precedenti', and 'Idem [i.e. Hilton] in anglicis quod anima humana sit ymago dei cum aliis.' The expanded version is found in London, British Library, MS Additional 15237, f.49r–v. The text has been subject to considerable textual smoothing and editorial expansion and has not been used in the collation of the texts in Appendix 1. For an account of the manuscript, which was clearly designed for a priest with the cure of souls, see Gillespie, *Literary Form*, pp.318–24 and pp.437–8.

[14] See Appendix 2. R.R.Raymo, 'Works of Religious and Philosophical Instruction', in *A Manual of the Writings in Middle English 1050–1500*, ed. A.E.Hartung, VII (1986), item 159, pp.2325–6 and 2538 describes this shorter text but only lists two copies, Cambridge, University Library, MS Dd. 14. 26 (3) and Cambridge, Trinity Hall, MS 16, to which should be added the Foyle copy of the *Speculum Christiani*. He draws attention to two other similar vernacular texts on the examination of conscience, one of which is preserved in four manuscripts containing Lollard material and the other in a single manuscript of the works of the *Cloud* author (Cambridge, University, MS Kk. 6. 26, f.26b), which is printed in a modernised version in *The Cloud of Unknowing and Other Treatises*, ed. J.McCann (London 1924), pp.243–6. Both texts use Augustine's *De Trinitate*, a major source of Hilton's doctrine of the image of sin. See also P.S.Jolliffe, *A Checklist of Middle English Prose Writings of Spiritual Guidance* (Toronto 1974), D.7 and D.3.

[15] V.Gillespie, 'The *Cibus Anime* Book 3: A Guide for Contemplatives?' in *Spiritualität Heute und Gestern*, Analecta Cartusiana, 35:3 (1983), 90–119, which also prints a list of manuscripts of the complete *Cibus Anime* and discusses the different recensions of the text and its possible development.

III

Hilton developed his doctrine of the *imago peccati* from a variety of patristic sources.[16] His first sustained account of it is found in *De Imagine Peccati*, his earliest extant Latin epistle, written as a solitary before joining the Augustinians. Illustrating the sense of inner struggle felt by some secular priests, internal evidence suggests that the recipient of Hilton's forthright analysis was 'a man of rank, an ecclesiastic who, like Hilton himself, renounced a worldly career' but had yet to find peace of mind.[17] Describing in terse and direct terms the corruption of man's soul and the occlusion of the image of God in it, Hilton analyses the erection in its place of an idol or lifeless simulacrum. His analysis, he writes, is based in self-examination: 'Inueni ydolum michi' he cries, citing the prophet Hosea:

> Et quid est hoc ydolum? Corpus peccati, viciis et concupiscenciis plenum
> . . . Et que est forma huius corporis? Amor et concupissencia inordinata
> ex fomite tanquam ex fonte scaturiens, teipsum deformans a vera forma
> que est ymago Dei, et falsam superducens formam, ymaginem videlicet
> diaboli. Et que est huius ydoli materia? Tuipse.[18]

Later he describes it as the 'idolum desolacionis positum in templo Domini quod est anima tua.'[19] This allusion to the 'abominatio in desolationem' of the prophet Daniel may have brought to Hilton's mind that other idol in the Book of Daniel, the statue which features in the dream of Nebuchadnezzar. Although not explicit at this early stage of the development of Hilton's thinking on the subject, Nebuchadnezzar's statue looms into focus later in Hilton's writing career.

In *De Imagine Peccati*, Hilton uses two unrelated analogies to describe the image of sin. He likens it to a well of corruption out of which flow seven channels, which represent the deadly sins and, more fundamentally, to a body (deriving from the Pauline *corpus peccati*) whose *capud* is pride. At this stage the other parts of this body of sin are not clearly described:

---

[16] The following discussion, like so much work on Hilton, is indebted to the learning of John Clark, especially his 'Image and Likeness in Walter Hilton', *Downside Review*, 97 (1979), 204–20, which illustrates and demonstrates the indebtedness to Augustine; see also *Walter Hilton's Latin Writings*, ed. J.P.H.Clark and C.Taylor, Analecta Cartusiana, 124 (1987), pp.335–60. On Augustine's doctrine of *renovatio*, see G.B.Ladner, 'St Augustine's Conception of the Reformation of Man to the Image of God', in *Images and Ideas in the Middle Ages*, 2 vols, Storia e Letteratura, 155 and 156 (1983), pp.595–608, esp. pp.600–5. For a general account, see W.Riehle, *The Middle English Mystics*, tr. B.Standring (London 1981), pp.142–64, esp. pp.144–8; 'Image et Ressemblance' in *Dictionnaire de Spiritualité*, 7(1971), cols 1401–72.

[17] *Latin Writings*, p.69; the text is edited on pp.73–102.

[18] *Latin Writings*, pp.73–4.

[19] *ibid*, p.98.

Ecce iam aliqualiter descripsi tibi partem suppremam huius ydoli, capud scilicet quod ex amore tui inordinato quantum ad sensum spiritualem, vt in superbia cum ceteris sibi conexis conficitur. Iam ventrem depingam cum membris sibi coniunctis, qui ex amore tui quantum ad sensum carnalem, vt gula et libidine cum quinque sensum effrenata delectacione compaginatur.[20]

But he does not here offer a systematic parallel between the parts of the body and the deadly sins: by the end he claims only to have offered 'aliquantulum formam ymaginis tue quam portas' (p.98). The *membra* of the body remain shadowy, even in his early formulation of what was to become his distinctive doctrine of reformation:

Faciet enim membra [anime tue] subiecta sibi saltim ex parte et membra corporis subiecta anime hic interim, et post hec reformabit corpus humilitatis tue configuratum corpori claritatis sue in eternum.[21]

Hilton returned to the theme at much greater length in *Scale* 1. Over the course of the last forty chapters of the book, Hilton's thinking on the *imago peccati* gradually comes into focus, as if he is feeling his way towards a formulation of this complex and difficult concept which will do justice to the sophistication of the ideas and at the same time be accessible to the limited theological and devotional literacy of his 'ghostly sister'. In chapters 52 and 53, he maps out the discipline required to see the 'ground of synne' in the soul. The withdrawal from bodily works and bodily wits should lead to an abandonment of all imagining of bodily things and lead to the discovery of:

a merk ymage *and* a peynfull of þin oun soule, whilk has neiþire liȝt of knowyng ne felyng of loue ne likyng. þis ymage (if þou behold it witterly) is al vmbilapped with blak stynkand cloþes of synne: as pryde, enuye, ire, accidie, couetise, glotonye *and* lecherie. (p.324b)[22]

This passage adds the image of stinking clothes (reminiscent of Julian of Norwich's 'dede-hame' assumed by Christ[23]) to the earlier image of a foul well (re-used

---

[20] *ibid.*, p.88.

[21] *ibid.*, p.101.

[22] All quotations from *Scale* 1 are taken from Cambridge, University Library, MS Additional 6686. Page references will be supplied at the end of each quotation. I am grateful to Dr Michael Sargent for giving me access to Professor Bliss's transcription of *Scale* 1 in this manuscript. Abbreviations have been silently expanded.

[23] 'it was the image and likenes of our foule blak dede hame wherein our faire, bryte, blissid lord God is hid', Long Text, chapter 10, *Julian of Norwich: A Revelation of Love*, ed. M.Glasscoe (Exeter 1976), p.12. This reading is found in London, British Library, MS Sloane 2499, which Glasscoe uses for her edition, and in Sloane 3705. It is not found in Paris, Bibl. Nat., MS fonds anglais 40.

here in chapter 55) and to the idea of the members of the *corpus peccati*. Perhaps not surprisingly, chapter 53 anticipates the pupil wondering what the image of sin is actually like. It is, Hilton tells her, 'like to no bodily thyng'. Rather it is 'Noʒt' (p.325a). Hilton, perhaps for good strategic reasons, still refuses to settle on one manner of description. If the soul were to be reformed to the image of God, then the ground of sin would be 'mykel abated *and* dried vp in þe' (a clear reference back to the well image), but the mirkness and heaviness of the body of sin affects the soul like 'stynkand smoke and a flitand wife' (p.325ab), which drive a man out of his house. Similarly, the soul finds 'blak reke of gostly blyndnes *and* grete flityng of fleschly thoʒtes.'

Only gradually over the next thirty chapters does one coherent and dominant image emerge, as Hilton develops and explores his anthropomorphic idol whose bodily parts can be linked to the deadly sins. The *imago peccati* is the basis for his extended forensic analysis of corrupt motivation and the occlusion of the image of God in man.[24] But such is the detail and subtlety of his exposition that even here he almost allows the detail to overwhelm the core idea: 'I haue nere forʒeten þis ymage, but now I turne aʒeyn þerto' (1.63: p.334b). Moreover his use of terminology is still occasionally ambiguous: the discussion of envy and wrath (distinctively linked together by Hilton) rather uncomfortably and unconvincingly blends the conceit of the *membra* or limbs of the idol with the traditional canonical concept of the *specie* of the deadly sins:

> Turne þis ymage up so doun *and* loke wel þerinne, and \þou/ schalt fynde [two] membres of enuy *and* ire festned þerto, with mony brounches spryngand out of hem. (p.335a)

By the end of his exposition of the deadly sins, *Scale* 1.84 reintroduces the term idol, used extensively in *De Imagine Peccati* but hitherto noticeable by its absence from the expanded *Scale* discussion:

> *Inueni idolum michi* – þat is forto sey, 'I haue founden a fals ymage þat men callen a mahmet in myself, wel foule desfigured and forschapen with wrecchednes of all þise synnes whilk I haue spoken of. (p.354b)

Now, finally, in *Scale* 1.85, the sins are explicitly linked with the parts of the human body. The head is pride; the heart is envy; the arms are wrath; the belly gluttony; the 'membres' (here tactically redefined to mean genitalia) are lust; the feet are sloth. Adopting this humanoid image requires him to invert the order of sloth and lechery from the earlier discussion, which suggests that he was not inevitably working towards this image as a crystallization of his incremental teaching, but rather that he came upon it late in his thinking as a way of codifying

---

[24] See Clark, 'Image and Likeness', pp.206–11; J.P.H.Clark, 'Intention in Walter Hilton', *Downside Review*, 97 (1979), 69–80.

what is often in danger of becoming an incoherent and metaphorically inconsistent exposition. In 1.84, he is still playing with the clothing imagery he had used earlier in his discussion of the 'cloþes of bestez hide' put on by the postlapsarian Adam and Eve, 'with þe whilk bestly cloþes we all are born and vm[bi]lapped and desfigured fro oure kyndely schappe' (p.355a). The kindly shape may offer a tentative link to the idol/image of 1.85, but a more likely inspiration for this final schema is Nebuchadnezzar's dream statue:

> The head of this statue was of fine gold, but the breast and the arms of silver and the belly and the thighs of brass. And the legs of iron, the feet part of iron and part of clay.[25]

The idol in the temple of the soul, the abomination of desolation of Daniel and the traditional moralization of Nebuchadnezzar as a type of pride may all have come together to recommend this model to Hilton as he looked to summarise his teachings in the first book of the *Scale*.[26] The remaining chapters of *Scale* 1 draw increasingly explicit contrasts between the *imago peccati* and the *imago dei*. The key new information in these chapters relates to the nature of the image of Jesus, which, by a contrasting analogy to the image of sin, 'is made of vertus, with mekenes and perfite loue and charite' (p.356a).

Hilton's didactic sense in *Scale* 1 is not entirely sure-footed. Perhaps the limitations of his audience posed a catechetic challenge which he only gradually mastered.[27] Certainly what he ends up with, perhaps reluctantly, is somewhat at odds with his earlier injunctions to abandon bodily imagining and his assertions that the image of sin is 'like to no bodily thyng.'

IV

The opening of *Scale* 2 may invoke a fictional audience. But it ostensibly responds to a desire for further exposition of the image of sin and perhaps to a request for greater clarity of focus than was achieved in *Scale* 1:

[25] *Daniel* 2. 32–3. I have used the Douay-Rheims translation.
[26] On Nebuchadnezzar as a type of pride, see P.B.R.Doob, *Nebuchadnezzar's Children* (New Haven 1974). Many manuscripts of Gower's *Confessio Amantis* have have an illustration of the dream showing the image, see J.Griffiths, 'Confessio Amantis: The Poem and its Pictures', in *Gower's Confessio Amantis: Responses and Reassessments*, ed. A.J.Minnis (Cambridge 1983), pp.163–78, and plate 1. Chaucer also refers to the tradition in the Monk's Tale (*Canterbury Tales*, VII, 2143–82). One of the Vernon lyrics also alludes to it: *Religious Lyrics of the Fourteenth Century*, ed. C.Brown, 2nd edn rev. G.V.Smithers (Oxford 1952), no.121, p.213. See also M. Camille, *The Gothic Idol* (Cambridge 1989), pp. 281–8, on the traditional political interpretation of the statue.
[27] On the original audience for *Scale* 1, see Hussey, 'Audience', pp.112–3, where it is also argued that *Scale* 2 'was addressed to a much wider audience than was *Scale* 1.'

> For as mykel as þou coueites gretly and askes it per charitee for to here more of an ymage þe whilk I haue bifore tymes in partie discried to þe ... I shal open to þe a litil more of þis ymage. (fol.63r)[28]

Perhaps reflecting the precise terms of the request, he continues:

> At þe bigynnyng, if þu wil wite pleynly what I mene bi þis ymage, I telle þe for soþe þat I vndirstonde noȝt elles bot þin owne soule. (fol. 63r)

All souls are the image of God, 'noȝt in þe bodili schape withouten bot in þe miȝtes of it within ... þis is þe ymage þat I haue spokyn of.' The fall has disfigured the soul into 'anoþer liknes' and the process of reformation is now 'þe entent of þis writynge.'

Scale 2 thus begins as a commentary on and 'pleyn' exposition of the two core images of the second half of *Scale* 1. Out of this Hilton builds his doctrine of reformation first by faith and then by faith and feeling. Reformation in faith is 'comun to alle chosen soules, þawȝ þei ben bot in þe lowest degre of charite.' (2.17, fol. 79r) Reformation in feeling is 'specialy of þese soules þat mowen comen to þe stat of perfeccioun' (*ibid.*). Although reformation in faith is sufficient for salvation, it does not eradicate the image of sin. Because his implied reader has aspirations to perfection, Hilton stresses the need to move beyond initial reformation. But for many of his subsequent readers this first stage was of particular importance for them as it pertains 'only of bigynnand and profitand soules & of actiue men' (2.5, fol. 67r). This stage of reformation relies on sacramental confession and on the impetus to systematic self-examination it provides (2.7):

> If þou wilt wite þan if þi soule be reformed to þe ymage of God or non, by þat I haue saide þu maiȝt haue entre. Ransake þin own conscience and loke what þi wil is, for þarin stondeþ al. If it be turnyd fro alle maner of dedly syn þat þou woldest for no þing wityngly and wilfully breke þe comaundement of God, and for þat þu hast misdon here biforun agayn his biddyng þou hast schryuen þe þerof mekely, with ful herte to lefe it and with sorw that þu dedist it: I say þan sikerly þat þi soule is reformid in faiþ to þe liknes of God. (2.9, fol.70r)

Virtue is the key to vanquishing the image of sin as it constitutes the image of Jesus.

Hilton's teachings on the *imago peccati* arc across the two books, despite the differences in tone and texture between them. He sees confession not simply as an instrument of sacerdotal diagnosis and prescription but, in line with canonical and pastoral developments in the fourteenth century, as a valuable arena for self-

---

[28] All quotations from *Scale* 2 are taken from London, British Library, MS Harley 6579. I am grateful to Professor Hussey for making available to me a copy of his transcription. Abbreviations have been silently expanded.

reliance and self-analysis on the part of the penitent.[29] For most Christians, baptism and penance were the major weapons to be deployed to control the image of sin and its associated vices:

> In þis reformyng, þat is only in faiþ, þe most part of chosyn soules ledyn here lif, þat setten here wil stedfast<li> for to fleen al maner of dedly syn, & for to kepyn hem in luf & charite to here euen-cristen, & for to kepe þe comaundementes of God vp her cunnyng; & whan it so is þat wicked stirynges & [yuel] willes rise in her hertes, of pride or of enuye, or ire or of leccherye, or of ony oþer hed syn, þei agenstonden hem & stryfen ageyns hem bi displesyng of wil, so þat þei folwe not in dede þese wicked willes. (2.10, fol.70r–v)

It is hardly surprising that this part of Hilton's programme of instruction should have attracted the attention of those adapting eremitical teachings for the use of people living the active life.

V

The prologue to the *Speculum Boni et Mali*, found only in the Lansdowne copy, shares with the *Cibus Anime* and the *Speculum Christiani* the same sense of the onerous burden of the priest's pastoral charge. The two opening authorities reflect the awesomeness of the task and the seriousness of the responsibility:

> *Si magnum gaudium fit in celo propter conversionem unius peccatoris, certe et indubitanter magna merces debetur illi qui fuerit causa convercionis illius. Augustinus: Magis est iustificare impium quam creare celum et terram.*

Both are drawn from book 1 chapter 3 of *Cibus Anime* (*Tria sunt genera elemosinarum*) which shares many authorities with book 2 chapter 30 (ominously called *De morte anime*). The same discussion of spiritual almsgiving in *Cibus Anime* contains

---

[29] Clark, 'Intention', 76–80; Hughes, *Pastors and Visionaries*, pp.196–7, 280. For brief surveys of the scene see Gillespie, '*Doctrina* and *Predicacio*', and J.Shaw, 'The Influence of Canonical and Episcopal Reform on popular Books of Instruction', in *The Popular Literature of Medieval England*, ed. T.J.Heffernan, Tennessee Studies in Literature, 28 (1985), pp.44–60. For more detailed discussions, see Gillespie, *Literary Form*, pp.94–187; L.E.Boyle, 'The *Oculus Sacerdotis* and Some Other Works of William of Pagula', *Transactions of the Royal Historical Society*, 5th ser., 5 (1955), 81–110, reprinted in *Pastoral Care, Clerical Education and Canon Law, 1200–1400* (London 1981); R.M.Ball, *The Education of the English Parish Clergy in the Later Middle Ages with Particular Reference to the Manuals of Instruction*, unpublished Ph.D thesis (Cambridge 1976), section iv (The Practice of the Cure of Souls); M.J.Haren, *A Study of the Memoriale Presbiterorum, a fourteenth-century confessional manual for Parish Priests*, unpublished D.Phil thesis (Oxford 1975).

an interesting parallel with Hilton's doctrine of the *imago peccati*, which illustrates the affinity of outlook between the two texts:

> Quomodo potest quis veraciter dicere se deum diligere et eius amorem appetere si eius ymaginem videat denigrari et in sterquilinio peccatorum iacere preciosissimum sanguinem christi, sub pedibus sponsam conculcari, spiritus sancti habitaculum pollui, sponsam christi prostitui, fidem catholicam deici, preceptum dominicum et totam eius beatitudinem pro vilibus voluptatibus et viciis contempni et ipse non curat nec clamat sed dissimulans solum suam quietem requirit.[30]

This chapter of *Cibus Anime* and the selections from it in *Speculum Christiani* also emphasise the value of a catechetically competent laity able to operate in cooperation with the clergy. This theme is reflected in the two vernacular couplets which illustrate the contrast between the *anima iusti et ymago dei* and the *anima impii et ydolum peccati*. The cryptic single word *sacerdos*, preceding the equally cryptic second couplet and linked with the singular imperative form of the invitation to penance, seems to be invoking the crucial role of the priest in administering the sacrament, but also to the heavy responsibility borne by 'bad' priests:

> *Speculum boni et mali. Sacerdos. Anima impii et ydolum peccati. The hed. Veni ad confessionem.* Fro þe prest drawe we hym faste. For in to helle he wolde ut caste.

Although the couplet is probably corrupt, the underlying sense of this passage may be compared with a section at the end of the prologue to the *Speculum Christiani*:

> *Crisostimus:* Multi sunt sacerdotes nomine et pauci in opere. *Gregorius:* Sacerdotes populorum iniquitate dampnantur, si eos aut ignorantes non erudiant aut peccantes non arguant. *Idem in pastoralibus:* Causa ruine populi sunt sacerdotes mali. *Dominus per Ysayam:* Propterea captiuus ductus est populus meus, quod non habet scienciam.[31]

The title *Speculum Boni et Mali*, which may be a deliberate echo of the title of its more popular sibling, is probably also an allusion to Hilton's description of the soul in *Scale* 2.30:

---

[30] All quotations from the *Cibus Anime* are taken from the early two-book copy preserved in Cambridge, Trinity Hall, MS 16, this quotation on f.2r. Cf. *Speculum Christiani*, H.5–7, with the Augustine quote on H.7.1–2. That the prologue also uses *auctoritates* from *Cibus Anime* is one argument for assuming that it is either part of the original conception of the text or was added to it before the work left the orbit of the milieu in which the *Cibus Anime* and *Speculum* were either produced or disseminated; see Gillespie, 'Cura Pastoralis', pp.177–81 and Hughes, *Pastors and Visionaries*, pp.196–7.

[31] H., p.7, cf. the same idea at the beginning of the *Dextera pars* of the *Oculus Sacerdotis*: 'Multi sunt sacerdotes et pauci sunt sacerdotes. Multi sunt nomine, pauci in opere', Oxford, New College, MS 292, f.34rb.

For þi soule is bot a mirrour in þe whilk þu schalt see God gostly. And þerfor þu schalt first fynde þi mirrour & kepen it briȝt & clene fro fleschly filþ & werdly vanitee, & holden it wel vp fro þe erþ, þat þu maiȝt seen it & oure lorde þerin also. (fol.102v)

VI

The first section of the *Speculum Boni et Mali* contains two series of seven couplets. Although *IMEV* describes the verses as 'the interpretation of Nebuchadnezzar's vision of the image', they in fact draw their inspiration from the chapters surrounding Hilton's final description of the image of sin at the end of *Scale* 1, though the influence of *Daniel* 2.25–49 on Hilton's thinking at this point of the *Scale* has already been suggested.[32]

The author of the couplets was obviously familiar with the core of Hilton's teaching on the image/idol theme in *Scale* 1 and, in particular, with his schematic summary of that teaching in 1.85–87. The first sequence of verses describes an 'image' composed of virtues and works of mercy, clearly a paraphrase of Hilton's *imago dei* 'whilk is þe ymage of vertus' (1.86, p.356b). The second set describes an 'ydoll' which is closely based on the summary of the *imago peccati* in *Scale* 1.85. In Lansdowne the series run in parallel; in the other two copies the *imago dei* sequence precedes the *imago peccati* verses. Each couplet is a rough but effective formulation and condensation of Hilton's teachings, producing in total an allusive but accurate précis of over forty chapters of *Scale* 1.

Three illustrations of the process must suffice.[33] The head of the image is faith and meekness, characterised by obedience to the decalogue and the teachings of the church. The idol's head, by contrast, manifests pride through disobedience to both. This derives from Hilton's discussion of heresy in 1.58:

and þerfor he þat seiz he louez God and kepez his biddynges, *and* despisez Holy Kirk *and* settez at noȝt þe lawȝes *and* þe ordinaunce of it made by þe hede *and* þe souereyn in gouernaunce of all Cristen men, he liȝez – he chesez noȝt God, [bot] he chesez þe loue of hymself contrarie to þe loue of God. (p.329a)

The same chapter makes the orthodox and commonplace link between pride and

---

[32] See above, p. 105; *IMEV* 3373.
[33] For reasons of space, it has not been possible to print all the supporting authorities for Text 1, but those couplets discussed in detail in this section have been supplied with their *auctoritates* in the edition printed in Appendix 1. In the illustrations here and in the edition in the appendix, source chapters from the *Cibus Anime* have been indicated in square brackets: for example [2.3] refers to book 2 chapter 3. The full list of chapters is printed in Gillespie, *Literary Form*, pp.402–7.

meekness, which is also emphasised in 1.86: 'Slee, þen, and breke doun pryde, and sett up mekenes' (p.356b).

The heart in the breast of the image is 'treuthe and charite' to God and our fellow Christians. Opposed to this, the heart of the idol is wrath and envy, manifested by 'hindringe and sclaunderinge, baningge and bakbitinge.' This linking of wrath and envy is not found in the summary of the idol in *Scale* 1.85 ('þe brest in þe whilk is þe hert is enuye' (p.355a)), but the sins are linked in the preceding discussion, especially in chapters 64 to 70. These chapters also emphasise the need for a man to 'kun loue his euencristen in charite' (1.67, p.337b). As the heading to chapter 68 in Harley 6579 puts it 'charite is noutes ellis bute for to lufe god and his euencristne as hym self.' Similar sentiments are expressed in 1.86: 'breke doun ire and enuye and reyse up loue and charite to þin euencristen' (p.356b).

The slothful feet and legs of the idol are reluctant to perform good works, whereas the image's feet and legs represent eagerness and readiness for the discreet performance of good deeds. Sloth receives little discussion in the earlier chapters of *Scale* 1, and 1.85 offers little elaboration, moving quickly on to the remedy: 'reyse up þi frende, whilk is Jesu, bi deuote preyere and meditacion.' Here Hilton's gloss, designed for his would-be contemplative, has been suppressed in favour of an active emphasis on the works of mercy, such as Hilton recommends in 1.87: 'in stede of accidie, feruour of deuocion, with a gladd redynes to all gode dedes' (p.356b).

As well as broadening the didactic thrust of the couplets, the latin *auctoritates* often demonstrate that their selection has been made with an awareness of the implications of Hilton's teachings. The proof-texts for the head of the image, for example, support the couplet's references to faith, meekness and obedience, but in so doing also reflect Hilton's emphasis on contemplative aspiration and on the soul as the *templum dei*:

> Unde *Bernardus*: Per humilitatem ascendite ad sublimitatem quia hec est via et non est alia propter eam. [2.3] *Augustinus*: Si altam domum volueritis fabricare virtutum humilitatis profundum faciatis fundam[e]ntum. [2.3] . . . *Gregorius*: Omnes qui divina metuunt precepta dei tabernaculum fiunt. [1.45]

There is here an interesting parallel with Hilton's reference to the *idolum desolacionis* in *De Imagine Peccati* which raises the intriguing possibility that the compiler may also have been familiar with this work.[34]

---

[34] 'Hoc est idolum desolacionis positum in templo Domini quod est anima tua, ad prouocandam emulacionem. Templum, inquit Apostolus, Domini, sanctum est, quod estis vos', *Latin Writings*, p.98 and note on this passage, p.356. The idea of the soul as the temple of God was, of course, a commonplace, but it was given extended treatment in Robert

The *auctoritates* for the head of the idol, by contrast, pick up Hilton's remarks about the diabolical tendencies of pride:

> *Augustinus*: Superbia angelum fecit diabolum humilitas hominem deum. [2.2] *Basilius*: Superbia ab angelis demones fecit, humilitas autem homines sanctis angelis similes reddit. [2.2] *Augustinus*: Quid celo securius quid paradiso iocundus; angelus tamen de celo homo de paradiso per superbiam lapsi sunt. [2.2]

This invites comparison with *Scale* 1.86: 'þis is noȝt þe ymage of Jesu bot it is lickere an ymage of þe deuel' (p.356a).

The proof-texts supporting the couplet describing the womb of the image similarly reflect Hilton's teaching on abstinence and discretion, especially his warnings against extreme mortification of the flesh:

> Vir discretus ad necessitatem ventrem reficit et a voluptate restringit. [2.18] . . . *Gregorius*: Ea sumenda sunt que nature necessitas querit non que edendo libido suggerit. [2.19]

In discussing avarice and covetousness, Hilton emphasises how hard these sins are to eradicate even for those who have formally died to the world:

> Lift up þis ymage *and* loke wel aboute, and þou schalt mo se couetise *and* loue of erthly thynges occupie a grete party of þis ymage, þoȝ it seme litel. þou hast forsaken ryches and mykel auere of þis world and art sperd in a dunion, bot hast þou forsaken clenly þe loue of all þise? (p.342b)

The authorities supplied here reflect the more worldly orientation of their intended audience of actives:

> *Augustinus*: Qui terrenis inhiat et eternis non cogitat utrisque in futuro carebit. [2.13] *Gregorius* in moralibus: Ve qui temporalia divinis preponitis fortes ad ambulandum in via mundi sed debiles ad aggrediendum viam mandatorum dei . . . Avaricia dicitur *ab apostolo* ydolorum servitus quia homo avarus exibet creature quod debet cr[e]atori scilicet fidem spem et dilectionem. Avarus plus diligit mundum et aliquando obolum unum quam deum creatorem suum et eius preceptum. [2.12]

Yet the image couplet's reference to 'wilful pouerte' (Hilton's own term) invokes *Scale* 1's teaching on attachment to worldly things:

> bot o thyng I sey to ilk man or woman þat has taken þe state of wilfull pouert (wheþere he be religiouse or seculere, or what degre he be inne),

Grosseteste's popular pastoral manual *Templum Dei*, which uses this Pauline quote as its starting point; *Robert Grosseteste: Templum Dei*, ed. J.Goering and F.A.C.Mantello, Toronto Medieval Latin Texts (Toronto 1984), p.29.

als long as his loue *and* his affeccion is bounden, festned and as it were gleymed with couetise of erthly gode þat he has or wold haue, he may no3t haue ne fele sothfastly þe clene loue and [þe] clere sy3t of gostly thynges. (p.343b)

The description of avarice as 'servitus ydolorum' is, therefore, typical of the allusive decorum of the work as a whole.

VII

A group of authorities towards the end of the first text acts as a bridge to the second by broadening the discussion away from sloth and its remedy to an Augustinian discussion of the fouling of the soul which parallels the account given by Hilton at the beginning of *Scale* 2:[35]

Anima vero christiana ante peccatum pulcra est et dei similis. Sed postquam peccaverit mortaliter perdi[di]t omnem pulcritudinem et redditur ita deformis et ita turpis sicut diabolus ymmo turpior ut dicit [Augustinus] in quadam oracione. (fol. 77v)

This passage also recalls *Scale* 2.14:

Alle þese & many oþer mo þat lifen <no3t> in drede of God bot breken his comaundementes, forschapen hemself fro þe liknes of God & maken hem like to bestes. 3e, & werre þan bestes, for þei are like vnto þe fende of helle. (fol. 76v)

But the first text ends on a more positive note with a series of authorities headed *Contra desperacionem*: 'Sicut scintilla in medio maris sicut omnis impietas viri ad misericordiam dei', and an exhortation to use confession ('Confitemini ergo peccata vestra, et penitenciam agite, et appropinquabit regnum celorum') which is entirely in keeping with Hilton's emphasis in the early chapters of *Scale* 2.[36]

---

[35] cf. *Scale* 2.1, ff.63r–v: 'þis ymage made to þe image of God in þe first schapynge was wnderly faire and bri3t, ful of brennande loue *and* gostly ly3t, bot þorw synne of þe first man Adam it was disfigured *and* forschapyn into anoþer liknes ...' On the Augustinian elements in this discussion, see Clark, 'Image and Likeness', *passim*. See also the extracts from Augustine's *De Trinitate* circulating as vernacular discussions of the image of God in man, cited in note 14 above. Cf the same phrase at the opening of the shorter version of Text 2 (Appendix 2).

[36] *Cibus Anime* 2.35; other chapters used here are 2.38, 39 and 43. A similar, but not identical selection of authorities in the same order is also found in the *Speculum Christiani*, H.73.19–25, including the exhortation to confession, which is not found in the *Cibus Anime* at the relevant points. cf also H.113.9–115.15. It may be that parcels of authorities circulated fairly freely inside the textual family.

Lansdowne does not mark the break between the two texts, but the other witnesses agree that the division comes after this pastorally responsible exhortation to hope in the mercy of God. The second text, on the examination of the conscience, is the logical and practical continuation of the forensic process initiated in the first. Hilton regularly emphasises the centrality of the will and intention in the process of reformation and this is reflected in the opening authorities of the new text:[37]

> *Gregorius*: Nihil deo dicius bona voluntate offertur. [1.48] Cum bona voluntate omnino perire non potes. [1.48]

The first vernacular passage is drawn, directly or indirectly, from *Scale* 2.9.[38] Although there has been some paraphrasing and editorial reshaping between the different versions, and some versions might even represent memorial reconstruction of Hilton's, the affinity is unmistakeable.

Hilton uses this chapter to emphasise how the process of reformation in faith is rooted in the teachings of *Scale* 1, particularly with regard to the avoidance of deadly sin. In chapter 10 he reminds his reader that reformation in faith is the state occupied by the majority of souls. The supporting authorities for the first extract, found both in *Cibus Anime* and in the *Speculum Christiani*, describe the reward awaiting the just, drawing on a section headed *De gaudiis celi*.[39] This reinforces Hilton's statement that this state, most commonly occupied by those in the active life, 'sufficeþ to saluacioun' (2.5, fol. 67r). Indeed the end of 2.10 emphasises how:

> simple soules þat trowen stidefastly as Holy Kirke trowes, & putten hem fully in þe mercy of God, & meken hem vndre þe sacramente & þe laghes of Holi Kirk' shall be 'mad sauf þorw praier & trowþ of her gostly modir whilk is Holi Kirk' (fol. 71v).

Clearly the new text is aimed at those in the world who will be engaged in the continual struggle against the image of sin rather than those who will aspire to the higher level of reformation through faith and feeling.

The second vernacular section contrasts those obedient and faithful servants of God and the church (amply characterised by the couplets of the image-head) with those whose behaviour typifies the head of the idol. This passage paraphrases *Scale* 2.14, omitting Hilton's use of the traditional analogy between the deadly sins and

---

[37] Clark, 'Intention', discusses this aspect of his teaching and the emphasis on confession in detail.

[38] The relevant portion is printed above, p.106. This second text, as it is in prose, was more susceptible to scribal substitution and corrupt reconstitution. The slight variations between the versions of the longer text and between the longer and shorter text suggest an incremental drift from a form close to Hilton's, particularly in the first prose passage.

[39] For the *Speculum*, see H.119.5–121.13.

animals. As adapted for this context, the similarity to the Latin passage from the end of text 1, cited earlier, and the opening of *Scale 2*, is clear:

> Oþir men þat drede nat god, þat lye in de[d]li sinne *and* wille nat knowe *and* kepe þe bidding*is* of god, þei disfigure *and* forschepe her soulis fro þe liknesse of god *and* make hem like to þe fendis of helle.

The supporting authorities naturally emphasise obedience to the commandments.

The final vernacular passage returns to the deadly sins, again drawing from 2.14. The supporting Bernardine proof-text succinctly expresses the point of the section:

> *Bernardus*: Quod enim quisque pre ceteris colit et diligit, id sibi deum constituisse probatur. [1.9]

Or, as Hilton himself puts it:

> Vnkyndely he doþ & vnresonablely he wirkiþ, þat lefiþ þe souerayn gode & aylastande lif þat is God vnso3t & vnlofed, vnknowen & vnworscipid, & chesiþ his reste & his blis in a passand delit of an erþly þinge. (2.14, fol. 76r)

Those who fail to reform to the image of God through the sacrament of Penance 'schul be dampned with þe deuyl into þe depnes of helle'(2.14, fol. 77r).

VIII

The *Speculum Boni et Mali* ends (in two of the three copies) with a rubric paragraph of authorities set apart from the rest of the text:

> *Paulus*: Erit enim tempus cum sanam doctrinam non sustinebunt. [1.1] *Salomon*: Fatui non poterunt diligere nisi ea que eis placent. *Gregorius*: Hoc certissime scito quod placere deo et pravis hominibus nemo potest. Deo gracias.

This serves as an epilogue to both texts, emphasising the urgency of reformation, the stupidity of worldly lovers and, in an allusive return to the concerns of the prologue, the need for self-reliance in an age when *sana doctrina* might be vulnerable.

The milieu which produced the *Cibus Anime*, the *Seculum Christiani* and the *Speculum Boni et Mali* clearly cared about the *cura animarum*, and worried about the quality of service offered by some priests. It also wanted to foster a spiritually responsible and self-aware laity. The accumulation of evidence points to the Carthusians and priests of York Minster as having a particular interest in the popular texts of this group, and nothing about either groups' activities in the late fourteenth and early fifteenth centuries makes such an association unlikely. Strikingly, the same groups had a demonstrable interest in the Latin and English writings of Walter Hilton. If, as has recently been claimed, 'between 1380 and 1430 households of York clergy had assumed responsibility for communicating and adapting eremitic teaching for the laity', it may be that the *Speculum Boni et Mali* represents one of the fruits of that new responsibility: a text formed in the image and likeness of Walter Hilton.[40]

---

[40] Hughes, *Pastors and Visionaries*, p.236; the evidence for the circulation of the *Cibus Anime*, *Speculum Christiani* and related texts is reviewed in Gillespie, 'Evolution', 'Cura Pastoralis' and 'Cibus Anime Book 3', cited in note 8. On Carthusian interest in Hilton's works, see Sargent, 'London Group', 189–90; on York interest, see Hughes, pp.213–6.

APPENDIX 1

Texts[41]

Three manuscripts contain both texts together:
1. London, British Library, MS Lansdowne 344, fols 70r–79r. (L)
2. London, British Library, MS Royal 8 F. vi, fols 25va–27rb.(R)
3. Oxford, Corpus Christi College, MS 132, fols 63v–69r.(C)

Only L preserves the prologue. R and C preserve the couplets in two separate sequences, the *imago dei* verses preceding those on the *imago peccati*. A heavily editorialised version of text 2 is preserved in London, British Library, MS Additional 15237, which adds extra authorities and smoothes and expands the vernacular sections.

Source chapters from the *Cibus Anime* are indicated in square brackets. Reference has been made to the copies preserved in Cambridge, Trinity Hall, MS 16; Oxford, University College, MS 60; and London, British Library, MS Harley 237. Many of the quotations are also found in the *Speculum Christiani*, but not enough to make that a source for the *auctoritates* in these texts.

It is significant that the material from or related to the *Speculum Christiani* in all the manuscripts listed in Appendices 1 and 2 (with the exception of Lansdowne) groups them together in Holmstedt's textual category C (H.pp.clv–clxxi), which preserves the work in its least stable state.[42] (Foyle (unknown to H.) can be assigned to category C3 and is related to Add. 15237 (Gillespie, *Literary Form*, pp.323–4)). It may well be, therefore, that Lansdowne preserves the *Speculum Boni et Mali* in a later, evolved form, just as its copy of the *Speculum Christiani* represents the text in its 'finished' and most widely represented form. This suggestion is supported by some of the verbal substitutions (e.g. *cherche* for *kyrke* in text 2) which lead away from Hilton's text and may explain its preservation in a non-northern dialect.[43]

---

[41] *Editorial Procedure*: Orthography of Middle English texts has been preserved. Latin texts have had u/v normalised. Lemmata have been standardised in the form *Gregorius*:. Scribal insertions are marked \.../. Editorial additons and emendations are enclosed by square brackets. Erasures, text over erasure, and other deficiencies are enclosed in angle brackets. Latin abbreviations have been silently expanded, vernacular abbreviations are expanded in italics. Rubric text is printed in italic. In Text 1, line numbering refers to the couplets only. In Text 2, the whole text is numbered. In Text 1, only substantive variants for the vernacular texts are recorded in the *apparatus criticus*.

[42] R does not contain any other material from or related to the *Cibus/Speculum* tradition. It contains *exempla* and miracles of the Virgin, a *Gesta Romanorum* and letter *formulae* relating to Lincoln diocese, one dated 15 March 1463. The text of the *Gesta* is signed several times by a Thomas Brewse 'de Kenforde' (ff.32r, 34r, 41r, 44r).

[43] I am grateful to Dr Margaret Laing of the University of Edinburgh for her opinion on the language of Lansdowne. On the limited available evidence, she suggests S.E. Lincolnshire/N.W. Norfolk for text 1 and 'the area just west of the Wash in the Spalding/Crowland environs' for text 2 (private communication, 21/7/89).

Nevertheless, L offers the best text of the Latin authorities and the metre and rhymes of the couplets are usually superior to the other versions. The dialect of the other copies is consonant with the dialect of the *Speculum*, which is North East Midlands, probably Lincolnshire.[44]

London, British Library, MS Lansdowne 344

Text 1

fol. 70r

Si magnum gaudium fit in celo propter conversionem unius peccatoris, certe et indubitanter magna merces debetur illi qui fuerit causa convercionis illius. [1.3] *Augustinus: Magis est iustificare impium quam creare celum et terram.* [1.3] *Anima iusti et ymago dei.* 3if þou in goodenesse lastinge be. In heuene þou schalt crounid be. *Speculum boni et mali. Sacerdos. Anima impii et ydolum peccati.* The hed. *Veni ad confessionem.* Fro þe prest drawe we hym faste. For in to helle he wolde ut caste.

1   T[h]e hede of þis ymage is stedefast fayth *and* mekenesse grete
     To goddis biddi[n]gge *and* holi kyrke ay sogette.

De fide dicitur in cimbalo *Athanasii:* Quicumque vult saluus esse ante omnia opus est ut teneat catholicam fidem. [1.4] *Galath. iii:* Omnes filii dei estis per fidem. [1.4] *Augustinus:* Beacior fuit Maria in percipiendo fidem christi quam in concipiendo carnem christi. [1.4] *Paulus:* Sine fide impossibile est placere deo. De humilitate dicit *Jeronimus:* Prima virtus est humilitas christianorum. Unde *Bernardus:* Per humilitatem ascendite ad sublimitatem quia hec est via et non est alia propter eam. [2.3] *Augustinus:* Si altam domum volueritis fabricare virtutum humilitatis profundum faciatis fundam[e]ntum. [2.3] Humiles sunt qui deum timent et diligunt et eius precepta fideliter custodiunt. *Unde per prophetam dicit dominus:* Super quem requiescit spiritus meus nisi super humilem et contritum spiritum et trementem sermones meos. *Gregorius:* Omnes qui divina metuunt precepta dei tabernaculum fiunt. [1.45] *Origenes:* Omnis qui [o]bedit verbo dei requiescit christus in eo. [1.45] *Beda:* Nichil salubrius observacione divina decalogi. *Augustinus:* Cicius exauditur una oracio obedientis quam milia contemptoris. [1.45] *Ysidorus:* Si id quod deus precepit facimus id quod petimus sine dubio obtinemus.

---

1. þis] þe RC. 2. To] of R.

---

44 M.Laing, *Studies in the Dialect Material of Medieval Lincolnshire*, unpublished Ph.D. thesis (Edinburgh 1978), pp.254–5; Gillespie, 'Cura pastoralis', pp.180–181. It is worth noting that Cambridge, University Library, MS Additional 6150 was owned by a chaplain in Walsingham, though it is unclear whether this is the Norfolk Marian shrine or in Durham.

The hed of þe ydole is hy pride and excellent
To goddis bidding and holi chirche ay inobediente.

Bernardus: Inicium omnis peccati et causa tocius perdicionis est superbia. [2.2]
Augustinus: Superbia angelum fecit diabolum humilitas hominem deum. [2.2]
Basilius: Superbia ab angelis demones fecit, humilitas autem homines sanctis
angelis similes reddit. [2.2] *Augustinus*: Quid celo securius quid paradiso iocundus;
angelus tamen de celo homo de paradiso per superbiam lapsi sunt. [2.2] Multi
enim sunt qui frequenter dicunt deo domine domine sed eius preceptis nolunt
obedire. *Quibus in evangelium dicit Dominus*: Quid vocatis me domine domine et
non facitis que precipio vobis. [1.45] *Item alibi*: Quare et vos transgredimini man-
datum dei propter tra[di]cionem vestram. [1.45] *Augustinus*: Contra deum super-
bire est eius precepta transcendere. [2.2] *Gregorius*: Evidentissimum signum
reproborum est superbia. Superba voluntas facit dei precepta contempni. *Unde
Bernardus*: O magnum malum proprie voluntatis que et tua bona tibi mala facit.
[1.45] *Idem*: Quid odit deus aut quid punit preter voluntatem propriam? Nichil
ardebit in inferno nisi propria voluntas; ipsa est que deum impugnat et adversus
eum extollitur. [1.45] *Augustinus*: Quemcumque superbum esse videris diaboli
filium esse non dubites. [2.2]

5   The herte in þe brest is treuthe and charite
     To god almy3ti and to al cristiante.

     The herte in þe brest is wrathe and gret enuie
     Hindringe and sclaunderinge, baningge and bakbitinge: moche lesis he.

     The bakke behinde is wilful pouerte
10   Alwey glad to spende wel superfluite.

     The bak is couetyse and streyte haldinge sinfulli
     To almus dede and trewþe a grete enmi is he.

Paulus: Radix omnium malorum est cupiditas. [2.12] *Idem*: Qui volunt divites fieri
incidunt in temptacionem et in laqueos dyaboli et in desideria iniusta que mer-
gunt hominem in interitum. [2.12] *Jeronimus*: Multis mortem generaverunt di-
vicie. [2.12] *Augustinus*: Qui terrenis inhiat et eternis non cogitat utrisque in
futuro carebit. [2.13] *Gregorius* in moralibus: Ve qui temporalia divinis preponitis
fortes ad ambulandum in via mundi sed debiles ad aggrediendum viam mandato-
rum dei. *Abacuc 2o*: Ve qui congregat non sua. [1.35] *Lincolniensis*: Ve illis qui
dicunt faciamus mala ut veniant bona quorum dampnacio iusta est. [1.35] Omne

---

3. þe] þys CR. and excellent] om. RC.   4. and] in R. 6. to] un to C. 8. baningge] om. R.
moche lesis he] m[i]schevusly C. 10. wel] om. RC. 12. a grete ... he] a full grete enmy C.

---

quod per peccatum adquiritur per diabolum datur illud autem quod sine peccato adquiritur per deum datur. De auro dicit *Jeronimus*: Avarus est sicut infernus insaciabilis. [2.14] Cor autem avari est quasi fovea sine fundo. *Augustinus*: Abundancia pecunie avaricie fauces non claudit sed extendit. [2.14] Avaricia dicitur *ab apostolo* ydolorum servitus quia homo avarus exibet creature quod debet cr[e]atori scilicet fidem spem et dilectionem. Avarus plus diligit mundum et aliquando obolum unum quam deum creatorem suum et eius preceptum. [2.12] *Tullius*: Deterius avaricia nullum vicium est. Avaricia facit hominem deo abhominabilem. [2.12] *Osee 9*: Facti sunt abhominabiles. [2.14] Avarus iniquus est in deum in seipsum et in proximum. [2.14] Nam deo retinet [d]ebita proximo denegat necessaria sibi ipsi subtrahit oportuna. [2.14] *Seneca*: Avarus nisi cum moritur nichil bene facit. [2.14]

The handis *and* þe armis ar þe werkis of merci
Alwey redi to do alm*us* dede wysli.

15 The handis *and* þe armis ar wreche *and* hastite
Alwey redi to veniaunse *and* fey3tinge folili.

[T]he wombe is discretiun *and* sobirte
Alwei gou*er*nid wel and discre[t]ly.

The wombe is excesse *and* gret glotenie
20 [Fulfilland ys lust alway gredyly].

Unde Apostolus: Quorum deus venter est. [2.16] *Bernardus*: Calix demonorum crapula et ebrietas. [2.16] *Augustinus*: Ebrietas confundit naturam, perdit graciam et perducit ad dampnacionem. *Gregorius*: Illa miseria plena est crudelitate que sic deseruit carni ut anima iuguletur. [2.17] *Paulus*: Si secundum carnem vixeritis moriemini. [2.17] *Jeronimus*: Qui post carnem ambulant in ventrem et libidinem provi quasi irracionabilia iumenta reputantur. [2.17] *Bernardus*: Edere laucius, potare sapidius, pulcrius vestiri, cubari mollius, orare brevius, vigilare parcius, coram deo nichil vilius. [2.17] *Gregorius*: Quasi per amenum pratum ad suspend[end]um vadit qui per prospera huius mundi ad interitum tendit. [2.17] Divitibus autem dicit *Augustinus de verbo domini sermo iiij*: Utere dives cibis electis et preciosis quia sic consue[vi]sti quia aliter non potes quia si consuetudinem mutas egrotas. [2.19] Discrete tamen bene agere debent et pauperes recreare quia secundum *Radulphum super levitici*: Qui ventris concupiscenciam amorem pecunie aut honoris appetitum divine preferunt caritati invisibiliter ydola pro deo colunt. [H.17.25]

---

13. þe] om. RC.   14. Alwey] be alway R. wysli] wylfully R.   15–16] om. R.   16. to] to do C.   18. wel] wysly R.   20] CR. Hatande ay godis lawe and chastite L.

The membris ar continence *and* chastite
Kepid ay wel from sinful lecheri.

The membris ar incontinense and lecher[y]
Hatyng ay goddis law and chastite.

25   The fete *and* þe leggis ar alwey redi
To werke al [þe] godenesse þat þei mai discretly.

The fete *and* þe leggis are slaw *and* ful heui
To goode werkys alwey froward *and* unlusti.

Text 2

Augustinus: Nullus sanctus et iustus caret peccato
nec tamen ex hoc desinit esse iustus vel sanctus cum affectu
(fol. 78r) teneat sanctitatem. *Bernardus*: Nichil querit deus
a te nisi cor tuum. [1.48] *Augustinus*: Omne enim quodcumque
5   vis ex toto corde et non potes perficere coram deo pro facto
reputatur. [1.48] *Gregorius*: Nihil deo dicius bona voluntate
offertur. [1.48] Cum bona voluntate omnino perire non
potes. [1.48]
    If þou coueite to knowe hou it standis *with* þi sowle
10   *and* qwhi it be like to þe ymage of god or noon, þou may
ransake þin owne conscience *and* loke what þi will is for
þerin standis alle. Yf þou be stedefast in þe feith of holi
cherche *and* turnid fro al dedeli sinne, *and* þat þou wolde
nat for no þing wetanli *and* wylfulli breke þe biddinge of
15   god; and for þat þou hast doon agayn his bidding þou has
schriuin þe fulli *with* meke herte *and* wil to forsake þi
sinne, and *with* sorwe þat þou dedist hit; þerin is þi soule
sykirli reformid in faithe to þe liknesse of god.
    De talibus per prophetam dicitur: Ego dixi dii estis et
20   filii excelsi omnes. [2.33] *Item in evangelio*: Fulgebunt
iusti sicut sol in regno patris eorum. [2.33] *Unde*

---

22. Kepid] Kepith CR. 24. ay goddis] ay dedely goddys CR. 26. al [þe]] CR. alwey L.
Text 2:
7–8. non potes] et sine bona voluntate omnino salvari non potes add. CR. 9. coueite]
wylt R; 'know to' couet C. 10. qwhi] weþir CR. 14. wetanli] wyttyngly C. 14. biddinge]
ordinans CR. 15. hast] om. R. 16. fulli . . . wil] mekely *with* ful herte *and* wylle RC.
17. *with* sorwe] wt so *subpuncted* be sory C. 17. þerin] þan C 18. in faithe] in þe faith R.

---

ancellmus: In die illa obediencium capita corona celestis
circumdabit et paciencium gloria inenarrabili gloria
fulgebit. [2.33]

25 Oþir men þat drede nat god, þat lye in de[d]li sinne
and wille nat knowe *and* kepe þe biddingis of god, þei
disfigure *and* forschape her soulis (fol. 78v) fro þe
liknesse of god *and* make hem like to þe fendis of helle.

Augustinus: Sicut mors corporalis seperat animam a
30 corpore, ita peccatum mortale animam a vera vita que est
deus. [2.30/1.3] *Unde David:* Maledicti qui declinant a
mandatis. [1.45] *Salomon:* Qui avert[a]t aurem suam, ne audiat
legem, execrabilis erit oracio ante deum. [1.1]

Sum men þer be þat chese to her god worschepe *and*
35 praysinge *and* vayn glori of þis wrechid world for þat þei
loue best *and* most bisi ar to winne *and* loþest to leese.
Enuious *and* wrathful men chese veniaunce *and* victorys of
þair aduersariis *and* enemiis. Couetise *and* hauerose men
chesin rychesse *and* [outrageus] hauy[n]g of worldli godis.
40 Glotons and lecherus [men] chesin sinful lustis *and* likynge
of þeir flesch. Sleutheful men chesin ydilnesse, ese *and* reste fro alle gode
dedis. And þus oni thyng þat a man fulli chesis *and*
louis more þan god *and* his bidinggis, þat þing
he makes his god.

45 *Bernardus:* Quod enim quisque pre ceteris colit et
diligit, id sibi deum constituisse probatur. [1.9]
Augustinus: Hoc ab homine colitur pre ceteris quod
diligitur. [1.9] *Dominus in evangelio:* Qui amat patrem et
matrem (fol. 79r) plus quam me non est me dignus. [1.9]
50 *David:* Perdidisti omnes qui fornicantur abs te. *Gregorius:*
Nemo potest in una et eadem re omnipotenti deo et eius
hostibus gratus existere. [1.9] *Jeronimus:* Unusquisque cuius
opera facit eius filius appellatur. [1.9]

*Paulus: Erit enim tempus cum sanam doctrinam non
55 sustinebunt. [1.1] Salomon: Fatui non poterunt diligere nisi
ea que eis placent. Gregorius: Hoc certissime scito quod
placere deo et pravis hominibus nemo potest. Deo gracias.*

---

25. Oþir men] O þe man R.   28. þe] om. R.   34. þer] om. CR. worschepe *and*] worshyp-
pyng C; *and* om. R.   36. bisi] besyste C. ar to] ar for to CR.   37. victorys] victorye CR.
and haverose] om. C.   39. [outrageus]] CR; honouris L.   40. [men]] CR; om. L. lustis] lust
CR.   41. þeir] þe R. Sleutheful] Synful R.   43. bidinggis] byddyng CR.   54–7] rubric] not
R.   54. *Paulus ... sustinebunt*] om. R.

C and R both preserve a short additional paragraph of authorities after line 53 and before line 54. The text is from R, with readings from C in square brackets.

Multa enim sunt qui retinent hominem in mortali peccato et tra[hu]nt eum a bono, scilicet malorum consorcium, pravorum adulacio, peccancium multitudo, peccandi consuetudo, peccati excusacio, aliorum peccatorum nam suorum consideracio, in mundanis occupacio, et emendacionis procrastinacio. [2.42] *Gregorius*: Cum miser homo in quantum peccato labitur suadet eum diabolus nec peniteatur [ne confitiatur] peccatum leve et modicum esse peccatum in corde eius affirmat, animam predicat, longum vite spacium promittit, permanere in peccato diucius suggeret ut sit in contemptum dei et disperacionem sui inducat et perdit. [2.42] *Eccl. 29*: Repromissio nequissima multos perdidit. [2.42]

APPENDIX 2

The Shorter Version of Text 2

The shorter version is preserved in three copies:
1. Cambridge, Trinity Hall, MS 16, fol. 92v. (T)
2. Cambridge, University Library, MS Dd. 14. 26 (3), fols 1v–2r.(Dd)
3. Beeleigh Abbey, Miss Christina Foyle's MS, fol. 45r. (F)

T is an important early copy of the *Cibus Anime*, Dd preserves a deviant copy of material from the *Speculum Christiani*, and F is a copy of the *Speculum*. They are scribally linked. Foyle and the bulk of T were written by the same scribe; Dd and a small section of T were also written by the same (perhaps different) scribe. This text was added in T apparently by a third hand. The text may have been designed to circulate separately from the longer version. The introductory Latin paragraph occurs at the end of text 1, which may be its immediate source. The opening sentence in Dd is translated, suggesting that it has been tailored into its context there. Dd's extra authorities are headed *De consciencia*, which may be a separate section of the compilation. F's reference to 'require supra' probably refers to the discussion of conscience in the *Speculum Christiani*, which precedes it in the manuscript (H.121.27–123.10.)

Cambridge, Trinity Hall, MS 16, fol. 92v.

Anima christiana ante peccatum valde pulcra est et
de[o] similis. Sed postquam peccaverit mortaliter perdidit

---

1. [deo]] F. dei T. 1–2] Euery clene crysten sowle is fulle fayre and lyke to ymage \of/ god Dd. 2–5. Sed . . . oracione] om. FDd.

---

omnem pulcritudinem et redditur ita deformis et ita turpis
sicut dyabolus, immo turpior, *ut dicit Augustinus in quadam*
5   *oracione.*

Now yf þou couet to know how it standes with þi sowle
and whether it be lyke to þe ymage of god or none, þou
mayste ransake þyn owen conscience *and* loke what þi wylle
is, for in þaym standes al. Yf þou be stedfastly gronded *in*
10 þe faythe of holy chirche, and sykerly *turned* fro al dedely
[synne], and þat þou woldes [not] for no thyng wytandely and
wylfully with deliberacioun breke þe byddyng of god, and for
þat þou has done agayne his byddyng þou has schryfen þe
wysely and mekely taken þi penau*n*ce with ful [herte] *and*
15 wylle to forsake þi sy*n*ne, and *with* contricioun and sorow of
hert þat þou has greved god *and* broken his byddyng and *with*
ful p*ur*pose *and* wylle to do no more, þen is þi sowle
reformed in feythe to þe lyknes of þe ymage of god.

Unde dicit Apostolus: Gloria nostra est testimonium
20 consciencie nostre. Qui habet bonam conscienciam audacter
conspiciet in deum in die iudicii, qui illam non habet
confusus cadet. [2.1] Nichil enim iocundius est neque securius
quam bona consciencia. [2.1] *Deo gracias.*

---

10. chirche] kyrke DdF.   11. [synne]] DdF. om. T [not]] Dd; no3t F; om. T.   12. with de-
liberacioun] *over erasure* Dd; om. F.   14. [herte]] DdF, purpose T (see 16).   18. in feythe]
om. DdF.   19.] *De consciencia* (margin) Dd.   20. Qui . . . consciencia] om. F which has *De
consciencia require supra in prima parte;* extra authorities Dd.

The Trinitarian Theology of Walter Hilton's Scale of Perfection. Book Two

J. P. H. Clark

Walter Hilton is a pastor rather than a speculative theologian. His higher education was in Canon Law rather than in Theology as such. But he is familiar with the commonplaces of technical theology, more specifically of a rather conservative Augustinian theology whose affinities have yet to be fully worked out, a task which can only be properly fulfilled as more of the Cambridge academic theology of his day is identified and studied. Beyond this, his contemplative interest leads him to become well grounded in monastic and especially Cistercian theology. It is within this framework that this Trinitarian theology needs to be viewed.

Hilton takes for granted the common teaching that man's soul is a created trinity, made in the image of God (cf. Gen. 1.26), in which the three faculties of *memoria*, reason (understanding), and love (or will) are a reflection of the Uncreated Trinity of Father, Son, and Holy Spirit,[1] to whom in Augustinian theology the characteristics of Power, Wisdom and Love (or Goodness) are respectively appropriated.[2] Through Adam's Fall, the 'likeness' of God (cf. Gen. 1.26) has

---

[1]   The common teaching on the image of the Trinity in man, derived from Augustine, is found in Peter Lombard, *Sententiae in IV Libros Distinctae*, Spicilegium Bonaventurianum 4–5 (Grottaferrata 1971, 1981), Liber 1, d. 3, cc. 2–3, (Vol. 1, Pars 2, pp. 71–76), with references to Augustine, *De Trinitate*.The trinity of *memoria, intelligentia, voluntas*, is described in *De Trinitate* 10.11.17 – 12.19. (In Augustine there are, of course, various 'trinities' in the human soul: M. Schmaus, *Die Psychologische Trinitätslehre des heiligen Augustinus* (Münster/Westfalen 1927), pp. 195–281).

Hilton repeats this in *Scale* 1, 43, Cambridge, University Library, MS Add. 6686 (= C), p. 314a; similarly in *Scale* 2, 31, London, British Library, MS Harley 6579 (= H), f. 106v. He uses 'reason' for the Augustinian 'intelligentia'. I am much indebted to the late Professor A. J. Bliss for advice on MS C, which is the base-text for his edition of *Scale* 1, to be completed by M. G. Sargent for EETS. For MS H, I have had the benefit of a gift of Stanley Hussey's edited transcript in 'An Edition . . . of Book II of Walter Hilton's *Scale of Perfection*' (London University Ph.D. dissertation, 1962), and have also worked directly from plates of the MS.

[2]   The theology of appropration is stated in e.g. Peter Lombard, *Sententiae* ed. cit. 1, d. 34 cc. 3–4, pp. 251–253, and is recalled in *Scale* 1, 43, MS C, p. 314a; cf. also *Scale* 2, 34, MS H, f. 112r taken up below.

been lost, and has to be recovered through receiving the effects of Christ's saving work.[3] In *Scale of Perfection, Book One*, Hilton sees the 'likeness' of God in Christ as expressed particularly in the virtues of humility an charity – love of God, and the others in God or for God; these virtues are both interdependent and 'inclusive' in the sense that they imply all the other Christian virtues.[4]

This being so, it is hardly surprising that the point of departure for the lofty teaching of *Scale of Perfection, Book Two*, where Hilton will go on to describe the progressive recovery of the 'likeness' of God in terms of a participation through grace in the Trinitarian life, should be once again the consideration of the nature and interdependence of humility and charity or desire for God. We shall see repeatedly that points made in *Scale 1*, are re-applied in the context of an even more profoundly intergrated Trinitarian spirituality.

It is from *Scale 2, 20* onwards that a more emphatically Christocentric and subsequently strongly Trinitarian emphasis appears.[5] Here an account of humility and desire for God is initiated, which goes far beyond what was written earlier in *Scale,1*. This is bound up with an understanding of the life of grace which lays the foundation for Hilton's subsequent exposition.

In *Scale 1*, Hilton takes it that the disposition of humility is the prerequisite for receiving the freely-given, infused virtue of charity. He even makes a distinction, in general terms, between 'imperfect' and 'perfect' humility and charity, and states that if one has imperfect humility – humility in the will but not in affection – one will have imperfect charity, but that if one has perfect humility one will have perfect charity.[6] In common with the *Cloud of Unknowing* – some of whose insights seem to be taken up in *Scale 2*[7] – Hilton echoes St Bernard's famous

[3] *Scale* 1, 43, MS C, pp. 314b–315a; *Scale* 2, 1, MS H, ff. 63r–v, with 2, 2, MS H, ff. 63v–65r.

[4] *Scale* 1, 51, MS C, p. 323b, with 1, 70, MS C, pp. 340b–342a; cf. 1, 18 MS C, p. 292a; 1, 62, MS C, p. 334a–b; 1, 77, MS C, p. 349b.

[5] Apart from combinations with 'oure Lord' or 'Crist', the name 'Ihesu' occurs four times by itself in *Scale* 2, 2; three times in *Scale* 2, 3; twice in *Scale* 2, 4; once in *Scale* 2, 10; in *Scale* 2, 20, it appears six times on its own; in *Scale* 2, 21, fifteen times on its own; in the rest of the book the Holy Name by itself appears very frequently, except in chapters 28, 29 and 31. In *Scale* 2, 42, it occurs thirty-three times by itself, and in *Scale* 2, 43, twenty-three times. The 'Christocentric' bias of *Scale* 2, 20 to the end is actually heightened in the contemporary Latin version by Thomas Fyslake, O. Carm.; see S. S. Hussey, 'Latin and English in the *Scale of Perfection*', *Mediaeval Studies* 35 (1973) pp. 469–470; J. P. H. Clark, 'English and Latin in *The Scale of Perfection*: Theological Considerations', *Analecta Cartusiana* 35: 1 (Salzburg 1982), pp. 205–212.

[6] If þou haue mekenes perfitely, þen schalt þou haue perfite charite, and þat is best: *Scale* 1, 68, MS C, p. 339a.

[7] J. P. H. Clark, 'Sources and theology in *the Cloud of Unknowing*', *Downside Review* 98 (1980), p. 109.

definition of humility: *Humilitas est virtus, qua homo verissima sui cognitione sibi ipse vilescit.*[8] 'He is meke þat sothfastly knowez and felez of hymself as he is.'[9]

In *Scale* 2, especially, Hilton's understanding of love of God presupposes the point of view found in St Bernard's *De Diligendo Deo* – a work with parts of which at any rate he seems to have been familiar.[10] True love of God is not without reward, but the reward itself lies in the possession of the Beloved. The Christian's reward is the possession of God, yet God is loved for himself and not simply as a recompense for labour undertaken. There is a loss of self-consciousness about one's deserts, yet this is far from any empty quietism. As Bernard writes, *Non enim sine praemio diligitur Deus, etsi absque praemii sit intuitu diligendus. Vacua namque vera caritas esse non potest, nec tamen mercenaria est: quippe NON QUAERIT QUAE SUA SUNT* (Cor. 13.5).[11]

But it is only possible for the possession of God to become a reward in so far as one dies to the false self, to that disordered *amor sui* which disfigures the image of God in the soul. The particular insight of *Scale* 2, 20 is that the radical death to the false self which is the very condition of attaining perfect love of God can only be received as a gift, as one is made aware of God in his immensity and love. This will lead to a reversal of the perspective of *Scale* 1, as Hilton sees that it is only through the unmerited gift of God's love that one can be made perfectly humble; there can be no question of 'acquiring' perfect humility.

Hilton points out that there are various acts through which, by grace, men may be led to conformity with God, according to their varying dispositions and situations; no single deed suffices. He insists that man cannot 'earn' the possesion of God as of right:

> he þat wil serue God wisely & come to þe þerfit luf of God, he schal coueite to haue none oþer mede bot him only. Bot þan for to haue hym may no creature deserue only bi his owne trauail . . . For he is soueren blis & eendeles godnes, & passeþ wiþ-oute comparisoun alle mennis desertes . . .[12]

Hilton holds a careful balance in insisting equally upon the gratuity of God's gift

---

[8] Bernard, *De Gradibus Humilitatis*, 1.2, *Opera*, ed. J. Leclercq et al., (Rome 1957 ff.), Vol. 3, p. 17. Recalled in *the Cloud of Unknowing*, ed. P. Hodgson, EETS (1944), Ch. 13, p. 40/8–9.
[9] *Scale* 1, 68, MS C, p. 339b.
[10] For instance, *Scale* 2, 40, MS H, f. 123v: grace losiþ þe heuy 3okke of fleschly luf fro þe soule . . ., recalling Bernard's treatment of the 'Grave . . . et importabile iugum super omnes filios Adam' (Ecclus. 40.1) in contrast to the spiritual liberty that accompanies Christ's easy yoke (*De Diligendo Deo* 13.36–14.37, *Opera* ed. J. Leclercq and H. M. Rochais (Rome 1963), Vol. 3, pp. 150–151); and earlier *De Imagine Peccati* in *Walter Hilton's Latin Writings*, edited by J. P. H. Clark and C. Taylor, *Analecta Cartusiana* 124 (Salzburg 1987), p. 78/91, with notes.
[11] Bernard, *De Diligendo Deo* 7.17 (*Opera*, Vol. 3, p. 133).
[12] *Scale* 2, 20, MS H, f. 83r.

of perfect love of himself, and upon the need for man to dispose himself to receive this unmerited gift.[13]

That contemplation is a gift of God which man may dispose himself to receive, but which remains a gift which God is in no way bound to bestow when man has done all in his power to receive it, is not a new idea. Some anticipation of this might be found in Richard of St Victor.[14] It was familar to the early Cistercians, including Gilbert of Holland,[15] to whom Hilton is indebted at so many points. But perhaps the closest parallel to Hilton's thought, as so often, is in William of St Thierry's *Epistola ad Fratres de Monte Dei*.[16]

Now Hilton takes up the definition of humility which he had given earlier in *Scale* 1 on the basis of St Bernard's words. But this time he relates it to that awareness of the life of grace which is to become so dominant a theme in the final part of *Scale* 2:

> He haþ not ful mekenes þat kan not felyn of hym-self soþfastly as he is, as þus: he þat doþ alle þe gode dedis þat he kan . . ., if he reste ay in hem & lene so mikel to hem & rewardeþ hem so gretly in his owne si3te þat he presumiþ of his owne desertes . . ., soþly as longe as he feliþ þus, he is not meke inow3 . . . Soþly, vntil a soule kan felablely þurw3 grace no3ten him-self, & baren him fro alle þe gode dedis þat he doþ, þurw3 behaldyng of soþfastnes of Ihesu, he is no3t perfitly meke.[17]

A humility that is based on the awareness of one's dependence on grace is dynamic, in that it makes one open to the work of grace:

> he þat þurw3 grace may see Ihesu, how þat he doþ al & him-self doþ ri3t no3t, bot suffreþ Ihesu wirken in him what him likiþ, he is meke . . . Soþly he þat haþ þis si3t schal neuer do þe lesse, bot he schal be stirid for to trauaile bodily & gostly mikel þe more & with þe better wil.[18]

In the following chapter Hilton distinguised explicitly between the two kinds of humility. The one is concerned in the first instance with one's own wretchedness; the second looks beyond the self to the greatness of God, as the sense of sinfulness is swallowed up in that of creaturely dependence:

> I mene not only of þat meknes þat a soule feliþ in þe si3t of his own syn or freltees . . . Bot I mene also þis meknes þat þe soule feliþ þurw3 grace,

---

[13] *Ibid.*, MS H, f 83r: he is free and gifiþ him-self where he wile & when he wil, neiþer for þis werk ne for þat . . . Nerþeles on þe toþer side I say also þat I hope he 3ifiþ it not, bot if a man wirke & trauaile al þat he kan and may . . .

[14] Richard of St Victor, *Benj. Min.* c. 73 PL 196.52; *Benj. Major* 5.4 PL 196.172–3.

[15] Gilbert of Holland, *In Cant.* 6.5 PL 184.41; 7.1 PL 184.43.

[16] William of St Thierry, *Epistola ad Fratres de Monte Dei (Lettre aux Frères du Mont Dieu)*, ed. J. M. Déchanet, Sources chrétiennes 223 (Paris 1975), c. 251, p. 344.

[17] *Scale* 2, 20, MS H, f. 83r–v.

[18] *Scale* 2, 20, MS H, f. 83v.

in si3t & beholdyng of þe endeles beynge & þe wundreful godnes of Ihesu
. . . For þurw3 si3t of his beynge, eiþer in ful feiþ or in felyng, þu scha[l]t
holden þi-self not only as þe most wrecche þat is, bot also as no3t in
substaunce of þi soule, þaw3 þu haddist neuer don syn.[19]

The distinction between imperfect and perfect humility matches exactly that
found in the *Cloud*.[20]

In the following chapters, Hilton describes the spiritual pilgrimage and the
purification that are necessary if one is to advance from the basic stage of 'reforming the faith' to the realisation of the life of grace, 'reforming in feeling'. He
then includes a careful account, using Pauline texts after the manner of Augustine, to explain how this 'reforming' takes place in the mind, *mens*, which is
properly the image of God.[21]

It is in *Scale* 2, 34, that Hilton's exposition becomes explicitly Trinitarian. He
takes up again the inter-relationship of knowledge and love in the search for God,
on which he had touched in *Scale* 1. In the earlier book he had said that the third
and highest degree of contemplation combines knowledge and love of God; his
words echo well-known teaching of Augustine.[22] But now he points out that there
has been (in *Scale* 2, 20 ff.) a call to seek only the love of God; how is this to be
harmonised with the doctrine that the knowledge of God is the soul's beatitude
and end?

The answer that he gives is finely balanced. He stands close to St Thomas as he
affirms that the vision of Jesus – that is, of God – is the full beatitude of the soul,
and that this is not only for the sake of the vision itself – considered, implicitly, as
an intellectual activity involving knowledge – but it is for the love that the
knowledge and vision of God is said to be the soul's principal beatitude, with love
attendant on this. Nevertheless, it is because one cannot come to this knowledge
or to the love that issues from it, without love, that Hilton has said that one
should seek only love.[23]

---

[19] *Scale* 2, 21, MS H, f. 85r–v.
[20] *Cloud*, ch. 13, pp. 40/8–41/6. this is a development from traditional teaching. Phyllis
Hodgson points to a possible affinity in Bernard, *Ep.* 393.3; a closer parallel is in Gilbert of
Holland, *In Cant.* 15.7 PL 184.78: *Infirmiores in vanitate sua humiliantur; perfectiores, in
veritate Dei.*
[21] *Scale* 2, 31, MS H, ff. 106r–v, citing Rom. 12.2; Col. 1.9; Eph. 4.23–24; Col. 3.9–10. For
related use of texts, cf. Augustine, *De Trinitate* 7.6.12; 12.7.12; 12.16.22 (C. Ch. Series
Latina, 50, pp. 265–7, 366–7, 451–4, citing Rom. 12.2; Col. 3.9–10; Eph. 4.23–24.
[22] *Scale* 1, 8, MS C, p. 282b: Thrid partie of comtemplacioun . . . lis boþe in cognicioun &
in affecioun; þat is forto sey, in knowyng & in perfite louyng of God. Cf. Augustine, *En. Ps.*
135.8: intellegimus sapientiam in cognitione et dilectione eius quod semper est, atque
incommutabiliter manet, quod Deus est. This passage was familiar to the Middle Ages,
being cited in Peter Lombard's discussion of the distinction between the Gifts of Wisdom
and of Knowledge (*Sententiae* 3, d.35, c. 1, n. 4 ed. cit., Vol. 2, p. 199).
[23] *Scale* 2, 34, MS H, f. 110v: Bot now wondrest þu, siþen þis knowynige of God is þe blis
& þe ende of a soule, whi þan haue I seid here bifore þat a soule schuld no3t elles coueite

From one point of view, one can once again find an antecedent in *Scale* 1. There, the second part of contemplation, intermediate between the initial stage of naked intellectual knowledge and the third stage which is properly contemplation, is said to consist principally in affection.[24] Nevertheless, Hilton goes beyond *Scale* 1, in what follows – in the careful distinction between Uncreated and created Love, and in the statement that it is God's gift of Himself, in the third Person of the Trinity, Uncreated Love, which enables man to come to the knowledge of God.

The heightened insistence that it is love which enables one to come to the knowledge of God at any rate poses the question whether Hilton may be responding to the *Cloud's* assertion that while God remains inaccessible to the intellect, he is fully accessible to love,[25] and whether he is adapting something of this within his own theological framework, while still refusing to set love against knowledge. If so, this would not be the only case where he adapts for his own purposes a perspective of the *Cloud's* author. The expression 'li3ty derknes', deriving from the writings of Pseudo-Dionysius, is found in the *Book of Privy Conselling*,[26] though not in the *Cloud* itself; Hilton uses the Dionysian expression in *Scale* 2 in a very un-Dionysian way.[27] But the suggestion should not be pressed too hard.

> þat lufe is not þe luf þat a soule haþ in it-self to God; bot þe luf þat oure Lorde haþ to a synful soule þat kan ri3t not lufen him is cause whi þis soule comiþ to þis knowynge & to þis lufe . . .[28]

In *Scale* 1 Hilton followed St Paul in recalling that the love of God is shed abroad in our hearts through the gift of the Holy Spirit.[29] Now, referring to the common distinction made by theologians between Uncreated and created Love, he points out (in line with the theology of appropriation deriving from Augustine) that God himself, and specifically the third Person of the Trinity, the Holy Spirit, is Uncre-

---

bot only þe luf of God. I spake no-þinge of þis si3t, þat a soule schuld coueit þis. Vnto þis I may say þus: þat þe si3t of Ihesu is ful blis of a soule, & þat is not only for þe si3t, bot it is also for þe blissed lyfe þat comiþ out of þat si3t. Nerþeles for lufe comiþ oute of knowynge & not knowynge oute of luf, þerfor it is seid þat in knowynge & in si3t principally of God with lufe is þe blis of a soule, & þe more he is knowen, þe better is he lufed. Bot for as mikel as to þis knowynge, or to þis luf þat comiþ of it, may not þe soule come with-oute luf, þerfore seide I þat þu schuldest only coueite luf.

[24] *Scale* 1, 5, MS C, p. 281a; principaly in affeccion.

[25] *Cloud*, Ch. 8, p. 33/11; cf. Ch. 6, p. 26/3–5.

[26] *Book of Priuy Counselling*, in *The Cloud*, ed. Hodgson, p. 154/17.

[27] *Scale* 2, 24, MS H, f. 90r: li3ty mirknes; 2, 25 and 2, 27, chapter-headings, MS H, f. 143r: li3tsom derknes; cf. J. P. H. Clark, 'The "Lightsome Darkness" – Aspects of Walter Hilton's Theological Background', *Downside Review* 95 (1977), pp. 106f. On the inter-relationship of *Scale* 1, *The Cloud*, and *Scale* 2, see further J. P. H. Clark, 'Sources and Theology', pp. 108–9.

[28] *Scale* 2, 34, MS H, f. 110v.

[29] *Scale* 1, 65, MS C, p. 336a, citing Rom. 5.5.

ated Love – *Deus dilectio est* (cf. John 4.8).[30] It is not created love which gives the soul the spiritual sight of Jesus, as if one could love God by one's own efforts, or deserve such a spiritual vision. Rather, it is the illumination given by the Holy Spirit, Uncreated Love, which discloses Christ in the life of grace, and so is the means of conferring that perfect humility which is no longer self-regarding. Thus at the higher level humility becomes no longer simply the disposition that is necessary in order to receive God's gift of love as it was in *Scale* 1, but it becomes the fruit of God's disclosure of himself in his love and grace.

In distinguising between Uncreated and created Love, Hilton appeals to 'holy wryters'. The distinction is indeed a common one, but on this point there was some difference of nuance between different writers. Augustine, accepting that we may in some sense participate in the life and love of God himself, took Rom. 5.5 to mean that the Holy Spirit does 'give' himself to us: *caritas . . . usque adeo donum Dei est, ut Deus dicatur.*[31] Passages in Augustine's *De Trinitate* make a like point.[32] Peter Lombard had boldly identified charity itself with the Holy Spirit,[33] but his view had been rejected, since it would have meant the annihilation of the human personality and of a freely given response to God. Hilton's words that 'þe gift of lufe is þe Holy Gost'[34] might, taken in isolation, seem to suggest Peter Lombard's doctrine, but his distinction between Uncreated and created Love obviates such a misunderstanding. He follows the line of development foreshadowed already in Bernard and William of St Thierry,[35] and developed by the scholastics, which distinguishes between the Uncreated Gift and our created participation in this, while seeing created charity as an intrinsic modification of the human personality.[36] Though there is no incongruity between the tradition represented by, say, St Bonaventure and St Thomas on this point, it is perhaps fair to point out, following Karl Rahner, that it is the *Summa Halensis* and St Bonaventure who in particular begin deliberately and firmly with the reality of *gratia increata* – just as St Paul – and St Augustine – begin with the fact that the Holy Spirit does in a real sense give 'himself' to us.[37]

Just so, for Hilton the fact of the Holy Spirit's giving 'himself' to us is the

---

[30] *Scale* 2, 34, MS H, ff. 110v–111r: Holy wryters seyn . . . þat þer is two maner of gostly lufe. On is called vnformed, an-oþer is callid formed. Lufe vnformed is God him-self, þe þridde Persoun in þe Trinite, þat is þe Holi Gost . . ., as Seynt Ion seiþ þus, *Deus dileccio est.*

[31] Augustine, *Ep.* 186.3.7 (CSEL 57, p. 50).

[32] Augustine, *De Trinitate* 15.17.31–18.32 (pp. 507–8), citing Rom. 5.5; *ibid.* 15.19.37 (pp. 513–4).

[33] Peter Lombard, *Sententiae* 1, d. 17, c. 1, nn. 1–4 (Vol. 1, pp. 141–3).

[34] *Scale* 2, 36, MS H, f. 115r.

[35] Bernard, *De Diligendo Deo* 12.35 (*Opera*, Vol. 3, p. 149); William of St Thierry, *Speculum Fidei* PL 180.395; *Aenigma Fidei* PL 180.399; *Expos. in Cant.* cap. 1, PL 180.506.

[36] Cf. St Bonaventure, *In Sent.* 2, d. 26, a un., q. 2, St Thomas, *ST* 1, q.38, a 1; 2–2 q. 23 a 2; a 3 ad 3; q. 24 a 2.

[37] Karl Rahner, 'Some Implications of the Scholastic Concept of Uncreated Grace', in *Theological Investigations*, Vol. 1 (ET London, 1961), pp. 324–5; 337–8.

primary consideration,a nd one which emphasises the priority and gratuity of God's gift.

> Lufe formed is þe affeccioun of þe soule, made bi þe Holy Gost of þe si3t & þe knowynge of soþfastnes, þat is God only . . . Now may þu see þat lufe formed is not cause whi a soule comiþ to þe gostly si3t of Ihesu, as summe men wolde þenken þat þei wolde luf God so brennandely as it were bi þeire owne mi3t, þat þei were worþi for to haue þe gostly knowynge of him . . . Bot luf vnformed, þat is God him-self, is cause of al þis knowynge . . . Bi-cause þat he lufiþ vs so mikel, þerfore he gifiþ vs his lufe, þat is þe Holi Gost. He is boþ þe gifer & þe gifte,[38] & makiþ vs þan bi þat gifte for to knowen & lufen him . . . For soþly a lesse þinge or a lesse gifte þan he is may not auailen vs for to bryngen vs to þe blissed si3t of Ihesu.
>
> And þerfore schul we fully desiren & asken of Ihesu only þis gift of lufe, þat he wulde for þe mikelnes of his blissed luf touchen oure hertes with his vnseable li3t to þe knowynge of hym, & departen with vs of his blissed luf, þat as he lufiþ vs, þat we mi3ten loue him ageyn . . . Nos diligamus Deum, quoniam ipse prior dilexit nos (Cf. 1 John 4.19) . . .[39]

God progressively reveals himself in his prevenient love. He loved us much in creating us in his likeness; he loved us more in the costliness of our redemption; but his greatest act of love is in the gift of the Holy Spirit, by which we know and love him, and are assured that we are his sons chosen to salvation.[40]

In redeeming us – and here Hilton must be referring to God's general gift to all mankind – God gave himself in the humanity of Christ; but the gift of himself to our souls for our salvation – and here the reference must be to sanctifying grace – is an even higher gift; it is God's supreme gift of love, for, Hilton repeats emphatically, it is God's gift of *himself*.[41]

Following the theology of appropriation, Hilton recalls that the creation of a soul is appropriated to the Father as Power (*potentia*); redemption is appropriated to the Son as Wisdom (*sapientia*), and the justification of the soul through the

---

[38] For orientation, with reference to the roots of this doctrine in Augustine, *De Trinitate*, 15.19.36, see Peter Lombard, *Sententiae*, 1, d. 18, c. 2, n. 2 (Vol. 1, Pars 2, p. 153).

[39] *Scale* 2, 34, MS H, f. 111r–v.

[40] *Scale* 2, 34, MS H, f. 111v: He loued vs mikel whan he made vs to his liknes, bot he loued vs more when he bo3t vs with his precious blode . . .: bot he lufiþ vs most when he gifiþ vs þe gifte of þe Holy Gost, þat is luf, bi þe whilk we knowen him & louen him, & are made siker þat we are his sones chosen to saluacioun.

[41] *Scale* 2, 34, MS H, ff. 111v–112r: þerfore þe most token of lufe schewd to vs, as me þinkiþ, is þis: þat he gifiþ him-self in his godhed to oure soules. He gaf him-self first in his manhede to vs for oure raunsoun . . . þis was a faire gift, & a grete tokne of lufe. Bot when he gifiþ him-self in his godhed gostly to oure soules for oure saluacioun, & makiþ vs for to knowe him & lufe him, þan lufiþ he vs fully . . . And for þis skil it is seide þat þe ri3tynge of a synful soule pur3 forgifnes of synnes is arettid and apropred principally to þe wirkynge of þe Holy Gost; for þe Holy Gost is luf . . .

application to it of Christ's work is appropriated to the Holy Spirit as Love (*amor*, *dilectio*). Creation is common to all human beings, and to irrational creatures as well. Redemption is common to all human beings – that is, it is a possibility for all. But it is the application of redemption to the elect which is a special gift, and is the work of the Holy Spirit, who is Love.[42] There is an extension here of St Augustine's observation that while the Trinity of Father, Son and Holy Spirit is substantial charity (*caritas*), there is a particular sense in which charity may be referred to the Holy Spirit.[43]

Anticipating what he will develop later, Hilton refuses to make any division in the life of grace; the realisation for oneself of adoption in Christ is the further development of the supernatural life which begins with justification. God's love, or grace – Hilton uses the terms interchangeably – is prevenient, so that the assent which the soul makes to God is an assent which he enables the soul to make. The experiential awareness of the life of grace is a further development, a disclosure of what had at first been imperceptible:

> þis luf vnformed, when it is gifen to vs, it wirkiþ in oure soule at þat good is . . . þis lufe lufiþ vs er þat we lufe him, for it clensiþ vs first of oure synnes . . . it stiriþ vs also for to forsaken þe luf & þe likynge of þe werld . . . We don ri3t no3t bot suffren him & assentyn to him . . . And 3it is þat wil not of vs, bot of his makynge,[44] so þat me þinkiþ þat he doþ in vs al þat is wel don, & 3it we seen it not. And not only doþ he þus, bot aftir þis lufe doþ more. For he opneþ þe ei3e of þe soule & schewiþ to þe si3t of Ihesu wundirfully . . ., how þat he is al & þat he wirkiþ al, & þat alle gode dedis þat are done & gode þou3tes arn only of him.[45]

The indwelling of Christ in the soul of the just is a familiar theme, for which a theological basis can be found in Ephesians 3.17, and especially in Augustine.[46]

---

[42] *Ibid.*, MS H, f. 112r: þe makynge of a soule is apropred to þe Fader, as for þe souereyn mi3t & power þat he schewiþ in makynge of it. þe byenge is aretted & apropred to þe Sone, as for þe souereyn wit & wisdom þat he schewyd in his manhed . . . Bot þe ri3tynge & þe ful sauynge of a soule bi forgifnes of synnes is apropred to þe pridde Persone, þat is þe Holy Gost. For þer-in schewiþ Ihesu most lufe vnto mannes soule . . . His makynge is comune to vs and to all vnresonable creatures . . . Also þe byenge is comune to vs & to alle resonable soules . . . Bot þe ri3tynge and þe halowynge of oure soules pur3 þe gift of þe Holy Gost, þat is only þe wirkynge of lufe; & þat is not comune, bot it is a special gifte only to chosen soules . . .

[43] Augustine, *De Trinitate* 15.17.29 (pp. 503–4).

[44] For orientation, see e.g. Peter Lombard, *Sententiae*, 2, d. 26, c. 2 (pp. 471–2); d. 27, c. 4 (p. 483) – with references to Augustine.

[45] *Scale* 2, MS H, f. 112r–v.

[46] E.g. Augustine, *De Trinitate* 4.20.27, cited by Peter Lombard, *Sententiae*, 1, d. 15, c. 8, n. 1 (p. 136). Augustine, *De Trinitate* 15.18.32 (p. 508) refers to the indwelling of the Trinity as such in the souls of the just; cf. Peter Lombard, *Sent.* 1, d. 17, c. 4, n. 2, (p. 145).

This is explicitly developed in the exposition of the Psalm *Qui Habitat*, a work which is closely related to *Scale* 2, and which may very well be Hilton's.[47]

It will be noticed that in the careful Trinitarian theology of *Scale* 2, 34, it is the Holy Spirit who discloses Christ. This is an emphasis that will be repeated later.[48]

Hilton has already recalled the common doctrine of the co-inherence of the Person of the Trinity, referring to 'Ihesu, in whome is alle þe blissid Trinite'.[49] Since the operation of the Persons of the Trinity is inseparable *ad extra*,[50] Hilton can speak equally of the operation of 'Jesus' as the Love which renews man to God's likeness and opens the way to spontaneous conformity to God's will.[51]

It is God's gift of his love and grace that Hilton sees in *Scale* 2, as making the casual link between contemplation, considered as 'reforming in feeling', the awareness of the life of grace, and the full development of charity and of all the other virtues which are implied in charity. The recognition that the gift of God's love is utterly unmerited casts one entirely upon the grace of God, so opening the way to the working of grace in what St Thomas knows as its 'operant' mode, where all is perceived as God's work, in distinction from the 'co-operant' mode, where there is consciousness of the deliberate conjunction of the human will with grace.[52] Once again, Hilton here marches closely with the *Cloud*, which sees 'operant' grace as ensuring that God directly governs the will in spontaneous conformity to himself.[53]

Hilton contrasts the receptiveness and spontaneity of the comtemplative with the self-conscious and laboured efforts of those who try deliberately to feel quasi-physical fervour. In doing so, he cites well-known words of St Paul on the Christian life as one of docility to the Spirit:

> a soule þat haþ þe gift of lufe þurȝ gracious beholdynge of Ihesu as I mene, or elles if he hafe it not ȝit bot wolde haue it, he is not bisy for-to streyne him-self ouer his miȝt as it were bi bodily strengþe for to han it bi bodily feruours & so for to felen of þe lufe of God . . . He seeþ wel þat

---

[47] An *Exposition of Qui Habitat and Bonum Est in English*, ed. B. Wallner, Lund Studies in English, 23 (Lund 1945), pp. 32/1–3; 37/12–13. On Hilton's probable authorship of this work, see J. P. H. Clark, 'Walter Hilton and the Psalm Commentary *Qui Habitat*', *Downside Review* 100 (1982), pp. 235–62.

[48] *Scale* 2, 37, MS H, f. 117r: þe Holy Gost liȝteneþ þe reasoun in-to þe siȝt of soþfastnes, how Ihesu is al & þat he doþ al; 2, 40, MS H, f. 124r: þis stilnes makiþ þe inspiracioun of þe Holy Gost in beholdynge of Ihesu.

[49] *Scale* 2, 32, MS H, f. 108v.

[50] For orientation see Schmaus, *Die Psychologische Trinitätslehre* . . ., pp. 151 ff., with references to other writings of Augustine as well as to *De Trinitate*.

[51] *Scale* 2, 34, MS H, f. 113r: þis luf is not elles bot Ihesu him-self, þat for lufe wirkiþ al þis in a mannes soule, & reformiþ it in felynge to his liknes . . ., þis luf bryngiþ in-to þe soule þe fulhed of alle vertues, & makiþ hem alle clene and trewe, soft and esy . . .

[52] St Thomas, *ST* 1–2 q. 111 a. 2.

[53] *Cloud.* ch. 34, pp. 70/12–71/1; cf. also *Book of Privy Counselling*, in *Cloud*, p. 164/4–6.

Ihesu is al & doþ al, & þerfor askiþ he no3t elles bot þe gifte of his lufe
. . .

þan is luf maister, & wirkiþ in þe soule, and makiþ it for to forgetyn it-self
& for to seen & beholden only how luf doþ. And þan is þe soule more
suffrande þan doande, & þat is clene lufe. þus Seint Poul mened when he
seide þus, *Quicumque Spiritu Dei aguntur, hii filii Dei sunt* (Rom. 8.14).[54]

This teaching in *Scale* 2, is closely matched in the Psalm commentary *Qui Habitat*.
Expounding Ps. 90.5, *Scuto circumdabit te veritas eius* – a text which Hilton will
take up in *Scale* 2, in a closely related manner – *Qui Habitat* explains that it is the
'shield' (*scutum*) of Christ's divinity, over and above the 'shadow' of his humanity,
which affords protection against spiritual enemies to the humble soul supernatu-
rally raised to the grace of contemplation.[55] This is expressed in terms that recall
St Bernard's teaching on the passage from the 'carnal' to the 'spiritual' love of God
in Christ – teaching which had become a commonplace of monastic spirituality,
but to which Hilton explicitly refers in *Scale* 1, and with which he shows his
familiarity elsewhere.[56] *Qui Habitat* goes on to describe a spontaneity in God's
service which matches that found in *Scale* 2, and is expressed in closely similar
terms:

He þat dispisiþ him-self as he haþ ben & as he is of Him-self soþfastliche,
& . . . fulliche hopeþ in me, . . . I schal dilyueren him from his enemyes, I
schal departe with him þe 3iftes of þe holi gost, and I schal maken him fre
& willi for-to loue me.[57]

In this passage, '3iftes' appears as plural in all extant manuscripts. But this is the
only passage in *Qui Habitat*, or in *Scale* 2, where this is so. In fact, the commentary
will go on to refer to the 'gift' (singular) of the Holy Spirit, just as *Scale* 2, does.
Qui Habitat describes how, as the meaning of the name of Jesus, who is both God
and man, is realised, so the *potentia, sapientia, amor* of the Trinity are reflected in
the soul's spontaneous conformity to God's will through the gift of the Holy
Spirit:

[54] *Scale* 2, 35, MS H, ff. 113v–114r.
[55] *An Exposition of Qui Habitat*, pp. 14/1–15/1. Cf. *Scale* 2, 37, MS H, f. 118r: þen forsakiþ
he vtterly him-self & vndirkestiþ him holly to Ihesu. & þan is he in a siker warde, for þe
schelde of soþfastnes . . . kepiþ him so wel þat he schal not ben hirt þurgh no stirynge of
pride, as longe as he beholdiþ him with-inne þat scheld, as þe prophet seiþ, *Scuto circumdabit
te veritas eius; non timebis a timore nocturno.*
[56] *Scale* 1, 35, MS C, p. 306b. St Bernard's teaching on this point is found especially in his
In Cant. 20.2.3–5.9 (*Opera*, Vol. 1, pp. 115–121). Cf. further *Walter Hilton's Latin Writings*,
p. 404, notes on *Ep. de Leccione*, 182 ff.
[57] *Qui Habitat*, p. 43/10–15.

... I schal make him mihti a3eynes alle synnes. And I schal make him wys in siht of so þfastnes. And I schal 3iuen him þe 3ift of loue, þat is, þe holi gost.[58]

It would be tempting to see in *Scale 2*, – and in *Qui Habitat* – a direct echo of the teaching of St Thomas concerning the gifts of the Holy Spirit: *secundum ea homo disponitur ut efficiatur prompte mobilis ab inspiratione divina*; in this very context St Thomas cites Rom. 8.14, the text used so emphatically by Hilton in *Scale* 2, 34.[59] But we should not locate Hilton precisely within the close-knit patterns which Neo-Thomist theologians have constructed on the basis of St Thomas' teaching, although Hilton's account of contemplation as a 'lifely felynge of grace'[60] is at any rate congruous with St Thomas' account of the Gift of Wisdom as giving an actual experience of divine things,[61] just as his description of the contemplative's insight into the spiritual meaning of Scripture could be matched with St Thomas' account of the Gift of Understanding.[62] In fact, Hilton's account of contemplation as an awareness of the life of grace can be matched in William of St Thierry.[63] And his subsequent statement of how docility to the Spirit, with the perfection of humility and charity, strikes down the capital sins at their root, has affinities not only with another strand of the early Cistercian tradition – as will be illustrated – but with a deeply-rooted element on the mediaeval teaching on the Gifts of the Holy Spirit, emerging in St Bonaventure and also in the well-known *Somme le Roy* (of which numerous Middle English versions exist), which sees the seven Gifts of the Holy Spirit as effective against the seven capital sins to which they are respectively opposed.[64]

For that matter St Thomas is himself in line here with the same twelfth-century monastic theology that nourished Hilton. St Bernard recalls Rom. 8.14 in a passage of *De Diligendo Deo*, referring to the liberty of spirit of the sons of God under Christ's easy yoke, which finds many echoes in Hilton, not least in the final

---

[58] *Ibid.*, p. 45/12–15.

[59] St Thomas, ST, 1–2 q. 68 a 1; Rom. 8.14 is cited *Ibid.* a 2.

[60] *Scale* 2, 40, MS H, f. 126r.

[61] St Thomas, ST 2–2 q. 45 a 2.

[62] *Scale* 2, 43, MS H, ff. 133r–136r. Hilton cites Luke 24.45 (f. 133v), as St Thomas does (ST 2–2 q. 8 a 2). But one can hardly plead specific dependence on St Thomas for such use of this verse.

[63] Cf. William of St Thierry, *Ep. ad Fratres de Monte Dei*, c. 298, p. 382: in ipso lumine veritatis undubitanter videt praevenientem gratiam.

[64] See below, pp. 138–9.

Cf. St Bonaventure, *In Sent*. 3, d. 34, p. 1 a 2 q. 1.

The teaching of the *Somme le Roy* may be found in *The Book of Vices and Virtues*, ed. W. N. Francis, EETS OS 217 (1942) p. 125. On the Middle English versions of the *Somme le roy*, see A. Barratt, 'Works of Religious Instruction', in *Middle English Prose*, ed. A. S. G. Edwards (New Brunswick 1984) pp. 416–7.

chapters of *Scale* 2.[65] The same text is also alluded to in a passage of William of St Thierry, *Epistola ad Fratres de Monte Dei*, which distinguishes 'perfect' from 'animal' and 'rational' souls.[66]

While allowing that God may grant the same heavenly reward to those who love and serve him by deliberate effort under the common grace, as to those 'perfect lovers' who receive the special grace of which he has spoken, Hilton affirms that is the 'special', operant grace, which for the duration of the experience ensures conformity to the will of God:

> in vnperfit lufers of God, luf wirkiþ al ferly bi þe affeccions of man; bote in perfit lufers lufe wirkiþ nerly bi his owne gostly affecciouns, & sleþ in a soule for þe tyme al oþer affecciouns . . .[67]

The reader should desire only the gift of God's love, that is, the Holy Spirit, who is both Giver and Gift. Again deepening a point made in *Scale* 1, Hilton contrasts this gift with the *gratiae gratis datae* of prophecy, working of miracles, knowledge, counsel, or fasting and penance; a condemned soul might have the latter as well as an elect soul.[68] It is the gift of God's love – the gift which is the Holy Spirit – which distinguishes between the elect and the condemned.[69] This gift enables one to love oneself and all one's fellow-Christians 'in God', thus effecting a union of the soul and of all those creatures who share in God's beatitude.[70]

Hilton stands close to Augustine's exposition of Ps. 45.11, *Vacate, et videte quoniam ego sum Deus* as he describes on the basis of this text how all the contemplative's good deeds are God's gift, and God's work in the soul that is prepared to still its own efforts and allow him to work in it.[71] He recalls something

---

[65] St Bernard, *De Diligendo Deo* 13.36 (*Opera*, Vol. 3, p. 151).
[66] William of St Thierry, *Epistola ad Fratres de Monte Dei* c. 43, p. 178.
[67] *Scale* 2, 35, MS H, f. 114v.
[68] *Scale* 2, 36, MS H, ff. 114v–115r: Aske þou þan of God no-þinge bot þis gifte of lufe, þat is þe Holy Gost . . . For þer is no gifte of God þat is boþ þe gifer & þe gifte, bot þis gift of luf . . . þe gifte of prophecie, þe gifte of miracles-wirkynge, þe gifte of grete knowynge & counseilynge, & þe gifte of grete fastynge or of grete penaunce-doynge, or ony oþer swilk, are grete giftes of þe Holy Gost: bot þei arne not þe Holy Goste, for a reproued & a damonable miȝt han alle þose giftes as wel as a chosen soule.
Scale 1, 47, MS C, p. 320a prefers desire for Christ to all the *gratiae gratis datae*, but does not refer to the gift of God's Uncreated Love as *Scale* 2 does: Sothly I hade leuere fele and haue a sothfast desyre and a clene longyng in my hert to my Lord Ihesu . . ., þen forto haue withouten þis desire al bodily penaunce of all men lyuand, all visiouns of aungels apperand, songes and sounes, sauours or smelles . . .
[69] *Scale* 2, 36, MS H, f. 115r: þis is þe gifte of lufe þat makiþ schedynge atwix chosen soules & reprefed: recalling Augustine, *De Trinitate* 15.18.32 (p. 507).
[70] *Scale* 2, 36, MS H, f. 115f: þis gifte makiþ ful pees atwix God & a soule, & oniþ alle blissed creatures holly in God. For it makiþ Ihesu for-to lufen vs. & vs him also, and ilke of vs for-to lufe oþer in him.
[71] *Scale* 2, 36, MS H, f. 115r–v: Vacate, et videte quoniam ego sum Deus . . . þat is, ȝe þat are reformed in felynge & han ȝour inner iȝe opned in-to siȝt of gostly þinges, cese ȝe

of the distinction that he made in *Scale* 1, between 'virtue in reason' and 'virtue in affection' – a distinction that finds a close parallel, once more, in William of St Thierry's *Epistola ad Fratres de Monte Dei* – as he contrasts the ease in the practice of virtue that comes with God's gift of love, the gift of the Holy Spirit, with the laboured efforts of those who work by the common grace and, like wrestlers, sometimes have the upper hand and sometimes are beneath. The loss of self-consciousness in the striving for virtue which Hilton describes is far from any empty quietism. A soul that has the spiritual vision of Jesus – as he is revealed in the life of grace – does not worry about striving for virtues, but sets his gaze on Jesus, who then becomes master in the soul and fights for it against all sins.[72]

Still the parallel with William of St Thierry remains close. Just so, in the *Epistola ad Fratres de Monte Dei*, William had described how, as the *imago Dei* is restored to the *similitudo Dei*, the practice of virtue becomes no longer a toil but spontaneous as *unitas spiritus* with God is realised.[73]

'Spiritual liberty' is a theme found in other twelfth-century Cistercians. There are suggestions of similar doctrine in some of Gilbert of Holland's sermons on the Song of Songs.[74] Hilton does not echo these particular passages, though his statement that through the awareness of grace:

> þus sleeþ lufe generally alle synnes in a soule, & reformiþ it in new
> felynge *of* vertues[75]

finds a close parallel in words of Gilbert of Holland on the dynamic force of the fire of love, the fire sent into the earth (cf. Luke 12.49) of the human heart.[76]

Hilton recapitulates the distinction that he has made earlier between imperfect and perfect humility. The first, bound up with the sense of one's own sinfulness, is due to the working of reason; perfect humility, in which the perception of Jesus in

---

sum-tyme of outwars wirkynge, & see þat I am God; þat is, seeþ only how I Ihesu, God, & man, do; beholde ȝe me, for I do al. I am lufe, & for lufe I do al þat do, & ȝe do noȝt . . ., for þer is no gode dede done in ȝowe ne gode þouȝte felt in ȝow, but if it be done þurȝ me . . ., Cf. Augustine, *En. Ps.* 70.1.18 (C. Chr. 39, p. 955).

72 *Scale* 2, 35, MS H, f. 116r: Oþer men þat stondiþ in þe commine wey of charite, & are not ȝit so fer forþ in grace, bot wirken vnder þe biddynge of resoun, þei strifen & feiȝten al-day ageyn synnes for þe getynge of vertues; & sumtyme þei ben aboue & sumtyme bineþ, as wrestellers arne. þose men don ful wel; þei han vertues in resoun & in wil, not in sauour ne in lufe . . .
Bot a soule þat haþ þe gostly siȝt of Ihesu takiþ no grete kepe of strifynge for vertues. he is not bisy aboute hem specially, bot he settiþ al his bisynes for to kepe þat siȝt and þat biholdynge of Ihesu þat hit haþ . . . And whan it doþ þus, þan is Ihesu soþfastly maister in þe soule . . .
For virtue in reason and in affection, cf. *Scale* 1, 14, MS C, pp. 287b–88a. An antecedent may be found in William of St Thierry, *Ep. ad Fratres de Monte Dei*, c. 43, p. 178.
73 William of St Thierry, *Ep. ad Fratres de Monte Dei*, c. 276, pp. 364–6; c. 286, pp. 372–4.
74 Gilbert of Holland, *In Cant.* 13.3; 39.4–5 (PL 184.65; 205–6).
75 *Scale* 2, 36, MS H, f. 116r.
76 Gilbert of Holland, *In Cant.* 15.5 (PL 184, 77).

his love and grace, and in his infinite being – *Et substantia mea tanquam nichilum ante te* (Ps. 38.6) – is the fruit of the special gift of God's love, and makes one forgetful of one's demerits or merits.[77] Such 'perfect' humility also enables one to love one's fellow-Christians equally 'in God', without passing judgement on them, so fulfilling what has been enjoined in *Scale* 1.[78] Through the gift of perfect humility – a gift which is due to the operation of the Holy Spirit, who is himself the Gift of Love – the root sin of pride is struck down, in varying degrees according to the recipient's stage of progress. In place of pride, humility is given. But the gift of perfect humility is dependent on god's gift of perfect love:

> þus is þe soule made meke . . . bi þe wirkyng of þe Holy Gost, þat is þe
> gifte of luf; for he opneþ i3e of þe soule for to seen & lufen Ihesu . . . & he
> sleeþ alle þe stirynges of pride . . . he þat lest haþ on þis maner . . ., soþly
> he haþe þe gifte of perfit meknes, for he haþe þe gifte of perfite lufe.[79]

From this point Hilton goes on to describe how 'Love' – by which he implies God's gift of Uncreated Love, the Holy Spirit – destroys the remaining capital sins and makes the practice of the coresponding virtues spontaneous.[80]

When Hilton goes on to describe the character of contemplation in its various facets, the Trinitarian pattern which has emerged so strongly persists as an under-current, emerging in such passages as:

> þus feliþ þe soule þanne *with* ful meek sikernes & grete gostly gladnes,
> & it conceifiþ a ful grete boldnes of saluacioun bi þis acorde-makynge,
> for it heriþ a pryuey witnesynge in conscience of þe Holy Gost þat he is
> a chosen sone to heuenly heritage. þus seint Poul seiþ, *Ipse Spiritus testi-*
> *monium perhibet spiritui nostro quod filii Dei sumus* (Rom. 8.16)[81]

– once again in line with the passage in St Bernard's *De Diligendo Deo* on liberty of spirit to which reference has already been made.[82]

Hilton repeats a catena of familair commonplace terms for contemplation, in

---

[77] *Scale* 2, 37, ff. 116v–117r: . . . þe first is inperfit; þat oþer is perfite. þe first meknes a man feliþ of beholdynge of his owne synnes & of his owne wrecchednes . . .
Perfit meknes a soule feliþ of þe si3t & þe gostly knowynge of Ihesu. For whan þe Holy Gost li3teneþ þe resoun in-to þe si3t of soþfastnes, how Ihesu is al & þat he doþ al, þe soule . . . forgetiþ it-self & fully leneþ to Ihesu *with* al þe lufe þat it haþ forto beholden him; it takiþ no kepe of vnworþines of it-self, ne of synnes bifore done, bot settiþ at no3t it-self *with* al þe synnes & alle þe gode dedis þat euer it did, as if þer ware no-þinge bot Ihesu. þus meke Dauid was whan he seid þus: *Et substancia mea tanquam nichilum ante te.* (Ps. 38.6).
[78] *Ibid.*, f. 117r: Also anentes his euen-Cristen he haþ no rewarde to hem, ne demynge of hem wheþer þei ben better or wers þan him-self is. Cf. *Scale* 1, 16, MS C, p. 290b, recalling the words of Abbot Pastor to Abbot Joseph in *Vitae Patrum* 5.9.5. (PL 73.910).
[79] *Scale* 2, 37, MS H, f. 118v.
[80] *Scale* 2, 38–9 passim.
[81] *Scale* 2, 40, MS H, f. 124v.
[82] Bernard, *De Diligendo Deo* 13.36 (*Opera*, Vol. 3, p. 151).

order to convey the many-sidedness of the experience and the inadequacy of any single term to convey what is strictly indescribable. Among these terms it is the 'lifely felynge of grace'[83] in particular which sums up those aspects of the contemplative experience which we have examined – the realised awareness of adoption in Christ, and of participation through grace in the life of the Trinity. Hilton refers to this as an awareness of 'þe presence of oure Lord Ihesu'.[84] Because the three Persons of the Trinity co-inhere, he can speak simply of 'Jesus' where before he has distinguished between 'Jesus' and the Holy Spirit. Subsequently he writes:

> Bot per-chaunce þou bigynnist to wundre whi I sey o tyme þat grace wirkiþ al þis, & an-oþer tyme I sey þat loue wirkiþ or Ihesu wirkiþ or God wirkiþ. Vnto þis I sey þus, þat whan I sey þat grace wirkiþ, I mene lufe, Ihesu & God; for al is on, & not bot on. Ihesu is lufe, Ihesu is grace, Ihesu is God; & for he wirkiþ al in vs bi his grace for lufe as god, þerfore may I vsen what worde of þese foure þat me list . . .[85]

At the conclusion of *Scale 2*, where he is referring to the possibility of intellectual visions of heavenly realities, Hilton says that the contemplative may be granted insight into the unity of substance and distinction of Persons in the Trinity, in accordance with the teaching of the Church's doctors.[86]

So there is the possibility of the verification of the Church's faith in the Holy Trinity. But Hilton is not in the first instance concerned with the verification of abstract metaphysical principles. Rather, he indicates that it is as conformity to God's will is attained that what is received from the Church through faith becomes an experienced reality, as the image of God in man, the *trinitas creata*, is renewed in his likeness, and faith is illuminated into 'feeling' and 'understanding'

> þe whilk vndirstondyng, þat I calle þe si3t of God if it be gracious a soule may not haue bot þorw3 grete clennes, as oure Lord saiþ, *Beati mundo corde, quoniam ipsi Deum videbunt* (Matt. 5.8) . . .; þat is, þei schul see God not with þeire fleschly hi3e, bot with þe innere hi3e, þat is vndirstondyng, clensid & illumined þurw grace of þe Holy Gost . . .[87]

Hilton's Trinitarian theology remains firmly in line with the wisdom of the monastic tradition – and of Augustine; and it is inseparable from his theology of grace.

---

[83] *Scale* 2, 40, MS H, f. 123v; cf. f. 126r.

[84] *Scale* 2, 40, MS H, f. 126r.

[85] *Scale* 2, 42, MS H, ff. 132v–133r.

[86] *Scale* 2, 46, MS H, f. 139r–v: þan is it opned soþfastly to þe ei3e of þe soule þe onhed in substance & distinccioun of Persons in þe blissid Trinitee, as it may be seen here, & mikil oþer soþfastnes of þis blissid Trinite pertinente to þis matere, þe whilk is openly declared & schewde bi writynge of holy doctours of Holy Kirk.

[87] *Scale* 2, 11, MS H, f. 73v. On faith and understanding in Hilton, see J. P. H. Clark, 'Augustine, Anselm and Walter Hilton', in *The Medieval Mystical Tradition in England – Dartington 1982*, ed. M. Glasscoe (Exeter 1982) pp. 102–26.

Time of Passion: Latent Relationships between Liturgy and Meditation in two Middle English Mystics

Marion Glasscoe

A study of meditations on the Passion in the vernacular designed to help those with little formal education in theology, whether lay or religious, to further their spiritual lives, points to a creative continuum between these and the liturgy of the Church – in particular that simplified form of the daily Office contained in the Hours of the Virgin and available in Prymers in the fourteenth and fifteenth centuries.[1] An awareness of this both enriches a reading of the meditations for a modern reader and sharpens their definition in a cultural context.

There is a natural affinity between liturgy and these meditations; both aim to mediate the truths of doctrine in a particular experiential way, and understanding of the significance of the Passion is at the heart of both. It is fundamental to the forms of the Church's worship both in the Mass and the daily Office throughout the year. Between them they enact and order for believers their common sense of how an ultimate reality engages with the processes of time: in the Mass, by a corporate sense of all life being a divine gift sustained in time by processes of death and resurrection; in the Office by a daily pattern of worship, which commemorates the Incarnation in the yearly cycle of time and links the activities of the Church in time present with the Saints. The complex, variable pattern of prayers, hymns, readings, versicles, responses, etc. enables a process in which private faith is projected into a communal experience and assumes a particular kind of ritualized existential quality. Underlying the whole structure of the Office, the complex traditions which rationalized the fixing of the Canonical Hours by the thirteenth century ensured a daily reminder of the events of the Passion counterpointed to the realities of the Resurrection, Ascension, Pentecost and the acts of the apostles. For behind the Hours of Lauds and Matins, Prime, Tierce, Sext, None, Vespers, Compline, that governed the daily structure of the life of religious,

---

[1] For a study of the way in which the Prymer acted as 'convenient quarry' for authors of Middle English Passion Lyrics, see A. Barrett, 'The Prymer and English Passion Lyrics', *Medium Aevum*, 44 (1975), 264–79.

lay a long accretion of teaching which found varied justification for these hours of prayer in both Old and New Testament. Allowing for some variations in the accounts, a general pattern emerged in which the hours were connected with the events of the Passion as follows: the betrayal of Christ at Matins, trial before Pilate and false accusation at Prime, crowning with thorns and condemnations to death at Tierce, the crucifixion at Sext, Christ's death at None, the deposition at Evensong and entombment at Compline.[2]

The whole life of the liturgy depends on balancing the discipline of habit with spontaneous renewal. It offers structures which interpret the meanings of the basic story of the faith it is designed to illuminate, and within which people can identify at various levels that interplay of faith and understanding that is called belief. Margery Kempe for instance, witnesses to the way in which visual icons of the Easter ceremonies activated her vibrant sense of the reality of the Incarnation. When she saw the priests kneel in the darkness, lit only by burning torches, to place the crucifix and host in the Easter sepulchre to symbolize the darkness of the physical death and burial of Christ prior to the joy of resurrection on Easter Day, the ritual precipitated in Margery an inner sense of the reality of the Passion and a corresponding outpouring of love and compassion in tears, as she spread her arms like her crucified lord.[3]

Not only was the organization of the Latin Office tied to a daily memorial of the Passion and its ultimate significance, by the fourteenth century there existed for the use of laity, or the uneducated religious, Prymers which contained less complex devotional structures for the Hours, and these were translated into the vernacular by the second half of the fourteenth century. The order of service in the Prymers had developed from monastic devotions added to the main Office from the eighth century onwards to remember the dead (the Office for the Dead) and to celebrate understanding of the role of the Virgin Mary in the operation of the faith – the Hours of the Virgin. These offices were generally adopted by the secular clergy and lent themselves to the purposes of lay piety particularly, because the Office for these Hours remained constant throughout the liturgical year and was not subject to the complex variations of the main Office.[4]

---

[2] For a full account of the development of the traditions and documentation of their sources see: Sister Mary Philomena, 'St Edmund of Abingdon's Meditations before the Canonical Hours', *Ephemerides Liturgicae*, 78 (1964), 33–57.

[3] 'whech syght & gostly beheldyng wrowt be grace so feruently in his mende, wowndyng hir wyth pite & compassyon, þat sche sobbyd, roryd, & cryed, and, spredyng hir armys abrood, seyd with lowde voys, 'I dey, I dey'. *The Book of Margery Kempe*, ed. Sanford Brown Meech and Hope Emily Allen, EETS OS 112 (London 1940) c.57, p.140, 11–15.

[4] For an account of the development of the Prymer see Edmund Bishop, 'On the Origin of the Prymer', *The Prymer or Lay-Folks Prayer Book*, (to be abbreviated *The Prymer*) ed. H. Littlehales, EETS OS 105 and 109 (London 1895–7) Vol.II, xi–xxxviii. The fact that in practice the Hours were not always said at the time of day designated as appropriate to

Thus at the Canonical Hours which govern the day of professional religious, these books provided orders of service in various uses besides Sarum and York with canticles, hymns, readings, responses and prayers in which the laity could follow the daily sanctification of time followed by priests and enclosed religious.

The Hours of the Virgin in the Prymer not only celebrate her as the instrument of the Incarnation and intercessor thoughout the day (she is, for instance, appropriately hailed at Evensong as a star 'Hail, sterre of þe þe see, holi modir of God!')[5] but they juxtapose this with a memorial of the events of the Passion story in a conflated Gospel sequence established in the well-known hymn *Patris Sapientia*.[6] Its verses appear individually at each of the Canonical Hours remembering the event traditionally appropriate to them, thus at Lauds, immediately following Matins the verses run:

> The wisdom of þe fadir
> Þe treuþe of þe hiȝ king,
> God and man was takun
> In þe morenyng.
>
> Of hise knowun disciplis
> Soone he was forsak;
> Sold and put to peyne,
> Mankynd saaf to make.

But although the verses call to mind the sequence of events of the Passion and emphasize the enormity of the situation in which the 'wisdom of the fadir' was subject to the destructive wills of violent and vacillating men, they are part of a wider structure which emphasizes that this monstrous outrage is seen to be part of the pattern of salvation. So after each Hour's verse there is the Versicle 'we worschipe þee, Crist, & blesse þee', and the Response 'ffor bi þi deeþ þou hast aȝenbouȝt þe world'. This in turn is followed by a prayer at each Hour which

---

them, (see for example: N. Orme, *Education and Society in Medieval and Renaissance England* (London 1989) p.183) does not destroy the validity of the theoretical pattern and its shaping influence.

[5] *The Prymer, op. cit.*, Vol.I, p.29.

[6] For the dating of this hymn to the fourteenth century see *Dictionary of Hymnology* ed. J. Julian (London 1908) p.886. The hymn has seven verses detailing the events of the Passion and ends devotionally in the eighth stanza:

> Has horas canonicas cum devotione
> Tibi Jesu recolo pia ratione
> Ut sicut tu passus es poenas in agone
> Sic labore consonans consors sim coronae.

See also J. B. L. Tolhurst, *The Monastic Breviary of Hyde Abbey*, Vol.6, Henry Bradshaw Publications, Vol.LXXX, 1942, pp.134–5. The text of the Middle English version appears in the Appendix.

brings to mind the glory, joy and life which was man's birthright, forfeited at the Fall, but renewed by all that is meant by Incarnation:

> lord ihesu crist, goddis sone of heuene, sette þi passioun, þi cros & þi deeþ, bitwixe þi iugement & oure soulis, now & in our of oure deeþ; & vouche-saaf to 3yue to lyuynge men merci & grace in þis liyf here; and to hem þat ben deed, for3yuenesse & reste; to þe chirche & to þe rewme, pees & acoord; & to us synful men, liyf & glorie wiþ-outen ende; þou þat lyuest and regnest god, bi alle worldis of worldis. amen!

In addition to these reminders of the redemptive purpose of the Passion there are also constant reminders of the cycle of salvation as the psalms celebrate God as defender and helper, and the anthems and hymns Mary as the willing instrument of the purposes of God. At Evensong she is remembered 'taking þat word "hail" [Aue] of gabrielis mouþ, . . . chaungynge þe name of eue' and at Sext, as Christ is nailed to the Cross, the anthem celebrates the burning bush which typifies the Virgin birth, and this reminds the worshipper that in God's ordinance destructive forces can be instruments of life not death.

Thus the devout laity, as well as the religious, were daily reminded of an archetypal pattern of suffering in time through which the nature of redemption was manifested and which established the means by which it would be experienced. This enters deeply in various ways into the structure of deliberately composed meditations on the Passion. For example, those in the *Speculum* of Edmund of Abingdon, originally a work of Victorine piety but translated into Middle English by the fourteenth century,[7] and those based on Bonaventura's *Vita Christi*,[8] are organized quite specifically in terms of the Canonical Hours. In the three meditations on which this paper focusses, this pattern is more submerged, but nevertheless importantly latent as a reference to be accessed.

Those who write in English about contemplative life in the medieval period witness to meditation on Christ's Passion as a fundamental activity in the development of an inward experience of the reality of God, although they differ in the way that they emphasize it. To define in general terms the *precise* connotations of words used by individual writers to clarify their understanding of the development

---

[7] See: 'The Mirror of St Edmund', ed. C. Horstman, *Yorkshire Writers: Richard of Hampole and His Followers* (London 1895) Vol.I, pp.219–61; Sister Mary Philomena, *op.cit.*; A. P. Forshaw, 'New Light on the *Speculum Ecclesie* of St Edmund of Abingdon', *Archives d'histoire doctrinale et litteraire du moyen âge*, 38 (1971), 7–33; A. P. Forshaw, 'St Edmund's *Speculum*: A Classic of Victorine Spirituality', *Ibid.*, 39 (1972), 7–40.

[8] e.g. 'The Privity of the Passion: Bonaventura de mysteriis passionis Iesu Christi' (Thornton Manuscript) in C. Horstman, *Yorkshire Writers*, *op. cit.*, I, pp.198–218; 'Medytacyuns of þe Soper of oure lorde Ihesu', (British Library, MS Harley 1701) ed. J. R. Cowper, EETS OS 60 (London 1885) pp.1–24; Nicholas Love, *The Mirror of the Blessed Lyf of Jesu Christ*, ed. L. F. Powell (Oxford 1908).

of contemplative life is to walk a mine-field; nevertheless it can safely be said that by the fourteenth century the term *meditation* had come to denote a willed mental concentration on aspects of the faith, either as formulated in Scripture, or prayer, or other devotional writing, hymns for example, which brings a quickening of love and understanding.[9] However, this actual process of coming alive which is at the heart of meditation is experienced not as a function of the effort of will itself, but as a gift from God.

Walter Hilton, perhaps the most systematic Middle English writer on the manner in which the soul comes to a mode of consciousness of God, which transcends the felt constraints of time and space, is hesitant about prescribing any strict rules for the practice of meditation, because, he says, it is the 'free gift of our Lord'[10] who bestows it in ways peculiarly appropriate to the make-up of the individuals involved. He is, nevertheless, clear that meditation is an exercise which enables the practiser to receive gifts of higher understanding, and he specifically recommends meditation on the Passion as a 'great help in destroying of great sins, and a good way to come to virtues. And so after to contemplation of the Godhead. For a man shall not come to ghostly delight in contemplation of Christ's Godhead but he come first in imagination by bitterness and by compassion and by steadfast thinking of his Manhood'.[11] As he explains, the light of the Godhead is known to us by the shadow it casts from the manhood of Christ, and we 'shall live under the shadow of His manhood as long as we are here';[12] though for Hilton the gift of the highest kind of knowledge of God pierces the shadow to the light itself.[13]

Since the author of *The Cloud of Unknowing* engages with this kind of level of contemplative experience and a sense of being, no longer subject to the fluctuations of death and resurrection in time in which it is first glimpsed, it is not surprising that meditations on the Passion and liturgical reference are not prominent in his writing. He recognizes their validity as a 'beme of the licnes of God'[14] but the greatness of the source of this light, experienced here as a blinding darkness,[15] is beyond any state where there is 'nede to use þe werkes of mercy, ne to wepe for oure wrechidnes, ne for þe passion of Criste'.[16]

Richard Rolle, a much more mercurial and poetic writer – he lacks Hilton's capacity for sustained analytical discourse, and is less stringent than the *Cloud*-author – creates in his vernacular writing on spiritual experience moments of flaring insight into the nature of the inward growth to the knowledge of God. He

[9] See further Simon Tugwell, *Ways of Imperfection* (London 1984) chapters 9–11.
[10] *The Scale of Perfection*, ed. E. Underhill (London 1923) 1, c.34, p.76.
[11] *Ibid.*, 1. c.35, pp.80–1.
[12] *Ibid.*, 2, c.30, p.362.
[13] *Ibid.*, 2, chapters 24–32.
[14] *The Cloud of Unknowing*, ed. P. Hodgson (Salzburg 1983) c.8, p.16, l.27.
[15] *Ibid.*, c.68, p.68, l.16–18.
[16] *Ibid.*, c.21, p.30, l.14–15.

too endorses meditation as a gift. In his *Emendatio Vitae* written for a young religious, but translated into English in the sixteenth century, he extends Augustine's distinction between reading scripture and prayer: 'In redynge, god spekis to vs: In prayer, we speke to god' continuing, 'In meditacion awngels to vs cum down & techis vs, . . . In prayer þa go vp & offyrs owr prayers to god'.[17] In the chapter on meditation he stresses meditation on the Passion as the 'moste profetabyll to þame þat nwly ar turnyd to criste':

> Þerfore truly is schewyd þe manhede of Ihesu criste, in þe qwhilk emong man suld be glad, in qwhilk he has mater of Ioy & also mournyng. Ioy for sikyrnes of owr gaynbiyng, heuynes for filth of owr synyng, for þe qwhilk it is to heuy þat so worþi a offirynge is offyrd. For þe boystus fleschly sawle in-to behaldyng of þe godhede is not rauischyd bot if it be gostely, all fleschly lettyngis vastyd.[18]

Here Rolle locates the familiar paradoxical response to the Passion of joy and sorrow, which also demarcates the human condition with which meditation engages.

In the little treatise the *Form of Living*, that he wrote for his friend Margaret, a nun who became a recluse, Rolle, like Hilton, is careful to say that he cannot be too prescriptive about the details of the practice of meditation since God will put the kinds of thoughts into her heart that are right for her: 'for I hope þat God will do swilk thoghtes in þi hert als he es payde of, and als þou ert ordaynde for'.[19] But he makes it clear that if contemplation is a direct experience of the joys of God's love, meditation is an exercise which prepares the ground for such experience.[20]

The treatise, *Ego Dormio*, that he wrote for another nun, explains that as she progresses in the love of Christ she will find that nothing matters to her but this love, and the sin of man which disfigures it, and that all this is focussed and enabled by thinking on the Passion of Christ: 'And I will þat þou have it mykel in mynde, for it will kyndel þi hert to sett at noght all þe gudes of þis worlde and þe joy þarof, and to desyre byrnandly þe lyght of heven . . . .'[21]

If, then, it is clear that in the fourteenth century the fruits of meditation were regarded as a divine gift, and that meditation on the Passion performs a dynamic function of activating a sense of the realities of God in such a way as to further the process of more contemplative knowledge, then it is surely the case that when,

---

[17] *The Mending of Life or The Rule of Living*, trans Richard Misyn, in *The Fire of Love and The Mending of Life or The Rule of Living*, ed. R. Harvey, EETS OS 106, London, 1896, c.XII, p.127, l.3–6. Augustine *Enarratio in Psalmum LXXXV*, PL 37, 1086: *Oratio tua locutio est ad Deum: quando legis, Deus tibi loquitur*.

[18] *Ibid.*, c.VIII, p.119, l.18–24.

[19] *English Writings of Richard Rolle Hermit of Hampole*, ed. H. E. Allen (Oxford 1963) c.vii, p.104, l.43–45.

[20] *Ibid.*, c.xii, p.118, l.35f.

[21] *Ibid.*, p.65, l.152–55.

despite his inhibitions about prescriptions for meditation, Rolle actually composes meditations on the Passion, he must see them as witness to the process of catalysis. The two isolated prose meditations on the Passion[22] and the meditation on the Passion embedded in *Ego Dormio* effect in literary terms an ascending scale in the meditative process. They point to his own meditational experience for others, and as such are part of the ethos of late medieval affective piety.[23]

The attribution to Richard Rolle of the two prose meditations in three of the four extant manuscripts of the long version, and the unique manuscript of the shorter version,[24] has been called in question because of the acute absence in the texts of that sense of joy springing from an inner knowledge of the reality of redemption which characterizes Rolle's work elsewhere.[25] Yet arguably the acute sense of deprivation of such joy embodied in these meditations can only be recognized through the possibility of its presence; 'absence is not non-existence, and we are therefore entitled to repeat, "come, come, come, come" ', cries God-bole to his Lord,[26] and Rolle's meditations on the Passion are powerful works in which he enacts a sense of the gap between the experience of sour sterility which is a concommittant of what St Paul calls 'the body of this death' (Romans 7:24) and the joy and creativity of God. The meditations project an experience of alienation and deadness from which the meditator longs to be released; he knows at one level that Christ's death is the key to such release, but in this work this knowledge is not projected as that of experience, though it depends on recognition of the possibility of such experience for its validity. One way in which this dimension of meaning is accessed in the text is through its structural links with the memorial of the Passion in the Canonical Hours. This paper will refer only to the shorter version of the meditations. Although the structure of both is in many essentials the same, the shorter version is on the whole superior in literary style[27] and points more clearly to the liturgical frame of reference which is important to both.

In the meditation the main events of the Passion story are isolated for attention in particular ways. First are those from the night of Christ's betrayal to his

[22] 'Richard Rolle's Meditatio Passione Domini', ed. C. Horstman, *Yorkshire Writers, op.cit.,* I, pp.83–103.
[23] For tangential studies see: V. Gillespie, 'Mystic's Foot: Rolle and Affectivity', *The Medieval Mystical Tradition in England,* ed. M. Glasscoe (Exeter 1982) pp.199–230; 'Strange Images of Death: the Passion in Late Medieval English Devotional and Mystical Writings', *Zeit, Tod und Ewigkit in der Renaissance Literatür,* Analecta Cartusiana, 117, ed. J. Hogg (Salzburg 1987) pp.111–59.
[24] For an account of the manuscripts see: H. E. Allen, *Writings Ascribed to Richard Rolle Hermit of Hampole and Materials for his Biography* (reprinted New York 1966) pp.278–87.
[25] *Idem.* See also, M. Morgan, 'Versions of the Meditations on the Passion Ascribed to Richard Rolle', *Medium Aevum,* 22 (1953), 93–101, p.101.
[26] E. M. Forster, *Passage to India* c.19.
[27] For a fuller analysis of the structure and style of the two meditations see M. Glasscoe, *Introduction to Five Medieval Mystical Writers in English* c.1, forthcoming, Longman.

condemnation to death. They include his prayer and agony in the garden of Gethsemane, his betrayal and capture as a criminal, the taunting before the authorities, the denial of Peter, the shame suffered, the appearance before Pilate, the scourging, the crowning with thorns, the scorning and condemnation to death. These events are framed as prayers:[28] Jesus is thanked for the particular incident under consideration which is then used in a prayer appropriate to aspects of the meditator's own experience and modulates into a set prayer indicated by the directives in the text *Adoremus* etc., *Pater*, *Aue*. Right at the start a connection is established between Christ's experience of death and a healing process. So, in the prayer which arises from the memory of Christ's anguish in the garden, the meditator thanks Christ that he sweated blood and identifies this sweat with that which marks the healing and turning point of human fever, conflating it with the sweat of human anguish struggling against evil, so that Christ's suffering from sin at the Passion and man's penance, are seen as part of one sacramental healing process. The meditator prays for help in all his temptations and for the comfort 'þat I my3te turne thorow þat swet owt of al sekenesse of soule in to lyf of hele of body'.[29]

At the point where the meditator presents to himself the death-sentence on Christ, he abandons the prayer structure and opens into a long passage of imaginative affective meditation, though it is still structured by emphasized moments in the Passion story, Christ's journey to Calvary, the Crucifixion and his words from the cross. As Christ's death comes nearer the meditator feels choked by sin and guilt which he sees killing Christ, not just once in time, but continually in inner experience:

> A, lord kyng of my3t, þat leuyn woldust þi my3t & os vnmy3ty become my wrongys to ry3te: what is it þat I speke & bete þe wynd? I speke of þe felyng of þe & fynde I no taste, I blondre in my wyrkyng os man þat is blynd, I studye in my thou3tes and þei wyrken al wast: it is tokenyng of my deth, and fylthe of my synne, þat slayn hath my sowle & stoke is þere-Inne, and stoppyth al þe sauoure, þat I may nou3t the fele, þat so schamely haue ben þi tretoure vntrewe; it mi3t be a prisoun, gloryouse lord, to þi godhed; þe stynke of my schame, þe sorwe of my soule, þe fylthe of my mouthe, 3yf I lykke þere-onne it fylyth þi name: so may I no manere þe swetnesse of the taste, þat I haue lost thorow synne to han lykyng of seyche comfort − for I blondre gladly in lustys of diuerse blamys.[30]

[28] For the close relationship between this element in the form of the meditation and a series of Anglo-Norman prayers in Cambridge, University Library, MS Ee vi 16, see M. Morgan, *op.cit.*, p.97f.

[29] *Meditatio Passione Domini*, *op.cit.*, p.83

[30] *Ibid.*, p.87.

But although he speaks of sin as a pollution that stops up the springs of life in the soul so that it cannot feel God immanent within it, he does also acknowledge the power of God's transcendence:

> But þou gloryouse lord, þou quykenyst þe dede, & tyrnyd hast þou many-fold and brou3t hem to heuenly mede: þe blynde-born þou ly3ted, in book os I rede: it betokynyth gostely werkys, it is no drede.[31]

As Rolle projects the meditator contemplating the appalling inversion of the created order, with its lord suffering greater deprivation than the foxes and birds as he hangs 'in þe eyre' on the cross with nowhere to lay his head,[32] he brings into play connotations from the Easter Office and the order for the Mass as Christ utters the words of reproach from Lamentations 1:12, Jeremiah 2:21 and Micah 6:3 there attributed to Him. They bring into focus the organic relationship be-tween man and Christ whose creativity is blasted by sin:

> Ihesu, why were it nou3t my deth þe dool and þe sorewe, whan I thenk in my thou3t whou reufully þou spake whan þou sayde: 'Alle 3e þat passyth be þe way, abydeth and byholdyth 3yf euere ony peyne þat euere soffred any man or ony wordely woo, be lyk þe sorwe þat I soffre for synful mannys sake'. Nay lord, nay, þere was neuere non so hard, for it was makeles; of alle peynys þat euere were, so hard was neuur fowndyn. And 3yt seydys þou, lord, so swetely and so mekely: *Vinea mea electa, ego te plantaui*: þat is 'My dere vyn3erde', seydust þou, þat is, my dere chosen, 'haue I nou3t my-self þe plauntyd? Why art þou so bytter?' *Populus meus, quid feci tibi*: þat is 'My swete, what haue I þe don? haue I þe wrathyd, þat þou dost me þis woo? haue I not 3euen þe al my self, and al þat euere þou hast, and lyf with-outen ende 3ef þou it wyl take, my body to þi foode, and to deth on rode, and hy3t þe al my-selue in heuene to þi mede? haue I with my gode, dede hyrtyd þe so sore, or with my swete dawntynge greuyd þin herte?'[33]

---

[31] *Idem.*

[32] A scriptural reference to Matthew 8:20 (cf. Luke 9:5) 'the foxes have holes and the birds of the air have nests, but the Son of man hath not where to lay his head', traditionally used to emphasize the poverty embraced by God at the Incarnation. See A. V. C. Schmidt, 'The Treatment of the Crucifixion in *Piers Plowman* and in Rolle's Meditations on the Passion', *Spiritualität Heute und Gestern*, Analecta Cartusiana, 35, ed. J. Hogg (Salzburg 1983) 174–86, esp. pp.188–92, and references cited.

[33] *Meditatio Passione Domine, op.cit.*, p.88. The following references to the liturgy are taken from *Brevarium Ad Usum Insignis Ecclesiae Sarum*, ed. F. Procter and C. Wordsworth (Cambridge 1882) Vol.I; *The Sarum Missal*, ed. J. Wickham Legge (Oxford 1916); *The York Breviary*, Surtees Society Publications, 71 & 75 (Durham 1879 and 1882); *The York Missal* Surtees Society Publications, 59, (Durham 1872).

The relationship of the passage from Rolle to the liturgy is as follows:

(a) 'Alle 3e þat passyth . . . mannys sake' based on Lamentations 1:12 used in Sarum Office for Good Friday, Matins, in primo Nocturno, lectio i: O vos omnes qui

The meditator acknowledges this as he indentifies himself with the penitent thief pleading for the pardon Christ extended to him, and confessing his failure to acknowledge Christ as the true source of his integrity:

Lord for þi mercy, þat welle art of mercy, say to me þat am þi thef þat þou to hym sayde – for I haue stole þi gode dedys, and vsyd mys þi grace, þe wyttus and þe vertues þat þou to me hast lent.[34]

As he sees his betrayal and sense of deprivation born by Christ in His words: 'My god, my dere god, why hastow al forsakyn me . . . ',[35] the meditator sees himself lying down among the bones of dead men on mount Calvary, taking the foot of the cross in his arms, the stench of death in his nostrils. It is a powerful icon: Christ and man identified in accepting the consequences of sin, but differentiated by the sign of the unfailing creativity of the love of God – life-blood; a creativity which the meditator longs for as he cries:

Come þanne at þi wylle, huenelyche leche, and ly3ten me sone os þou my nede knowyst; a sparkle of þi passyoun, of loue and of reuthe, kyndele in myn herte to quycnen it with: so þat al brennyng in loue ouur al thynge, al þe world I may forgete, and baþe me in þi blood.[36]

The meditation ends with the description of the deposition at 'os it were tyme of evynsonge',[37] and entombment, and this mention of not just a time of day but a Canonical Hour links this particular meditation on the Passion, which engages so devastatingly with the condition that meditation is designed to help, with the wider liturgical pattern of a daily memorial of the Passion.

In fact the Evensong reference is particularly potent. In the Prymer the deposition belongs to Evensong, the entombment to Compline. In Rolle, after the sorrow of these events, the meditation ends quietly: 'Þenne was þere warde set of

transitis per viam, attendite et videte si est dolor sicut dolor meus. (I. dcclxxxvii). Cf. *York Breviary*, 71, 401, Sabbato Pasche, Lauds, Antiphon.

(b) *Vinea mea electa . . . so bytter'* based on Jeremiah 2:21 used in Sarum Office for Good Friday, Matins, in secundo Nocturno, after Lectio iii: Response 4. Vinea mea electa ego te plantavi. Quomodo conversa es in amaritudinem: ut me crucifigeres et Barrabam dimitteres. Versicle. Ego quidem plantavi te vinea mea electa omne semen verum. Quomodo conversa es. (I, dcclxxxix). Cf. *York Breviary*, 71, 390, Good Friday, Matins, in Primo nocturno, Response and Versicle after Lectio iii.

(c) *Popule meus . . . þe don?* based on Micah 6:3 used in Sarum Mass on Good Friday in the Reproaches which occur after the Epistle, Gospel and subsequent prayers: Populus meus, quid feci tibi aut in quo contristavi te? (*Sarum Missal*, p.112). Cf. *York Missal*, 105. This is also an Antiphon at Lauds on Passion Sunday in the Sarum Office (I, dccxxviii).

[34] *Meditatio Passione Domini*, op.cit., p.88.
[35] *Ibid.*, p.89.
[36] *Ibid.*, p.90.
[37] *Ibid.*, p.91.

armede kny3tes, to kepe þe monument tyl þe thrydde day. &c Amen'.[38] The scene is a counterpart to the inner penitential awareness of the meditator. But at the heart of the darkness there is a certainty of light in the Resurrection of the 'thrydde day', and in contemplative understanding the historical Resurrection of love is experienced as an inner reality more powerful than the block of sin (guarded tomb) that separates man from Christ. The Prymer too expresses the faith that the most negative moment of withdrawal contains the potential for new growth. In the Sarum Evensong man is reminded that as Christ was taken down from the cross 'Power of resureccioun / Was hid in goddis mynde': in York that 'his myght was in his godhede, so gracius & god';[39] and at Compline in both, the tomb is a trigger for awareness of the means of salvation.[40]

The mystics are those who witness to a sense that the real meaning of the story of the Incarnation is known in terms of an inner dynamic in a constant cycle of Incarnation in time in which the being of God is known intimately both within and above the structure of the personality, integrating all its energies and redeeming them from loss and waste. For Rolle, meditation is one way to enable this process, and he tries to enact in his own meditational writings his sense of how it works: in the prose meditations by creating a horrifying consciousness of the gap between sterility and creativity, the bridging of which is potentially achieved even in the moment of recognition – the very sense of the absence of God is assurance of his presence – but this presence is realized only by a divine gift. But by linking his particular meditation with the whole cycle of the liturgy, he accesses a dimension of meaning which can remain latent in the form. This dimension is also present in the meditation on the Passion in *Ego Dormio* which engages with the sorrow and potential joy of the Passion at a different level of meditative experience. The following argument will be easier to follow if the text is given in full.

> My keyng, þat water grette and blode swette;
> Sythen ful sare bette, so þat hys blode hym wette,
> When þair scowrges mette.
> Ful fast þai gan hym dyng and at þe pyler swyng,
> And his fayre face defowlyng with spittyng.
>
> Þe thorne crownes þe keyng; ful sare es þat prickyng.
> Alas! my joy and my swetyng es demed to hyng,

---

[38] *Idem.*

[39] York Hours of the Cross, *The Lay Folks Mass Book*, ed. T. F. Simmons, EETS OS 71 (London 1879) p.86. Cf. the Latin p.87:

> De cruce deponitur hora uespertina,
> Fortitudo latuit in mente diuina:
> Talem mortem subiit vite medicina,
> Heu corona glorie facuit supina.

[40] See Appendix.

Nayled was his handes, nayled was hys fete,
And thyrled was hys syde, so semely and so swete.

Naked es his whit breste, and rede es his blody syde;
Wan was his fayre hew, his wowndes depe and wyde.
In fyve stedes of his flesch þe blode gan downe glyde
Als stremes of þe strande; hys pyne es noght to hyde.

Þis to see es grete pyte, how he es demed to þe dede
And nayled on þe rode tre, þe bryght aungels brede.
Dryven he was to dole, þat es owre gastly gude,
And alsso in þe blys of heven es al þe aungels fude.

A wonder it es to se, wha sa understude,
How God of mageste was dyand on þe rude.
Bot suth þan es it sayde þat lufe ledes þe ryng;
Þat hym sa law hase layde bot lufe it was na thyng.

Jhesu, receyve my hert, and to þi lufe me bryng;
Al my desyre þou ert, I covete þi comyng.
Þow make me clene of synne, and lat us never twyn.
Kyndel me fire within, þat I þi lufe may wyn,
And se þi face, Jhesu, in joy þat never sal blyn.

Jhesu, my saule þou mend; þi lufe into me send,
Þat I may with þe lend in joy withowten end.
In lufe þow wownde my thoght, and lyft my hert to þe.
My sawle þou dere hase boght; þi lufer make it to be.

Þe I covete, þis worlde noght, and for it I fle.
Þou ert þat I have soght, þi face when may I see?
Þow make my sawle clere, for lufe chawnges my chere.
How lang sal I be here?

When mai I negh þe nere, þi melody to here,
Oft to here sang,
Þat es lastand so lang?
Þou be my lufyng,
Þat I lufe may syng.

As reproduced here, the text has been represented by its editor, Hope Emily Allen, in stanzas[41] but it does not appear as verse in all the manuscripts.[42] In *The*

[41] *English Writings, op.cit.*, pp.67–9.
[42] See Oxford, Bodleian Library, MS Rawlinson A. 389 ff.77–81; Vernon Sum. Cat. 3938, ff.389–70; Cambridge, University Library, MS Dd V 64 111, ff.22b–9. London, British Library, MS Add. 22283 f.150b–1b; Add. 37790 f.132–5b.

Fire of Love Rolle defines his mystical experience of the joys of God's love as one in which he became aware in a special way of the Word that informs all words, the harmony behind all music, so that 'my meditation became a poem and I began to sing what I had previously spoken'.[43] This meditation, if written as prose, though heard or read as poetry, would enact the surprise of speech become song, meditation become poem, and point the disciple to a contemplative understanding of this exercise of her faith.[44] Furthermore, the stanzas obscure the fact that the use of rhyme shapes significant units of sense, since the rhyme scheme then cuts across the stanza forms. This becomes clearer by looking at the first two stanzas.

Here the first rhyming unit on *grette* brings to mind both interior and exterior pain: Christ's solitary agony in the garden and the pain of scourging. It nevertheless addresses the sufferer as *king* thus defining a relationship between the meditator and Christ and establishing the twin poles of thought, sovereignty through patient suffering. The second rhyming unit on *dyng* emphasizes the deforming physical violence which precedes the final judgement to death, and provides the stark reminder that this action kills joy: 'alas! my joy and my swetyng es demed to hyng'. The third unit rhyming on *fete* isolates the image of the five wounds and modulates into an extended description of this on a new rhyme. This fourth unit, edited as the third stanza, is in fact borrowed from a current Middle English verse paraphrase of lines in a Latin meditation[45] and is some justification for printing out the whole piece in stanza form. The description of the five wounds prepares for the fifth unit, which fuses memory of the outrage of the historical Passion story with its sacramental meaning, as the bread of heaven, is, in effect, rubbished on the cross. The sixth unit rams home the enormity of such an act, but the sacramental references have already introduced the joy latent in the horror. For the mystics, the Passion focusses the terrifyingly destructive forces in human nature, but it also signals the one way by which they are to be rendered ultimately ineffective, through a love which ventures all in faith, a way which is not isolated in history but constantly to be repeated. In this meditation, just at the moment when the full sacriligious horror of what happened is described, there is a change of tone as Rolle initiates the seventh rhyme scheme chiming with *ryng*, and refocusses the actions of hideous brutality as the means by which the voluntary ring-dance of love is patterned in time: the leader has shown the way and the dancers respond:

---

[43] *The Fire of Love*, trans. C. Wolters (Harmondsworth 1972) c.15, p.93.
[44] Further justification for the argument that this meditation is cadenced prose is the fact that lines 20–21 are translations from Rolle's Latin prose in *Incendium amoris* ed. M. Deanesley (Manchester 1915) cap.42, 1.237–8.
[45] See *Religious Lyrics of the Fourteenth Century*, ed. Carleton Brown (Oxford 1952) p.1: it appears to derive ultimately from lines in *Liber Meditationum* attributed to St Augustine, see *PL* XI, 906.

> Bot suth þan es it sayde þat lufe ledes þe ryng;
> Þat hym sa law hase layde bot lufe it was na thyng.

> Ihesu receyve my hert, and to þi lufe me bryng;
> Al my desyre þou ert, I covete þi comyng.

The meditator's projected response 'I covete þi comyng', works at several levels: that of the reality of the sacraments, the promise of the second coming, and the anticipation of a coming in mystical experience which is longed for. All three are part of one pattern, defined by Christ, but experienced within the penitential life of the meditator: no resurrection without death, no joy without sorrow, no feeling of the presence of love without sometimes consciousness of its absence, and all three comings relate to an overcoming of sin.

So the rest of the meditation turns on overcoming separation from God through the fire of love. The tenth rhyming unit on *thoght* and *þe* brings together the Passion which started the meditation and the inner desire of the speaker through the image of the wound of love which will impel the soul to God. Stressed monosyllables enforce the recognition of Jesus as the goal of longing: 'þou ert þat I have soght'. The last seven lines on three rhymes break the pattern of units of sense on single rhymes as the meditator signals by means of the present tense: 'lufe chaunges my chere', the possibility of transformation to a state where he can hear the melody to which love dances, and he ends with a statement of faith 'þou be my lufyng, þat I lufe may syng'. This meditation works by recalling the familiar isolated moments of the Passion story – the agony in the garden, the scourging, the crowning with thorns, the crucifixion itself – and using the resources of rhetoric to embody a sense of the joyful reality behind the story which such meditation is designed to enable. It is devotional art work which enacts in its form that faith that the experience of broken suffering in time is in reality the choreography and notation for the dance and music of love, which is implicit in the whole order of the Hours of the Virgin.

This movement between painful penitential awareness of the historical reality of suffering as a concommittant of time and embracing it as the medium for redemption and the resurrection of love, governs the order of the liturgy and is particularly clearly distilled in the Hours of the Virgin; it is at the heart of Rolle's understanding of the role of meditative experience; it is also central to the visionary experience of Julian of Norwich. The core of the series of visions which she calls showings are centred on icons of the crucified Christ. They assume sharper definition when related to the liturgy and the meditative tradition. The physical conditions in which the revelations occurred, that of remission from a critical illness from which she suffered in early May 1373,[46] are emblematic of their content. At a point when she is given over for dead, and a priest brings a crucifix

[46] *Julian of Norwich: A Revelation of Love*, ed. M. Glasscoe (Exeter 1976) (to be abbreviated *Julian*) c.2, p.2.

before her, she is suddenly released from all pain and has a series of fifteen distinct showings which last until 'none of the day overpassid'.[47] There are twelve showings linked with the physical disfigurement of Christ in the Passion and the processes of death, staining blood and drying flesh, but just as Julian expects to see them culminate in death, as in the meditative tradition of the Hours of the Passion, the whole scene is transfigured to one of spiritual life and joy in which she shares. Then follow three more showings, one of a wedge of sin that seems driven between man and God in time, but which nevertheless is the very medium through which he is known; the next, depending on this, relates to how prayer can develop techniques for digesting this barrier[48] and the fifteenth is of man finally and permanently delivered from the wretched filth of the waste product which inevitably attends this process: this is visualized as the body of a child ascending from the stinking corruption of a corpse. She then experiences a brief return to, and remission from, her sickness, before the final revelation during the following night when she experiences her soul in a way that is not constrained by the dimensions of time but is 'as it were an endles world and as it were a blisfull kyngdom'[49] in which Christ is king.

The basic shape of the showings relates to the way the Office in the Prymer celebrates the meaning of life in time. They start early in the morning about 4 a.m., so somewhere around Lauds, and the first fifteen last until 'none of the day overpassid'. If this is None and not noon, and since she also refers to Prime[50] it is likely to be so, then the first group of showings presumably ended before Evensong. These are the ones centred on the images of the Passion, though the visionary nature of Julian's showing is emphasized by the breaking of the pattern of the Hours of the Cross with an experience of the salvation that the context of these Hours celebrates.

This is particularly potent in the seventh, eight and ninth showings which involve Julian in the dynamic experience in which opposed positions are reconciled in transfiguration, an experience to which Rolle's meditations on the passion witness in different ways. She experiences in herself the opposition of the weakness of insecurity and the secure strength of assurance of the reality of the love of God which is known only through the suffering it transforms,[51] and she sees this movement through failure and loss to strength and renewed life as central to the meaning of the Incarnation. In so far as sin kills love it threatens the whole universe,[52] in so far as it affords the opportunity for love to manifest its greater strength, it becomes the very means by which 'al shal be wel'[53] and transformed to

---

[47] Ibid., c.65, p.81.
[48] See further c.5, *Introduction to Five Medieval Mystical Writers in English, op.cit.*
[49] *Julian, op.cit.*, c.67, p.82.
[50] Ibid., c.69, p.84. See below.
[51] Ibid., c.15, p.17.
[52] Ibid., c.18, p.20.
[53] Ibid., c.27, p.28.

bliss 'by vertue of Criste'.[54] She does not see Christ's death for, 'sodenly, I beholdyng in the same crosse, he chongyd his blissfull chere . . . and I was as glad and
mery as it was possible'.[55] In the visions, the death of Christ and thoughts on the
deposition and entombment proper to Evensong and Compline are bye-passed.
Christ remains alive manifesting the ultimate realities of love and joy.[56] But
before the final showing she experiences a period of time when her visions cease
and she is assailed by nightmare doubt from which she is delivered by faith,[57] an
experience which represents in its own way both the desolation of the loss of
Christ and his power to Harrow Hell not inappropriate to the Canonical time of
day.[58]

During the following night she has a vision of just that 'liyf and glorie wiþ-
outen ende' and Christ who 'lyuest and regnest god' which are prayed for repeatedly in the prayer which follows the memorial of the Passion in the Hours of
the Virgin.[59] This is followed by another period of temptation until she is finally
freed from this 'about prime day;' in terms of the passage of time in early May,
sun-rise, and as a Canonical Hour, associated with the Resurrection appearances
of Christ;[60] the Prymer celebrated then the strength and efficacy of God's indwelling help: 'In alle þingis y souȝte reste; and in þe eritage of þe lord y schal dwelle.
Þanne þe makere of alle þingis seide to me; & he þat made me restide in my
tabernacle'.[61]

The link between the cycle of Julian's showings and the order of the Hours in
the Prymer becomes even more pertinent in a closer study of the first showing. It
contains three distinct elements: (1) the bleeding which results from the cruel
pressing home of the crown of thorns 'as it were in the time of his passion'[62] which
makes her marvel that 'he that is so reverend and dredfull wil be so homely with a
synfull creture liveing in wretched flesh';[63] (2) the Annunciation to Mary whose
meek assent to God's will enables him to be born and who marvels at the
familiarity of the creator with his creatures;[64] (3) a sense of the sustaining love of
God focussed in the image of the world, small as a hazelnut held in the palm of her
hand, but sustained by the buoyancy of God's love in a void which would otherwise destroy it.[65]

---

[54] *Ibid.*, c.19, p.22.
[55] *Ibid.*, 8th showing, c.21, p.23.
[56] *Ibid.*, 9th showing, c.22 and 23, pp.24–25.
[57] *Ibid.*, c.66, p.81.
[58] See Appendix, verse for Compline.
[59] See above p.144.
[60] *Julian, op.cit.*, c.69, p.84; for the association of Prime with the Resurrection see, Sister
Mary Philomena, *op.cit.*
[61] *The Prymer, op.cit.*, I, p.18 (Capitile, Prime).
[62] *Julian, op.cit.*, c.4, p.4.
[63] *Idem.*
[64] *Ibid.*, c.4, p.5.
[65] *Ibid.*, c.5, p.5.

These three elements which are the essence of her vision combine to express the essential message of the Incarnation, the sustaining love of the Creator born in time as a saving power, which is expressed through its capacity to suffer and survive. This conflates elements in the Prymer from Matins to Tierce and, significantly, the subsequent icons of the Passion in Julian's text relate to the crucifixion itself, remembered at Sext and None. The crowning with thorns was remembered at Tierce, but specific remembrance of the overwhelming contrast between the greatness of God and the processes of Incarnation are particularly remembered at Matins and Lauds; the psalms are chosen to stress God as the creator of the whole Universe[66] while the celebrations of Mary stress the incredible paradox of the unmade creator consenting to be constrained to the processes of birth: Leccio 3 at Matins has:

Holi modir of God, þat worþli disseruedist to conseyue him þat al þe world my3te not holde![67]

Even more significant is the wording of the Matins hymn:

Blessed modir, bi goddis 3ifte! In whos wombe was closid, he þat is hi3este in alle craftis, & holdiþ þe world in his fist.[68]

The Hour of the Cross at Lauds echoes this contrast in a sober reminder of how such a gift was betrayed by men:

The wisdom of þe fadir,
Þe treuþe of þe hi3e king,
God and man was takun
In þe morenyng.[69]

The psalms at Lauds which continue the celebration of God as creator are also mixed with those stressing God as the source of life for individuals,[70] preparing the way for those at Prime and Tierce which stress his saving power in time of trouble; just as the anthems to Mary start to celebrate her as the means by which man is penetrated by the grace of the Godhead:

Þe makere of mankynde, takynge a body wiþ a soule . . . 3af to us his godhede.[71]

---

[66] They are in modern numbering, 95, 8, 19, 24, 93, 100, 148, 149.
[67] The Prymer, op.cit., I. p.6.
[68] Ibid., p.2.
[69] Ibid., p.15.
[70] 63, 67.
[71] The Prymer, op.cit., I, p.18.

Whanne he was born wonderfulliche of a maide, þanne was fulfillid holi
writ. Þou cam doun as reyn in-to a flees, for to make saaf mankynde.[72]

It is as if the elements held in solution in the Office (themselves the product of
meditative understanding) are, quite literally, transformed in Julian's visionary
mode of knowing. In all her showings she comes to understand personally the
means of activating the potential for the transfiguration of suffering in time
implicit in her understanding of the Incarnation. The Passion is absolutely central
to all that she understands, and she feels it inappropriate to contemplate directly
the joys of heaven, although she is aware of the possibility of that experience.[73] In
her showings the contemplative potential of meditations on the Passion which
Rolle gestures towards in his *Ego Dormio* example is realized. All time is seen as
sanctified as it becomes the medium for the realization of divine love. For Julian
the only way to 'endles knowyng in God'[74] is by what she calls, with a resonance
which embraces a wide range of reference both within her showings, within the
context of the liturgy of the church and within other meditative writings on the
Passion: 'time of passion as he bare in this life and his crosse, . . . '.[75]

APPENDIX

The text of the Middle English version of *Patris Sapientia* relating to the Hours in
the Sarum Rite

Matins

Lauds   The wisdom of þe fadir,
                  Þe treuþe of þe hiȝ king,
                  God and man was takun
                  In þe morenyng.

                  Of hise knowun disciplis
                  Soone he was forsak;
                  Sold and put to peyne,
                  Mankynd saaf to make.

Prime   Ihesu, at oure of pryme,
                  Was led to fore pilat;

[72] *Ibid.*, p.21.
[73] Julian, *op.cit.*, c.19, p.21.
[74] *ibid.*, c.21, p.23.
[75] *Idem.*

Wiþ false witnessyng
Michel accused for hate;

Buffetid; hise hondis weren boundun:
Þei spaten in his face;
Þus þei biseien foule,
Oure lord, king of grace.

Tierce

At vndren þe false iewis
Crieden with hiჳ vois,
'Delyuere vs baraban,
And do þis on þe cros!'

A sharp coroun of þornes
Þei diden on his heed;
And dide him bere his cros.
Þere he schulde be deed.

Sext

At myddai, oure lord ihesu
Was nailed on þe rode,
Bitwixe twey þeeues hangid;
His bodi ran al on blood.

Him þirstide for peyne;
Þei ჳauen him drynke galle.
Al þis peyne he suffride,
Ffro deeþ to bie us alle.

None

At noon diede oure lord ihesu,
Þat was of myჳtes moost;
He criede 'heli' to his fadir,
And so he lefte his gooste.

A spere in to his side
Was þrillid of a kniჳt;
And þanne þe erþe quakede;
Þe sunne wiþ-drowne his liჳt.

Evensong

Fro cros, crist was takun doun
At euesong tyme, we fynde;
Power of resurreccioun
Was hid in goddis mynde.

159

Þe medicyn of liyf, bi storie,
Took sithe deeþ out of toun.
Allas! þe coroun of glorie.
Was þus cast vpsedoun.

Compline   At our of comepelyn
Þei leiden hym in graue,
Þe noble bodi of ihesu,
Þat mankynde schal saue.

With spicerie he was biried,
Hooli writ to fulfille.
Þenke we sadli on his deeþ;
Þat schal saue us from helle.

Margery Kempe's Scribe and the Miraculous Books

Roger Ellis

I

This paper has, if not its origin, possibly its inspiration, in a recent remark by the friend whose birthday it commemorates: in 'The Audience for the Middle English Mystics' Stan has written, of the *Book* of Margery Kempe, that 'it reads like a despairing attempt to bring some order to a kaleidoscope of journeys, visions, accusations and sobbings'.[1] In this paper, I wish to consider an obvious way in which the second scribe does just that, in ch. 62:[2] and to ask how satisfactory is the result.

Ch. 62, you will remember, tells how the scribe was tempted to abandon Margery in the face of sustained criticism of her from the pulpit by a friar (? the Franciscan William Melton: so n. to 148/28–9) newly arrived at Lynn in 1420–21, famous for his preaching, and impatient of interruption. The friar has put up with Margery's first noisy outburst ('sche brast owte wyth a gret cry & cryid wondyr sor', 149/16) when he is preaching about the Passion, but grows angrier as the outbursts continue, and finally he bans her from his preaching. Matters reach such a pass that he directs one of his sermons against her – though not by name – and when Margery's friends, understanding his drift, raise their voices in protest, he thumps on the pulpit and says that if he hears another word he 'xal so smytyn þe nayl on þe hed. . . þat it schal schamyn alle hyr mayntenowrys' (152/27–9). At that point, with a fine biblical cadence (cf. John 6:66) the priest-scribe tells how he was among those who turned back, intending never again to trust her.

The following abbreviations are explained in the notes:
A (see n. 16), Ar (n. 11), ASS (n. 16), DSp (n. 12), IA (n. 5), JV (n. 16), LA (n. 7), MQ (n. 17), Ol (n. 11), RG (n. 10). Riehle (n. 8), VB (n. 19), Vetter (n. 9).
Where not otherwise indicated, translations, not literal, are my own.

[1]   *De Cella in Seculum: Religious and Secular Life and Devotion in Late Medieval England*, ed. by M. G. Sargent (Cambridge 1989), p. 117.
[2]   In this paper, references to *The Book of Margery Kempe*, ed. by S. B. Meech and H. E. Allen, EETS OS 212 (1940), are by page and line number.

As in two earlier episodes where he appears as a distinct character (the Proem and ch. 24), the scribe's doubts are confuted by a miracle: this time one he reads in a book. An unnamed 'worshepful clerk, a bacheler of diuinite' (153/29), presses a book upon him, and this leads him to other books, in all of which he finds support for Margery's tears and loud sobbings. The book is the *Vita* of the beguine St Mary of Oignies by her confessor and mentor Jacques de Vitry, and the episode, in ch. 18–19 of the scribe's copy of the text, that of the miraculous draught of tears obtained by her for a priest who had asked her to cease from weeping so loudly in church. The parallel – Margery/Mary, the friar/the priest, the priest-scribe/de Vitry – must have seemed irresistible: not least, when a subsequent revelation to Margery includes a promise that her opponent 'xal be chasti3ed scharply' (156/18). So too the material from the other books, though none of them presents so directly the threefold relationship of total faith (the narrator) and unbelief (the antagonist) that we find in Margery's *Book*. There is 'þe Prykke of Lofe. . . þat Boneauentur wrot'; 'Richard Hampol, hermyte, in Incendio Amoris'; and a 'tretys' alleging that 'Eli3abeth of Hungry cryed wyth lowde voys' (153/38–154/14). 'þe Prykke of Lofe' is presumably a Middle English translation of the *Stimulus Amoris*, but not the one ascribed to Walter Hilton.[3] From it the scribe copies a passage from chapter 2, describing how the writer, 'ouyrcome thorw desyr', runs madly through the streets and scandalises the observers: blending in his own person the roles of both visionary and scribe, and opposing to both that of his ignorant opponents. So too with the *Incendium Amoris*, though what, in that text, the 'leche mater þat meuyd hym to 3euyn credens' the scribe doesn't tell us.

The importance of the first three witnesses is further indicated by their citation elsewhere in the *Book*. On one occasion Margery approaches, with enquiries about her spiritual life, a Dominican, 'a worschepful doctowr. . . hite maistyr Custawns', who has come to Lynn for a general Chapter of the Dominicans (165/27 ff); he validates her experiences by referring to the same episode that our scribe has found (or will find, for we cannot date the two events relative to one another) in the book of 'Maria de Oegines'. And some years previously, while she is still bearing children (therefore some time before June 23 1413, see n. to 23/9), Margery has herself cited 'Stimulus Amoris [and] Incendium Amoris', in an attempt to validate her own experiences, at her first meeting with Richard of Caister, the Vicar of St Stephen's Norwich (39/24–5). From these same two texts a young priest reads to her shortly after his arrival at Lynn, some (little?) while after her return from the Holy Land in 1414; he continues reading them to her

---

[3]   I read the reference to 'Stimulo Amoris & capitulo ut supra' (154/10) as referring to the Latin original of the translated material: which makes easiest sense if we suppose the scribe was not directly translating from the *Stimulus* but copying from an existing translation (better punctuated at 154/6 as 'wylte I bowe. Lord,'). For the corresponding passage in the Hilton version, see *The Prickynge of Love*, ed. by H. Kane, Elizabethan and Renaissance Studies 92:10 (Salzburg 1983), 20/6–16, and for an assessment of Hilton's claim to authorship, *ibid.* xxii–xxiv.

during his time there 'þe most part of vij ʒer er viij ʒer' (143/25–35).[4] On the principle that to say a thing three times is to make it true, these citations appear to guarantee the truth of Margery's claims. Devil's advocates, however, may beg leave to doubt: how carefully, they may ask, has the scribe read the texts which he is offering as miraculous proof of Margery's practices?

The question was answered, with respect to the *Incendium*, by Hope Emily Allen (n. to 154/10–12).[5] Miss Allen adduced as a parallel, in *Incendium* ch. 34, what Rolle calls a great shout ('clamor') uttered by the loving soul, as a way of describing the gift of *canor* so important to him. If not the sole reference to the phenomenon in the *Incendium* (see also *IA* ch. 32, p. 238), it is certainly one of the most arresting. Yet, in Allen's words, 'Margery's friend has misunderstood Rolle, who is probably. . . describing an ineffable mystical experience'. Rolle's shout is an inner one, 'clamorem illum canorem ab extrinsecis auribus omnino absconditum arbitr[o]r' (*IA* p. 244) [I judge that that shouting song is altogether hidden from outward ears]. It *can* be spoken aloud, but only by and to one like Rolle himself, as a way of clarifying the nature of the gift to the recipients ('in hac equidem apercione exultarem amplius aut certe uberius emularem; quoniam mihi ostenderetur incendium amoris et sonora iubilacio euidenter effulgeret', *ibid.* [in his expounding I should rejoice more fully or more copiously imitate him since I should have been shown the fire of love and the sonorous jubilation would have plainly burst forth]). Likewise, when talking in ch. 40 of tears, which would combine with Margery's 'gret cry' to produce a sign of such offence, Rolle describes them, much as the *Cloud* author will describe acts of discursive meditation, as inferior to the graces he has himself experienced:

> Lacrime lauare solent a delictis. . . sed ardens amor omnia excedit inex-cogitabiliter. . . Non aio fletum esse inutilem, nec dolorem cordis dico indecentem, aut non diligendum in hoc exilio; sed admiror aliquem in tantum raptum amoris iubilo, quod. . . uel orando uel meditando flere non possit. . . quasi abstractis lacrimis, in ipso fonte ueri et eterni gaudii iugiter iocundetur (*IA* pp. 269–70)[6]
> [Tears do customarily wash you from faults. . . but burning love surpasses all things unimaginably. . . I don't say weeping is useless, nor sorrow of heart unfitting or unworthy of love in this exile: but I am struck by the

---

[4] On this chronology, see n. to 142/29–31 ('he came to Lynn about 1413, or perhaps a little later'): the priest begins to read to Margery only after the death of her first confessor, the anchorite (142/24–7), who was still alive when she set out for the Holy Land in 1413 (60/26–7, and n. to 60/18–9).

[5] Reference to the *Incendium* in the present work, abbreviated *IA*, is to *The Incendium Amoris of Richard Rolle of Hampole*, ed. by M. Deanesley, University of Manchester Publications XCVII (Manchester 1915).

[6] On tears, linked with meditation and prayer as a lower, purgative, stage of the spiritual life, see *IA* chs 14 (p. 183), 31 (p. 235), 32 (p. 235), 42 (p. 276).

man so caught up in the song of love that praying or meditating he cannot weep. . . but perpetually rejoices, his tears, so to speak, dried up, in that fountain of true and endless joy]

II

As with Rolle, so with 'Eliȝabeth of Hungry. . . in hir tretys', though here matters are complicated because we don't know for certain who this Elizabeth of Hungary was nor what the 'tretys' written by or about her. If we follow Meech's note, this Elizabeth was

> St Elizabeth of Hungary (b. 1207), daughter of King Andrew II of Hungary and wife of Landgrave Ludwig IV of Thuringia (d. 1227), and a religious of the Third Order of St Francis from 1228, [who] died 17 Nov., 1231, and was canonised 28 May 1235 (n. to 154/13–14).

Her 'tretys' might then be the *Vita* produced by Jacques de Vitry and preserved in the *Legenda Aurea* of James of Varaggio: a text known in East Anglia because of Bokenham's translation of it as one of his *Legendys of Hooly Wommen* (Allen's n. to 154/13).[7] But another candidate has been advanced by Riehle and, in an as yet unpublished paper, by Alexandra Barratt: a great-niece of the Saint, also called Elizabeth, daughter of Andrew III of Hungary.[8] Born c.1294, this Elizabeth 'entered the famous Dominican nunnery of Töss' in 1309 and died there in 1337. In this case the 'tretys' might be some version of 'the book of the Sisters of Töss' produced by Elsbeth Stagel and featuring prominently 'a *vita* of Elizabeth, who appears to have been the pride of the nunnery' (Riehle p. 31).[9] This Middle High German text does not appear to have been translated into Middle English, but, given the close links between Lynn and Germany during the 14th century (*Book*, p. liii), and evidenced repeatedly in the *Book*, it could have been known to our scribe. To complicate matters still further, a text exists, in both Latin and several medieval vernaculars – widely known from the use made of it in the pseudo-

---

[7] For the former, abbreviated *LA*, see *Jacobi a Voragine Legenda Aurea*, ed. by Th. Grässe (Dresden and Leipzig 1846), pp. 752–71; for the latter, *Legendys of Hooly Wummen by Osbern Bokenham*, ed. by M. S. Serjeantson, EETS OS 206 (1938).

[8] W. Riehle, *The Middle English Mystics*, trans. by B. Standring (London 1981), pp. 31–2, and A. Barratt, 'Cherchez la femme: the revelations of St Elizabeth of Hungary', kindly supplied, with other material, by the writer.

[9] For an edition of this work, see *Das Leben der Schwestern zu Töss*, ed. by F. Vetter, Deutsche Texte des Mittelalters, VI (Berlin 1906), pp. 98–122; a modern translation, which I have not been able to consult, is in M. Weinhandl, *Deutsches Nonnenleben*, 'Katholikon Werke und Urkunden', Bd. II (Munich 1921); another in J. Ancelot-Hustache, *La vie mystique d'un monastère de Dominicaines au moyen âge d' après la chronique de Töss* (Paris 1928), pp. 178–221, was kindly drawn to my attention by Dr Barratt.

Bonaventuran *Meditationes Vitae Christi* [10] – of revelations to a 'seynt Ely3abeth'.[11] 'This work of uncertain origin is often ascribed to St Elizabeth of Hungary' (Allen's n. to 154/13) but by Dr Barratt to Elizabeth of Töss since she also was a 'kynges doughter of Hungarye' (Ar 392/2) and because one of the oldest manuscripts describes the visionary as a virgin (Ol p. 31): which the great-aunt was not, and the great-niece was. The principal difficulty with this hypothesis concerns the use of the revelations in the ps.-Bonaventuran *Meditationes*, which are variously dated, but, most authoritatively, 'début du 14e siècle'.[12] Even if the Dominican Elizabeth of Töss had by then received the visions that were to circulate in the name of 'Elysabeth the kynges doughter', I doubt that she would also have achieved the celebrity that would guarantee them a place in a Franciscan compilation originating, it is generally held, in Tuscany. (And the Elizabeth whom the *Vita* of Elsbeth Stagel presents doesn't, so far as I can determine, have any particularly compelling links with the visionary 'Elizabeth'.) In any case, the Franciscan interest and connection would seem weightier arguments in favour of the great-aunt's involvement in the work: which explains how the two Middle English versions of the text end by referring to the end of the visionary's life 'the yere of our lorde a MCCxxxj' (Ar 400/19, cf. CUL Hh 1.11 f. 127v).[13] But this

[10] See *Sancti Bonaventura. . . Opera Omnia*, ed. by L. Peltier, 15 vols (Paris 1864–71), XII, 513; and, for a modern translation, *Meditations on the Life of Christ*, trans. by I. Ragusa and R. B. Green, Princeton Monographs in Art and Archaeology 35 (Princeton 1961), abbreviated *RG*, pp. 10–12.

[11] For an edition of this text, abbreviated *Ol*, see F. Oliger, 'Revelationes B. Elisabeth', *Antonianum* I (1926), 24–83. (Allen's references to this text, in her notes, do not agree with mine.) To Oliger's list of manuscripts can be added (so Barratt) another version of the text in Cambridge, Magdalene College MS F. 4. 14, identified as source of the two Middle English versions in Cambridge, University Library, MS Hh. 1. 11, ff. 122r–7v, and a de Worde printing of 1492–3 (sig. p[v]v–q[iv]r); for a modern edition of the de Worde text, see C. Horstmann, 'The reuelacions of saynt Elysabeth of Hungary', *Archiv* 76 (1886), 392–400, abbreviated *Ar*. The precise relation of the two versions of the Latin text has yet to be determined.

[12] So *Dictionnaire de spiritualité ascétique et mystique* (Paris 1937–), abbreviated *DSp*, X (1980), 914. Earlier datings include the second half of the 13th c. (*RG* p. xxii: the author was 'a Franciscan monk living in Tuscany'); the end of the 13th c. (Oliger, *DSp* VIII (1974), 325, and *Ol* pp. 24–5), 'before 1330' (*New Catholic Encyclopedea* 9 (1967), 614), 'before 1335' (Fischer, *DSp* VIII, 325). See also *Meditaciones de Passione Christi*. . ., ed. by M. J. Stallings, Studies in Medieval and Renaissance Latin Literature XXV (Washington DC 1965), p. 10 n. 22 (explains 1335 as the latest date for its appearance, since by then it is being quoted in ME). See also *DSp* I (1937), 1848–53.

[13] MS copies of the revelations consulted (e.g. Oxford, Bodleian Library, MS Canon. Misc. 525) further witness to this Franciscan connection (so also *Ol* p. 30). Of particular interest, Bod. Canon. Misc. 257 establishes links between the *Meditationes* and the 'revelations', both copied in the MS, by cutting from the former all material deriving from the latter, so as to avoid duplication; the copy of the 'revelations', ff. 181v–197v, uses the same phrases to introduce revelations and text as are normally found in the *Meditationes* at this point ('cuidam. . . deuote s[c]ilicet beate Elysabeth ut creditur', 'predicta christi filia').

conclusion can be opposed – and is, by Barratt – on internal grounds. Possibly, therefore, we have to do with a text produced by an unnamed woman sometime in the thirteenth century and published under the name of the famous Franciscan tertiary. We have, then, not one but three texts to consider, each with some claim to be regarded as the 'tretys' which Margery's priest-scribe was citing.[14]

First, Stagel's *Vita*. This certainly includes tears (for example, Elizabeth's grief for the death of a loved sister, Vetter p. 109, though I get the sense that more tears are shed by others when she dies, p. 117, than by her in the course of her life); and it features many of the elements of a saint's life which Margery has taken care to include in her Book: patient endurance of protracted illnesses; miracles; and so on. This could very well have been the 'tretys' our scribe encountered (though, if so, and given his difficulties with the language and handwriting of his predecessor, 4/14–17, not in its original German). But, though I speak under correction in this matter – my comprehension of Elsbeth Stagel's German is little better than our priest-scribe's would have been – I do not find Stagel's text particularly relevant to this enquiry.

A stronger case can be made out for the *Vita* of the great-aunt by de Vitry: not least because she is offered as one of two saintly exemplars to an unnamed queen in a revelation of St Bridget of Sweden, which Margery will surely have known, given her interest in 'Bridis boke' (39/24, 143/27).[15] As in Margery's story, de Vitry's narrative creates a powerful ecclesiastical antagonist for the saint, in the person of her confessor Conrad of Marburg (no comparable figure occurs in the other two texts). More to the point, de Vitry's heroine has the same abundance of tears as Margery. If this were the text our scribe had in mind, though, he must have read it almost as selectively as he read Rolle. For Elizabeth of Hungary, tears are one of three linked graces of contemplation (the others are 'coelestes visiones crebro videre et ad amorem alios inflammare' [frequent heavenly visions and the capacity to set others afire with heavenly love]), and unlike Margery's tears, they generally express not pain but joy:

---

[14] I agree with Barratt in opposing Oliger's ascription of the work (p. 50) to Elizabeth of Schönau, because of the differences, in tone and content, between the work and those of Elizabeth of Schönau. Nor do we need to consider the claim of Elizabeth of Schönau's writings to be those the scribe had in mind, though the two Elizabeths, of Hungary and Schönau, are sometimes confused in manuscript (*Ol* pp. 25, 34–5, 45).

[15] 'Audiui. . . quod sancta Elizabeth filia regis Vngarie delicate enutrita et nobiliter nupta magnam sustinuit paupertatem et deiectionem; que maiorem consolationem obtinuit a Deo in paupertate. . . quam si mansisset in omni honore' (*Revelationes S. Birgitte*, impressit B. Ghotan (Lübeck 1492), IV. ivE) ['O þou hase herde told of Elizabeth, þat was þe kynges doghtir of Hungary, þat was noriste in grete delytes and nobilly wedded, bot scho was eftir right pore and law. And ʒitt had scho more comforth in hir pouert þan euir scho had in wardly wyrschipe' (EETS 291 (1987), 255/16–20)]. See also *Medium Ævum* 52 (1983), 154–5 (my review of Riehle).

tunc jucundae devotionis lacrymas emittebat, ita ut lacrymae de vultu ejus jucundae tanquam de fonte serenissimo effluere viderentur (*LA* p. 761) [then she wept tears of joyful devotion, such that the joyful tears flowed from her face as from a most pure fountain]

Occasionally, it is true, they strike a darker note: in one vision tears alternate repeatedly with laughter (rather like Julian's important seventh showing), and are later explained, the tears as her reaction to the withdrawing of Christ's presence, the laughter as her pleasure at his return (*ibid*). Overall, though, they are not much like Margery's tears: their origins and effects are different; there is no loud crying to offend the neighbours.

Stronger than the claim of either to be the text our scribe was referring to, and so recognised by Allen (n. to 154/13), is the anonymous revelations-text. This shares a number of features with Margery's *Book*. In both, Christ forgives the visionary all her sins on more than one occasion (revs 11–13, *Ol* pp. 76, 78, *Book* 16/34–5 and n.); in both St John the Evangelist is called, in the absence of a priest (in Margery's case, a priest who understands English), to be the visionary's confessor (rev. 10, *Ol* p. 74, *Book* 81/4 and n.); Margery is as afraid to answer a divine invitation (to marry God the Father, *Book* 87/7–8) as 'Elizabeth' to answer a question from the Virgin (do you love God?) either affirmatively or negatively (rev. 8, *Ol* p. 70). Most notably, the anonymous revelations regularly originate with, or produce, tears (revs. 1,3, *Ol* pp. 52, 54): tears which sometimes express grief for particular sins (rev. 6, *Ol* p. 60), for the saint's sinful state (revs. 2,12, *Ol* pp. 54, 76), or for a wrong done her (rev. 11, *Ol* p. 74); and tears which, at other times, are caused by fervent prayer and expressive of devotion (*Ar* 393/6, wanting in *Ol*). And the Virgin Mary, who is for most of the time the only speaker, offers herself in this respect as model (rev. 7, *Ol* p. 66). These tears look much closer to the ones that Margery weeps than those of Franciscan great-aunt or Dominican great-niece (though, as earlier noted, the Middle English translation, which our scribe might have been reading, identifies 'Elizabeth' with the great-aunt).

'The reuelacions of saynt Elysabeth' deserve a better press than they seem until now to have received. (As a sign of that, we may note that some manuscripts conclude with additions from the Book of Angela of Foligno (*Ol* p. 80), with no great crashing of theological gears, or glaringly obvious join.) They have a double shape of progressive revelation about the life of the Virgin and the birth of Christ (revs. 4–7, 9), and, parallel to the Virgin's spiritual development, a growth of Elizabeth herself in holiness. The former may now – does – seem, via the familiar lens of pseudo-Bonaventura, a typically medieval development and not especially significant or interesting. The latter is something else. It is marked by a repeated pattern of promised or actual forgiveness (see above) in counterpoint with a wrong committed and (a mark of increasing holiness) another patiently endured (revs. 6, 11, *Ol* pp. 60, 74). What is most exciting about this forgiveness, of all sins ever committed by the Saint, is not its repetition (that, after all, the text shares with Margery); nor its traditional understanding that such is achieved by the

Passion of Christ (rev. 12, *Ol* pp. 76, 78); but the awareness that such a forgiveness does not take away the human capacity to sin again. An early promise of forgiveness explains, in response to the Saint's expressed fear that she has not kept the previous counsels of the Virgin, that the Virgin did not choose her because of her ability to remain sinless (rev. 2, *Ol* p. 54). Again, at the end of the story, Christ guarantees Elizabeth's forgiveness for a third time, and, when Elizabeth asks plaintively why she goes on sinning, answers that she acquires greater humility and love as a result: sin, we are reminded, is very behovely. In such a context expressions of a sense of personal unworthiness, however earnest – and Elizabeth makes them several times – are besides the point, a mark only of her capacity for endless argument (cf. rev. 5, *Ol* p. 60: 'tu semper litigas'): and, indeed, may get in the road of the very graces being offered, such as tears.

If this were the text our scribe had in mind, it would be unfair to complain that he had neglected its spirit in relentless pursuit of its letter: saints are proved to be saints by reference to the example and practice of other saints. Equally, it may be argued that only the spirit guarantees the practices of the letter, and it is the spirit which crucially requires to be demonstrated in any analysis of sanctity. It would be a pity if the modern reader were to depend on our scribe, or even on Allen's notes, for an appreciation of 'the revelations of Elizabeth'.

III

No such problems of identification attend the defence's principal witness. We can identify very precisely the text being referred to. The *Vita* of Mary of Oignies was written in 1215, two years after she died, and directed, we learn from the prologue, to Bishop Fulco of Toulouse.[16] This original form of the *Vita*, in two Books each with thirteen chapters, is represented in England by two copies of the Latin, and a Middle English translation, with clear Carthusian connections.[17] 'Maistyr Custawns', who, as earlier noted, resolved Margery's doubts by referring to the life of

---

[16] In this paper quotation from the *Vita*, abbreviated *JV*, is taken from *Acta Sanctorum*, abbreviated *ASS*: see *ASS* June, ed. by G. Henschenius *et al.* (Antwerp 1695–1717), IV, 636–66, cited by Book, chapter, and numbered paragraph (de Vitry's book and chapter divisions are in the margin). Translation is provided from MS Douce 114, in 'Prosalegenden', ed. by C. Horstmann, *Anglia* VIII (1885), abbreviated A, 134–84 (Horstmann's emendations silently accepted). For a modern English translation, see F. M. Chaugy, *The Lives of S. Jane Frances de Chantal [etc.]*, 2 vols (London 1852), II. 315–447.

[17] For information about these manuscripts, and comment on the relation of the *Vita* to contemporary heretical developments, see P. Deery Kurtz, 'Mary of Oignies, Christine the Marvelous, and Medieval Heresy', *Mystics Quarterly*, abbreviated *MQ*, XIV:4 (1988), 186–96. The Carthusian connection, observable in MSS Douce 114 and Oxford St John's College 182 (so Deery Kurtz), is reinforced in the MS Bodley 240 copy of the life of St Christina Mirabilis, often linked with the *Vita* of Mary (see further below): the original 'est apud Lond. inter monachos Cartus.' (*Nova Legenda Anglie*, ed. by C. Horstmann (Oxford 1901), I, lxi, a text drawn to my attention by Dr Bruce Barker-Benfield, Bodleian Library.)

Mary of Oignies, may have known the work in this form: but since the work circulated in other forms – and since, moreover, two of them witness to a specific and ongoing Dominican interest in the work – he's likelier to have encountered it in one of these latter.[18] These were both produced by Dominicans. The first was the work of Vincent of Beauvais, who inserted an abbreviated version of de Vitry's *Vita* into what became the fourth part of his *Speculum Maius*, the *Speculum Historiale*, composed between 1244 and 1259 (Book XXX, chs x–li: ch. x, Vincent's own prologue; chs xi–xv, de Vitry's prologue).[19] The second was produced c.1309 by Arnold of Liège, who quarried the *Vita* for a dozen *exempla* in his popular *Alphabetum Narrationum*.[20]

Whatever the form in which Custawns knew the *Vita*, Margery's scribe read it either in a manuscript of the *Speculum* or in a form deriving directly from it. His references to 'þe xviij capitulo [of the *Vita*] þat begynnyth, "Bonus es, domine, sperantibus in te", and also. . . þe xix capitulo' (153/10–12) match those in the *Speculum* but not in the standard text (where the quoted words appear at the start of I.v).[21] Nor do they match those in the *Alphabetum*, where the *exempla* are cited only by author e.g. London, British Library MS Harley 268 f. 163v, 'Iacobus de Uictriaco'; London, British Library MS Royal 15 D v, f. 282r, 'Jaques de Vitry raconte').

I said 'a form deriving directly from' Vincent's text – for example, a *Vita* extracted from it – because one such exists in MS Bodleian Canon. Misc. 205, ff. 128r–139r, a manuscript which illustrates yet again the links between Mary and

---

[18] This 'Dominican interest' may have begun soon after Mary's death. Fulco provides a link between Mary, of whom he was a close friend, and the founder of the Dominicans (fuller details below). On Fulco, see further J. A. Herbert, *Catalogue of Romances in the British Museum*, 3 vols (London 1883–1910), III. 494. A third version of the *Vita*, dependent on Vincent's, appears in the *Historia Aurea* of John of Teignmouth. I have consulted the MS Bodley 240 copy of this work (pp. 475–80, drawn to my notice by Mr Martin Kauffmann, Bodleian Library).

[19] For these dates, see *The Oxford Dictionary of the Christian Church*, ed. by F. L. Cross, 2nd ed. (London, 1974), p. 1441, and M. Paulmier, 'Etude sur l'état des connaissances au milieu du XIIIe siècle: nouvelles recherches sur la genèse du *Speculum maius* de Vincent de Beauvais', *Spicae: cahiers de l'atelier de Vincent de Beauvais*, 1 (1978), 91–119. I have consulted the *Speculum Historiale*, abbreviated VB, in the 1591 Venice edition, pp. 431r–5v.

[20] For date and author, see Herbert, *Catalogue of Romances* III. 423–8. For a Middle English translation, see *An Alphabet of Tales*, ed. M. M. Banks, EETS OS 126–7 (London 1904–5), where the relevant items are 21, 136, 145, 268, 273, 323, 588–9, 616, 660, 670, 789. See also Allen's n. to 153/10.

[21] A shared error also links Book and VB rather than JV at 153/15 (see further below, and cf Allen's n. to this line). On 'sperantibus', ASS edition of JV reads 'spirantibus' in error: MSS of JV consulted, and VB, read 'sperantibus', the latter clearly required by the context. The version of Vincent's *Vita* in the *Historia Aurea* (see above, n. 18) wants this material – as also Vincent's chapter numbers – and so cannot have been the text to which the scribe was referring. For a later use of Vincent's version of JV, see the prologue to *The Mirror or Glass of Christ's Passion* (1533), by the Syon monk Fewterer (sigs. aiiiv–ivr).

the Dominicans. The manuscript emanates from the Dominican scriptorium in Venice c.1407–10;[22] it contains exclusively Dominican material, and describes how Mary's Life, taken from Book XXXI of the *Speculum Historiale*,[23] has been included

> non solum ex deuocione ad supradictas. . . sed eciam. . . de magna con-
> ueniencia supradicte sancte et aliarum predictarum ad beatam
> Katherinam de Senis quoad quam plurima prout diligenter inspicienti
> poterit faciliter apparere (f. 128r) [not only out of devotion to the afore-
> said women (i.e. the holy women of Liège: see further below) but also
> from the great harmony between the aforesaid and other foresaid saintly
> women to the blessed Katherine of Siena (represented in MS, *inter alia*,
> by Raymond of Capua's *Legenda* and an excerpt from his translation of
> the *Dialogo*) in respect of very many features, as a careful study will easily
> reveal]

Jacques, as we shall see, had presented Mary in company with other holy women of Liège, in particular, though he did not name her, St Christina Mirabilis. Thomas of Cantimpré makes this link explicit in the prologue to his life of the latter,[24] and, as in A, manuscripts regularly add a third life to those of Mary and Christina (MQ 14, 186–7, 195): this, of St Elizabeth of Spalbeck, also takes place 'in þe prouince of Leody [Liège]'. Vincent made Mary's life part of the history of his times, including, in Book XXX, reports of the Lateran Council (Fulco travelled there with St Dominic, ch. lxv) and of the crusades against the Albigensians, a brief account of St Elizabeth of Hungary derived 'ex cronicis' and 'ex gestis eius' (ch. cxxxvi),[25] and, above all, the story of the establishment of the Dominicans. MS Canon. Misc. 205 returns Mary to her original context of saintly women, this time all Italians and all Dominican tertiaries: Joan of Orvieto, Margaret of Castel-lo, Mary of Venice, and St Catherine,[26] whose canonisation was being energeti-cally pursued at this time in Venice by the collection of testimony in its support (n. to 65/38). Mary's place in this new anthology seems designed to further that cause by virtue of the 'magna conueniencia' held to exist between her and St Catherine. Margery's scribe may have read Mary's life in such an anthology as

---

[22] For date and place of composition, see C. Huter, 'Cristoforo Cortese in the Bodleian Library', *Apollo* (Jan. 1980), 11–17.

[23] This error (XXXI for XXX) is shared by the *titulus* to the Book (but not the running title) in VB.

[24] See Thomas of Cantimpré, ASS 24 July Bd. V, 650 (quoted A p. 104, and translated A 119/3ff).

[25] This abbreviated narrative cannot be identified with the 'tretys' of 'Elizabeth', since it does not refer to the gift of tears.

[26] This linking of Mary and Catherine provides a parallel with the linkage of the two in the Douce 114 translation (cf. MQ 14, 187).

this.[27] And Margery's interest in and knowledge of Mary – which, like that of her scribe, looks to have come through Dominican channels – was very probably given an increased impetus, and maybe even generated, during her stay in Venice in 1414 (ibid.), shortly after the production of the manuscript.

Yet if the identification of the text has proved unproblematic, the scribe's use of that text is a very different matter.

The original was a clear repsonse to the troubled times in which its author was living (DSp VIII, 60–2). In the prologue de Vitry reminds bishop Fulco how, when the heretics had driven him out of his diocese, he made his way to Liège, attracted there by the reputation of the crusaders against the heretics and of the holy women whose impeccable orthodoxy stood as such a reproach to the latters' errors: 'magis pro uno veniali lugentes quam homines in partibus tuis pro mille mortalibus' (JV §2, VB ch. xi) [weeping more over one venial sin than the men of your region for a thousand mortal sins]. He found in Liège a Promised Land (Toulouse having be⌞ ⌟e Egypt of the Pharaohs with the arrival of the heretics) and a garden full of lilies. Even when Liège was sacked, and later, when there was a famine lasting three years, he saw, and could witness, to the virtues of those lilies of God. Mary's story is one among many. One woman, for instance, was for many years confined to bed suffering from no other illness than her desire to be with God; another, like Mary, was renowned for her tears, which 'tamen caput non evacuabant sed [VB scilicet] quadam plenitudine mentem refovebant' (JV §6, VB ch. xiv) [did not dull the mind but nourished it completely]; still another (Christina Mirabilis) died and was resurrected before burial so that she could have her purgatory on earth. Miracles are also recorded in connection with the Eucharist, which ought to be a reproach to those heretics 'qui cibi [VB sibi] huius suauitatem nec fide nec corde percipiunt' (JV ibid., VB ch. xv) [who neither believe in nor experience in the heart the sweetness of this food]. This concern to restate orthodox values against the spread of heresy is reflected regularly in the Vita: most notably, when Mary proposes to undertake a pilgrimage to the site where a massacre of crusaders took place, and prophetically anticipates a future Crusade, though at that time, three years before it was called, there was no mention of heretics in the locality (II.vii, JV §82, VB ch.xli).

But de Vitry was not writing only to give orthodoxy a shot in the arm; his prologue tells of enemies within as well as without: worldly men who defame the holy women and call them by new and insulting names, even as the Jews called Christ a Samaritan and his disciples Galileans.[28] That new and insulting name, Beguine, Jacques does not permit himself to repeat in the Vita: when first it appears, near the end of the twelfth century, the word carries a pejorative sense (of 'heretic', because of its supposed derivation from 'Albigensis/Albeghini') that

---

[27] But not this one: Dr Barker-Benfield informs me that it did not come to the UK till 1817.

[28] See DSp I (1937), 1314ff for information in this paragraph.

it begins to lose only after ecclesiastical approval for the inauguration of a common life for the beguines reduces the perceived dangers of heresy. At the outset, it needs only certain tendencies, such as fervent worship, mystical leanings, and even chastity, to give rise to a suspicion of heresy: not for the first time the ultra-orthodox are in danger of being identified with that very error against which they are reacting. To defend orthodoxy against the heretics therefore carried with it, for Jacques, the secondary duty of offering Mary as a model of orthodoxy to the lazy and the worldly.

Hence Mary's example is positively and insistently affirmed. As is usual in writing of this sort (sermons and penitential manuals, for example),[29] the text creates a hypothetical reader by projecting outwards from the narrative, at appropriate points, its own negatives. De Vitry regularly addresses this reader, directly and indirectly, urging upon him/her the challenge of Mary's example (many of these figures of rhetoric are wanting in Vincent's version of the text). Mary's chastity warns lechers to repent (I.iii, JV §14); her modesty of dress is a reproach to fashionable women (I.xi, JV §37); chatterers should learn from her silence (I.xii, JV §38, VB ch. xxvi); those covetous of worldly wealth should remember how her love of poverty led her to cut her headcloths in two so as to share them with the poor (II.ii, JV §46): and so on. All the same, the worldly are likely to find fault: a revelation from Mary to a priest not to accept a second, better-endowed, benefice is likely to arouse objection among priestly readers whose knowledge of Gratian, and their own dues, so much exceeds their interest in this present book that, should they chance to read it, they will, he tells them,

> ancillae Christi visiones phantasmata seu somnia, ridendo more vestro repudiatis (II.vi, JV §78) [count þe visyouns of Crystes mayden fantoms, or ellis, as ȝoure maner is, scorne hem as dremes (A 167/46–168/2)]

Nor is the writer above reproach; like Margery's scribe, de Vitry lets himself be seen more than once in a poor light. In company with others, for example, he laughs at her for making so much in confession, so exhaustingly, and so often, of the slightest fault: and so, by implication, passes a judgement on himself for preferring his own ease and creature comforts to the truths and duties of his faith (I.vi, JV §19, VB ch. xx).

Yet it does not seem, either, that we are authorised to follow Mary all the way in her practice. De Vitry's account of her early married life (I.ii, JV §12, VB ch. xvii) includes what one might have reckoned unexceptionable – and not even, in context, especially exceptional – expressions of piety, worthy of imitation by heretic and worldly Christian alike. Mary spends the great part of the night in manual work and prayer; the little sleep she permits herself she takes on boards on

---

[29] See examples in R. Ellis, *Patterns of Religious Narrative in the Canterbury Tales* (London 1986), p. 32 n. 75.

the floor; she wears a knotted cord about her body. This account carries the equivalent of a government health warning:

> nec hoc dixero [VB dixerunt] vt excessum commendem, sed ut fervorem ostendam. In iis [VB his] autem et multis aliis quae privilegio gratiae operata est, attendat lector discretus quod paucorum privilegia non faciunt legem communem. Ejus virtutes imitemur: opera vero virtutum ejus sine privato privilegio imitari non possumus [VB om. Eius. . . possumus] (*ibid.*) [I seye not þis, preisynge þe exces, but tellynge þe feruoure. In þis and many oþer þat she wroghte by priuelege of grace, lat þe discrete reder take hede þat priuilege of a fewe makiþ not a commun lawe. Folowe wee hir vertues; þe werkes of hir vertues wiþ-outen specyal priuilege folowe maye wee not. (A 136/4–9)]

Mary's 'exces', that is – and the narrative does contain 'many oþer' instances – is praiseworthy only as a sign of fervour, or, as we shall see, as a mark of the Spirit's dealings with her: we should imitate her virtues but not 'þe werkes of hir vertues' without ' specyal priuilege' (a phrase repeated in II.iv, *JV* §64, A 162/37). One of the more dramatic of these 'werkes' consisted of a habit of self-mutilation: Mary punished herself for sensual delight in her food by cutting off and burying great gobbets of her flesh (I.vii, *JV* §22, VB ch. xx). This physical excess is described first in traditional negative terms ('carnes suas fastidiens' [loþinge hir fleshe]); then, more importantly, in positive: while she so mistreats her body, she is enflamed with a huge heat of love and sees one of the Seraphim standing by her 'in hoc mentis excessu' [in þis excesse of mynde]. Physical excess, that is, is validated by a partnering spiritual excess: and this latter may be safely applauded. All the same, both are dangerous in inexperienced hands: a friend seizes Mary's hand in an excess of spiritual affection and finds himself subject to stirrings of a very unspiritual sort (II.c, *JV* §75, VB ch. xxxviii). Indeed, it is one of the marks of Mary's sanctity that she is anxious to observe a mean and avoid excess (Ii.ii, *JV* §43, VB ch. xxix: excessive abstinence, for instance, I.viii, *JV* §23, VB ch. xxi). Yet undeniable excesses ('modum non habebat') may be justified in terms of their proposed ends (the salvation of souls, for example, II.ii, *JV* §56, VB ch. xxxiii), or by contrast with the Saint's public demeanour towards her neighbours:

> Licet autem quantum ad proximos. . . mira discretione pacem custodiret, sibi tamen soli indiscreta valde [VB valde indiscreta] seipsam nimis abiiciens, et supra modum affligens nobis aliquando videbatur. Ipsa tamen circa se tanto discretior erat quanto nihil de se nisi a Spiritu sancto familiariter edocta aliquid facere praesumebat (II.iv, *JV* §63, VB ch. xxxv) [And þof she kepte pees wiþ a wondir discrecyone anent hir neighbors. . . to hirselfe she was ful vndiscrete, settynge ouerelitil by hirselfe and turmentynge aboue mesure, as it semyd to vs sumtyme. In so myche she was more discrete anenste hirselfe, in as myche as she pre-

sumed to do nothinge of hirselfe but famylierly taghte of þe holy goste (A 162/23–9)]

This passage draws a fine line between 'turmentynge aboue mesure' and being 'more discrete': how you interpret Mary's practices depends partly on the spectacles you happen to be wearing ('as it semyd to vs sumtyme'). 'In as myche' as Mary was divinely inspired, any appearance of excess reflects merely the limited viewpoint of the bystanders. The text, that is, manages to keep all its options open.

The options are not, however, equally open to all. At the same time as he is positively recommending Mary's example to his readers, de Vitry is systematically placing it beyond the reach of most of them (though not Fulco, the book's first reader, who is accorded an exemplary walk-on part, in a sort of spiritual coda, near the end of each book).[30] You can see this most easily by comparing the discretion Jacques allows the reader with the discretion he describes in Mary, in the previous quotations from I.ii and II.iv respectively. The reader's discretion is called into being only to acknowledge the impossibility and undesirability of imitating Mary's practices à la lettre; Mary's is presented rather as an expression of obedience to the Spirit and duty to the neighbour. In other words, de Vitry is both affirming a literal example and constraining most of his readers to a metaphoric reading of it.

This is some way from how Margery's scribe read the story: though, to be fair, part of the responsibility for his misreading lies with the version of the story he was following. It was Vincent, after all, who gave Mary such a dramatic exit from the church in response to the priest's request that she refrain from weeping: where Jacques had described a secret withdrawal ('clam egressa'), Vincent created a noisy one ('clamans egressa'): and it was this version that our scribe faithfully reported ('went owt. . . wyth a lowde voys crying', 153/14–15).[31] And it was Vincent who tipped the balance of elements in Jacques' original from the arguing of a case to the reporting of a miraculous and incident-filled life: an emphasis which, followed to its logical conclusion, made Mary and the other saintly women of Liège items in an alphabet of preachers' tales (Arnold's). All the same, Vincent did not destroy the balance between argument and narrative: he retained most of the passages warning aspiring saints against the dangers of excess. Such warnings Margery's scribe seems to have had no time for: caution in religious matters would seem for him, as for Margery, to indicate not care for the complexities of truth but faintheartedness and cowardice.[32] As with 'the revelations of Elizabeth' he got the

---

[30] These are I.xiii (JV §41), II.xii (JV §104, VB ch. xlix).

[31] 'Clamans' also occurs in the story as preserved in Arnold's Alphabetum (e.g. London, British Library MS Harley 268 f. 138f), though whether or not this points to derivation of the Alphabetum from VB cannot be determined on present knowledge. The ME translation reads 'rase vpp' (EETS, OS 127 p. 294), perhaps derived from a reading like 'eleuans'; London, British Library MS Harley 4725 copy of JV, f. 164v, reads 'iam'.

[32] To be fair, Jacques himself is trenchant in criticism of those who dismiss the visions of

letter of his text bang to rights; he just missed its spirit. (And a similar conclusion could, I think, have been reached, had space permitted, with respect to 'Boneauentur' and 'þe Prykke of Lofe'.)

Perhaps the greatest irony in this transformation of woman into first argument, and then simple exemplum, of sanctity is the existence of a deeper parallel between the two women than the scribe's concentration on their physical symptoms could reveal: simply, the situation of holy women (of any age) labelled heretics by the worldly. As Mary to the Albigensians, so Margery to the Wycliffites (e.g. 28/28–29/3, 112/1–2, 129/22–31). Our priest, however, was no de Vitry: that role had been assumed by a previous generation of English mystics (Walter Hilton, the *Cloud* author) who had reacted to the outbreak of the new heresy with warnings against excess and literalmindedness like those of de Vitry. It had also been incarnated by Julian of Norwich, from whom Margery sought confirmation of her own practices. After all, it was Julian who, in ch. 72 of the long version of her *Shewings*, wrote of tears that 'we should not stynten of moning ne of gostly weping, that is. . . of peynfull longing':[33] whether actual or not, tears finally signify, like roarings in Church, only as metaphors.

Mary as 'phantasmata seu somnia' (II.vi, JV §78): as is the Douce translator in an addition to the text (A 182/12–15).

[33] *Julian of Norwich: A Revelation of Love*, ed. M. Glasscoe (Exeter 1976), p. 87.

Additional note: the ascription of the *Vita* of Elizabeth of Hungary, in *Legenda Aurea*, to Jacques de Vitry depends solely on Allen's n. to 154/13. Conceivably, as Sarah McNamer has pointed put to me, Allen may have meant to write 'Jacobus da Voragine'. My argument remains unaffected by this finding, fortunately.

The Latin Mirror of Simple Souls:
Margaret Porette's 'ultimate accolade'?

Edmund Colledge

Connoisseurs of recent studies in medieval letters will recognise in this title the allusion to Professor Hussey's seminal study,[1] in which he presented, with the quiet lucidity and authority which we have learned to expect of him, the evidence for the manuscript tradition of Walter Hilton's *Scale*, and the conclusions to be reached from it. With great probability he argued that for a spiritual work to have been translated into Latin and then, usually, to have been circulated among readers, learned but without command of the vernacular tongue in which it was first composed, was to award it 'the ultimate accolade'. Here one wishes to argue against an opinion that this accolade was so bestowed on Margaret Porette's *Mirror of Simple Souls*.[2]

The facts concerning her *Mirror* can be stated briefly. She seems to have been a French-speaking native of Valenciennes, where, before 1307, the bishop of Cambrai ordered a copy of the *Mirror*, which had been condemned as heretical, to be publicly burned in her presence. She was then warned what would be the consequences for her if she persisted in publishing her book. From this we may guess that those responsible for her prosecution had discerned in her few marks of repentance or submission; and later events confirm that such was her disposition. She sent other copies of her book – which she had been expressly forbidden to do – to three theologians, one of whom, Godfrey of Fontaines, was a celebrated teacher of the University of Paris whose historicity is well-attested. All three sent

---

[1] 'Latin and English in the *Scale of Perfection*', *Mediaeval Studies* 35 (1973) pp. 456–76.
[2] This brief discussion is derived from the writer's introduction to the modern English translation which he has made, in collaboration with Judith Grant and J. C. Marler, from the only identifiable surviving manuscript, which we call 'MS C', Chantilly, Musée Condé, MS F. xiv. 26. My thanks are due to Mlle. Amélie Lefébure, conservateur des collections at Chantilly, for kindly allowing me access to MS C at a time not especially convenient to her, to Miss Winefrede Cobb for her generosity and expert typing, to Dr Frank Mantello, chairman of the Department of Greek and Latin at the Catholic University of America, and to Fr. Alberico de Meijer and Fr. Martijn Schrama at the Augustinian Provincial Library at Eindhoven, for putting their bibliographical skills and resources unreservedly at my disposal.

Margaret certificates of qualified approbation, even though one of them confessed that he could not understand the *Mirror*; and she was urged to exercise caution in distributing it too widely. Instead she formed a plan which was in the end to prove fatal to her. She had new copies made with the theologians' certificates inserted as a prologue (the only available manuscript of the original French, now in the Condé Museum at Chantilly, lacks these, but they do appear in the Middle English translation), and sent one to the bishop of Châlons-sur-Marne, evidently hoping for a favourable verdict from him with which she might circumvent the Valenciennes condemnation.

This stratagem did not succeed. Instead, the bishop placed the matter, and the book, in the hands of the Inquisition, already well informed of its history. So it was that Margaret was arrested and sent to Paris for imprisonment, to await interrogation by France's chief inquisitor, William Humbert, universally known as 'William of Paris'.

It is in no way partisan to add to this 'of evil memory'. He had become notorious for the leading part which he had played in the infamous proceedings against the French Templars, which culminated in a hideous auto da fè when more than fifty of them perished in Paris. Even in an age not conspicuous for humanitarianism, public opinion had so turned against the Inquisition and its works that William, it is very evident, perceived that in Margaret's case justice – or what in those days passed for justice – must be shown to have been done. This accounts for the care with which each stage in her trial was recorded and re-counted before, in June 1310, she was 'handed over to secular power' and burned at the stake. Few heresy prosecutions of the Middle Ages are so lavishly docu-mented; and there is no condemned work for which such a plethora of evidence survives.[3]

The pioneers in calendaring and editing this were Paul Frédericq and H. C. Lea, although they both presumed that Margaret's book had not survived, it being the Inquisition's policy ruthlessly to destroy all such writings. We shall see that William attempted to do this for the *Mirror* but that he failed. In our own time, we owe a huge debt to Romana Guarnieri for the enterprise and assiduity which enabled her to make, in 1946, her sensational announcement that the *Mirror* had survived, and to follow this with her transcript of 'MS C', Chantilly, Musée Condé, MS F.xiv.26.[4] More recently, valuable work on the *Mirror* and its back-ground has been published by Robert E. Lerner;[5] and Paul Verdeyen of the Dutch

[3] The most up-to-date bibliography of the trial documents is found in Paul Verdeyen: 'Le procès d'inquisition contre Marguerite Porete et Guiard de Cressonessart (1309–1310)' *Revue d'histoire ecclésiastique* 81 (1986) pp. 47–94.

[4] *Le mirouer des simples ames anienties et qui seulement demourent en vouloir et desir d'amour* (Rome, 1961); 'Il "Miroir des simples ames" di Margherita Porete', *Archivio italiano per la storia della pietà* 4 (1965) pp. 501–648 (French text).

[5] 'An Angel of Philadelphia ... the Case of Guiard of Cressonessart' (in *Order and Innovation in the Middle Ages: Essays in Honor of Joseph R. Strayer*, ed. William C. Jordan,

province of the Society of Jesus has frequently engaged our attention with the competence with which he has demonstrated the many resemblances between Margaret and spiritual writers of unimpeachable orthodoxy in the Netherlands, notably Hadewijch of Brabant.[6] Elsewhere we shall discuss how such resemblances between authors writing in Dutch and in French may have originated; and it is not germane to our present purposes to raise here the question, to which so many contradictory answers have been offered, of whether Margaret's condemnation and barbarous execution were justified. Instead, we shall offer our chief criticism of Verdeyen's work, and endeavour to show, using Hussey's criteria, that it contains one fundamental misconception.

It is in Fr. Verdeyen's 'Essai de biographie critique'[7] that one finds the first record of his interest in Margaret. He calls her 'a Beguine of Valenciennes', whereas there is no contemporary evidence that that is where she was born; and in our forthcoming work we give our reasons for thinking that the attribution to her of a Beguine's status, for which we have only William Humbert's word, may be no more than casual denigration. We describe the evidence we found in the Valenciennes municipal archives to show that even if she had been a Beguine there, she might have lived free of every restriction, beyond those which bound every baptised Christian. In 1987 Professor Henri Platelle made the same point, though without producing documented evidence, in his article, subtle and well-informed, though not wholly disingenuous, 'Porete (Marguerite)'.[8]

Whatever criticisms we may offer of Fr. Verdeyen's already published contributions to this debate, they have earned him the gratitude of scholars who are concerned. He has given us a careful and precise description of the documents of Margaret's trial,[9] in which he followed Robert Lerner's good example[10] by taking account of the puzzling case of Guiard of Cressonessart, also tried in Paris in 1310 by France's chief inquisitor, William Humbert.

The chief charge against Guiard, that he 'favoured and supported' Margaret, seems to mean little more than that in other parts of France he had defended the doctrines of 'the Brethren of the Free Spirit', that – very probably – he knew Margaret to be the author of the anonymous Mirror, which Romana Guarnieri justly called the 'Bible of the "Brethren" ', and that he had denounced William's proceedings, once they were under way, as contrary to justice.

Yet Fr. Verdeyen's major achievement to date must be regarded as his critical

Bruce McNab, Teofilo F. Ruiz (Princeton 1976) pp. 343–64, 529–40; and see also The Heresy of the Free Spirit in the Later Middle Ages (Berkeley 1972).

[6] See note 3: 'Le procès . . .' contains the most complete list of writings concerning Margaret, including Verdeyen's own.

[7] In Jan van Ruusbroec: The sources, content and sequels of his mysticism, ed. P. Mommaers and N. de Paepe (Louvain 1984) p. 8.

[8] Catholicisme hier aujourd'hui demain, fasc. 51, coll. 646–7.

[9] See note 3.

[10] See note 5.

Latin text in the 'Continuatio Mediaeualis', and its critical apparatus, which collation with Dr Guarnieri's edition of the French shows to be a frequent and necessary help in the difficult task of interpreting the often enigmatic *Mirror*. It is only to be regretted that the apparatus is incomplete; some significant omissions of French words and phrases from the Latin are not recorded.

The apparatus given often shows us what seem to be defects in MS C. Towards the end of the prologue we read: '. . . loing du palais ouquel les tres nobles amis de ce seigneur demourent', 'far from the palace where the very noble friends of this lord dwell'; yet the Latin gives this as: 'longe ab illa pace in qua nobilissimi amici illius principis commorantur'.[11] Evidently this derives from a crux 'palais/pais' (which in Old French can mean either 'peace', feminine, or 'land', masculine).

At times, however, the French seems to be superior to the Latin. In chapter 11 Love observes: 'C'est a dire que cestse Ame est de si grant constance que se elle avoit toute la congnoissance de toutes les creatures . . .' ('This means that this Soul is so very constant that though she had the knowledge of every creature . . .') where as the Latin merely reads: 'Hoc est dictum quod si ista anima haberet omnem notitiam omnium creaturarum . . .'.[12] The Latin translator may have been working from a defective French copy, or perhaps he did not understand 'est de si grant constance'.

In places it may seem that he considered it prudent not to translate over-literally. In chapter 19, when again Love is speaking, she observes: 'Icelluy seul Dieu . . . qui les a creees et rachetees et par auenture maintes foiz recreees', the Latin omits 'and, it may be, recreated them again and again'.[13] This omission, we suggest, may have been made because it was thought that this notion of Margaret smacked of 'Priscillianist pre-existentianism'; or it may have been caused through homoeotopy between 'creees' and 'recreees'.

Chapter 25 concludes, in the French, with: '. . . et elle est commune a tous par la largesse de parfaicte charité, set seule en Dieu par la divine emprise de Fine Amour', ('and she [such a Soul] is common to all through the generosity of perfect charity, and alone in God, since Perfect Love has taken possession of her'). Yet the Latin translates this: '. . . by the divine intention of Perfect Love',[14] and all the manuscripts support this. We have observed that a difficulty here is the correct interpretation of medieval French 'emprise': 'emprise' in courtly literature can mean the undertaking to which a knight has bound himself, wearing some token to show that he was so bound; but later contexts suggest that 'has taken possession', is intended here. The Latin may indicate that the translator was in a quandary over how to understand 'emprise'.

[11] Ed. Guarnieri (note 4), p. 22; ed. Verdeyen: *Margaretae Porete: Speculum Simplicium Animarum* (parallel with R.G's French) Corpus Christianorum Continuatio Mediaeualis LXIX (Turnhout, 1986) p. 15

[12] Ed. Guarnieri, p. 530; ed. Verdeyen, p. 43.

[13] Ed. Guarnieri, p. 539; ed. Verdeyen, p. 77.

[14] Ed. Guarnieri, p. 544; ed. Verdeyen, p. 93.

When in chapter 27 Margaret wrote: 'Meditation of Love knows well . . . that she must not exert herself' ('que elle ne se doit exonier') – one of many manifestations of her expressions of sympathy for Quietist teachings – the Latin has 'that she must not intrude herself' ('non debet se intromittere').[15] Again all the Latin manuscripts support this, suggesting that the translator himself did not understand the exact meaning of 'exonier'.

The brief chapter 28[16] contains a quite exceptional number of errors in both the French and Latin versions. Love's opening statement, 'Such a Soul, says Love, swims in the sea of joy', has in R. Guarnieri's edition been silently emended from MS C's 'Telle Amour', 'Such a Love'; and the French 'swims' is replaced by the Latin 'sinks', 'drowns'. The French continues: '. . . she feels no joy, for she herself is joy', which in the Latin becomes 'for she dwells in joy'. The French goes on: 'Now they [the Soul and joy] have one common will . . .', which the Latin changes to: 'Now they are one and indivisible'. The conclusion of the Latin is: '. . . and I am changed into that which I love more than I love myself', which the French omits, though we in our translation have supplied it. All this may point to some damage, never adequately repaired, in the French archetype.

In chapter 32, where Margaret makes the Soul say: 'Je n'ayme ne moi ne luy ne ses oeuvres', 'I do not love myself, or him, or his works', two Latin manuscripts have the correct 'amo nec me', but a third has 'amouet me', which Verdeyen has mistranscribed as 'amonet me'.[17]

In chapter 33, where Dr Guarnieri edits MS C to read 'La cognoissance des anges, des ames et des sains', we have preferred the Latin, and have emended to 'the knowledge of the angels and of the holy souls'.[18]

Editing chapter 39, Dr Guarnieri accepts MS C's 'comme sa pure serve' without question; but the Latin, 'eius humilis ancilla', suggests that this was made from a French text with the more probable 'poure', 'as his humble serving-maid'.[19]

Occasionally we find the Latin agreeing with MS C in readings which may be considered defective. For example, in chapter 51, the French has: 'O tres precieuse Hester', 'O most precious Esther', which the Latin also has: 'O pretiosissima Esther'; whereas we have suggested that in this context any allusion to the story of Esther is quite inappropriate, and have preferred the reading of the medieval English translation, 'O most sweet and precious being', which suggests a crux 'estre/Hester'.[20]

In chapter 59, the logical sequence of the dialogue between Reason and Love – 'When is such a Soul without herself? – When she does not belong to herself – And when does she not belong to herself?' is destroyed in MS C by the repeated

---

15 Ed. Guarnieri, p. 544; ed. Verdeyen, p. 95.
16 Ed. Guarnieri, p. 545; ed. Verdeyen, p. 96.
17 Ed. Guarnieri, p. 548; ed. Verdeyen, p. 107.
18 Ed. Guarnieri, p. 549; ed. Verdeyen, p. 113.
19 Ed. Guarnieri, p. 553; ed. Verdeyen, p. 122.
20 Ed. Guarnieri, p. 561; ed. Verdeyen, p. 153.

omission of 'not'. Verdeyen emends his Latin to 'et quando est sui ipsius', mistakenly in our opinion.[21]

In chapter 94, where Margaret wrote: 'ce vous convient il avoir, car c'est le sentier de divine vie', 'it is right that you should have this, for it is the path to the divine life', the Latin has: 'Ita oportet, quia istud est fundamentum diuinas uitae',[22] although the French 'sentier' is an evident allusion to Matthew 7.14 which, one again suspects, the Latin translator did not grasp.

In Verdeyen's extracts from the Latin trial documents there occurs one mistranscription, when one reads: '. . . presente . . . Guilelmo dicto Fratre, archidiacono Landonie in ecclesia sancti Andree in Scotia'.[23] 'Landonie' should be 'Laudonie'. In the introduction to our translation we have shown, from medieval Scottish documents, the historicity of the canonist William Frere, archdeacon of Lothian in the diocese of St Andrews.

We have until now delayed what constitutes our chief criticism of Verdeyen's work on the *Mirror*. In his first declaration of his intention to collate Vatican Library, MS Vaticana Chigiano B. iv 41 with the other known copies and to publish a text, he wrote: 'The first Latin version has a special interest . . . because it was made before 1310, while the author was still alive'.[24] One might surmise that this claim was based on his discovery of a manuscript which could be so dated; but that is not so. It is derived from an assumption, in our opinion erroneous, that Margaret's French has been turned into Latin to help the Inquisition's assessors in Paris to understand her book and to pass judgment on it; yet it was not the Inquisition's practice to require assessors to read the whole of suspect works, but only propositions, considered as dubious, which had been extracted from them. In particular, had Verdeyen been familiar with the case of Meister Eckhart, whose condemnation was separated from Margaret Porette's trial by less than twenty years, he might not have fallen into the error, as we consider, of believing that this Latin translation had been made as a preliminary document on which to base her prosecution. During Meister Eckhart's trial, during the late 1330s, at Cologne, the German vernacular works examined were not translated, but had German extracts only prepared from them.

It is true that not all of those appointed by William Humbert to serve on his canonists' and theologians' commissions were native speakers of French; yet we regard it as improbable that more was done with the *Mirror* than was usual in the scrutiny of writings suspected of heresy: that sentences, *articuli*, which seemed suspect to the scrutineers were drawn up in lists for submission to the commissioners, who were only required to read the lists, not the works from which

---

[21] Ed. Guarnieri, p. 567; ed. Verdeyen, p. 171.
[22] Ed. Guarnieri, p. 593; ed. Verdeyen, p. 265.
[23] Paris, National Archives Box J. 428 no. 165; Verdeyen, 'Le procès' (note 3), pp. 56–58.
[24] This is in Verdeyen's preliminary announcement of his intentions in *Ons Geestelik Erf* 55 (1981).

they were extracted. The authority on such procedures is still Josef Koch's important essay, 'Philosophische und theologische Irrtumslisten von 1270–1329'.[25] We can be virtually sure that the *articuli* were extracted from the French *Mirror*, and only then converted into Latin, because we know that that happened when the case against Eckhart was being prepared.

In recent editions of the Denzinger-Schönmetzer *Enchiridion Symbolorum*, the constitution *In agro dominico* of 27 March 1329, in which twenty-eight such Eckhart *articuli* were rehearsed and pronounced on, the contexts from which they were taken are identified. This we owe to the learned Dominican M.-H. Laurent.[26] Thus we find that twelve articles seem to come from Eckhart's Latin works, but fifteen from his German writings. Though his dossier, originally vast, was sent to Avignon, where it was much reduced, we may be sure that the articles which *In agro dominico* quotes are from the work of the first scrutineers, and that this work was done in Cologne by German speakers.

We find it difficult to suppose that anything different happened in the case of the *Mirror*. The existence of this Latin translation testifies rather to the vitality of Margaret's book, and shows that even after it had been condemned, twice, other clerics – for the Latin translator was surely such – could be convinced that it was a work of edification, as its author had claimed that the three theologians to whom she had appealed had judged. Nor need we be surprised that the translator was unaware of the Mirror's condemnation. Elsewhere we have shown how, one hundred and twenty years after Margaret had perished, a faction of the Council of Basle, intriguing against Eugene IV and claiming, falsely it would seem, that he had shown favour to the *Mirror* and to those who esteemed it, sought to have it condemned by the Council, plainly in ignorance of what had happened in Paris.

Furthermore, Verdeyen has overlooked another germane consideration. He assumed that the Inquisitors' assessors would be asked to read entire books which had been denounced as suspect; but Josef Koch has shown, to one's complete satisfaction, in 1930, that this was not so.[27] Nonetheless, we reiterate our gratitude to him for his valuable contributions to the further knowledge of this case, so perplexing and fascinating.

[25] Reprinted from *Mélanges Mandonnet* 2, 1930, in Koch's *Kleine Schriften*, 2 vols (Rome 1973) 2, 423–50.
[26] 'Autour du procès de maître Eckhart. Les documents des archives Vaticanes', *Divus Thomas* 39 (1936) pp. 331–48, 430–47.
[27] See note 25.

Notes on Some Medieval Mystical, Magical and Moral Cats

Douglas Gray

At first sight, medieval cats are rather an unreligious lot. Whenever they find themselves in holy pictures, they often seem uneasy or inattentive. One of Leonardo's pen and ink sketches of a Virgin and Child shows the Child grasping a large cat, which seems to be straining to escape from the Holy Infant's clasp.[1] Sometimes in Annunciation scenes we see a somnolent cat: a black cat will sit quietly in a corner of the scene, under a bench, or at the back of the scene directly under the hovering white Dove of the Holy Spirit, apparently unmindful of what is going on. Is this a detail which suggests that the great spiritual event takes place in the midst of ordinary life and domestic unconcern, a case of 'the Old Masters' understanding, as Auden says, that it takes place 'while someone else is eating or opening a window . . . in a corner . . . Where the dogs go on with their doggy life'?[2] Such a 'literal' reading would be charitable to the cats, and I think could be defended as sensible. But others would urge us to remember the possibility of symbols disguised under the apparently insignificant realia of life, and the demonic associations of the cat. Can it suggest the sleeping devil, unaware that he has been tricked? Or does the cat correspond to the symbolic mousetrap in which the devil is caught (in which case the cat is presumably playing a 'good' role)? But it does not seem clear which of these symbolic readings we should prefer, or indeed whether we should accept a symbolic reading at all. There is a similar ambiguity in an early sixteenth-century Annunciation by Lorenzo Lotto where the cat does react – it is startled by the angel and makes off rapidly.

Perhaps we need to admit at the outset that the significance of the cat may be ambiguous, and even complex. This impression is strengthened as we look further. Sometimes in scenes of the Last Supper a cat and a dog fight over food: they fight over the bones in that of Cosimo Roselli (1484) in the Sistine Chapel, and in that of Pietro Lorenzetti at Assisi (early fourteenth-century) the dog is eating scraps of

[1] One of a series of sketches for a Madonna with Child and cat. The pictures mentioned below can be found (with discussions by S. Rossi, S. S. Thaller, A. Cavallero, and others) in *Gatti nell'arte. Il magico e il quotidiano* (Rome 1987 [exhibition at the Palazzo Barberini]).
[2] 'Musée des Beaux-Arts'.

185

food which the servants are clearing away, watched closely by a cat with his ears laid back in hostility. Is this a symbolic suggestion of the working of the curse of original sin which is present in the main scene in the treachery of Judas, or, more simply (and to my mind more credibly), another example of a 'realistic' setting in the surrounding circumstances of ordinary life? This latter explanation seems likely to be the case in the Van Eyck miniature in the early fourteenth-century Turin Hours, where in the peaceful scene of the birth of John the Baptist there is a dog with a bone and a cat with a bowl – yet the fact that slippers are also visible has suggested a symbolic reading of a kind more favourable to the cat: humility / slippers; faithfulness / dog; prudence / cat. And what are we to make of the small figure of the cat which looks on without curiosity at the scene of female vanity in 'Pride' in Bosch's Seven Deadly Sins, where the woman is looking into a mirror held by a devil? Is it implicated in the vice, or a moral comment on it, since a natural animal needs no such beautification? Or of the Holy Family of Dosso Dossi, where a cat stands in front of the scene? Can this cat, once revered in Egypt, be a prophetic intimation of the Flight into Egypt? *Tot catti quot sententiae*, one is inclined to think.

In such scenes, however, the cat is individual and 'other'. This is so even in that archetypal scene of animal harmony in Paradise when God has just created the natural world with all its species. In a fine illustration in an early sixteenth-century French Book of Hours now in the Bodleian Library,[3] we see God surrounded by his newly made creatures, all in attitudes of restful harmony. In the bottom right-hand corner sits the cat, and, just in front of it, the mouse. Even before the Fall, the cat is giving the mouse a decidedly sinister look, and has its claws unsheathed in readiness for the moment. And in the equivalent scene in the left-hand section of Bosch's 'Garden of Earthly Delights', the cat has 'jumped the gun' and is carrying off a mouse.[4] It may be that here, ignoring the theological problem posed by the cat's action, Bosch is giving us a premonition of the Fall, or it may be another ironic parallel with 'real life' – the cat gets on with its work even in Eden.

A popular dictionary of symbols produces a brief and bare list of the significances of the Christian cat – 'Christian: Satan; darkness; lust; laziness'.[5] It has much more to be said for it than this, but it is true that it does not achieve the mythological variety and splendour which it did in other religions, especially that of Egypt.[6] There are some memories: a medieval Christian writer records the two

---

3   MS Douce 135, f. 17v.
4   See C. de Tolnay, *Hieronymus Bosch* (New York 1966), p.205.
5   J. C. Cooper, *An Illustrated Encyclopedia of Traditional Symbols* (London 1978) s.v. 'cat'.
6   The Egyptian cat-goddess Bastet is the first recorded example of the often-noted connection of the cat and the female or female principle. The sacred cats of Eygpt appear briefly in the *Bibliotheca Historica* of Diodorus Siculus, which was translated (from a humanistic Latin version) into English by Skelton; unfortunately, although he had a sound knowledge of cats, he seems to have been misled into confusing the Latin word involved:

mythological Scandinavian cats which drew the goddess Freyja, and tells the story of how the giants threatened by Thor tricked him by challenging him to lift a large and hefty grey cat, which arched its back as the god raised his arm, so that he could only manage to make it lift one of its paws – it was in fact the great serpent that encompasses the earth.[7] In the Irish *Tain* there is a rather mysterious reference to 'the feat of the cat' among the extraordinary skills of Cuchulain.[8] And cats retained something of their ancient mystery. They had occult powers.[9] According to Cornelius Agrippa they are among the animals subject to Saturn: 'also all creeping Animals, living apart, and solitary, nightly, sad, contemplative, dull, covetous, fearfull, melancholly, that take much pains, slow, that feed grossly, and such as eat their young. Of these kinds therefore are the Mole, the Ass, the Wolf, the Hare, the Mule, the Cat, the Camel, the Bear . . .'[10] etc.; he also remarks that 'cats also are Lunary, whose eyes become greater or less, according to the course of the moon'.[11] There is apparently an alchemical cat – its association with night is appropriate for such experiments, and its ability to see through darkness makes it an appropriate symbol for the practitioner of this arcane mystery. Since it is subject to the influence of the Moon, it can represent the Luna or Mercury of the

he renders it once as 'hyndes', elsewhere cautiously as 'a beest called feles', 'that beest that named is felis' (see the edition of F. M. Salter and H. L. R. Edwards, vol. II, EETS OS 239, 1957), p.402).

[7] Snorri Sturluson, *Gylfginning* (trans. J. I. Young, *The Prose Edda*, Cambridge 1954, pp.53, 78). King Arthur also has a battle with giant cat, a figure, say his barons, of God's vengeance. In the long and vivid account in the English *Prose Merlin* (ed. H. B. Wheatley, EETS OS 36 (1899), pp.665–9), a fisherman repeatedly broke his vow to give the first fish that he caught to God. The third time that he cast his net, instead of a fish, he 'drough oute a litill kyton as blakke as eny cool. And whan the fissher it saugh, he seide that he hadde nede therof in his house for rattes and mees, and he norisshed and kept vp in his house till it strangeled hym, and his wyf and his children, and after fledde in to a mountayn that is beyonde the lak'; it was 'grete and horible that it is merveille . . . to se', and destroyed everything it could catch (though it still retained one or two more or less cat-like habits: it came out of its cave when Merlin whistled, and in the course of the fight it paused to lick its claws that were wet with blood). In the Egerton MS of Mandeville's *Travels* there is a mysterious transformation of Lot's wife into 'a salt cat' (ed. M. Letts, London 1953, p.72); it is not clear whether this is a term for a mass of salt, or 'the likeness of a cat' (there seems to have been something strange about the statue: Theodoricus (*De locis sanctis*) says it waxed and waned with the moon).

[8] *The Tain*, trans. T. Kinsella (Dublin, London 1969), p.34.

[9] In the sixteenth century, Erastus explains that some men dislike cheese, and others abhor cats because of 'occult virtues' (L. Thorndike, *A History of Magic and Experimental Science* (New York 1923–58), vol. V. p.662); this belief goes back to the Middle Ages (see G. R. Owst, 'Sortilegium in English homiletic literature of the Fourteenth Century', *Studies Presented to Sir Hilary Jenkinson* ed. J. Conway Davies (London 1957), p.283).

[10] *Of Occult Philosophy*, trans. J. F. (London 1651) I, ch. xxv. Hence the cat appears in G. B. Castiglione's sixteenth-century 'Melancholy'.

[11] I, ch. xxiv. Cf. W. B. Yeats, 'The Cat and the Moon' in *The Wild Swans at Coole* (1919).

philosophers.[12] Just such a cat is found in the sixteenth-century scene of the Alchemist's Laboratory by Jan Van der Straet or Stradano[13] – though, again, it would be possible for a sceptic to think that it is looking on in some amazement. The darker associations of the cat undoubtedly encouraged medieval moralists to link it with death or (constantly) with the devil: 'þe cat of helle' in *Ancrene Wisse*; in the *Ayenbite of Inwyt* the devil is said to play with the sinner as the cat does with the mouse; in *The Castle of Perseverance* Belial threatens to bind Mankind in hell 'as catte dothe þe mows'.[14]

It is not at all surprising that with such sinister associations the cat later figured prominently in witchcraft. It appears in Hans Baldung Grien's early sixteenth-century 'Witches', now in the Louvre; and frequently as an alleged 'familiar' in later sixteenth-century witch-trials (witches went to the Sabbat on animals or in the form of animals, including cats). The first recorded cat in an English witch-trial is a rather striking creature belonging to Elizabeth Francis, who was examined at Chelmsford in 1556. It was given to her by her grandmother: she had to renounce God, and give of her blood to Satan 'whiche she delyuered her in the lykenesse of a whyte spotted Catte, and taughte her to feede the sayde Catte with breade and mylke, and she dyd so, also she taughte her to cal it by the name of Sathan and to kepe it in a basket'. Satan speaks to her 'in a straunge holowe voice', and has remarkable powers, producing sheep, two husbands, and sundry acts of destruction for her and for Mother Waterhouse to whom she later gave him.[15]

Although the Middle Ages did not see anything like the spectacular persecution of witches in the sixteenth and seventeenth centuries, the unfortunate reputation of the witch-cat has some clear medieval antecedents. There is for example the spectacular heretical cat in Walter Map's twelfth-century *De nugis curialium*. He says that a group of heretics called Publicani or Paterini recently arrived in England indulge in nocturnal orgies – the houses are closed up, and

> each family sits waiting in silence in each of their synagogues, and there descends by a rope which hangs in the midst a black cat of wondrous size. On the sight of it they put out the lights, and do not sing or distinctly repeat hymns, but hum them with closed teeth, and draw near to the place where they saw their master, feeling after him, and when they have found him they kiss him. The hotter their feelings, the lower their aim: some go for his feet, but most for his tail and privy parts. Then, as though

---

[12] 'Il représentait la Lune ou Mercure Philosophique, parce que le Chat semble ressentir les effets des influences lunaires', A.-J. Pernety, *Dictionnaire mytho-hermétique* (1787), s.v. 'Chat'.

[13] Reproduced in *Gatti*, pl. 8.

[14] *Ancrene Wisse* EETS OS 249 (1962), p.54; *Ayenbite* EETS OS 23 (1866), p.179; *Castle of Perseverance* EETS OS 262 (1969) p.31, ll. 951–2.

[15] C. L'Estrange Ewen, *Witch Hunting and Witch Trials* (London 1929), Appendix VIII (I am indebted to Dr Clive Holmes for this reference).

this noisome contact unleashed their appetites, each lays hold of his neighbour and takes his fill of him or her for all his worth.[16]

This piece of anti-heretical propaganda was often repeated,[17] and though the animal involved is not always a cat, it was prominent enough to furnish one of the suggested etymologies for the name of the 'Cathar' sect.[18] And already in this period we find recorded stories of shape-shifting. Gervase of Tilbury mentions in his *Otia Imperialia* that 'women have been seen and wounded in the shape of cats by persons who were secretly on watch' – and revealed by the wounds and mutilations.[19] This belief surfaces again in a story in that book which had such an influence on later witchcraft-trials, the *Malleus Maleficarum* (1486). A workman who was chopping wood was attacked first by a large cat, then by a second, and a third. He managed to drive them away by beating them on their heads and bodies. After only an hour, much to his amazement, he found himself arrested and brought before the magistrate to answer a charge that he had beaten three respected women. Eventually the judge was persuaded of the truth of his story about the cats, and that it was the work of the devil.[20] Such shape-shifting is attested in the testimony of the witches recorded by Ginzburg in his study of the sixteenth-century *benedanti*, where it is understood as a separation of the spirit from the body: one witch, after using a magic ointment 'was transformed into a cat, left the body at home . . . and went out by the door'; another expresses the fear that if the spirit did not return before dawn or cockcrow it would not change back, and the body would remain dead and the spirit remain a cat.[21] Even before the great witch-craze, in one of the rare cases where accusations of sorcery were treated as heresy, the proceedings against Alice Kyteler in Ireland in 1324, it is alleged that she had an 'incubus' which could appear in the form of a cat: 'quandoque sibi apparet in specie cati, quandoque in specie canis nigri et pilosi, quandoque in specie cujusdam aethiopis cum duobus sociis.'[22] It seems clear that the witches' cat of the Renaissance descends from a combination of anti-heretical propaganda and ancient folk-beliefs about the magic and sometimes sinister power of a predatory creature associated with night and darkness.[23]

[16] Ed. and trans. M. R. James, revised by C. N. L. Brooke and R. A. B. Mynors (Oxford 1983), pp.119–21 (I, ch. 30).

[17] I. von Döllinger, *Beiträge zur Sektengeschichte des Mittelalters* II (Munich 1890), p.293.

[18] Alan of Lille, quoted in A. Vacant and E. Mangenot, *Dictionnaire de Théologie catholique*, s.v. 'Lucifériens', ix. 1044 ff.

[19] III, 93 'De phantasiis nocturnis opiniones', ed. F. Liebrecht (Hannover 1856), p.45.

[20] Trans. M. Summers (London 1948) p.127.

[21] C. Ginzberg, *The Night Battles, Witchcraft and Agrarian Cults in the Sixteenth and Seventeenth Centuries* (1966; trans. J. and A. Tedeschi, London 1983), p.19.

[22] *A Contemporary Narrative of the Proceedings against Dame Alice Kyteler (1324)* ed. T. Wright (Camden Society 24, 1843). Again, it is interesting to note how often cats are associated with women (and in this context, old women).

[23] Cats were used in necromancy and witchcraft in the Middle Ages; see Thorndike, II,

The cat of folklore has a heavy symbolic charge (which sometimes involved it in cruel rituals and games);[24] people obviously found it 'good to think', especially, perhaps, because of its 'liminal' nature – belonging, more than other domestic animals, both to the world of the tame and the wild, both to the world of day and of night. While it is often not clear how far back particular details of folk-belief[25] can be traced, the essential paradox that the cat is potentially both maleficent and beneficent seems to be a medieval one. Cats are associated with healing;[26] they have prophetic power and may be used to foretell the future: 'whan ye se a cat syt in a wyndowe in the sonne & that she lycke her ars, and that one of her fete be aboue her ere ye nede not to doubte but þat it shall rayne that daye. . .'[27] In folk-tales we often meet a decidedly nicer kind of cat, one which is both magical and helpful. Again, this material is difficult to date, but some of it is certainly medieval. The fact that an analogue to 'Puss in Boots' is found in the mid sixteenth-century collection of Straparola suggests that stories like this are of some antiquity. This version is set in Bohemia. A poor widow bequeathes to her three sons her three solitary possessions; the third son, Costantino, receives her female cat. When he is mistreated by his older brothers, the cat takes pity on him, urges patience, and by a series of ingenious tricks – she kills a hare, puts it in a bag, takes it to the king as a present from Costantino; she takes back to her friend (to the mortification of his brothers) some of the splendid dinner she has been given; she magically removes the ugliness which has come from his poverty; stages a 'rescue' of Costantino from the river so that he is received by the king with favour and splendid clothes – ensures that Costantino comes to wealth and fortune, is

pp.781 (Liber Vaccae), 964 (Cecco d'Asoli, burnt in 1327). The witch-like bawd Celestina keeps her ointments in a black cat's skin: Celestina trans. L. B. Simpson (Berkeley 1955), p.43.

[24] See, for instance, R. Darnton, The Great Cat Massacre (London 1984), pp.83–5, 90–96 (the massacre was early eighteenth century); Thorndike IV, p.277; K. Thomas, Man and the Natural World (London 1983), pp.109–110. There is a rather nice later belief (mentioned by H. R. Patch, The Other World, Cambridge, Mass. 1950, p.53) that 'on the bridge . . . that led to heaven . . . a one-eyed dog kept watch on one side and a one-eyed cat . . . on the other . . . and allowed no one to pass to heaven who was unkind or cruel to cats and dogs on earth'.

[25] On general folk-beliefs, see K. Briggs, Nine Lives (London 1980); Bächtold-Stäubli, Handwörterbuch des deutschen Aberglaubens s.v. 'Katze' (IV, 1109–1123).

[26] Bächtold-Stäubli, 1122; P. Dale-Green, The Archetypal Cat (Guild of Pastoral Psychology, Guild Lecture 124, London, 1963), pp.7–8 (including the rural belief that a stye rubbed with a tom-cat's tail (cf. Map's story?) will disappear). Thorndike (V, p.432) records a remarkable recipe for rheumatism from Fries's Spiegel der Artznei (pr. 1518): a goose is stuffed with a mixture of chopped up cat, incense, wax, mutton-fat and other ingredients, roasted, and the fat used to anoint the limbs.

[27] The Gospelles of Dystaues (translated from French; printed c. 1507–9), f. c i; cf. Thorndike IV, p.277; Bächtold-Stäubli 1107.

married to a princess, and finally made king.[28] This magic cat is said to be a fairy; she is certainly a very different creature from Elizabeth Francis's Satan.

If it was not notably visionary or mystical, the medieval cat was a companion of recluses. Everyone has heard of the cat which was the only beast allowed to an anchoress by the author of *Ancrene Wisse*. An earlier animal, celebrated in poetry by his Irish hermit companion, is 'white Pangur', Pangur ban, who is perhaps a remote ancestor of Christopher Smart's Jeffrey, though it is not clear that his especial skill in hunting is a celebration of the Almighty. It is presented as a parallel pursuit to the scholar's pursuit of knowledge – 'he directs his bright perfect eye against an enclosing wall. Though my clear eye is very weak I direct it against keeness of knowledge. He is joyful with swift movement when a mouse sticks in his sharp claw. I too am joyful when I understood a dearly loved difficult problem. . .',[29] and the harmony comes from the shared intensity devoted to their differing tasks. Another Irish cat does not seem to have quite entered into the religious spirit of the pilgrimage on which it was taken. According to a story in the Book of Leinster, three students went on pilgrimage (the austere *peregrinatio pro amore dei*: they cast away their oars), taking with them only three loaves and their cat. They were cast up on a beautiful island on which they built a church, and their cat set about providing food for them, bringing in up to three salmon every day. With an unworldly lack of gratitude, they decided that this way of life was no true pilgrimage and that they would eat no more of the cat's food. They were rewarded after six days with food sent from heaven, and lived on to a pious death in old age, but the unfortunate cat ate so much salmon that it became a monster, a giant sea-cat, and was finally put down under the eyes of the wide-voyaging St Brendan.[30] Another example of pious meanness on the part of holy humans occurs in the life of the obscure Breton saint Cadoc, who tricked the devil into building a bridge on condition that the first creature which passed over it should belong to him; the saint arranged that it should be a cat! It is not surprising that cats are not prominent among the menagerie of animals who help, feed, and protect saints.[31]

---

[28] *Le piacevoli notti* XI, story 1. Cf. Aarne-Thompson, *The Types of the Folktale* (revised edn, Helsinki 1964) 545 'The Cat as Helper'; 545B 'Puss in Boots'. Dick Whittington's cat seems to date from the sixteenth century.

[29] Trans. G. Murphy, *Early Irish Lyrics* (Oxford 1956), p.3.

[30] Robin Flower, *The Irish Tradition* (Oxford 1947), pp.26–7.

[31] Some other cats achieved some proximity to sanctity. A cat is found (among other animals and birds) on a cope of English workmanship now in the cathedral of St Bertrand de Comminges (A. G. I. Christie, *English Medieval Embroidery* (Oxford 1938), pp.11, 127, pl. lxxvii). There is a sixteenth-century Madonna del Gatto (with the cat gazing upwards to the Virgin and Child) by Federico Barocci, now in the National Gallery (see M. Oldfield Howey, *The Cat in the Mysteries of Religion and Magic* (London 1930), ch. ix). (A pious legend says that at the moment when the Virgin gave birth to Christ, a cat lying under the manger gave birth to a kitten.) Dale-Green (p.11) mentions an Italian legend about St Francis concerning the occasion on which Satan sent hundreds of mice to distract him from prayer: suddenly a cat sprang out of his sleeve, and wrought such havoc that only two of the

But there is one conspicuous example in the painting of St Jerome in his study by Antonello da Messina, now in the National Gallery, London. Here, the cat sits placidly on the floor of the scholar's cubicle, and it is most unlikely that it has any symbolic significance. It just seems to like being there.[32]

This cat is close to the actual cats of ordinary medieval life, which were prominent in most households. The evidence seems to show that they were numerous. The excavation of the cesspit of Richard of Southwick, a thirteenth-century burgess of Southampton, shows that he had cats (as well as dogs and a small monkey).[33] At Cuxham, in Oxfordshire, a twelfth-century lease of a manor includes in its stock one 'cattus senex' and two 'juvenes catti'.[34] They were part of everyday life. The author of Hali Meiðhad vividly imagines the domestic chaos that surrounds the over-worked wife: she hears her children screaming, and 'sið þe cat et te fliche.'[35] The same is implied by the instructions in courtesy books not to make 'cat nor hound your companion at table, nor to stroke a cat or dog while eating, and to clear them from bedrooms: 'dryue out dogge and catte, or els geue þem a clout'.[36] In his Miller's Tale Chaucer refers in passing to 'an hole. . . ful lowe upon a bord, / Ther as the cat was wont in for to crepe' in the house of his Oxford carpenter.[37] That it was a familiar domestic animal is also indicated by its frequent visual representation, especially in the humbler kinds of medieval art. We find a graffito of a cat's head in a church at Stetchworth, Cambridgeshire,[38] and sculptured cats' heads in Norman arches. There are many examples in carved misericords: at Rodez in France a depiction of cats in basket; in England, at, for instance, Minster (Isle of Thanet), an old woman with a distaff, and a cat and a dog; at Worcester, a domestic scene in which a man is stirring a pot beside the fire and

---

mice escaped by taking shelter in a crack in the wall – 'and it is said that descendents of this holy cat still sit motionless before holes and crevices, waiting to catch the fugitives'. (Official hagiography has a less spectacular conclusion: according to the Speculum Perfectionis (100), the saint accepted the plague of mice as a trial of his patience.) Odder still is the case of 'The Cat Saint' described by V. Alford in Folklore 52 (1941) 161–83. St Agatha appears in cat form in the Pyrenees (partly because of the similarity of her name to 'santo gato', but she is associated with women, the weather, and death). She is a worthy companion to the greyhound saint (see J.-C. Schmitt, The Holy Greyhound. Guinefort, Healer of Children since the Thirteenth Century (trans. M. Thom, Cambridge 1983)).

[32] See H. Friedmann, A Bestiary for Saint Jerome (Washington 1980), fig. 119, pp.162–3.

[33] C. Platt, Medieval Southampton (London 1973), p.104.

[34] P. D. A. Harvey, A Medieval Oxfordshire Village, Cuxham 1240 to 1400 (Oxford 1965), p.63n. A later cat ate a cheese, recorded in 1293–4: '1 caseum comm' per catum'. Ships' cats also seem to have been well established (see K. Thomas p.98 and n.: in 1532 a fishing ship had 'a dog and a cat, with all other necessaries').

[35] Ed. B. Millett, EETS OS 284 (1982), p.19.

[36] The Babees book ed. F. J. Furnivall, EETS OS 32 (1868), pp.25, 182, 283, 302.

[37] Canterbury Tales I, 3441: The Riverside Chaucer ed. L. D. Benson (Cambridge, Mass. 1987), p.71. On Chaucer's cats generally see Beryl Rowland, Blind Beasts (Kent, Ohio 1971), pp.67–73, and Animals with Human Faces (London 1974), pp.51–3.

[38] V. Pritchard, English Medieval Graffiti (Cambridge 1967), p.61, fig. 83.

warming his feet; on one side hang two flitches of bacon; on the other 'a gigantic cat is basking in the warmth of the chimney'. There is a crouching cat (at Godmanchester); a cat playing a fiddle; an ape riding a cat and combing it with a large comb; two cats walking upright.[39] By far the greatest number, however, show the cat holding a mouse,[40] or sometimes pouncing on it or tossing it (as at Beverley) (and sometimes in playful reversal of the roles of these natural 'contraries', a scene of the 'world upside down' in which the mice or rats hang the cat).[40] This illustrates its most important function in the medieval house, which was to catch mice and rats (a function it shared with the domesticated weasel) rather than to be a 'pet' in the modern sense. But it is a narrow line that divides companions – like Pangur ban – from pets, and that cats were given names (admittedly traditional ones) – like Gib (from Gilbert),[42] or Scots Bawdronis, or French Tibert – indicates some kind of familiarity. And familiarity can easily pass into affection. At St Andrew's church in Old Cleeve (Somerset) there is a stone memorial to a civilian who is shown with his feet resting not on a hound or a lion but on a cat, which in turn is 'resting' its paws on a mouse.[43] There is a signet-ring with 'a most spirited and beautifully engraved figure of a cat devouring a mouse', with the legend '*gret : wel : gibbe : oure : cat'.[44] And the occasional remarks of moralists imply the same; there is a story of a hermit[45] who was brought to Rome by the fame of St Gregory's sanctity, who, when he saw the pope in splendid procession with his cardinals, went home brooding on whether humility could reign with such glory; as he slept he was answered by a voice singing the verse 'Pluris habes catum quam praesul pontificatum', for, it is explained, 'habebat enim bonus vir ille catum, cum quo quandoque ludendo post manuum labores et orationes se recreare solebat' (yet another cat-companion). Familiarity certainly meant knowledge: 'What beest is it that hath her tayle bytweene her eyen?' asks

---

39 See V. H. Debidou, *Le Bestiaire sculpté du moyen âge en France* (Paris 1961), fig. 123; G. L. Remnant, *Catalogue of Misericords in Great Britain* (Oxford 1969), pp.68, 137, 173, 193; T. Wright, *Essays on Archaeological Subjects* (London 1861) II, p.118; J. Clutton-Brock, *The British Museum Book of Cats* (London 1988), p.48 (with the cat and the fiddle, cf. the cat playing the tabor in Queen Mary's Psalter, p.46; a tenement called 'le Catfithole' is recorded, *MED* s.v. 'cat').

40 This is also frequently found in MS illustrations; see Clutton-Brock, pp.42, 47, 48.

41 Great Malvern; see Wright, II, pp.116–7, fig. 2.

42 'Gib' is also used as a term of reproach, especially for an old woman; Skelton's phrase 'tonnish gyb' (*Elynour Rummynge* 99) may rather nicely suggest that the cat, like the proverbial mouse, likes an occasional tipple of the stronger stuff. The female connection is revealed in the phrase 'cat's tail' for 'prostitute' (attested in the fifteenth century).

43 See *Proc. Somerset Arch. Soc.* 68 (1922), 56, pl. x, figs 2, 3; Clutton-Brock, p.19.

44 *Proc. of Soc. of Antiquaries* 11 March, 1886, p.97.

45 Told by Gerald of Wales, *De principis instructione liber*, in *Opera* ed. G. F. Warner, VIII, RS 21 (1891), pp.121–2. Salimbene reproves friars who 'love to play with a cat or a whelp or some small fowl but not as the Blessed Francis was wont to play with a pheasant and cicada, rejoicing the while in the Lord' (G. C. Coulton, *From St Francis to Dante* (London, 2nd edn. 1907), p.90).

the *Demaundes Joyous*: 'it is a catte when she lycketh her arse'.[46] And many of the visual images show accurate observation. There are some excellent drawings of cats in the Pepysian Sketchbook,[47] And in Italy even before Leonardo, Pisanello was experimenting (c.1440) with studies of cats in different positions.[48]

Observation of this kind is also found in the scientific books and encyclopedias. There is a splendid encyclopedic cat in Bartholomew's *De Proprietatibus Rerum*, translated by Trevisa:

> The catte hatte *mureligus* and *musio* and hatte also *catus*. And haþ þat name *mureligus* for he is enemy to mys and to rattes, and communliche ycleped *catus* and haþ þat name of rauenyng, for he rauyssheþ mys and rattes. Oþer he haþ þat name *catus* of *catat* þat is 'for to see', for he seeþ so scharpliche þat he ouercomeþ derknesse of þe night by schynyng of þe light of his yhen. And þe name *catus* cometh of grew and is to menynge 'sly and witty', as Ysidorus seiþ *libro xii°*. And is a beste of vncertayn here and colour. For som catte is whyte, som reed, and som blak, and som scowed and splenked in þe feet and þe face and in þe eeren, and is most yliche to þe lepard. And haþ a gret mouþ and sawe teeþ and scharpe and longe tonge and pliaunt, þynne, and sotile. And lapeþ þerwiþ whanne he drynkeþ as oþere bestes doon þat hauen þe neþer lippe schorter þan þe ouer, for bycause of vneuenesse of lyppes suche bestes souken nou3t in drynkynge but lapeþ and likkeþ, as Aristotil seiþ and Plinius also. And he is a ful leccherous beste in 3ouþe, swyfte, plyaunt, and mery. And lepeþ [and] reseþ on alle þyng þat is tofore him and is yladde by a strawe and playeþ. And is a wel heuy beste in eelde and ful slepy. And liþ sliliche in awayte for mys and is ware where þey ben more by smelle þan by sight. And hunteþ and reseþ on hem in priuey place. And whanne he takeþ a mous he pleyeþ þerwiþ and eteth him after þe pleye. And is as it were wylde and goþ aboute in tyme of generacioun. Among cattes in tyme of loue is hard fightynge for wyues, and oon cracceþ and rendeþ þe oþer greuousliche wiþ bytyng and wiþ clawes. And he makeþ a reweliche noyse and horrible whan oon profreþ to fighte wiþ anoþer. And is a cruel beste whanne he is wilde and wonyeþ in wodes and hunteþ þanne smalle wilde bestes, as conynges and hares. And falleþ on his owne feet whanne he falleþ out of highe place and is vnneþe yhurte whanne he is yþrowe down of an high place. His drytte stynkeþ ful foule and þerfore he hydeþ it vnder erþe and gadereþ þervpon couerynge wiþ feet and clawes. And whanne he haþ a fayre skynne he is as it were prowde þerof and goþ faste

---

46 Pr. 1511, facs. ed. with introduction by J. Wardroper (London 1971). The scene is depicted (though the cat's tail is not between its legs) in the Ashmole Bestiary (see Clutton-Brock, p.48).

47 See M. R. James, 'An English Medieval Sketch-book, No. 1916 in the Pepysian Library, Magdalene College, Cambridge', Walpole Soc. 13 (1924–5), pp.1–17; F. Klingender, *Animals in Thought and Art* (London 1971), fig. 258.

48 *Gatti*, p.40.

aboute; and whanne his skynne is ybrende þanne he abydeþ at home. And is ofte for his fayre skynne ytake of þe skynnere and yslayne and yhulde.[49]

This admirably compendious account of the nature of the cat is less moralistic than that of the first edition of the *Encyclopedia Britannica* (1773), which declares that 'of all domestic animals, the character of the cat is the most equivocal and suspicious' (notice, for instance, the quasi-scientific aside – 'as it were' – which qualifies one of the writer's rare moral terms 'proud'). It is worth quoting in full, because the best moral cats are based on the actual cats. Of course, since nature was a 'mirror' for man, it was meaningful, and often symbolic. But generally the most effective moral use of cats by writers is when they are close to actuality, when they are using similes (the author of an Italian *lauda* compares his soul to 'an old limping cat'[50]) or the humbler didactic forms of 'wisdom' literature.

Proverbial cats, for instance, are more numerous and distinctly more interesting than bestiary cats.[51] Here particularity of observation is generalized (with varying degrees of earnestness or irony) to human experience – 'when all candles are out all cats are grey'.[52] A number of the animal's characteristics are the source of proverbial similes: its behaviour when confronted by its natural 'opposites' – 'hound and cat kiss, but are not the better friends'; 'by scratching and biting cats and dogs come together';[53] 'the cat often mouses after her mother'; 'two women in one house, two cats and one mouse'[54] – or rivals of its own kind – 'to agree like two cats in a gutter'. (Its function as a mouser is implied in a number of proverbs: 'let no man buy a cat unless he sees the claws' etc.) The common simile 'as a cat plays with a mouse' is put to a variety of literary uses. As we have seen, it is used of the devil; but Chaucer brilliantly adapts it to Absolon, the predatory parish clerk in the *Miller's Tale* as he observes the luscious Alison in church:

> I dar wel seyn, if she hadde been a mous,
> And he a cat, he wolde hire hente anon[55]

---

[49] *On the Properties of Things* ed. M. C. Seymour et al. (Oxford 1975), pp.1228–9.

[50] Quoted by P. Diehl, *The Medieval European Religious Lyric* (Berkeley 1985), p.214 (*Laudi spirituali del Bianco da Siena* ed. T. Bini (Lucca 1851) p.29 'va zopicando come vecchia miccia').

[51] The Bestiaries make much more of their exotic wild relatives, like the Panther. However, the cat is used in *Li response du bestiaire* (*Li bestaires d'amours* de Richart de Fornival, ed. C. Segre (Milan 1957) p.123) to illustrate the importance of 'soft words': it 'a ore mout simple chiere, et du poil au defeus est il mout soues et mout dous. Mais estraigniés li le keue, il getera ses ongles fors de ses .iiij. piés, et vous desquirra les mains se vous ne le laissiés aler.'

[52] B. J. Whiting, *Proverbs, Sentences, and Proverbial Phrases from English Writings Mainly before 1500* (Cambridge, Mass. 1968), C 27. Unless otherwise noted, the proverbs come from the section in Whiting C 80–110.

[53] H 563, S 99.

[54] W 500.

[55] CT I, 3346–7.

– perhaps without over-long 'playing'. 'What may the mouse against the cat?' asks one proverb.[56] A certain amount, but usually in fantasy, unless the cat is away (i.e. the medieval 'mice play where no cats are' or 'the mouse goes abroad where the cat is not lord').[57] Adages of this sort are easily adapted to political satire, as the well-known proverb-fable 'to hang a bell about the cat's neck'.[58] Langland, who is one of the many users of this, also adapts another proverb – 'woe to the land where the child is king' – in a feline way: '. . . there the catte is a kitoun the courte is ful elyng'.[59] Similarly used are 'let the cat wink', 'for he hath awaked the slepynge catte' (a variant of the dog-adage), and the heraldic 'the cat, the rat, and lovell our dog rule all England under a hog'.

Other proverbial characteristics include its agility ('a cat falls on its feet'[60] – just as Bartholomew had observed), its sight ('to see like a cat in the night'), or its habit of playing with a straw ('as the cat plays with a straw', 'to draw the straw before the cat'). Henryson puts this (rather nicely) into the mouth of a wolf conversing with a cunning fox: 'It is an auld dog, doutles, that thou begylis; / Thow wenis to drau the stra befoir the cat!' (alluding to the view that 'a young cat will jump at a straw drawn before her but not an old one').[61] He is tricked even so. It is intelligent – or cunning ('well wot the cat whose beard he licks'). This again lends itself to sardonic use: it is applied in one of Marie de France's fables (no.40) to the crow which sits on the ewe's back, cruelly pecking out wool. That tribute to its independence – 'a cat may look at a king' – is attested in the early sixteenth century. Another adage, alluding to the practice, mentioned by Bartholomew, of 'singeing' its skin in order to keep it at home, finds its way into anti-feminist polemic; it is attibuted by the Wife of Bath to one of her old husbands:

> Thou seydest this, that I was lyk a cat;
> For whoso wolde senge a cattes skyn,
> Thanne wolde the cat wel dwellen in his in;
> And if the cattes skyn be slyk and gay,
> She wol nat dwelle in house half a day,

---

56 M 745.

57 M 736–7.

58 B 232. This is illustrated in Brueghel's 'Netherlandish Proverbs' (see Clutton-Brock, p.52); cf. Also Baum, *MLN* 34 (1919), pp.462–70.

59 B Prol. 189 ff. Gower, *Vox Clamantis* I, ch. 6 uses the idea of the cat abandoning its task of catching mice as an image of the world upside down.

60 The Laud Troy Book (ed. J. E. Wülfing, EETS OS 121 (1902)) has a couple of nice variations: Achilles unhorsed by Hector 'fel to the gounde as a cat, / Wel euen vpon his ketil-hat' (6136–8), and Hector lays low the Greeks by giving them 'suche pattis / That thei fel doun as dede cattis' (8841–2).

61 S 818. Henryson ed. D. Fox (Oxford 1981), *Fables* 2010. Cf. M. P. Tilley *Dictionary of the Proverbs in England in the sixteenth and seventeenth centuries* (Michigan 1950), p.406.

> But forth she wole, er any day be dawed,
> To shewe hir skyn and goon a-caterwawed.[62]

Still others allude to the dangers of its life ('a cat that has good skin shall be flayed' [cf. Langland's 'I have as moche pite of pore men as pedlere hath of cattes, / That wolde kille hem, yf he cacche hem myghte, for coveitise of here skynnes'] or 'brennyd cat dredith feir', a variant of the burnt child). That Heywood (1546) has 'a woman has nine lives like a cat'[63] suggests that another well-known saying was also current. One or two refer to it as a thing of little worth ('not avail a cat's tail'; 'a piece of a kid is worth two of a cat'), and it is perhaps worth noting that although its keen eyes may be used as a favourable comparison, its distinctive nose seems to be a popular similitude in the description of human ugliness: the giant herdsman in *Ywain and Gawain* has ears like an elephant, a broad and flat face, and 'his nese was cutted als a cat', and in a satirical lyric, a lady says of her lover: 'your forehed, mouth, and nose so flatte, / . . . best lykened to an hare / Of alle lyvyng thynges, saue only a catte.'[64] Its well-known desires and dislikes appear, often satirically: 'Who shall find a cat true in keeping milk?' is glossed by Berners 'wysdome is greate if the cat never touched mylke; as much to say as, whan love toucheth, wysedome is than oftentymes overcome' (cf. 'little and little the cat eats the bacon').[65] One very common proverb alludes to its liking for fish and its dislike of water 'the cat would eat fish but would not wet its feet' (which is echoed by the fox when he speaks to the wolf in the Henryson fable mentioned above: 'I can not fische, for weiting off my feit'); another to its habit of sitting where the matron was sitting ('iam catus resedet ubi iam matrona sedebat'). Proverbial cats are a very moral collection (or 'kyndyll', 'cloudyr' or 'gloryng', to use contemporary 'terms of association'[66] of cats), and the lessons they are made to teach are not only monitory and uplifting, but are often expressed in memorable and vivid form – the masterful cat 'sneezes at his own will'; a less masterful one is 'turned in the pan'. Sometimes the proverbial phrase will achieve a kind of exhilaration, whether in the delight of a comparison – 'thei lay ston-stille as two cats'; 'he is as clene as cattus hadde lykkyd hym' – or in the delight of sound – 'clym! clam! cat lep over dam!'[67]

Cats in adages are close cousins of cats in exempla. Henry of Lancaster in his

---

[62] CT III, 348–54.
[63] W 510.
[64] *Ywain and Gawain* ed. A. B. Friedman and N. T. Harrington, EETS OS 254 (1964), l. 260; *Secular Lyrics of the Fourteenth and Fifteenth Centuries* ed. R. H. Robbins (Oxford 1952) No. 208. In *Arthour and Merlin* (ed. O. D. Macrae-Gibson, EETS OS 268 (1973)), there is a wild man, a bold knight, 'ac he hadde nose as a cat'. Dunbar's 'Blak Moir' also has a 'schort catt nois.'
[65] L 396.
[66] J. Hodgkin, 'Proper Terms' Philological Society Supplement, 1907, pp.18, 88 ('gloryng' = 'brightly shining', a reference to cats' eyes).
[67] At the end of Bozon's version of belling the cat (*Les contes moralisés*, ed. L. T. Smith,

fourteenth-century *Livre de Seyntz Medicines*[68] adapts the idea of the house of the soul in the image of a poor man's house, which, when it is visited by a great lord, has to be cleared of all its furniture. When the lord leaves, it is put back, often in worse array than before, and the cat, which had fled outside for fear, comes back in and sits in the place where the lord himself had sat (cf. the proverb mentioned above). The cat here is the devil – and, as often, when an exemplum begins to develop a kind of literary 'realism', the morality comes as something of a shock – but often, it must be said, the symbolic role of the cat as a figure of death or the devil is far from inappropriate, given its rapidity and efficiency as a hunter (and the ease with which its victims could be seen as blind or foolish). Rather different, however, is this merry folk-tale adapted to exemplary ends in the English *Gesta Romanorum*:

> A mowse on a tyme felle into a barell of newe ale, that spourgid, and myght not come oute. The cate come beside, and herde the mouse crie in the barme, pepe! pepe! for she myght not come oute. The cat seide, 'Why cries thou?' The mouse seide, 'for I may not come oute.' The catte saide, 'if I delyuer the this tyme, thou shalte come to me when I calle the.' Þe mouse seide, 'I graunte the, to come when thou wilte.' The catte seide, 'Thou moste swere to me' and the mouse sware to kepe coue-naunte. Then the catte with his fote drew oute the mouse, and lete hym go. Afterward, the catte was hongry, and come to the hole of the mouse, and called and bade hire come to hym. The mouse was aferde, and saide, 'I shall not come.' The catte saide, 'Thou haste made an othe to me, for to come.' The mouse saide, 'Broþer, I was dronkyne when I sware, and therfore I am not holdyn to kepe myn othe,'[69]

The moral of this not that cats should not trust mice, or (as Aesop might have had it) that you can always get out of a tricky situation by your wits, but that many people when they are in tribulation promise to amend their lives, yet when things have improved they see no reason to keep their promise. The cat, in fact, is close to God.

In fables, which are close to proverbs as well as to exempla, the cat is an equally appropriate figure, but here its ambiguity will sometimes creep out. In Henryson's very fine version of the ancient 'Country Mouse and Town Mouse', the cat represents death – in a wonderfully final morality: 'the cat cummis and to the mous hes ee'. Marie de France's 'del gupil e del chat' adapts the widespread

---

Paris 1889, p.145): many people promise to right the wrongs of their rulers, but when they see them, then it's a case of 'watch out, here comes the cat!'.
[68] Ed. E. J. Arnould (Oxford 1940), p.101.
[69] Ed. S. J. H. Herrtage, EETS ES 33 (1879), pp.364–5. It appears in Odo of Cheriton's *Fables* (and in the Spanish adaptation *El libro de los Gatos*). (In these collections, the cat can play a variety of roles, from the hypocritical clerk to God.)

traditional tale of the cat's single trick:[70] the fox boasts that it knows a hundred, but when the dogs come it is the cat who escapes by jumping. It remarks with some self-satisfaction 'suvent est ateint li gupilz, / Tut seit il quointes par ses diz!'; it is here rather charitably moralized as the 'leial humme' (as against the liar). In another, 'del chat, del mulet, e de la suriz', we find a cat sitting quietly on 'sove' [fur] – a nice domestic touch – until he sees a vole and a mouse. He says that he is their bishop, and that they should be confirmed by him; but they are not tricked and run away from the bishop and hide in the wall. The moral relates this to law and injustice: confronted by someone who wishes you ill, the best course is simply to take refuge. A similar Aesopic prudence is urged by one of Rinuccio's fables, Englished by Caxton.[71] The cat in a certain house played havoc with the rats, and eventually they held a council. An old rat said that they needed to stay up on the high beams so that the cat would not be able to catch them. The cat soon became aware of their plan, and hung himself up on a beam, pretending to be dead. But one of the rats looking down began to laugh and said to the cat 'O my frend yf I supposed that thow were dede I shold goo down, but wel I knowe the so fals & peruers that thou mayst wel haue hanged thy self faynynge to be dede, wherfore I shall not go doune'. He that has once been beguiled should not let it happen again. This is close to some of the folk proverbs and tales dealing with the battle of wits between cats and their natural opposites noted above – notably to the story of the 'Cat's Funeral', where the mice preparing to bury the cat find (with fatal results for them) that she is not dead but only sleeping. This is depicted at Tarragona Cathedral: in the first scene the cat is carried in a litter by rats and mice (one of the rats is carrying a shovel – or, possibly, an axe, which would suggest an execution rather than a burial); in the next scene the cat springs up and catches the rat while the rest run off.[72] The folktale found its way to the Spanish New World (it has been recorded in Puerto Rico).[73]

Literary cats are a sophisticated breed, but they usually derive their strength from the other kinds we have been discussing. The best-known examples come from later periods when the cat had firmly established its status as 'pet'. But Pangur ban is a distinguished early example, and there are others. Two mid sixteenth-century cats celebrated by the poets of the Pléiade deserve to be better known. Ronsard's Le Chat[74] firmly states the animal's prophetic powers ('sur tous

---

[70] No. 99. Arne-Thompson 105. It is found in The Owl and the Nightingale (809 ff.), and travelled eventually to the New World (T. L. Hansen, The Types of the Folktale in Cuba, Puerto Rico, the Dominican Republic, and Spanish South America (Berkeley 1957), p.10).

[71] Caxton's Aesop ed. R. T. Lenaghan (Cambridge, Mass. 1967), p.170.

[72] E. P. Evans, Animal Symbolism in Ecclesiastical Architecture (London 1896), p.207.

[73] Arne-Thompson 113*; cf. Hansen, p.10.

[74] In 'Le Sixiesme Livre des Poemes'. A hostile Protestant pamphlet compared Ronsard to a cat playing with its victims (H. Nais, Les animaux dans la poésie française de la Renaissance (Paris 1961), p.525. On allergy to cats, see K. Thomas, p.109; cat brains were used in poisons (Thorndike III, pp.533 ff.).

l'animal domestique / Du triste Chat, a l'esprit prophetique'), and just as firmly states his aversion to it ('Home ne vit qui tant haisse au monde / Les Chats que moy d'ne haine profonde, / Je hay leurs yeux, leur front & leur regard: / Et les voyant je m'enfuy d'autrepart, / Tremblant de nerfs, de veines, & de membre . . .'); when a white cat sleeping on his pillow suddenly wakes him up, his servants suggest optimistic significances, but Ronsard knows that 'le Chat devin miaulant signifie / Une facheuse & longue maladie', and that he must keep to the house for a long time, like the cat, which never leaves its master's house in any season, '& jamais ne s'enfuit, / Faisant la ronde & la garde eternelle / Comme un soldat qui fait la sentinelle. . .' (a fine passage which suggests that aversion was not unmixed with affection). Du Bellay, in his *Epitaphe d'un chat*,[75] writes an affectionately playful elegy for his little grey cat Belaud, a creature of exquisite grace and excellence, who would indulge in such 'mignardises' as stealing the meat his master was eating, but who never did 'plus grand dommage / Que de manger un vieux frommage, / Une linotte & un pinson, / Qui le faschoient de leur chanson'. Belaud, who loved playing with his master – 'alors qu'on l'animoit, / A coups de patte il escrimoit, / Et puis appaisoit sa cholere / Tout soudain qu'on luy faisoit chere' – was his 'cher mignon', his 'compagnon / A la chambre, au lict, à la table': Du Bellay prays that he may celebrate him 'd'un vers aussi mignard que toy' and that he will live on 'tant que sur terre / Les chats aux rats feront la guere'.

Back in England, and moving backwards in time, we have Skelton's Gyb, that 'cat of carlyshe kynde' which devoured Jane Scrope's pet sparrow – 'Gyb, our cat savage, / That in a furyous rage / Caught Phyllyp by the head, / And slew him there starke dead' – an atrocity which provokes a marvellously operatic imprecation directed against the whole nation of cats.[76] Earlier still, in Scotland, Henryson in his 'Two Mice' catches the 'poetic reality' of the cat which has caught a mouse:

> Fra fute to fute he kest hir to and fra,
> Quhylis vp, quhylis doun, als tait as ony kid.
> Quhylis wald he lat hir rin vnder the stra;
> Quhylis wald he wink, and play with hir buk heid;
> Thus to the selie mous grit pane he did;
> Quhill at the last throw fair fortune and hap,
> Betwix the doser and the wall scho crap[77]

in a gruesome imitation of the game, which is also exemplary, suggesting the instability of Fortune and the uncertainty of life under threat from Death, when it comes 'and to the mous hes ee'.

---

[75] In 'Divers Jeux Rustiques (1558).
[76] 'Phyllyp Sparowe', ll. 273 ff., in *John Skelton. The Complete English Poems* ed. J. Scattergood (Harmondsworth 1983).
[77] Henryson, *Fables* 330–336.

The most famous literary cat of the Middle Ages appears even earlier in the *Roman de Renart*. The ingenious Tibert is associated with the arch-villain Reynard, and sometimes takes his side. However, in one celebrated episode, even the wise and cunning cat is worsted. Tibert is sent by the King to tell Reynard that he must answer the summons to Court. Bruin has just returned after his attempt to bring Reynard back has ended in disaster, and Tibert is most unwilling. Although he claims (I quote from the late version translated by Caxton (1481)) that he is 'little and feeble', the king insists that he is 'wise and well learned'; and he departs with a heavy heart – and being a cat, he can understand the unfortunate significance of one on St Martin's birds flying and settling on his left side rather than on his right. 'Nevertheless he did as many do, and gave himself better hope than his heart said'. At Maleperduys Reynard welcomes him – 'though he said well, his heart thought it not' – and tries to persuade him to stay the night. Tibert has no difficulty in rejecting the offer of a honey-comb, but his resolution wavers at the thought of a good fat mouse for supper – and there are many of these to be found, he is told, in the priest's barn nearby. As always, Reynard has found a weak spot, and the nature of the cat's dominating passion is demonstrated in a way that is both comic and exemplary in a lovely piece of dialogue:

> 'O, dere Reyner, lede me thyder for alle that I may doo for yow!' 'Ye, Tybert, saye ye me truth? Loue ye wel myes?' 'Yf I loue hem wel?' said the catte, 'I loue myes better than ony thyng that men gyue me! Knowe ye not that myes sauoure better than veneson – ye, than flawnes or pasteyes? Wil ye wel doo, so lede me theder where the myes ben, and thenne shal ye wynne my loue, ye, al had ye slayn my fader, moder, and alle my kyn.' Reynart sayd: 'Ye moke and jape therwyth!' The catte saide: 'So helpe me God, I doo not!' 'Tybert,' said the Fox, 'wiste I that veryly, I wolde yet this nyght make that ye shuld be ful of myes.' 'Reynart!', quod he, 'Ful? That were many.' 'Tyberte, ye jape!' 'Reynart', quod he, 'in trouth I doo not. Yf I hadde a fatte mows, I wold not gyue it for a golden noble. 'Late vs goo thenne, Tybert,' quod the foxe; 'I wyl brynge yow to the place er I goo fro you.'[78]

But of course, disaster lurks in the barn. Overcoming Tibert's distrust of these priests that 'are so wily and shrewish', Reynard persuades him to leap into a hole, where his neck is caught in a snare: 'thenne began he to wrawen [*screech*], for he was almost ystranglyd. He called, he cryed, and made a shrewd noyse'. As always, Reynard savours the situation with cruel glee: 'Tybert, loue ye well myes? Be they fatte and good? Knewe the preeste herof, or Mertynet, they be so gentyl that they wolde brynge yow sawce. Tybert, ye synge and eten – is that the guyse of the court?' And Tybert's mewing and crying rouses Mertynet and then the priest, who runs there 'all mother-naked', thinking that the fox has been taken. Tibert is

---

[78] Caxton, *The History of Reynard the Fox* ed. N. F. Blake, EETS OS 263 (1970), p.21 (punctuation modernised).

cruelly beaten, and loses an eye, but fights back in self-defence: 'the naked preest lyfte vp and shold haue gyuen a grete stroke to Tybert, but Tybert, that sawe that he muste deye, sprange bytwene the prestes legges wyth his clawes and with his teeth that he raught out his ryght colyon or balock-stone'. In the midst of the resulting commotion, Tibert manages to extricate himself from the snare, and makes his escape back to the court 'as a poor wight'. (Tibert later is part of the hanging party which takes Reynard to the gallows, but, not surprisingly, the vengeance never takes place; Reynard lives on and even in a later speech recalls how the false deceiver Tibert, having escaped from the hounds by his one trick of climbing, jeered at his father as he ran away from the hounds – 'and though I should hate Tybert herefor, is it wonder? But I do not. . .') Tibert is not as complicated a character as Reynard, but clearly a well-known one (scenes from this adventure are found depicted on the stalls of Bristol Cathedral), and gives his name to other later cats (and to that later warlike figure Tybalt in *Romeo and Juliet*, described by Mercutio as 'you rat-catcher . . . Good king of cats . . .').[78a]

If this prince of cats receives less than fair treatment at the hands of Reynard and his creators, let us turn finally to Chaucer to give us a more sympathetic and deeply moral emblem, in which the cat is used as a comment on erring humans. At the beginning of the *Summoner's Tale* the house of the sick man Thomas is visited by a friar;

> '*Deus hic!*' quod he, 'O Thomas, freend, good day!'
> Seyde this frere, curteisly and softe.
> 'Thomas,' quod he, 'God yelde yow! Ful ofte
> Have I upon this bench faren ful weel;
> Heere have I eten many a myrie meel.'
> And fro the bench he droof away the cat,
> And leyde adoun his potente and his hat,
> And eek his scrippe, and sette hym softe adoun.[79]

This is the friar, who, a few lines later, when he embraces and kisses the wife, 'chirketh as a sparwe'. Our opinion of him as a thoughtless, self-obsessed and self-important man is already forming. Surely here his gesture is not simply a piece of domestic realism or a rhetorical 'circumstance': it seems more like what Joyce would call an 'epiphany' – 'a sudden spiritual manifestation, whether in the vulgarity of speech or of gesture. . .' This cat is being pushed out of the (not very holy) picture by a distinctly unholy man.

[78a] Hoc est nomen illustrissimi catti Lancastriensis.
[79] CT III, 1770–77.

The Rhetoric of Ancrene Wisse

T. P. Dolan

Parts Six and Seven of *Ancrene Wisse* have often been celebrated for the stylistic skills which the author has displayed in them,[1] in particular his astonishing range of rhetorical devices. This paper will consider the styles of Parts Two, Three, Four, and Five in order to furnish a more comprehensive account of the author's achievement. He was clearly familiar with the traditional teaching of classical and Christian rhetoricians. Twice, indeed, he cites rhetorical figures by name ('antonomasice', f.1a 25–26; 'ywallage' (i.e. Hypallage),[2] f.20a 6), but throughout the text he shows himself to be a master of rhetoric, inasmuch as he consistently and skilfully adjusts his style to the tone and quality of the subject-matter. The first and last Parts, which he calls the 'Outer Rule', are almost completely devoid of stylistic colour,[3] whereas all the other sections, which he calls the 'Inner Rule', derive their effect from a judicious use of rhetorical devices. It is true to say that Part Six and, more especially, Part Seven contain the highest concentration of

[1] For a general account of recent stylistic and literary analyses of AW see Roger Dahood, 'Ancrene Wisse, Katherine Group, Wohunge Group', in *Middle English Prose: A Critical Guide to Major Authors and Genres*, ed. A.S.G.Edwards (New Brunswick 1984), pp.15–16. See in particular *Ancrene Wisse: Parts Six and Seven*, ed. Geoffrey Shepherd (London and Edinburgh 1959), pp.lix–lxxiii, also Dennis Rygiel, 'The Allegory of Christ the Lover-Knight in *Ancrene Wisse*: An Experiment in Stylistic Analysis', *SP* 73 (1976), 343–364, and Rygiel, 'Structure and Style in Part Seven of *Ancrene Wisse*', *NM* 81 (1980), 47–56. J.A.W.Bennett is more modest in his praise for AW: see his *Middle English Literature*, ed. and completed by Douglas Gray (Oxford 1986), pp.271–275. Compare his remarks with those of Janet Grayson, *Structure and Imagery in Ancrene Wisse* (Hanover, New Hampshire 1976) and of Cecily Clark, 'Early Middle English Prose: Three Essays in Stylistics', *EIC* 18 (1968), 363–375.

[2] For definitions and examples of these rhetorical devices see [Cicero] *Ad C. Herennium De Ratione Dicendi (Rhetorica ad Herrennium)*, ed. and trans. Harry Caplan (London 1958) and also Richard A.Lanham, *A Handbook of Rhetorical Terms* (Berkeley 1968). The terms used in this paper are those most generally accepted (e.g., Prosopopoeia rather than Sermocinatio). All quotations from AW are taken from *Ancrene Wisse*, ed. from MS. Corpus Christi College Cambridge 402 by J.R.R.Tolkien, with an Introduction by N.R.Ker, EETS 249 (London 1962 for 1960). The abbreviation 'þ' is expanded to 'þet'.

[3] For a detailed account of Part One see *Ancrene Riwle: Introduction and Part I*, ed. and trans. with Commentary by Robert W. Ackerman and Roger Dahood (Binghampton 1984).

stylistic features associated with the Grand Style, but he never resists using a Figure of Speech or a Figure of Thought, or a Trope, when the occasion demands it in the other less celebrated Parts. To give one instance of this at the outset of this paper, there is a flawless example of Climax (mounting by degrees) in Part Two:

> Eue þi moder leop efter hire ehnen. from þe ehe to þe eappel. from þe eappel iparais. dun to þer eorðe. from þe eorðe to helle.
>
> (f.14a 5–7)

Here each phrase ends with a word which is immediately taken up to head the next syntactical unit. In using such a memorable device the author draws attention to Eve's spectacular fall from Grace as a striking example of what can happen to an anchoress if she looks at a man.[4]

Although the most obvious debt to the rhetorical tradition can be identified in an author's use of stylistic devices, such as Repetition, Antithesis, Rhetorical Question, Asyndeton, Metaphor, Simile, and so forth, it is also important to recognise the help which that tradition gave an author in amplifying his work (in the section of the manuals dealing with *Inventio*). As regards amplification of material, the author of *Ancrene Wisse* seems to be closely familiar with the advice provided by classical authorities and handed on by their Chrisian successors, notably those concerned with instructing preachers in the numerous *Artes Praedicandi*.[5]

The commonest methods used by the author of *AW* to amplify his material may be examined under the following headings:

1. Citation and concordance of biblical and other authorities.
2. Definition, derivation, or interpretation, of words and names.
3. Analogies, comparisons, anecdotes, *exempla*.
4. Degrees – positive, comparative, and superlative.
5. Exegesis and interpretation of texts, including Allegory.

Firstly, as regards the use of authorities, the author supports his text with a rich selection of citations from biblical, classical, and patristic sources. In this practice

---

[4] On this passage see Linda Georgianna, *The Solitary Self: Individuality in the Ancrene Wisse* (Cambridge, Massachusetts 1981), p.157, fn.46.
[5] See Th.-M.Charland, *Artes Praedicandi: Contribution á l'histoire de la rhétorique au moyen âge*, Publications de l'Institut d'études mediévales d'Ottawa 7 (Paris 1936); also Harry Caplan, 'Classical Rhetoric and the Medieval Theory of Preaching', *Classical Philology* 28 (1933), 73–96, and Caplan, 'Rhetorical Invention in Some Medieval Tractates on Preaching', *Speculum* 2 (1927), 284–295. A good translation of a representative Art of Preaching (fourteenth century) is given by Leopald Krul in *Three Medieval Rhetorical Arts*, ed. James J.Murphy (Berkeley 1971), pp.114–215. See also Bennett, p.272 and Shepherd, p.lix.

he seems to be fulfilling the advice of St Augustine who approved of preachers using the words of Scripture to enrich and corroborate their own words, which in his opinion were inadequate in comparison with those of the Bible:

Huic ergo qui sapienter debet dicere, etiam quod non potest eloquenter, verba Scripturarum tenere maxime necessarium est.[6]

In Part Two of AW, for instance, the wide range of authorities quoted includes Solomon, Isaias, Matthew, John, Luke, Augustine, Bernard, Anselm, *The Lives of the Fathers*, Gregory, and Seneca. Solomon alone is cited ten times. Similar references to authorities of the past occur throughout the sections dealing with the Inner Rule (not in the Outer Rule). Usually the quotations are organically connected with the subject-matter and supply authority for the author's words. Often the same quotation occurs several times within a relatively short space. For example, in Part Two, Solomon's words *Omni custodia serua cor tuum* are employed three times, with telling effect, in the passage dealing with the Five Wits (f.12b 1–5; 27b 1–6; and f.32a 6–10).[7] This repetition of authorities serves several functions. It helps to bind the material together and has the mnemonic effect of assisting the anchoresses to assimilate important points in the argument. Often two or more authorities are used to complement each other. Elsewhere in Part II, for instance, when he is describing the sufferings of Christ on the cross he cites Augustine, Bernard, and Luke in succession, with an extended paraphrase on each occasion (f.30b 1–15).

Similarly traditional is his habit of interpreting words and names, often with symbolical implications, e.g.,

Þes eappel leoue suster bitacneð alle þe wa þet lust falleð to & delit of sunne.

(f.13b 21–22)

Þurh blod is i hali writ sunne bitacnet.

(f.31a 3–4)

Frequently he defines a word without symbolical overtones and invests that word with a particular connotation which is relevant only to the surrounding context:

Scheome ich cleopie eauer her. beon itald unwurð. & beggin as an hearlot ȝef neod is hire liueneð ...

(f.96b 15–17)

---

[6] Quoted by Josephine G.Cooper (Sister Ethelbert), 'Latin Elements of the "Ancrene Riwle" ', Birmingham University Ph.D. Thesis (1956), p.viii, from *De Doctrina Christiana*, IV, Cap. V, n.8 (*PL* XXXIV, 92).

[7] For a close analysis of this passage see Georgianna, pp.59–61.

His etymologies are often false, but are rhetorically effective because they frequently involve some sort of repetition. For instance, in the following example he plays on the root-syllable of the word for anchoress:[8]

> for þi is ancre ancre bicleopet. & under chirche iancret as ancre under schipes bord forte halden þet schip. þet uþen ant stormes hit ne ouerwarpen. Alswa al hali chirche þet is schip icleopet. schal ancrin o þe ancre.
>
> (f.39a 2–6)

The commonest form of definition concerns biblical names (e.g., 'Iosue spealeð heale', f.81b 23–24; 'Galilee spealeð hweol', f.88a 3–4).

The author is obviously very fond of issuing instruction through the medium of narrative – analogies, comparisons, anecdotes, *exempla*, and so forth. Time and again he introduces passages with such remarks as

> cunneð þis essample. A mon þe leie in prisun ...
>
> (f.34a 16–17)
>
> Ah neomeð ȝeme hu hit feareð bi a forbisne. Hwen a wis mon neowliche haueð wif ilead ham ...
>
> (f.59a 2–3)
>
> þenched her of þe tale hu þe hali mon in his fondunge ...
>
> (f.63a 13–14)

Sometimes he takes a word from a quotation and amplifies it into an anecdote. For instance, on one occasion he takes the word *refrenans* from a citation he gives from St James and applies it in a description of the way a horse's bridle sits not only on the horse's mouth, but also over its eyes. Again he plays on the root-syllable of the key-word: *bridli, Bridel, ibridlet*: f.18b 21 – f.19a 4. He is always at pains to make reference to things or people with which or whom the anchoresses are familiar. Even 'sluri þe cokes cneaue' is brought in to illustrate a point (f.103a 3–6). Sometimes he decides not to waste time over relating stories they might hear elsewhere. For instance, when he is referring to God's revelations to Moses and Elias, he simply says

> Me schal leoue sustren þeose estoires tellen ow. for ha weren to longe to writen ham here.
>
> (f.42a 19–20)

The most famous *exemplum* is the one of the besieged lady in Part Seven (f.105 a 18 – f.105b 18), but often his use of what he calls *forbisne* or *essample* involves briefer references. Even so, many instances of this method of amplification are quite long, for example, the story in Part Six of the three holy men who were

---

[8] On this word see Ann K. Warren, *Anchorites and Their Patrons in Medieval England* (Berkeley 1985), p.8.

visited by the Queen of Heaven (f.100a 12–24). This particular story also includes speech ('Nai qð ure leafdi ...'), which is a rhetorical device in its own right (Prosopopoeia).

A fairly common method of amplification is the use of degrees – positive, comparative, and superlative, with which he introduces a passage and then proceeds to expand the material along the same lines, e.g.,

> Idel speche is uuel. ful speche is wurse. Attri is þe wurste.
>
> (f.20b 25–26)
>
> Fikeleres beoð þreo cunnes. þe forme beoð uuele inoh. þe oþre þah beoð wurse. Þe þridde þah beoð wurst.
>
> (f.22a 11–13)

After making these introductory divisions the author goes on to discuss each of them in turn, thereby amplifying and illustrating his material.

Perhaps the most obvious and traditional form of amplification used in the text is the allegorical interpretation of scriptural and patristic texts, all of which contain hidden meanings which he sets out to reveal. For instance in Part Two he cites Canticles 2.10 and says about its meaning:

> hit is bileppet & ihud. but ich hit wulle unualden.
>
> (f.26a 27)

Often the explanation does not have to be as elaborate as in the previous instance, e.g.,

> bi þet te folc of israel wende ut þurh þe reade sea þet wes read & bitter. is bitacnet þet we moten þurh rudi scheome. þet is isoð schirft. & þurh bitter penitence passin to heouene.
>
> (f.89b 22–25)

There is no need to give any more examples of this method of amplification. Suffice it to say that the author is as much indebted to the traditional methods of amplification described and advocated in classical and medieval rhetorical theory under the section concerned with *Inventio*,[9] which he could copy and develop from the techniques he found used in his sources, as to the theory of *Elocutio*, to which we shall now turn.

The commonest of the Figures of Speech used in AW all derive their effect from some form of repetition. Sister Humbert's great pioneer work[10] on this aspect of the author's style is still useful but, as we shall see, it has to be used with caution, because she was frequently misled by the modern punctuation put in by

---

9 See Caplan (1927).
10 Agnes Margaret Humbert, *Verbal Repetition in the* Ancren Riwle (Washington 1944).

Morton in his edition[11] which she used for her dissertation. The author's favourite device seems to be Anaphora (initial repetition), e.g.,

> 3e schulen iseon ... 3e schulen bihalde ... 3e schulen gasteliche iseon ...
>
> (f.24a 18–23)
>
> Hercnið nu ... Hercnið nu ...
>
> (f.26a 13–15)
>
> Fondunge liht & dearne. Fondunge liht & open. Fondunge strong & dearne. fondunge strong & openlich.
>
> (f.59b 16–17)

The main purpose of this figure is to convey emphasis and to draw particular attention to the clauses which the repeated words introduce.

Sister Humbert found eighty examples of Antistrophe (final repetition),[12] but analysis of the authorial punctuation presented in the EETS edition of the Corpus text reveals that there are very few indisputable examples of this device. In the following example, the first quotation is the one cited by Humbert, and the second is taken from the EETS edition. This will help to show the problems involved in identifying this figure:

> ... sitte þe þridde? bute þe ilke þridde, oþer stu(n)de trukie.
>
> (AR, p.68, l.6)
>
> ... sitte þe þridde. bute 3ef þe ilke þridde oþer stude trukie.
>
> (AW, f.17a 6–7)

Here the repeated word in question is 'þridde', but the author may not have intended it to have final place in the second clause. Practically all Humbert's examples of Antistrophe may be queried for this reason. Certainly there is repetition, but it is usually of a general nature, not specific placing in final position.

General random repetition is widespread throughout the text and there is no need to do more than give a few instances, e.g.,

> we ahen him blod for blod. ant ure blod þah a3ein his blod þet he schedde for us. were ful unefne change.
>
> (f.85a 26–28)
>
> ha beoð þes deofles gongmen & beoð aa in his gong hus. Þe fikeleres meoster is to hulie þe gong þurl.
>
> (f.21b 26–28)
>
> þet dunt of alle duntes is him dunte laðest.
>
> (f.89a 4–5)

---

[11] *The Ancren Riwle*, ed. James Morton, Camden Society 57 (1853). Note that his text is based on the Nero version.

[12] pp.107–108. Shepherd, p.lxviii, relies quite heavily on Sister Humbert's treatise when dealing with instances of repetition in AW (he reproduces, for instance, her misspelling of 'epanodos' ('epanados', p.111).

Very often, as in the last two examples cited here, the stem or root syllable of the key-word is repeated. This is the figure known as Polyptoton. Frequently it extends over a considerable period, for example, in a passage in Part Five, where he is telling his audience to beat the hound of hell and plays on the words 'beat', 'ibeaten', and 'beatunge' (f.89a 4–12).

Anadiplosis (final-initial repetition) is quite a common figure and is used to great effect for emphasis throughout the whole work, e.g.,

& schunen þet ha ham ne iheren. iheren ich segge

(f.21a 25)

Na þing ne awealdeð wilde flesch ne ne makeð hit tomre. þen muche wecche. wecche is in hali writ i feole studen i preiset.

(f.39a 22–24)

Another figure of this type, but involving the repetition of sound rather than of meaning, is Homoioteluton, the effect of which is usually derived from adverbial endings (e.g., 'se scheomliche ituket. se sorhfulliche ipinet', f.99a 4).

The effect of similar sounds also plays its part in the device of Paronomasia, which is a prominent feature of the author's style and displays the subtlety of his mind and his mastery of the language, inasmuch as he seems to be able to choose vocabulary which binds style and matter together without any forcing (e.g., 'feond þe þuncheð freond', f.25b 9; 'mon schal wreien him i schrift. nawt werien him ne seggen ...', f.82b 12).

We shall now leave devices based on patterns of repetition and indicate other types of Figures of Speech, one of the most frequently occurring of which is Antithesis. All sections of the Inner Rule are enriched by examples such as

ischrud mid lombes flees. and beoð wedde wulues.

(f.16b 9)

for ase soft as he is her. as heard he bið þer. ase milde as he is nu. ase sturne þenne. lomb her liun þer.

(f.83a 9–10)

The second of these two examples clearly demonstrates how Antithesis can also affect the syntax of the phrases in which it is used. Here the author deliberately balances the antithetical elements ('her'/'þer'; 'nu'/'þenne'; 'soft'/'heard'; 'milde'/'sturne'; 'lomb'/'liun') so that both the vocabulary and the syntax work together to produce emphasis and rhetorical colour.

The author presumably expected that his book would be read out loud, as Shepherd noted,[13] and this expectation conditions the way the material is presented. Devices such as repetition and balanced phrasing produce satisfying sounds, but the author also employs many other figures which derive their effect

[13] p.lxv.

from the sounds of imaginary speech. One of his favourite habits is to ask Rhetorical Questions, which are very useful for sustaining the reader's attention and emphasizing a particular point in the argument, e.g.,

> Nis þis large relief? nis þis muche laue?
>
> (f.45a 28 – f.45b 1)

Sometimes he answers the question himself, as in the following instance:

> Hweder þe cat of helle cahte eauer towart hire ... ȝe soðes ...
>
> (f.26b 19–20)

The use of *Sententia* is a very common feature of *AW*, though whether it can be claimed as an example of classical influence is an arbitrary matter since ordinary conversation abounds in proverbial statements, which are often made unconsciously. Phrases such as the following are ubiquitous in the text: 'ofte a ful haher smið smeoðeð a ful wac cnif', f.13b 2–3).

The author varies his syntax in such a way as to diversify the speed of his discourse. Often his sentence are quite long because he attaches strings of subordinate clauses which capture the inventive process of construction which people use in ordinary speech. This is a major feature of his stylistic achievement; every section of the text bears witness to this, so that it would be a distortion to single out one sentence for demonstration. Even so, one could look, for example, at a hypotactic sentence in which he gives a symbolical interpretation of a night-bird (f.38b 26 – f.39a 2). Here the clauses follow on casually as in speech. Often the author abandons conjunctions altogether to effect Asyndeton, and this accelerates the rate of his address, e.g.,

> Ich am an ancre. a nunne. a wif iweddet. a meden. a wummon.
>
> (f.86b 12)

Often he uses phrases of similar length for this device, and this produces an attractive rhythmical balance, e.g.,

> Þe ealleofte hwelf is ifed wið supersticiuns. wið semblanz & wið sines. as beoren on heh þet heaued. crenge wið swire. lokin o siden. bihalden on hokere. winche mid ehe.
>
> (f.53a 15–17)

Here he deliberately chooses phrases made up of similar units to give balance to the Asyndeton. The opposite figure to Asyndeton is Polysyndeton, which derives its effect from the accumulation of words, phrases, or clauses. In the following example the gravity of the man's loss is indicated by the repetition of 'and':

ȝef a mon hefde ilosed in a time of þe dei his feader ant his moder. his
sustren & his breðren. & al his cun & alle his freond þet eauer hefde
weren asteoruen ferliche.

(f.84a 18–21)

Another characteristic figure is Synonymy, with which the author puts down
one word and immediately re-inforces it with one of similar meaning. This feature
is very common in works translated from Latin into English, but here the main
purpose seems to lend extra force to the original word, e.g.,

þe heorte edfleo & wende ut ...

(f.13a 14–15)

unlideð hit & openeð ...

(f.22a 3)

Our final common Figure of Speech which should be noted is Alliteration.
This occurs much less frequently than in the three saint's lives of the Katherine
Group,[14] but it is still a major characteristic of this text, e.g.,

ower sawle seccli sone se heo is ute.

(f.13a 15)

wringeð ut þet wursum biuoren al þe wide worlt

(f.87b 16)

The incidence of this figure increases in Part VII, as in the celebrated

help of his hehe hird to halden hire castel.

(f.105a 23–24)

which is obviously deliberate, and which is completely lost in the Latin version
('auxilium sui excercitus ad castellum ipsius tenendum', The Latin Text of the
Ancrene Riwle, ed. C.D'Evelyn, EETS 216, p.153).

Turning now to Tropes, the author uses a number of different types of this
category. Antonomasia (use of an extraneous epithet to designate something)
occurs quite frequently when he refers to the devil (e.g., 'þe feond of helle', f.18b
13; 'te beast of helle', f.102b 20). The figure of Hyperbaton (upset of regular
word-order) is very common since the author often re-arranges his normal syntax
in the interests of emphasis e.g.,

Nu mine leoue sustren monie temptatiuns ich habbe ow inempnet under
þe seoue sunnen.

(f.61a 24–25)

---

[14] The differing levels of Alliteration in this group of texts are discussed by Dorothy
Bethurum in 'The Connection of the Katherine Group with Old English Prose', JEGP 34
(1935), 553–564.

Here he introduces the sentence with a strong adverbial headword, follows this with a direct address to his readers, and then puts the object followed by the subject, thereby giving emphasis to 'monie temptatiuns'. Examples of this kind of syntactical manipulation are very common. For prose of this period, the normal order here would be *'Nu ... habbe ich ow inempnet monie temptatiuns ...', where 'Nu' would cause the inversion.

Metaphor is also an extremely common device in *AW*, and there is no need to cite more than two typical instances ('þe heorte is a ful wide beast', f.12b 9; 'ha makeð of hire tunge cradel to þe deofles bearn', f.21a 18–20).

The final Trope we should mention here is Hyperbole, which the author mainly likes to use about Christ (e.g., 'forlure ure lauerd þet is hundred siðen, ʒe þusent siðen betere þen is al þe world', f.85a 5–6).

Finally we come to Figures of Thought. Simile is common throughout the Inner Rule. A typical example is the following: 'þis stiche wes þreouald. þe ase þreo speren smat him to heorte', f.30a 20. Here he combines it with another of his favourite devices, which is to split up his material for mnemonic purposes into numerical divisions.[15]

Perhaps the most striking instance of these Figures of Thought is Prosopopoeia (imaginary speech). The commonest form is his invention of queries, comments, and questions for his audience, e.g.,

> Me leoue sire seið sum & is hit nu se ouer uuel forte totin utwart?

> (f.13a 22–23)

Sometimes such speech is very robust as when, for example, he is telling the sisters what to say in Confession:

> Sire godes are ich am a ful stod meare. a stinkinde hore.

> (f.86a 25–26)

This analysis of the stylistic devices used in *AW* has shown that they occur throughout the Inner Rule. (By contrast, the Outer Rule, Parts One and Eight, is written in an abstemiously plain style, thereby demonstrating the author's sensitivity to the relationship between style and content). It is true, nevertheless, that his use of the Grand Style, with its rich clustering of different types of figures and tropes, is more deliberate in Parts Six and (especially) Part Seven. In the earlier Parts there is nothing as powerful as Christ's wooing speech in Part Seven (f.107b 4 – f.108a 19), with its balanced phrasing ('oðer hit ... oðer hit ... oðer hit'); Rhetorical Questions ('hwer ... Nam ... nam ...' etc.); Anaphora 'Nam ... nam ... nam ...' etc.); word-play ('swotest & swetest'); numerical division and Asyndeton ('Ah ha is þreouald. i widewehad. i spus had. i meidenhad'); Polyptoton ('bugge ...

---

[15] See R.A.Waldron, 'Enumeration in *Ancrene Wisse*', *Notes and Queries* 214 (1969), 86–87.

buggen'); alliteration ('wult tu wealden al þe world'); balanced syntax with Anti-strophe ('nan uuel ne schal nahhi þe. na wunne ne schal wonti þe'); Homoioteu-leuton and Asyndeton ('unmeteliche. vneuenliche. unendliche mare'); *Exempla* ('Creasuse weole ... Absalones schene wlite ... Asaeles swiftschipe ... etc.), and so forth. Even Litotes (denial of the contrary) features here: 'ant alle somet aȝein mi bodi, ne beoð nawt wurð a nelde.' Here the author is obviously stressing the importance of his instruction concerning Christ and the wayward soul and he accordingly produces a stylistic *tour de force*. Elsewhere, in earlier Parts of the book, he uses rhetoric more loosely.

It cannot be claimed that the author's style is original because he is obviously heavily indebted to the mannered style of his biblical and patristic sources[16] and he is also presumably under the influence of contemporary writers in Latin who favoured an artificial prose style. Although the *Moralia super Evangelia*[17] has been discounted as a direct source of *AW* it bears witness to the type of writing which was acceptable for similar material. The full extent of the *AW* author's originality in content and style will only become apparent when Bella Millett's critical edition of the text is published by EETS. Nevertheless, at this stage it is possible to show that, granted the author's debt to his sources and training[18], he has carried out his task with consummate skill and discrimination and has had sufficient confidence to choose when and where to use rhetorical figures throughout the Inner Rule. In this exercise of choice lies his originality.

[16] On the influence of the author's sources on his style see Cecily Clark, 'As Seint Austin Seith ...', *Medium Ævum* 46 (1977), 212–218. See also the important reservations stated by Bella Millett in ' "Hali Meidhad", "Sawles Warde", and the Continuity of English Prose', in *Five Hundred Years of Words and Sounds: A Festschrift for E.J.Dobson*, ed. E.G.Stanley and D.Gray (Cambridge 1983), pp.101–102.

[17] E.J.Dobson *Moralities on the Gospels A New Source of Ancrene Wisse* (Oxford 1975), pp.126–182. See the review of this book by Richard H. Rouse and Siegfried Wenzel, *Speculum* 52 (1977), 648–652.

[18] See Dennis Rygiel, 'A Holistic Approach to the Style of Ancrene Wisse', *Chaucer Review* 16 (1982), 275.

I wish to acknowledge the generous help I was given for my work on *Ancrene Wisse* by the late Professor Shepherd, the late Professor E.J. Dobson and Professor R.M.Wilson.

'Maiden In The Mor Lay' and the Religious Imagination

Ronald Waldron

Maiden in the mor lay,
   In the mor lay,
Sevenyst fulle,
Sevenist fulle,
Maiden in the mor lay,   5
   In the mor lay,
Sevenistes fulle ant a day.

Welle was hire mete;
   Wat was hire mete?
Þe primerole ant the, –   10
Þe primerole ant the, –
Welle was hire mete;
   Wat was hire mete? –
The primerole ant the violet.

Welle <was hire dring>;   15
   Wat was hire dring?
<Þe chelde water of þe –
Þe chelde water of þe –
Welle was hire dring;
   Wat was hire dring?>   20
Þe chelde water of <þe> welle-spring.

Welle was hire bour;
   Wat was hire bour?
<Þe rede rose an te –
Þe rede rose an te –   25
Welle was hire bour;

Wat was hire bour?>
Þe rede rose an te lilie flour.[1]

The Middle English lyric to which Sisam gave the title *The Maid of the Moor* is tantalizing in its isolation and brevity, in the tentativeness of its quasi-hesitant repetitions, and its perplexing form; it has, not surprisingly, challenged the inter-pretative powers of a number of present-day critics. The critical discussion cen-tring on the poem over the last forty years will be sufficiently familiar to readers of this volume to make it unnecessary for me to review it in any detail. In barest outline, it may be recalled that the poem has been read by D.W.Robertson Jr. as an allegory referring to the Virgin Mary and by Joseph Harris as a ballad of the conversion and penance of Mary Magdalene which has been re-written as a Marian poem, while R.L.Greene, E.T.Donaldson, Siegfried Wenzel, and more recently John Burrow have defended a non-exegetical approach.[2]

Superficially the strength of the exegetical interpretations is their greater co-herence. For every feature of the poem, Robertson, for instance, has an allegorical significance which cancels the strangeness of the literal narrative structure:

> The number seven indicates life on earth, but life in this instance went on at night, or before the Light of the World dawned. The day is this light, or Christ, who said, "I am the day". ... The moor is the wilderness of the world under the Old Law before Christ came. The primrose is not a Scriptural sign, but a figure of fleshly beauty ... we are also told that she ate or embodied the violet, which is a Scriptural sign of humility. The maiden drank the cool water of God's grace, and her bower consisted of the roses of martyrdom or charity and the lilies of purity with which late medieval and early Renaissance artists sometimes adorned pictures of the Blessed Virgin Mary, and, indeed, she is the Maiden in the Moor ...[3]

Donaldson protests: 'I cannot find that the poem, as a poem, makes any more "sense" after exegesis than it did before, and I think it makes rather more sense as it stands than the critic allows it.'[4] Yet his vindication of the sense of the poem as

---

[1]   Oxford, Bodleian Library, MS Rawlinson D. 913; text printed from *Fourteenth Century Verse and Prose*, ed. Kenneth Sisam (Oxford 1921), p.167, the later stanzas expanded on the pattern of the first; line 8 *was*: MS *wat*.
[2]   D.W.Robertson Jr., 'Historical Criticism', *English Institute Essays, 1950*, ed. Alan S.Downer (New York 1951), pp.3–31 (esp. 26f.); Joseph Harris, ' "Maiden in the Mor Lay" and the Medieval Magdalene Tradition', *JMRS* 1 (1971) 59–87; Richard L.Greene ' "The Maid of the Moor" in the *Red Book of Ossory*', *Speculum* 27 (1952) 504–06; E. Talbot Donaldson, 'Patristic Exegesis in the Criticism of Medieval Literature – The Opposition', in *Critical Approaches to Medieval Literature: Selected Papers from the English Institute, 1958–1959*, ed. Dorothy Bethurum (New York 1960), pp.1–26; Siegfried Wenzel, 'The Moor Maiden – A Contemporary View', *Speculum* 49 (1974) 69–74; John Burrow, 'Poems without contexts: the Rawlinson lyrics' in *Essays on Medieval Literature* (Oxford 1984), pp.1–26, (first published in *EC* 29 (1979) 6–32).
[3]   D.W.Robertson Jr., 'Historical Criticism', p.27.
[4]   E.T.Donaldson, 'Patristic Exegesis in the Criticism of Medieval Literature', p.23.

it stands is finally an assertion of its qualities of mystery and suggestivity. In a similar vein, Silverstein says: 'Incremental repetition and refrain produce the disclosure of this poem but what is disclosed beyond the romantic reality is not within the limits of proper inference ... .'[5] Aside from Christian allegory or legend, the only actual *interpretations* of the poem's narrative have been based on specula-tion that the maiden was a fairy or water-sprite of pre-Christian folk-belief.[6] Burrow's conclusion, despite his conviction that the poem is a popular secular dance-song, is that the context of the poem is now so obscure that we may never be able to find the right literal interpretation. Indeed 'one suspects ... that the singers of the *karole* may themselves not have known the significance of their mysterious damsel who lay in the moor – or in the Worcester variant, "by wood". Originally, perhaps, she *was* a water-sprite; but for the carollers she may well have been, as she is for us, a creature of mystery.'[7]

I wish in this note to propose a specific context for the poem in the singing-games of children. In spite of the scarcity of parallels from the Middle Ages it is hardly doubtful that such pastimes (collected in large numbers by the folklorists of the nineteenth and twentieth centuries) had their medieval counterparts, or indeed that some individual examples have come down through many generations by an oral tradition existing entirely within the world of children's play. My argument for assigning the poem to this genre, however, rests principally on the coherence and (to me) persuasiveness of the resulting reading and not on the discovery of precise analogues.

A number of nineteenth-century children's singing-games (*Booman, Green Grass, Green Gravel, Jenny Jones, Old Roger, Wallflowers*) are categorized by Alice B.Gomme as Funeral Games.[8] These are dramatic games in which the text is potentially the script for the enactment of a funeral, usually of a young person, often a young maiden or her bridegroom-to-be. Some may be ring-games, like *Green Gravel* (Gomme, p.170), in which details of the funeral of the maiden, including the washing and laying out of the corpse, and communication with the lover, are described in a mixture of the past and present tense.

> Green gravel, green gravel, your grass is so green,
> The fairest young damsel that ever was seen;
> We washed her, we dried her, we rolled her in silk,
> And we wrote down her name with a glass pen and ink.
> Dear Annie, dear Annie, your true love, is dead,
> And we send you a letter to turn round your head.

[5] *Medieval English Lyrics*, ed. Theodore Silverstein (London 1971), p.83.
[6] See John Speirs, *Medieval English Poetry: The Non-Chaucerian Tradition* (London 1957), p.63; Peter Dronke, *The Medieval Lyric* (London 1969), p.195f.
[7] John Burrow, 'Poems without contexts: the Rawlinson lyrics', p.20.
[8] Alice Bertha Gomme, *The Traditional Games of England, Scotland and Ireland* (1894–98, repr. 1984), p.462.

In *Jinny Jo* (the *jo* of some versions is obviously the Scottish dialect word meaning 'dear' – cf. '*dear* Annie' in the poem above; other versions have *Jenny Jones*) the text takes the form of a dialogue, dramatically performed (as the descriptions of the nineteenth-century informants show), of a group-courtship followed by a funeral.

> We've come to court Jinny jo,
> Jinny jo, Jinny jo,
> We've come to court Jinny jo,
> Is she within?
>
> Jinny jo's washing clothes,
> Washing clothes, washing clothes,
> Jinny jo's washing clothes,
> You can't see her to-day.
>
> So fare ye well, ladies
> O ladies, O ladies,
> So fare ye well, ladies
> And gentlemen too.

[These verses are repeated for:
>> (1) drying clothes,
>> (2) starching,
>> (3) ironing,
>> (4) ill,
>> (5) dying.   Then –]

> Jinny jo's lying dead,
> Lying dead, lying dead,
> Jinny jo's lying dead,
> You can't see her to-day.
>
> So turn again, ladies,
> Ladies, ladies, ladies,
> So turn again, ladies,
> And gentlemen too.
>
> What shall we dress her in?
> Dress her in, dress her in?
> What shall we dress her in?
> Shall it be red?
>
> Red's for the soldiers,
> The soldiers, the soldiers,
> Red's for the soldiers,
> And that will not do.

[Various other colours are suggested in the same way, but are found unsuitable – black because "black's for the mourners," green because "green's for the croppies," and so on till at last white is named.]

> White's for the dead people,

Dead people, the dead people,
White's for the dead people,
And that will just do.

Belfast (*Notes and Queries*, 7th series,
xii.492 [1891], W.H.Patterson).[9]

I am not suggesting that *Jinny Jo* or *Green Gravel* is descended from or directly connected in any way with *Maiden in the Mor Lay*; I cite them merely to show that the Middle English poem has some characteristics in common with the nineteenth-century children's singing-game and may have originated in a similar context.

The question-and-answer form, and the repetitions with variation are, of course, common features of ballad-form; they are, in fact, so essential to the structure of the Middle English poem (as they are to the later children's play-song quoted) as to suggest that, instead of seeking to interpret *Maiden in the Mor Lay* on the basis of the Mary Magdalen ballads, we should regard the features which they have most strikingly in common as having been welded to the legend of Mary Magdalene's penance in the wilderness from just some such source in popular song as *Maiden in the Mor Lay* itself.[10]

In *Jinny Jo* the unusually long drawn-out question-and-answer form serves the

---

[9]   Gomme, pp.260–83. For records of these two games in New Zealand, see also Brian Sutton-Smith, *The Folkgames of Children*, Publications of the American Folklore Society, Volume 24 (Austin 1972), pp.25–28.

[10] In the standard medieval form of the legend, as represented in the *Legenda Aurea* (and by the Middle English miracle play *Mary Magdalene*) Mary spends a period of contemplation in the wilderness, during which she is attended by angels and sustained by purely heavenly food. In the ballad-versions, the period of contemplation (probably, as Child suggest, under the influence of legends of other female saints, such as that of her sister Martha) has become a seven-year period of *penance* imposed on her by her confessor (Jesus, or an old hermit or palmer), a penance which is repeated when she shows herself insufficiently purged of worldliness. See *Jacobi a Voragine Legenda Aurea*, ed. T.Graesse (1846), p.413; *The Digby Plays*, reissued from the plates of the text edited by F.J.Furnivall for the New Shakespeare Society in 1882, EETS ES 70 (1896); Francis James Child, *The English and Scottish Popular Ballads*, 3 vols (New York 1957; reprint of the 5 vol. edn of 1882–98), i, p.229. It is in this section of the ballad-legend (in some versions – though *not* the Catalan ones which Doncieux regards as closest to the original) that the questions and answers which so much resemble those of *Maiden in the Mor Lay* appear. Harris declares: 'it is unthinkable that the ballad can have derived from the lyric' and in the sense that there is no specific Mary Magdalene material in the lyric he is undoubtedly right; all that *may* derive from the lyric is the form and substance of some of the questions and answers as to her experience in the wilderness. The alternative genetic explanation – that the lyric, although written down approximately two centuries earlier than the date of 1526 at which the particular form of the Magdalene legend represented in the ballad can be first documented, is nevertheless an attenuated form of this ballad – seems considerably less convincing, whether the lyric is thought to have been 'ground out of the ballad by the friction of oral transmission' or (according to the theory Harris finally adopts) the result of conscious adaptation by a learned poet. See Harris, ' "Maiden in the Mor Lay" and the Medieval

poetic and dramatic function of delaying the recognition of the maiden's death and of mitigating its horror (though emphasizing its poignancy) when at length revealed. A similar poetic function is performed by the continuity of imagery between the courtship and funeral scenes: the care in dressing the corpse recalls the preoccupation with clothing of the young bride-to-be, while the quasi-incidental variation 'Red's for the soldiers', 'Blue's for sailors', and so on, to 'Black's for the mourners' and 'White's for the dead people', poignantly suggests the contrast between the funeral that is and the wedding that might have been. What makes it, in Gomme's words, 'perhaps the most realistic of all the singing games' (p.280) makes it also perhaps the most moving. After the repeated 'And that will not do' of these closing stanzas, the last line: 'And that will just do' falls as a perfect expression of rueful acceptance.

It is, of course, intrinsic to my argument that *Maiden in the Mor Lay* is also this kind of poem that the first line may be read quite literally as '(A/The) maiden lay (buried) in the ground'. Sisam's title *The Maid of the Moor* seems to have pre-empted the interpretation of this line: no subsequent editor or critic appears to have doubted that the maiden was one who, in some sense, 'dwelt on the moor'.[11] The Middle English verb *lie(n)/ligge(n)* is frequently used in the sense 'live, dwell' in Middle English, as it is, for instance, in *Pis kyng lay at Camylot vpon Krystmasse* (*Sir Gawain and the Green Knight*, 37). This is *OED* **Lie** v.[1] Sense 5. 'To dwell or sojourn; *esp.* to sleep or pass the night (in a place), to lodge temporarily. Now *rare* or *arch*.' (cf. *MED* **lien** v.(1), Sense 7(b)). Indeed, if 'Maiden in the mor lay' is read in the way I am proposing, there is every reason to admit the poetic resonance contributed by this sense of *lay* (cf. the obviously metaphorical *bour* in the last stanza). I suggest, however, that the primary meaning of the word in this line is the much older 'lay dead, lay buried': *OED* Sense 1d. 'Expressing the posture of a dead body: To be extended on a bier or the like; to be buried (in a specified place). ... †In OE. and early ME. also, To be dead.' (cf. *MED*, Sense 3(e)). A contemporary parallel use of the word is *William of Palerne* 166: *Pe king edwardes newe at glouseter pat ligges*, which (by a coincidental irony in the present discussion) the *OED* erroneously cites for Sense 5. As is pointed out by Thorlac Turville-Petre, *at glouseter pat ligges* has as its antecedent not *newe* ('nephew', i.e.

Magdalene Tradition', 69ff.; George Doncieux, 'Le Cycle de Sainte Marie-Madeleine', *Revue des Traditions Populaires* 6 (1891) 257–76 (date of origin, p.273).
[11] Tolkien's glossary, while not giving specific support to the interpretation suggested by the title, glosses **Ligge(n)** as 'to lie (down, idle, &c.), be (lodged, situated, &c.)'. *The Oxford Book of Medieval English Verse*, chosen and edited by Celia and Kenneth Sisam (Oxford 1970), p.167, glosses *lay* in line 1 as 'dwelt', and adopts the same title as *Fourteenth-century Verse and Prose*. The title which R.T.Davies gives to the poem, *The maiden lay in the wilds*, postulates the same narrative structure (*Medieval English Lyrics: A Critical Anthology*, ed. with introduction and notes by R.T.Davies (London 1963) p.102,320f.).

Humphrey de Bohun), as was formerly thought, but *king edward* and refers to the tomb of Edward II in what is now Gloucester Cathedral.[12]

Given this alternative sense for *lay*, it is, of course, still possible to take *in the mor* in the way it has always been understood – as 'on the moor': the maiden was lying in a moorland grave (perhaps in a churchyard which, like many Dartmoor or Exmoor village churchyards, was on the edge of the moor). We should remember, however, that in both Old English and Middle English the word had various potential meaning-components (relative flatness, elevation above sea-level, dampness or swampiness) which were blended in different proportions in different contexts, making it difficult in many instances of its use to specify an exact sense. The *OED* (s.v. **Moor** *sb.*[1]) distinguishes two principal senses: '1. A tract of unenclosed waste ground; now usually, uncultivated ground covered with heather; a heath; ...' and '†2. A marsh (*obs.*); *also dial.*' The *MED* closely follows this division of senses, but provides earlier Middle English examples of Sense 2, for which, oddly, the earliest citation in the *OED* is dated 1441, although the sense is common in Old English. The *OED* also has a third sense, attested only from 1596: '3. *dial.* The soil of which moorland consists; peat.' The *MED* offers no Middle English examples of the use of the word in this sense. (Close, perhaps, is the single instance it cites as '1. (b) *fig.* the earth' ... *Cleanness* 385: *Pe moste mountaynez on mor þenne watz no more dry3e.*) It may, however, already have been a possible sense in Old English. The evidence for this is in an additional citation in the Bosworth-Toller *Supplement*[13] from *The Old English Version of the Rule of Chrodegang*, ch.81. Hypocritical teachers are like frogs who *quasi in aqua sapientie esse uidentur, et in luto heresis tamen uersantur: swilce hi an wisdomes wætere wunian, 7 swaþeah eardiaþ an þæs gedwildes more 7 meoxe*, where *more 7 meoxe* 'moor and dung' translates L. *luto*, abl. of *lutum* 'mire'.[14] The first line of our poem could well mean 'A/The maiden lay buried in the mire'.

While the poem may not be complete as we have it, there is nothing to suggest that it is defective at the beginning. If the first line is read in either of the two ways now newly proposed, the poem appears (like the nineteenth-century Funeral Games cited) as the effort of a child's mind to take in and comprehend the fact of death (specifically the death of another child). The ambiguous and hesitant approach to the subject is comparable to that in *Jinny Jo*[15], while the note of

---

12   *The Alliterative Revival* (Cambridge 1977), p.135.
13   Joseph Bosworth, *An Anglo-Saxon Dictionary* (Oxford 1882); *Supplement* by T.Northcote Toller (1921), s.v. *mór*.
14   Ed. A.S.Napier (EETS, OS 150, 1916), p.95f.
15   Patterson's descriptions show that the players were well aware of these implications in the text, e.g.: 'Something tragic has happened; but the father and mother wish to temporize, so they sing in answer: Jinny Jo's washing clothes, *etc.* ... till at last the parents are forced to announce the sad fact that
  Jinny Jo's lying dead.'
(*Notes and Queries*, 7th series, 12 (1891) 492f.) In the version of the game described by

acceptance struck by the repeated *Welle was hire* ... is found in the later poem in the final *And that will just do*.

This sheds a very different light on the poem from that of the doctrinal interpretations,[16] but I would contend that as an attempt to meet a profound and universal human need for reassurance in the face of mortality it is a kind of religious poem. We may be distantly reminded of another fourteenth-century maiden who has gone *þur3 gresse to grounde* (*Pearl*, 10)[17] and another mourner (not a child but child-like) whose naive questions, even after his partial enlightenment, are curiously similar in their range:

> I wolde bysech, wythouten debate,
> 3e wolde me say in sobre asente
> What lyf 3e lede erly & late
>
> (390–92)
>
> Haf 3e no wonez in castel-walle,
> Ne maner þer 3e may mete & won?
> . . .
> So cumly a pakke of joly juele
> Wer euel don schulde ly3 þeroute
>
> (917f., 929f.)

He has to learn, through his vision, that celestial food is altogether different from that on earth:

> Þe Lombe vus gladez, oure care is kest;
> He myrþes vus alle at vch a mes.
>
> (861f.)
>
> Þe Lombe þe sakerfyse þer to refet.
>
> (1064)

The images of life on earth, *Blomez blayke and blwe and rede* (27), can be no more than metaphors for life in heaven. *Maiden in the Mor Lay* goes little further than the viewpoint of the *Pearl* dreamer in his garden state of disconsolate grief. It is nevertheless, I suggest, a touching expression of the limited religious imagination of the child.

Patterson – not the most common, according to Gomme (*Traditional Games of England, Scotland and Ireland*, p.277) – there is a resurrection: 'suddenly Jinny comes to life again, and springs up, when the play ends amid wild rejoicing.'

[16] Donaldson comes close to reading the poem in a similar way when he compares the maiden to Wordsworth's Lucy, though his remarks indicate that he is thinking of Lucy's secluded life rather than her death.

[17] Quotations from *Sir Gawain* and *Pearl* are taken from *The Poems of the Pearl Manuscript*, ed. Malcolm Andrew and Ronald Waldron, York Medieval Texts, second series (London 1978).

Elementary Teaching Techniques and Middle English Religious Didactic Writing

Marie Denley

The stylistic and structural principles of later Middle English religious didactic writing are primarily traceable to the rhetoric of the pulpit, sometimes joined to the rhetoric of the letter-writer. The following discussion will make no attempt to diminish the clear pre-eminence of the *ars praedicandi* and, to a lesser extent, the *ars dictaminis*, in this respect, but will suggest an additional, though humbler and smaller, pervasive influence on religious didactic writing, that of simple pedagogic processes encountered at very elementary stages of medieval education. Certain didactic and expository techniques, themselves undeniably standard rhetorical equipment, were used by religious teachers to make their work accessible; such use may or may not have been conscious, but it made capital of the powerful impact of structures and processes familiar from early stages of learning (in some cases, even before a medieval child's formal education programme began). It is widely recognized amongst educational and developmental psychologists nowadays that the *processes* by which we learn from an early age are far more crucially formative than the actual content of what we learn, in establishing processes of learning and evaluation later in life. Medieval educationalists may not have evolved an analytical theory of early learning-processes, but both at the commonsense proverbial level, and in more formal statements, there is evidence of awareness that, educationally, the child is father of the man. In a late fifteenth-century Oxford school-master's collection of *vulgaria* we are told:

> It is a thynge not litell to be caryde for in what auctorys a childe is customyde in youghe, for then the myn of a yong mann is as waxe, apte to take all thynge ...
> They ar happy, mesemyth, that upon the begynnynge of ther abses have hapynede upon goode maisters, for if thei fro thensforth contynewe as thei have begune, lukkynge alway upon goode maisters acordynge after the diversite of connynge to be lurnede, and therselfe lurnynge with as

goode a diligence as thei be tought, withoute doubte, yf thei shall want
no wytt, they shall prove within fewe yeres excellently connynge.[1]

While being cautious of according the status of an educational manifesto to a
practical teaching aid, a collection of *vulgaria*, we can reasonably note that a
practising schoolmaster felt it worth commenting on the impressionability of the
young mind, and on the formative importance of early good teaching, in a manual
aimed at his actual 'customers'; although the emphasis is practical, on offering the
right kind of syllabus and the right kind of staff, the comments show implicit
awareness that *processes* instilled at the elementary stage have a lasting effect on
the education of a child.

The wide interpretation of 'education' in this discussion, and the diversity of
material considered, requires some comment. In selecting a sample of basic educational devices for examination, attention has not been confined to formal educa-
tion-towards-literacy, though that plays a significant part. Material concerning
the early socialization of the young child within the household, courtesy-book
literature dealing with the social and moral grooming of the slightly older child,
and elementary religious education, whether aimed at children or at untutored
adults, also come within the province of this discussion. The more one considers
what can be gleaned about the basic education of medieval children, the more
apparent it becomes that it is a continuum in which the intellectual, the religious,
the moral, the social and the practical cannot be separated without doing violence to the beliefs of medieval educators. The formation of the virtuous Christian from the untutored child is the unifying aim. The primary purposes and
indeed the primary tools of acquiring literacy were religious, as has been amply
demonstrated by historians of education and literacy, notably Nicholas Orme, Jo
Ann Hoeppner Moran and William J. Courtenay.[2]

The essential religious drive of elementary education is apparent from the
teaching-materials used to start off the novice reader. Apart from actual service-
books and psalters in Latin, which with their clear and large format were ideal for
encouraging recognition of letters and the ability to reproduce sounds (in a
language as yet unknown to the learner), small booklets known as 'primers', some
Latin, some English, were used as reading-manuals. Such booklets were copied in
quantity between the thirteenth and the sixteenth centuries. They were antho-

---

[1] William Nelson, ed., *A Fifteenth Century School Book* (Oxford 1956), pp.20–21.
[2] See Nicholas Orme, *English Schools in the Middle Ages* (London 1973) (henceforth
English Schools) esp. ch.2; ibid., *From Childhood to Chivalry: the Education of the English Kings
and Aristocracy 1066–1530* (London and New York 1984), esp. ch.4; Jo Ann Hoeppner
Moran, *The Growth of English Schooling 1340–1548: Learning, Literacy and Laicization in
Pre-Reformation York* (Princeton, N.J., 1985) (henceforth Moran), esp. ch.2; William
J.Courtenay, *Schools and Scholars in Fourteenth-Century England* (Princeton, N.J., 1987) esp.
ch.1. See also W.J.Frank Davies, *Teaching Reading in Early England* (henceforth *Teaching
Reading*) (London 1973), esp. ch.2.

logies of the essential prayers and liturgical devotions useful to the laity, and they appear to have been used as elementary readers, often beginning with the alphabet before moving on to the essential prayers which a clergyman acting in the spirit of the Fourth Lateran Council and subsequent episcopal constitutions would have wished his flock to know. Lay people seem to have been very attached to their primers in later life, often leaving them by specific mention in their wills, which might suggest that their early impact, combining instruction in literacy and in the elements of the faith, was considerable.[3]

The spirit of the courtesy-books, where manners are the outward and visible sign of inward and spiritual grace, reaches its most idealized expression in the *Gawain*-poet's complex concept of *cortaysye*, which in *Cleanness* stands for the Christ-like nature to be imitated by man. The notion of courtesy, as purveyed by the (admittedly slightly later) medieval courtesy-books, seems already to have been an accepted means towards, and expression of, godliness. For example, *The Babees Book*, while offering much practical advice about etiquette, specifically links courtesy with the attainment of virtue at its opening, and concludes:

> And myhtefulle god, that suffred peynes smerte,
> In curtesye he make yow so experte,
> That thurhe your nurture and youre governaunce
> In lastynge blysse yee mowe your self auaunce![4]

Similar minglings of practical advice on etiquette with elementary spiritual advice can be found in many other courtesy-books, including the later fifteenth-century *The Lytylle Childrens Lytil Boke, The Young Children's Book* and the Sloane *Boke of Curtasye*,[5] which cheerfully mingles precepts of Christian behaviour with extremely prosaic instruction on how to be a good gatekeeper or butler, without any sense that it is breaching decorum or confusing categories. The ideological symbiosis of the education of a Christian and the social education offered in courtesy books has recently been very fully discussed by J.W.Nicholls.[6] The general peda-

---

[3]   See Henry Littlehales, ed., *The Prymer or Lay Folks' [sic] Prayer Book*, Part II, EETS OS 109 (London 1897), pp. xlii–xliii. One wonders if a liking for anthologies of shorter pieces and extracts such as those classified by Robert Raymo as 'miscellaneous manuals' was fostered by the anthology-like character of primers. See Robert R. Raymo, 'Works of Religious and Philosophical Instruction', ch.XX of Albert E.Hartung, ed., *A Manual of the Writings in Middle English 1050–1500*, vol.7 (New Haven, Connecticut, 1986), p. 2273, item 24. On primers, see Moran, pp. 42–3 and notes, and *Teaching Reading*, pp. 99–109.
[4]   Frederick J.Furnivall, ed., *Early English Meals and Manners*, EETS OS 32 (London 1868, repr. 1894) (henceforth *Meals and Manners*), p. 258, ll.214–218 of *The Babees Book*.
[5]   *Meals and Manners*, pp.265–274 (*The Lytylle Childrens Boke/ The Young Children's Book*) and pp.177–205 (*The Boke of Curtasye*).
[6]   J.W.Nicholls, *The Matter of Courtesy: A Study of Medieval Courtesy Books and the Gawain-Poet* (Woodbridge 1985).

gogic point to be extracted from the education-for-life manuals is that they demonstrate how children were themselves programmed from an early age to see the content of their 'curriculum' as a continuum and not to separate, or to be surprised at the conjunction of, religious and practical educational matter. Similarly, the inseparability of basic reading instruction from religious materials, and from a religious didactic purpose, encouraged an implicitly holistic view of elementary education.

Awareness of the 'holistic' basis of medieval elementary education, viewed in conjunction with explicit medieval perception that what first goes into a child's head, and the processes whereby it is inculcated, are crucially formative for later development, leads on to speculation about evidence of didactic capitalization on early learning-processes and materials. In religious didactic literature mainly aimed at a lay audience, an examination of four sample basic teaching-devices or groups of related devices, namely (i) the alphabet, (ii) catechetical processes involving question-and-answer, the subdivision of material, and repetition, (iii) rhymes and (iv) proverbs, yields results suggesting that at least some such capital was consciously or unconsciously made by spiritual instructors. The familiarity and accessibility of devices from the early (in our terms, very roughly 'primary' and 'junior') educational stages offered a handy vehicle for conveying points of religious instruction in a clear, comprehensible form.

It is often pointed out that the alphabet was first presented to the medieval child, certainly by the fourteenth century, in a form in which he, or less frequently she, could not avoid confronting Christian symbolism at the beginning and end of its traditional layout. The alphabet opened with a cross and ended with 'amen'; its enclosure by specifically Christian material symbolizes the subsuming of literacy in the scheme of Christian education; it is unsurprising to find that the alternative English name for the ABC, 'abece' or 'absey' is the 'cross-row'.[7] Although the alphabet was first learnt to acquire passive literacy in Latin, that is, the ability to read out loud (without comprehension) the sounds of Latin psalms and other service-book material, it also provided a framework for vernacular literacy. Inculcating the alphabet appears to have been accomplished by a variable combination of phonic and look-and-say memorial methods. Once learned parrot-fashion, it could provide a useful mnemonic framework for religious and moral teaching; equally, a vernacular alphabet-verse, offering a conceptually meaningful alliterative or rhymed sequence with moral or religious content, could reinforce the trainee literate's grasp of the alphabet itself. Examples of alphabetic arrangement for both the reinforcement of ethical teaching, the reinforcement of basic literacy, and the combination of the two, can be found.

Chaucer's ABC, a translation of a prayer in Deguilleville's Le Pèlerinage de la Vie Humaine, an aureate hymn to the Virgin in which each 8-line decasyllabic

---

[7] English Schools, p.61.

stanza opens with a successive letter of the alphabet, is too complex an art-lyric to be viewed in the mainstream mnemonic didactic tradition.[8] Nonetheless, an early tradition recorded in Speght's 1602 edition relates it to the religious edification of a distinguished lay person. It was

> made, as some say, at the request of Blanche, Duchess of Lancaster, as praier for her privat use, being a woman in her religion very deuout.[9]

Whatever the historical accuracy of this, the early categorization of Chaucer's *ABC* as a piece suitably framed for the prayers of a pious aristocratic laywoman is itself of interest; the alphabet forms a useful structured progression for meditation based on the earliest external pattern acquired during elementary education. Its structural familiarity facilitates the apprehension of what it carries, rather than obtruding itself distractingly. On a much more mundane level, the alphabet-sequence is expanded in the so-called *ABC of Aristotle*, where moral teaching of the courtesy-book type is combined with the psycholinguistic reinforcement of alliteration in each line on successive letters of the alphabet. Its recommendation of moderate behaviour (somewhat reminiscent of the gnomic sanctions of Old English sapiential poetry) tells its audience not to be

A to amerose, to aunterose, ne argue not to myche.
B to bolde, ne to bisi, ne boorde not to large.
C to curteis, to cruel, ne care not to sore.
D to dul, ne to dreedful, ne drinke not to ofte.[10]

And so on, systematically dinning in its alliterative advice, further reinforced by parallel syntactic structures.

The expanded alphabet or cross-row remained current enough as a religious teaching-device until the earlier sixteenth century for the Bridgettine monk, Richard Whitford of Syon, to produce both prose and verse versions. Whitford produced many works for the early printing presses aimed at a diverse audience, starting with his original small monastic audience amongst the nuns of the double monastery at Syon, Isleworth, and proceeding to a wider audience of both lay people and other religious; this wider audience received his (usually revised) works in printed versions either directly, or indirectly if relayed by a literate intermediary (not necessarily clerical, since anyone who had the money could buy a printed book).[11] Whitford's work shows special interest in giving the spiritually-

---

[8] Larry D.Benson, general ed., *The Riverside Chaucer* (Third edition; Oxford 1988), pp.637–40.
[9] Ibid., p.1076.
[10] *Meals and Manners*, p.260.
[11] Discussed in my forthcoming 'Teaching through Print: Bridgettine Religious Didactic Writing, its Audiences and its Dissemination'.

inclined layman the means to better his or her own spiritual condition (and, in *A Work for Householders*, that of those in a layman's charge). Whitford's cross-row verse-translation of a piece by St Bonaventure combines mnemonic alphabetic arrangement with the psycholinguistic reinforcement of heavy caesural breaks and end-rhyme:

A ¶Alway loue pouerte/ with vyle thinges be content.
B Be also in good workes: busy and dilygent.
C Couet nat moch to speake: but rather to kepe sylence.
D Deme in euery place 7 tyme: y[t] god is in presence.[12]

Whitford does not content himself with progressing through the alphabet, but even works the miscellaneous paraphernalia at the end of the traditional model alphabet into his religious didactic rhyme:

(Con)ceyue here .ii. tytles mo.
.ii. preceptes/ for ten.
Loue god and your neyghbour both:
so conclude Est. Amen.[13]

Although Whitford claims to be translating St Bonaventure's alphabetic teaching for its *spiritual* value to the devout, he adds a final practical comment on it as an aid to literacy:

If you lerne perfectely this crosrowe you may the better spell and do to gyther/ and so more redyly rede.[14]

Spelling and 'doing together',[15] as part of literacy, are all ultimately a means to further religious education, as Whitford elsewhere makes plain:

---

[12] There is a prose cross-row (*The Crossrowe or A.B.C*) published with this verse cross-row ('An other alphabete .A.B.C. or crosrowe') printed by Waylande in 1537 (*RSTC* 25413.5) with other pieces including *A dialoge or co(m)municacion … For preparacion vnto howselynge*, a pastoral treatise preparing the parishioner for the sacrament. The quotation is from K. vi.a.

[13] Ibid., K. vii.a.

[14] Ibid., K. vii.a.

[15] I take 'do together' to mean 'make out syllables and be able to pronounce them out loud from written versions', as in the syllabary method of learning to read by progressing from recognition of single letters to recognition of them in conjunction. Michael Clanchy agrees with this interpretation (oral comment on my paper on Bridgettine views of literacy given at the Warburg Institute in June 1988). The syllable-building method of learning to read forms the basis of jokes in *Love's Labour's Lost* V.i.49–55.

For the occupacion of redynge 7 meditacion: shal teche the what to fle, and auoyde, and whyther thou shuldest intende and passe. By redynge: and lernynge: thy wytte, and vnderstandynge shall increase. And much mayst thou p(ro)fet therby yf thou warke 7 do therafter.[16]

The second group of teaching-devices with which this paper will deal takes together, as catechetical techniques, processes involving question-and-answer exchanges, subdivision of the subject-matter, and repetitive structures involving some degree of response on the part of the pupil. Catechetical question-and-answer technique is as appropriate for the instruction of pre-literates and illiterates as of novice literates; as an elementary religious didactic device, it appears just as suitable for adults as for children. In John Mirk's *Instructions for Parish Priests*, a rhymed vernacular manual to help the lower echelons of the clergy instruct their parochial charges, the section *Quod sufficit scire in lingua materna* uses a very basic instructive method, the leading question, in which information is carried in a question requiring the answer 'yes'. Mirk envisages parishioners as subjected to a systematic and internally informative series of questions, as for example when he breaks up the intimidating bulk of the Creed into manageable bits:

> Be-leuest þow on fader & sone & holygost,
> As þou art holden, wel þow wost,
> Thre persons in trynyte,
> And on god (vnsware þow me),
> Þat goddes sone monkynde toke,
> In mayde mary (as seyth þe boke),
> And of þat mayde was I-bore:
> Leuest þow þys? telle me by-fore,
> And on crystes passyone
> And on hys resurrexyone,
> And stegh vp in-to heuen blys
> In flesch and blod (beleuest þow þys?) ...[17]

The effect is unintentionally comic, taken out of the context of pastoral education; there is little the catechumen can reply but a bemused 'Yis' like Geoffrey in *The House of Fame* left speechless by the eagle! The repetition by the priest of the information-carrying, loaded question must have been considered useful for dinning in necessary teaching to unsophisticated minds, when systematic 'apposing' or catechizing was carried out regularly by a conscientious instructor.

---

[16] Richard Whitford, *An instructyon to auoyde and eschewe vices* in *Dyuers holy instrucyons* (Myddylton, 1541) (RSTC 25420), f. 69r.

[17] Edward Peacock, ed., *Instructions for Parish Priests by John Myrc*, EETS OS 31 (London 1868), p.26, ll.815–26.

Modern educational theory might look down upon the process, since it leads to rote-learning rather than profound understanding, but it does at least provide a memorial basis on which later understanding can be built; in any case, medieval attitudes to rote-learning valued it as a constructive process, not separable from understanding (see the passage from Henry VIII's 1536 *Injunctions* quoted at notes 19 and 21 below). In fairness, it should be observed that this 'interrogative sausage-machine' technique offers, as well as the potential educational value inherent in repetition and clear subdivision, the chance of briefly and appositely amplifying the basic material at the appropriate point. For example, in the same section of Mirk's *Instructions*, the credal clause concerning Christ's coming in judgment is amplified to make a particular application to the individual's case:

> And [he] schal come with woundes rede
> To deme þe quyke and þe dede,
> And we vch one (as we ben here)
> In body and sowle bothe I-fere,
> Schule ryse at þe day of dome
> And be redy at hys come,
> And take þenne for oure doynge
> As we haue wroȝt here lyuynge,
> Who so has do wel schale go to blysse,
> Who so has do euel to peyne I-wysse.[18]

(In passing, we should not neglect the two-way educational function of the teaching-devices in Mirk's *Instructions*; their unpretentious vernacular, mnemonically-effective verse, homely diction and simple schematism must have reinforced both the didactic processes and the basic doctrinal learning of minimally or inadequately educated parish clergy, as well as inculcating learning-patterns in their charges.) The importance of repetition, and of the subdivision of material into manageable chunks by clergymen, for lay instruction, is still being emphasized at the turn of the Reformation in Henry VIII's 1536 *Injunctions*; while listing the essential basics of the faith to be taught to children and servants, they recommend:

> And the same so taught, shall cause the said youthe ofte to repete and vnderstande. And to thintent this may be the more easily done, the sayde curates shal in theyr sermons deliberately and plainly recite of the said pater noster, articles, or commaundementes, one clause or artycle one daye, and another an other daye, tyll the hole be taught and lerned by lytell and lytell.[19]

---

[18] Ibid., p.26, ll.827–36.
[19] T.W.Baldwin, *William Shakspere's Petty School* (Urbana, Illinois, 1943) (henceforth Baldwin), p.32.

Although the major responsibility for the elementary religious education of unsophisticated laymen belonged to the clergy, there is evidence that, from an early date, religious educational strategies derived from the Fourth Lateran Council were, within limits, to be deputed to responsible members of secular households. In the fourteenth-century Northern English translation of Archbishop Thoresby's catechism known as *John Gaytryge's Sermon*, the Archbishop exhorts pastors to

> Enioyne þair parischennes and þair sugettes þat þay here and lere þise ilke sex thynges and oftesythes reherse þam till þat þay cun þam, and sythen teche þam þair childir, if þay any haue, whate tym so þay are of elde to lere þam ...[20]

Such practices are still being enjoined in Henry VIII's 1536 *Injunctions*:

> Also in the same theyr sermons and other collations, the persons, vycars, and other curates aforesaid, shal diligently admonishe the fathers and mothers, maisters, and gouernours of youthe, beynge within theyr cure, to teche or cause to be taught theyr chyldren and seruantes, euen from theyr infancy, theyr Pater noster, tharticles of our fayth, and the tenne commandementes in theyr mother tonge: And the same so taught, shal cause the sayd youthe ofte to repete and vnderstande ...[21]

It is demonstrably assumed that basic catechetical processes will be encountered at home, as well as from pastors, from an early age, and that lay heads of households and parents are expected to have assimilated some very basic religious educational techniques. An example of how such domestic elementary religious education is envisaged as working is provided by Richard Whitford in his earlier sixteenth-century printed treatise *A Work for Householders*,[22] where the Bridgettine monk, for all his claustral seclusion, shows remarkable common sense and basic awareness of educational psychology. The basic learning-device recommended is repetition (which may involve some one-to-one work for the head of the secular household, but which should also be daily and communal, to help the old, who are too shy to show their ignorance, to learn painlessly and inconspicuously). Such texts as the Creed and Paternoster are broken down into small meaning-units which can then be briefly expanded upon, in a less bald manner than that exemplified by Mirk's *Instructions*, albeit by the same technique. Particular emphasis is given by Whitford to starting early with the young, for, as the

---

[20] George G.Perry, ed., *Religious Pieces in Prose and Verse*, EETS OS 26 (London 1867 and 1914), p.2, ll.26–30.
[21] Baldwin, p.32.
[22] *A Work for Householders* is known in several prints and was very popular. See RSTC 25421.8, 25422, 25422.3, 25422.5, 25423, 25425, 25425.5.

English proverb has it, 'yᵉ yonge cocke croweth as he doth heare 7 learne of the olde'.[23] There is considerable likelihood that a child in a secular household, whether its own or one to which it had been sent for its education, would in the course of daily life encounter several catechetical teaching-devices (such as question-and-answer, repetition and subdivision) which, along with short rhymes and popular proverbs, to this day remain common features of adult discourse to children.

The question-and-answer format already encountered in crude form in Mirk's *Instructions*, in collocation with analytic subdivision of the material, is a widespread teaching and reinforcing device which can be given more interesting, lively forms, allowing the pupil a less passive role. Question-and-answer format is common in the elementary grammatical treatises (which by modern educational divisions might be seen as belonging to the 'junior' rather than the 'primary' stage of education); although in all probability the questions are there envisaged as posed by the master for answer by a model pupil into whom the right answers have previously been hammered, it would be possible for them to be used as frameworks legitimating genuine discipular enquiry and re-enquiry for information from the master, though this is less likely. John Drury's *De Comparacione*, an English treatise of the 1430s on the comparison of Latin adjectives and adverbs,[24] and a short anonymous fifteenth-century grammar now preserved in Trinity College Cambridge, provide typical examples, as in the following extract from the latter, on concord in Latin grammar:

> How many acordys hast thou in grammer?
> ffoure: on by twene the nominatyf case and the uerbe, the secunde by twene the adiectyf and the substantyf, the thrydde by twene the relatyf and the antecedent, the fourthe by twene the noune partytyf, the noun dystributyf, the noune of superlatyf degre and the genityf case that folweth'.[25]

The treatise then takes these categories in order, with examples, of which the following is from the section on agreement between adjective and noun:

> The secunde acorde is by twene the adiectyf and the substantyf. In how many maners schul they acorde? In thre, in case, gender, and noumber.

[23] Richard Whitford, *A Work for Householders* (Wynkyn de Worde, 1533) (*RSTC* 25423), B.ii.a.
[24] Sanford Brown Meech, 'John Drury and his English Writings', *Speculum*, 9 (1934), pp.70–83, esp. pp.79–82.
[25] Sanford Brown Meech, 'An Early Treatise in English Concerning Latin Grammar', *University of Michigan Publications: Language and Literature*, vol. 8: *Essays and Studies in English and Comparative Literature* (Ann Arbor, 1935), pp.81–125. This quotation is from pp.98–9.

Ensaumple, as thys good man ȝaf me a fayre ȝyfte, iste bonus homo dedit michi pulchrum donum. In how many maners may they be lette? By foure: by particion', as my brother is on of creatours, ffrater meus est vna creaturarum; by dystribucion, as nouthyr of thys twey stones is cristall', neuter istorum duorum lapidum est cristallum ... (etc.)[26]

The question-and-answer analytic subdivision of elementary catechetical and secular pedagogical technique may have reinforced the traditional analytic subdivisions of religious exegetical writing and of evolving penitential practice, as a useful and accessible teaching device in religious didactic treatises; the predisposition of teachers to use a technique familiar from early stages of education need not have been at the conscious level, since the process was encountered at every turn. Systematic subdivisive and interrogative procedure can be exemplified from a short anonymous fifteenth-century decalogue treatise:

Worschippe þi fadir and þy modyr. þat þou be of longe lyffe upon the lond þat þe Lord þi God wole yeue to þee. ¶ Who brekyth this heest. vnkynde men, frowarde men. and rebel men. ¶ Why vnkynde men. for þey helpen not her eldres as þey schullen/ for þe Wise Man seiþ Ecc'. iij.cº. he is cursed of God that terriþ þe fader or moder to wrathe.
¶ Why frowarde men. for þei wollen take no goostly techinge as Ysaie seiþ in the .xxx. cº. sones of frowardnes not willynge to here þe lawe of God seien. speke ye to us plesaunt þingys þouȝ þei ben errouris. ¶ Why rebel men. for þei ben vnbuxum to Crist and to His Chirche for Goddis lawe tellith that Daton and Abiron for vnbuxumnesse to Moises and Aaron sonkun down to helle al quike wijff and child and alle þat longen to hem.[27]

The interrogative formula is more attractive and effective when mingled with other modes of discourse. In the massive, wide-ranging, early fifteenth-century decalogue treatise *Dives and Pauper*, which deals accessibly with far more sophisticated material than the bare essentials of the faith, the dialogue-structure between the rich pupil and his poor religious mentor is varied. Usually, exposition of some aspect of a commandment is triggered by a question from Dives eliciting a lengthy answer from Pauper, but the format varies. Dives is permitted interruptions, objections and longer comments which add more dramatic interest to the dialogue and allow the entertainment-factor into teaching in a very welcome fashion. Nonetheless, the sheer familiarity of the underlying interrogative elementary teaching-formula allows the audience to feel at home, to concentrate on the content because undistracted by unfamiliar formats:

[26] Ibid., p.99.
[27] Carl F.Bühler, 'The Middle English Texts of Morgan MS. 861', *PMLA* 69 (1954), pp.686–92. This quotation is from p.690.

DIUES. What 3if he seye þe Pater noster or oþer holy wordis or som oþer holy preyere pryuely or apert for to don þe peple wenyn þat it is don be weye of miracle and for his preyere and his holynesse, whan he doth it be resoun and werkyng of kende? PAUPER. Þan is it a wol gret ypocrysye and wel greuous synne in hym þat doth it on þat maner and for þat ende. But wychecraft is it non, for it is no worchepe to þe fendis craft ne þe peple is nou3t steryd þerby to trostyn in þe fend but raþere in God. DIUES. Is it ony wychecraft to charmyn nedderys or oþer bestis and bryddis with holy wordis of holy writh or with ony oþer holy wordis? PAUPER. 3if man or woman take hede in his doynge only to þe holy wordis and to þe my3t of God, it is non wychecraft... DIUES. Is it ony peryl to man or woman to charchyn his frend in his deyynge to comyn a3en and tellen hym how he faryth?/ PAUPER. It is a wol gret peryl, for, as Sent Powyl seyth, þe fend oftyntyme makyth hym lyk an angel of ly3th ...[28]

The third 'sample' elementary teaching device, rhyme, is a widespread feature of religious didacticism for its mnemonic function. At the popular level, short rhymes have a long history in the informal education of children, who take great pleasure in sound-patterning from an early age. Children will happily accept both nonsense and entertaining rhymes for their amusement, and 'educational' rhymes, offered by parents and teachers, which contain useful information or received wisdom and make capital of the child's delight in aural design. Such rhymes are even now of practical value; which of us, however sophisticated, would be without 'Thirty days hath September' or 'I before E/ Except after C', for example? Iona and Peter Opie have amply demonstrated that successive generations of children retain their attraction to rhyme and other small-scale aural patterns in an active subculture of invented and transmitted formulae.[29] Brief snatches and tags of useful, aphoristic, gnomic and mnemonic verse of kinds which, though not specifically designed for children, could be, and probably were, used in their informal education, are to be found in the most miscellaneous places, embedded in other verse, fossilized in sermons, scribbled in margins and painted on walls. A couple of brief tags from a mid-fifteenth-century Latin manuscript provide examples of the type:

> Dere is that hony bought
> That on the thorn is y-sought

and

---

[28] Priscilla Heath Barnum, ed., *Dives and Pauper*, Vol.I, Part 1, EETS OS 275 (London 1976) (henceforth *Dives and Pauper*), p.169.
[29] Iona and Peter Opie, *The Lore and Language of Schoolchildren* (Oxford 1959).

Wist ever any man how brechel were his shinne-bon,
Wold he never lepen there that he mighte gon.[30]

That short rhymes were used in basic education-for-life in courtesy-training is
evidenced by two verses, now lost, painted on the wall of Launceston Priory
dining-hall:

Who so cometh to any hous,
Ne be he nought daungerous –
Take that he findeth;
And but a wil do so,
Resone wolde accorde therto
To take that he bringeth

and

Who so wil his worship save,
Honest maners he most have.
It falleth to a gentilman
To say the best that he can
Of every man in his absènce
And say him sooth in his presènce.[31]

Even the humble non-didactic rhymes made up by children to amuse themselves
or braintease each other are sometimes put to use in the early stages of Latin
grammar teaching. Nicholas Orme draws attention to a few examples from the
vulgaria section of a fifteenth-century grammatical miscellany from Bristol and
Wiltshire; there we find a collateral, or distant ancestor, of 'Who killed Cock
Robin?' in

Y say a sparw
Schotte an arow
By an harow
Into a barow[32]

rendered usefully into Latin as *vidi passerem sagittare sagittam per herpicam in baiula-
torium siue in cineuectorium*! In the same collection there are a couple of not very
taxing rhyming riddles with the answer 'four':

---

[30] Celia and Kenneth Sisam, eds, *The Oxford Book of Medieval English Verse* (Oxford 1970)
(henceforth *OBMEV*), p.561, items 307 (v) and (viii).

[31] *OBMEV*, p.562, items 311 (i) and (ii).

[32] Nicholas Orme, 'A Grammatical Miscellany from Bristol and Wiltshire', reprinted as
ch.6 of *Education and Society in Medieval and Renaissance England* (London 1989) (henceforth *Education and Society*), pp.87–112; for this rhyme see pp.98–9 and p.102, no.25. 'A
Grammatical Miscellany ...' was originally published in *Traditio*, 38 (1982), pp.301–26.

> On feler þen thre *and* fewer þan fyvy,
> y hadde vpon my cule stro*kes* ful ryve[33]

and

> On feler þen thre *and* fe[w]er þan fyve,
> y plokkyd appullys ful ryve.[34]

Schoolmasters clearly did not entirely disdain the use of children's own lore for teaching them.

In basic religious didactic works, whether aimed at adults or the young, we find the sheer mnemonic qualities of verse (usually end-rhymed, but occasionally alliterative) themselves a valued educational tool. The vernacular pastoral manuals contain numerous versifications of the basic short prayers of the faith, a large number of which have been collected by George Russell.[35] Capital is made of the suitability of rhyme for the moral and religious education of children in the context of the home by the Bridgettine Richard Whitford in his *A Work for Householders*, who adds to it a touch of play-acting likely to appeal to the young. Whitford makes up 'a prety lesson' in rhyme for the householder to teach his children, as a mnemonic for the culpability of bad behaviour; it is a lesson ascribing an enlightened degree of moral responsibility to the child, who is envisaged as reciting to its mother or governess a rhyme *requesting* punishment for offences committed:

> yf I lye/ backebyte or stele/
> yf I curse/ scorne/ mocke/ or swere
> yf I chyde/ fyght/ stryue/ or threte
> Than am I worthy to be bete
> Good mother/ or maystresse myne
> yf ony of these nyne
> I trespace to your knowynge
> With a newe rodde and a fyne
> Erly naked before I dyne
> Amende me with a scourgynge.[36]

Whitford's approximately contemporary fellow-Bridgettine, William Bonde, produced a long printed treatise on the monastic life, *The Pilgrimage of Perfection* (1526), intended for reading by pious lay people as well as by its original audience of female Bridgettines. Bonde comments on the mnemonic usefulness of rhyme in

[33] *Education and Society*, p.111, no.105.
[34] *Education and Society*, p.111, no.106.
[35] G.H.Russell, 'Vernacular Instruction of the Laity in the Later Middle Ages in England: Some Texts and Notes', *Journal of Religious History*, 2 (1962), pp.98–119.
[36] Richard Whitford, *A Work for Householders* (Wynkyn de Worde, 1533) (RSTC 25423), D.ii.a.

the verse-summary which he appends to his prose discussion of five points to be remembered by the devout:

> Consyder well these .v. poyntes/ 7 often recorde them in thy mynde/ that thy seruyce be neuer without feare/ ne thy loue 7 ioye without reuerence. And for that thou mayst the better beare them in mynde/ here I haue drawen them to the agayne in ryme/ after my symple maner.
> Recorde these fyue poyntes/ as ofte as thou may
> Howe thy lyfe is shorte/ and slypper is the way
> Thy deth is vncertayne/ remember the ende
> Euer ioye or payne/ the one shalt thou fynde.[37]

The only thing to recommend such verse, as Bonde would have been the first to admit, is that it rhymes – more or less – and may therefore lodge in the memory. Both Bonde and Whitford make notable use of interspersed mnemonic didactic verse, probably because they are both conscious of writing for a mixed audience of less as well as more educated nuns and lay people, some of whom may have access to their work only through the medium of being read to by others and who therefore have practical need of memorial hooks to hang instruction on.[38]

Vernacular religious didactic treatises with more sophisticated structures and content than an archiepiscopal syllabus of pastoral education are not above the interspersion of mnemonic verse. For example, both the original Latin and the unique Middle English translated versions of the *Speculum Christiani* contain brief versified renderings of each of the Ten Commandments, heading the discussion of each decalogue article, as here with the fourth commandment:

> Thyne fadyr and moder thou schalt honoure,
> Not alonly wyth dewe reuerence;
> Bot in ther nede thou hem socoure,
> And kepe ay gude obedience.[39]

Here the vernacular rhyme spells out the practical implications of the commandment briefly. The same work heads the discussion of each capital sin with a vernacular verse of self-description by each sin, as, for example, Accidia:

> Me thynke3 ful heuy of goddes seruyce.
> Gudnes to wyrke wyl I no wyse.

---

[37] William Bonde, *The Pilgrimage of Perfection* (Wynkyn de Worde, 1531) (STC 3278), f.lxi.a. The first edition of the *Pilgrimage* was printed by Pynson in 1526 (STC 3277).
[38] See the discussion in my forthcoming article under note 11 above. There is a not inconsiderable body of scraps of verse and of proverbs in the work of Bonde and especially Whitford, as was demonstrated in a paper to the London Medieval Society in autumn, 1986, which I intend to publish in modified form.
[39] Gustaf Holmstedt, ed., *Speculum Christiani*, EETS OS 182 (London 1933 for 1929), p.22.

Idelnes and slepe I loue beste,
For in hem I fynde moste reste.[40]

English verse, in the Latin original as in the Middle English translation, forms a large proportion of Tabula VII, dealing with moral and sapiential matters, and Tabula VIII, dealing with prayers to the Sacrament, Christ and Mary, in the *Speculum Christiani*. The moral rhymes often have a pat, world-weary wryness, as in the verse-rendering of St Paul's 'Wysdome of this worlde es bot foly a-for god':

Hys ryches riche and worschype grete
Es bot fauntome and dysseyte,
Wher-wyth he has many man defylede,
And at the laste hem by-gylede.[41]

Even the relentless allegory of *Jacob's Well*, where the normal device to hold the attention is vivid exemplary narrative, breaks into verse on a few occasions to highlight major topics. The recommendation of humility to counter pride turns to verse:

þis lownes, here in oure lyuyng,
þat we mowe be heyghed in heuen, in oure endyng,
graunte vs he
þat for vs deyed on rode tre.[42]

The drama of a formal dialogue between devils and angels contending for the soul of a dying rich man is cast in short verses, built up of translations of Psalm xxxv 2–8.[43]

Verse is often used as the vehicle for the last sample category of basic didactic device, proverbial, gnomic and aphoristic material. The proverb or *sententia* has a wide variety of uses in formal rhetoric, but that need not exclude its everyday use to encapsulate and tersely communicate received wisdom about the creation and ways of the world. Children inevitably acquired some familiarity with proverbial wisdom from an early age in colloquial speech, given the still-traceable plethora of popular medieval proverbs, many sanctioned by unhistorical association with King Alfred;[44] many of the miscellaneous rhyming tags and *tituli* preserved by accident in odd locations are proverbial or semi-proverbial, like the two fifteenth-century examples quoted above at note 30, which offer gnomic generalizations

---

[40] Ibid., p.64.
[41] Ibid., p.150.
[42] Arthur Brandeis, ed., *Jacob's Well*, Part I, EETS OS 115 (London 1900), p.76.
[43] Ibid., pp.139–40.
[44] For the major repository of medieval English proverbs see B.J. Whiting, *Proverbs, Sentences and Proverbial Phrases from English Writings Mainly Before 1500* (Cambridge, Massachussetts 1968). For proverbs ascribed to Alfred, see O.Arngart, ed., *The Proverbs of Alfred*, Skrifter utgivna av Kungl. Humanistiska Vetenskapssamfundet i Lund 32 (Lund 1942–55).

about human conduct, or the following pair from the same manuscript, offering wisdom ranging from an observation on nature's ways (with an implicit human moral) to a satiric antifeminist false analogy:

>   (a) Winter alle etes
>   That summer begetes

and

>   (b) The smallere peses, the mo to potte;
>   The fairer woman, the more giglotte.[45]

The educational use of proverbs can be evidenced from both the teaching of manners and the teaching of letters; their force lies in ready familiarity coupled with terse, pungent style. Many of the proverbs cited in such contexts are scriptural and sapiential in origin, but their concrete down-to-earth expression accords with that of native proverbs. For example, in *Symon's Lesson of Wysdome for Children* (c.1500), both popular and scriptural proverbs are adduced to recommend good behaviour as the way for a child to avoid beatings, and to justify beatings as valuable for the truly refractory child:

> My chyld, y rede þe be wys, and take hede of þis ryme!
>   Old men yn *prouerbe* sayde by olde tyme
>   'A chylde were beter to be vnbore
>   Than to be vntaught, and so be lore',[46]

and

>   And as men sayth þat ben leryd,
>   He hatyth þᵉ chyld þat sparyth þᵉ rodde;
>   And as þe wyse man sayth in his boke
>   Off *prouerbis* and wysedomes, ho wol loke,
>   Vnder a man that shold werre wynne,
>   'As a sharppe spore makyth an hors to renne
>   Ryȝt so a ȝerde may make a chyld
>   To lerne welle hys lesson, and to be myld.'[47]

Briefer didactic uses are made of proverbs in the elements of Latin grammar-teaching, as the scatterings of them in school *vulgaria* show. In the fifteenth-century miscellany from Bristol and Wiltshire quoted above at note 32 there occurs the rhymed proverb

> Schort hors sone y-whyped, lytell mete sone y-flypyd.[48]

---

[45] OBMEV, pp.560–61, items 307 (i) and (vi).
[46] *Meals and Manners*, p.399.
[47] *Meals and Manners*, p.402.
[48] *Education and Society*, p.100, no.1.

A more learned but still lively example occurs in another schoolbook, a late fourteenth- or early fifteenth-century collection of *vulgaria* from Magdalen College, Oxford, where a greedy drinker is reproached with a proverb-like analogy taken from Horace:

> Me semeth [thu hast] the properti of an hors lech, for lykwese as horase sayth as a horse leche wyll not go fro the skyne tylle he be full of blode, so thu wylt neuer leue the cuppes except thu be ful of drynke.[49]

The process of latinizing English proverbs, familiar to the medieval schoolboy, is recalled in an insulting use by the vice Nowadays in *Mankynde*, when he asks Mercy to translate a scatological couplet:

> 'I haue etun a dyschfull of curdys,
> And I haue schetun yowr mowth full of turdys.'
> Now opyn yowr sachell with Laten wordys
> Ande sey me þis in clerycall manere!'[50]

Nicholas Orme comments that the vernacular couplet recalls a common formula ('I have something nice and you have something nasty') current in medieval schoolboy insults.[51]

In religious didactic treatises, scriptural and popular proverbial material go hand-in-hand, though the punchy immediacy of the popular type has a snappier clinching effect. An amusing conscious variation on this process is executed in the decalogue treatise *Dives and Pauper*. The instructor Pauper, quoting the Book of Proverbs, cites the maxim that 'a man in his elde goth nought lyghtly awey from þe weye of his 3ougthe', when discussing the dangers of a wilful and unchastised early life. His rich pupil Dives cockily interjects 'And þow it is a comoun prouerbe: 3ong seynt, eld deuyl', apparently confuting his master with a conclusive saw. Pauper is stung into expostulating against this 'synful prouerbe' and counters it with a rhymed Latin proverb and its English translation:

> And as þe poete sey3t, Quod noua testa capit, inueterata sapit, Sueche as þe sherd or þe shelle or þe vessel taky3t qhanne it is newe, sueche it sauoury3t qhanne it is eld.[52]

The joke is based on the disruption of an accepted didactic practice: a *sententia* from a teacher, judiciously placed in his discourse, is intended to round off a precept authoritatively. Dives steps out of line by turning his master's proverb-

---

[49] *Education and Society*, p.149, no.86, in ch.8, 'An Early Tudor Oxford Schoolbook', first published in *Renaissance Quarterly*, xxxiv (1981), pp.11–39.
[50] Mark Eccles, ed., *The Macro Plays*, EETS OS 262 (London 1969), p.158, ll.131–4.
[51] *Education and Society*, p.77, in ch.5, 'Early School Notebooks', first published in *The Yale Library Gazette*, lx (1985), pp.47–57.
[52] *Dives and Pauper*, p.128.

citing technique back on him, and promptly gets his knuckles rapped like a cheeky schoolboy. Even in the rarefied air of Syon Monastery, the popular proverb sustains a vigorous existence as a religious didactic device in the printed works of the Bridgettine Richard Whitford as he aims at his mixed audience of nuns and lay people; and as in *Dives and Pauper*, the tendency is to use proverbs to clinch a discussion or carry a point snappily. Such is Whitford's awareness of the potential force of the demotic proverb that when he gives English renderings of Latin proverbs, he either chooses, or possibly himself provides, catchy rhymed translations with a colloquial native ring to them. For example, in *An instructyon to auoyde and eschewe vices*, Whitford

> shortly conclude[s] with the old blunt prouerb:
> *Est et semper erit: similis similem sibi querit.*
> This is to say:
> Hyt hathe bene euer, and euer shall be
> That the lyke wyl seke, with the lyke to be.
> In man and beast, In herbe and tre
> Where they be bredde; lyke shal they be.[53]

My conclusion is cautious. This paper is not trying to make a case for a radical revision of the view of sermon rhetoric as the mainspring of persuasive didactic strategies in late medieval vernacular religious instruction. Rather, it tries to raise consciousness of the less obvious, indirect, almost 'osmotic' influence of early educational processes, which coincide with, and reinforce, rhetorical processes formally recommended for their immediate communicative effectiveness; simple strategies encountered during the early stages of education are easily internalized and can, if activated later, be useful to promote the ingestion and digestion of further instruction. In our more sophisticated studies of the rhetoric of religious writings, we should not overlook these humbler didactic processes, which have lasting power, for

> *quod noua testa capit*
> *inueterata sapit.*

or, in Richard Whitford's translation,

> ... it is an olde sayenge. The pot or uessell shall euer sauour or smel of that thynge wherwith it is fyrst seasoned.[54]

---

[53] Richard Whitford, *Dyuers holy instrucyons* (Myddylton, 1541), f.73a–b (from *An instructyon to auoyde and eschewe vices*).
[54] Richard Whitford, *A Work for Householders* (Wynkyn de Worde, 1533), B.ii.a.

The Quatrefoil of Love

Helen Phillips

The Quatrefoil of Love survives in two fifteenth-century manuscripts of northern provenance, London, British Library MS Additional 31042 (the London Thornton Manuscript) and Oxford, Bodleian Library MS Additional A 106, and in an edition by Wynkyn de Worde for which dates between the late fifteenth century and 1532 have been suggested.[1] The poem was composed in northern Middle English, in alliterative thirteen-line stanzas, probably in the second half of the fourteenth century.[2]

Norman Blake has shown that de Worde's text had been recast into a more southern and modern English, either at the time of printing or by an earlier revisor, for a southern readership, and that this 'unique early printing of a Northern alliterative poem' contradicts the assumption that there was no market for alliterative verse in Tudor southern England.[3]

It also indicates that the work had qualities that could continue to find it readers from the time of its composition until almost the eve of the Reformation, and beyond the areas where alliterative poetry and its associated vocabulary were traditional: northern grammar and vocabulary have often been altered in the printed text.[4] In fact, it is a skilful and lively poem, deserving something better than the neglect or patronizing dismissal it has usually received.[5]

---

[1]   *The .iiii. leues of the trueloue*, London, British Library, Huth 102. On dates see: A.W.Pollard and G.R.Redgrave, *Short-Title Catalogue of Books Printed in England, Scotland & Ireland . . . 1475–1640*, vol. 2 (London 1926) 53 [1530?]; rev. 2nd edn (1976) [1510?]; N.F.Blake, 'Wynkyn de Worde and the *Quatrefoil of Love*', *Archiv* 206 no. 3 (1969–70) 189–200 [1500–1532?]; J.A.W.Bennett, *Middle English Literature*, ed. and completed by Douglas Gray (Oxford 1986) 50 n. [fifteenth century?]; *British Museum Catalogue of Printed Books* vol. 132 (London 1962) [1530?]. Between 1510 and 1532 seems likely.

[2]   *The Quatrefoil of Love*, ed. Sir Israel Gollancz and Magdalene M.Weale, EETS OS 195 (1935). For dates see: Gollancz and Weale xxii; Thorlac Turville-Petre, ' "Summer Sunday", "De Tribus Regibus Mortuis" and "The Awntyrs off Arthure": Three Poems in the Thirteen-line stanza', *Review of English Studies* NS 25 (1974) 1–14, p.9. Quotations are from Gollancz and Weale or, where indicated, from the manuscripts.

[3]   Blake 190, 200.

[4]   Blake 191–9.

[5]   E.g. Gollancz and Weale xx–xxiv; Bennett 49–50.

It is one of a number of mystical and devotional works published by de Worde, including major northern mystical writers like Rolle and Hilton.[6] Sue Ellen Holbrook has suggested that as early as 1501 'de Worde had become a regular publisher of books of use and special interest to readers of Carthusian and Briget-tine literature, including the monks and nuns of Syon Abbey and his patron, Lady Margaret Beaufort'.[7] The *Quatrefoil*, though not a mystical work, would suit such a clientele. It draws on images which are *inter alia* symbols in the mystical tradition for contemplative union: the divine Lover, the love-knot, the dove and a maiden seeking love.[8] Its narrator is presented as a devout layperson or member of a religious order: he or she enters 'bedande myn hourres'. It looks as if it were composed with a female religious audience in mind, with its appeal to a girl to reject earthly love for a spiritual 'trewe-lufe', its emphasis on Mary's role in the scheme of salvation, its teasing (?) references to women's 'witte' at 53 and 292 (and in 292ff. woman's wit is proved right, against its detractor), and the dispro-portionate space it gives to descriptions of women and girls in the Doomsday scenes, 456–61, 471–81. The poem's subject is Justice and Mercy and it seems to fit into what John J. Thompson has suggested is a distinct group of poems on the theme of mercy in the London Thornton Manuscript. Thompson has tentatively linked this group to other clusters of short didactic pieces on the themes of mercy, Mary, repentence, and transience in several manuscripts, including the Vernon and Simeon manuscripts.[9] It is interesting to note that G. R. Keiser has suggested that several texts in Robert Thornton's other manuscript, Lincoln Cathedral MS 91, might have come from a female religious house.[10]

Like several late medieval didactic poems, the *Quatrefoil* is a *chanson d'aventure* with an admonitory bird. In a 'mery orcherde' in May the narrator overhears a girl lamenting her lack of a sweetheart. A dove sent by Mary expostulates, offering a 'trewe-lufe' that will never fade, and then launches into an exposition of the four-fold love shown to man by the Trinity and Mary. These four persons are

6   George R.Keiser, 'The Mystics and the Early English Printers: the Economics of Devo-tionalism', *The Medieval Mystical Tradition in England, Dartington: 1987*, ed. Marion Glass-coe (Woodbridge 1987) 9–26.

7   Sue Ellen Holbrook, 'Margery Kempe and Wynkyn de Worde', Glasscoe 1987, 27–46, esp. p.41.

8   Wolfgang Riehle, *The Middle English Mystics*, trans. by Bernard Standring (London 1981) 37–8; 43–4; 51–2. See also Aelred of Rievaulx, *Speculum Charitatis*, PL 195, 530–1, 535; Bernard of Clairvaux, *Sermones in Cantica Canticorum*, 7, 27.6, 40, 57, 59, PL 183 806–10, 915–16, 981–4, 1050–5, 1062–6. In curious anticipation of the poem's use of dove-expositor and flower-emblem, Bernard in sermon 59.9 (1065–6) calls the dove and the flower complementary witnesses to Redemption, addressing the ear and the eye respec-tively.

9   John J.Thompson, 'Literary Associations of an Anonymous Middle English Paraphrase of Vulgate Psalm L', *Medium Aevum* 57 no. 1 (1988) 38–55.

10 George R.Keiser, 'More Light on the Life and Milieu of Robert Thornton', *Studies in Bibliography* 36 (1983) 111–19.

represented by the four leaves of the Quatrefoil, which the poet calls by one of its other names, the Truelove Grass. The exposition ends with a long section on Doomsday and the plea that we should pray for mercy now, for 'nowe es mekill mercy *and* þan sall nane be', 498.

Medieval writings designed to a numerical scheme like this often have a predictable, mechanical air to modern readers, but the *Quatrefoil* combines the potentially static scheme of the four-leaved flower with the dynamic of a narrative moving from Creation to Judgement in brief, rapidly shifting scenes.

De Worde's title, *The iiii leues of the Trueloue*, is preferable to Gollancz's *Quatrefoil of Love* because the whole poem constitutes a multiple pun on the term *trewe-lufe* in its several senses: (1) 'faithful love', (2) 'lover', (3) the Truelove knot, (4) the Truelove flower (whose names include Truelove Grass, True Lover's Knot, Herb Paris Quadrifolia and One Berry).[11] 'Trewe-lufe' also aptly describes the poem's expositor, the 'trewe turtyll', 507, a 'faire foulle full of lufe', 40.

The versatile motif of the Truelove facilitates the poet's fusion of many literary and theological traditions, the most important of which are the images of the divine Lover and of a plant, multi-branched or otherwise articulated, extending through history. The latter is an image with a complex biblical ancestry, indebted particularly to the Tree of Jesse and the Mystic Vine. It is occasionally a structural principle in other lyrics.[12]

We should consider first the poet's use of the 'trewe-lufe' in sense (4) the flower. Magdalene Weale, the *Quatrefoil*'s EETS co-editor, believed that Mary is 'exalted into a fourth person of the Trinity' in the first part of the poem.[13] Certainly the four leaves joined on one root, 142–3, seems to symbolise a heretical Quaternity, giving symmetrical, equal status to Father, Son, Spirit and Mary. Is the poet deifying Mary, by taking the excesses of popular devotion to their logical conclusion or by a radical extension of orthodox concepts like the *Regina Coeli* or *Mater Misericordiae*? Is the *Quatrefoil* a bizarre recrudescence of Collyridianism or Gnostic Tetrads, or an offshoot of the idea of the Motherhood of God sometimes found in the mystics,[14] putting the feminine back into the divinity? Although one should not disregard the feminine bias of the poem, the answer seems to be that the *Quatrefoil* offers a kind of literary *trompe l'œil*: while as a visual symbol the flower does imply symmetrical status for the four persons, and a heretical Four-in-

---

[11] Geoffrey Grigson, *The Englishman's Flora* (London 1959) 412–13; Roger W.Butcher, *A New Illustrated British Flora*, vol. 2 (London 1961) 666.

[12] For example, Richard L.Greene, *The Early English Carols*, 2nd rev. edn (1935 Oxford 1977) 26, 115–18; *Religious Lyrics of the XIVth Century*, ed. Carleton Brown (Oxford 1932) 112, pp.181–5; *The Poems of John Audelay*, ed. Ella Keats Whiting, EETS OS 184 (1931) 202–3.

[13] Gollancz and Weale xxiii. The idea of a Quaternity was occasionally discussed by theologians, e.g. Peter of Celle, sermon 13, *In Capite Jejunii*, PL 202, 674–6.

[14] E.g. *A Book of Showings to the Anchoress Julian of Norwich*, eds Edmund Colledge and James Walsh (Toronto 1978), chs 58–9 (revelation 14) vol. 1, 151–60; vol. 2, 589–93.

One analogous to the orthodox Three-in-One, yet verbally the poet never gives Mary divine authority, denying her even the power to intercede at Doomsday, something many medieval artists accorded her.[15]

Against this it might be argued that in lines 309–21 Mary, having ascended to Heaven, becomes part of a four-fold God:

> Appon his fadir right hand hire son may scho see
> And þe hende haly gaste vn-to þam bathe b[elde]
> Now are þay samen in a gode þase persouns iij
> And scho es mayden of myght and modyr ful myl[de]
> Swilk anoþer trewlufe grew neuer on tre . . .   London MS, 315–9

Scho, 318, however, should probably be distinguished from þase persouns, 317: three persons unite 'in a gode' but four create the Truelove.[16] The flower does not symbolise a deity, but the conjunction of Mary with the Trinity: a conjunction of unequal powers and natures.

The four leaves represent not God but a love-union. The words used of the flower characterise it as a love-relationship rather than as a deity: its leaves are called felawes, frende, felawe and fere; they are several times called leues of loue and their conjunction is louely, gentill, a faire felauchip. The poem's frame story of a maiden seeking love provides a key for recognising many later allusions – literal, metaphorical and typological – in the narrative to a whole set of mystic unions: the union of two natures in Christ; of three persons in God; of Mary with God; the Church with God; and the individual soul with God. Since in exegesis Mary prefigures both the Church and the soul, and since it was she who gave Christ his human nature, she is a figure of more than individual significance in the poet's vision of a union of love which joins the human to the divine – a divinity which is itself a union of distinct persons.[17]

The single root probably symbolises love itself, reflecting Luke 10:42 unum est necessarium or Ephesians 3:17–19 in charitate radicati et fundati, Ut possitis com-

---

[15] See Avril Henry, Biblia Pauperum: A Facsimile and an Edition (Aldershot 1987) 149 .r. 12; Sermon 6, attrib. Bonaventure, De Assumtione B. V. Mariae, Opera, vol. 9 (Quaracchi 1901) 703; Eamon Duffy, 'Mater Dolorosa, Mater Misericordiae', Aquinas Lecture 1988, New Blackfriars (Summer, 1988); Sandro Sticca, The Latin Passion Play: Its Origins and Development (Albany 1972) 66–78.

[16] Ronald Waldron points out to me that 'in a gode' ('in one God') echoes the Nicene and Athanasian creeds: further evidence of Trinitarian orthodoxy; the EETS text omits iij, 317. (De Worde implies that the Quatrefoil is God at 514, having 'iiii leues', where Bodley MS has 'iii' and BL 31042 garbles the passage.

[17] Honorius of Autun, Expositio in Cantica Canticorum, PL 172, 494; Aquinas, Summa Theologiae 3a art. 4 (Rome 1962) 2018–19; Peter Damian, Sermon 45, In Nativitate B. V. Mariae, PL 144, 740–1. Ephraim the Syrian calls Mary mortalium cum Deo conjunctio, Opera Omnia vol. 3, ed. J.Asseman (Vatican 1846) 525, 528. See Francis Cunningham, 'The Relationship between Mary and the Church in Medieval Thought', Marian Studies 9 (1958) 52–78.

prehendere . . . supereminentem scientiae charitatem Christi.[18] The flower as an emblem thus of simultaneous plurality and unity may have behind it an idea akin to Richard of St Victor's argument that it is love, in its plenitude, that creates the God who is both plural and single.[19]

The fourth leaf, then, is not the apotheosis of Mary: Magdalene Weale's equation of the poet's attitude with that of the naive mariolatry of Sicilian peasants was probably rash.[20] A Quaternate God was heresy, and theologians were so ready to condemn speculations that might be suspected of tending in that direction, and proofs of the logical necessity of the Trinity were so thoroughly rehearsed, that it is unthinkable that a theologically sophisticated writer could have drifted carelessly into such a position.[21] In fact, the significance of the fourth leaf seems to have been very carefully worked out and it appears to represent not an apotheois of Mary but the entirely orthodox concept of the deification of humanity in Mary.[22] In Mary at the Nativity and Assumption man is restored to the Image of God, and Mary's Assumption foreshadows the elevation of all redeemed humanity. St Bernard said of the Assumption *Absorpta videtur in deitatem humanitas, non quod mutata sit substantia sed affectio deificata.*[23] The source of the doctrine of deification is 2. Peter 1:4, *ut per haec efficiamini divinae consortes naturae,* and is best epitomised in Athanasius' 'For he was made man that we might be made God'.[24] The recurrent descents and ascents in the poem, between heaven, earth and hell, as God draws back to himself his lost human 'frendys' (103), represent just such a rapprochement between human and divine. In stanzas xi and xxv we are shown that the full Quatrefoil comes into being through the descent of the Incarnation and the ascent of the Assumption. The conjunction of four leaves which is also a 'trewe-love' represents a union of human and divine: that *admirabile commercium* to which the antiphon for the Feast of the Circumcision refers – Versicle: *Tanquam sponsus . . .,* Antiphon: *O admirable commercium: Creator generis humani animatum corpus sumens . . . largitus est nobis suam deitatem.*

[18] Gregory the Great, *ut enim multi arboris rami ex una radice prodeunt sic multae virtutes ex una charitate generantur, Homilia in Evangelia* 2. 27 (1). *PL* 76, 1205.
[19] Richard of St Victor, *De Trinitate* 3, ch. 2; 5, chs 16–17, *PL* 196, 916–18, 961–2; for the bonds and 'glue' of love, uniting the persons of the Trinity, Christ's two natures, and man and God, see *De Gradibus Charitatis,* ch. 4, *PL* 196, 1204–8 (cf. Hosea 11:4).
[20] Gollancz and Weale 20–1 n. 42.
[21] Bernard, *De Consideratione,* 13 book 5, ch. 7, *PL* 182, 797–9 (against Gilbert de la Porrée); Richard of St Victor, *De Trinitate, PL* 196, 961–7 (argument against four persons); for attacks on Peter Comestor see Edmund J.Fortman, *The Triune God: A Historical Study* (London 1972) 186–7, 196–9.
[22] Hippolytus (attrib. Origen), *Omnium haereseon refutatio,* 10, *PG* 16, 3452–3; Irenaeus, *Contra Haereses,* 5 Preface, *PG* 7, 1120; Peter Damian, *In Nativitate,* 738–40; *The Cloud of Unknowing,* ed. Phyllis Hodgson, Analecta Cartusiana 3 (Exeter 1982) 67, ll.18–19.
[23] Bernard, sermon 2, *Dominica infra Octavam Assumptionis B. V. Mariae, PL* 183, 429.
[24] Athanasius, *De Incarnatione Verbi Dei* 54.3, *Select Works and Letters,* ed. Henry Wace and Philip Schaff, Select Library of Nicene and Post-Nicene Fathers 4 (Oxford 1892) 62.

The Truelove is both the eternal bridegroom and the conjunction of the triune God with humanity, the *commercium* of redemptive love.

This is theological art: the energy that shapes it is a pattern-perceiving intelligence, and the aspects of the flower that most inspire the poet are its name and geometrical design. With its more organic properties – growing, fading, etc. – he does little, though that little demonstrates his habitual theological deftness. The contrast in the frame-story, for instance, between earthly and eternal love is presented by a contradiction between the flower's organic, mutable, nature and its name: *trewe* [= 'faithful', 'unchanging'] *lufe*. The girl finds both many Trueloves and none: none 'Withowtten diffadynge' (44–5, 58). The image of a flower or leaf falling is employed twice: for Adam's sin and Second Adam's death (102, 205–8), moments when the human and divine are sundered.[25] The flower 'sprynges' twice: at the Nativity (138–43) and Assumption (305) – when it 'sprynges all new[e]'.[26] The moment when the complete Quatrefoil springs into being is explicitly defined as the joining of God and man: 'With myrthe in a mayden es god *and* man mett ... Swilk anoþer trewlufe was neuer in lande sett' (134, 138).

This preoccupation with conjunctions between God and man, and body and spirit, is one of the principles of selection for the poem's biblical episodes. (The other main themes are kingship and the Trinity: for example, the Trial and the Harrowing of Hell both bear witness to Christ's kingship, and the Baptism, and the Creation of man in God's image (90–1) are particularly associated with the manifestation of the Trinity.[27]) The biblical episodes are short and their details purposefully chosen. Many of them involve references to, or images of, the union of divinity and humanity: for example, Longinus' spear and Thomas's hand brought revelations that the man Jesus was also God (see Mark 15:39, John 20:28), and the reference in line 315 to Christ on God's right hand signifies exegetically the elevation of his human nature.[28] The Holy Innocents rejoice because through death they are drawn to Christ: 'Hym-selfe walde þam haue', 169, an echo of Mark 10:14, *Sinite parvulos venire ad me*, quoted in the antiphon for Lauds on Holy Innocents Day, and in some Latin plays on the subject.[29] The

---

[25] The common image of humanity as leaves derives from Isaiah 64:6.

[26] For Christ's flesh flowering a second time see Bernard, Sermon 59.8, *In Cantica*, 1059; on Redemption as revived growth see Gerhart B.Ladner, 'Vegetation Symbolism and the Concept of Renaissance', *De Artibus Opuscula XL: Essays in Honour of Erwin Panofsky*, ed. Millard Meiss (New York 1961) 303–22; Bonaventure, *Vitis Mystica* 41, PL 184, 731–6; Guillaume de Deguileville, *Le pèlerinage de l'âme*, ed. J.J.Stürzinger, Roxburghe Club (London 1895) 187–230, ll.5633–6702.

[27] The Harrowing of Hell was associated with Psalm 23 (AV 24), 7, 9; see *The Chester Mystery Cycle*, ed. R.M.Lumiansky and David Mills, EETS SS 3, 328, l.89; 351, l.156.

[28] Jean Daniélou, 'La session à droite du Père', *The Gospels Reconsidered: A Selection of Papers read at the International Congress on the Four Gospels* (Oxford 1960) 68–77.

[29] *Liber Responsalis*, PL 78, 740; Karl Young, *The Drama of the Medieval Church* vol.2 (Oxford 1933) 56; Gustave Cohen, *Anthologie de drame liturgique en France au moyen-âge* (Paris 1955) 203.

Magi episode ends with a similar statement: 'To blysse he þam broghte', 156, probably because in exegetical tradition the Magi prefigure the Church, and the gentiles in particular, brought into union with Christ. The Homily for Lauds on Epiphany used the imagery of union with the Bridegroom: *Hodie caelesti sponso juncta est ecclesia.*[30]

The leitmotiv of the joining and dividing of human and divine, and body and soul, recurs in the Doomsday episode. The poet plays on *sere*, *sam*, *sembelee*, *fere*, *geder*, and *sonder* in lines 406–11:

> The saule and þe body þᵗ lang has ben sere
> Behoues to be sam at þᵗ sembelee
> Ilke a saule sale be sent to seche hys awn fere
> When criste wyll vs geder a gret lord is he
> Wᵗ owyr felsch and owr fell als we in warld were
> And neuer sal sonder efter þᵗ day be   Bodleian text

Christ's death and Resurrection are also presented in terms of joining and dividing. His death is a splitting of the flower: 'Allas for þat trewlufe þat it sulde twyn swa', 216, leaving the fourth leaf 'allan', 'allanly', 196, 209, and the fellowship 'torn', 197. In 213–14 the piercing of Christ's body is tellingly juxtaposed with the splitting of the temple rock.[31] In death his body and soul divide, 241–2. In contrast his Resurrection is an act of union: body and soul rejoin, 271–2, and the raising of Christ is a collaborative effort between the persons of the Trinity, 276–9. The picture of his soul (*with þe godhede*, as the poet carefully puts it, making the parallels body / soul and man / God) dividing from the body (*with þe manhede*) and rejoining, 241–2, 271–2, comes from a well-established theological and dramatic tradition.[32] It is significant that this tradition arises from Canticles 5:2 *Ego dormio et cor meum vigilat: vox dilecti mei pulsantis: Aperi mihi, . . . amica mea, columba mea.* The poem is steeped in Canticles and its exegesis.

When we consider this theme of conjunction, and further themes of the divine Lover and of number symbolism, we are in the area of knot imagery: the *trewe-lufe* as a love-knot. It was the Truelove knot that gave the Truelove flower its name. 'Truelove Grass' and 'Herb Paris' ('paired', 'equal') refer to the symmetrical pattern of four leaves, which resembles a Truelove knot.[33] This knot, with four

---

[30] *Liber Responsalis* 743.

[31] The piercing of the body and the cleft rock were associated with Cant. 2:14, *columba . . . in foraminibus petrae*: e.g. Bonaventure, *Lignum Vitae*, Quaracchi ed., vol. 8, 79–80; see Rose Jeffries Peebles, *The Legend of Longinus in Ecclesiastical Tradition and English Literature and its Connection with the Grail* (Baltimore 1911) 5–43, 80–141.

[32] J.A.McCulloch, *The Harrowing of Hell* (Edinburgh 1930) 95–7, 109, 120–1, 128, 330 n. 5. The separation of body and soul appears in the *Passion du Palatinus* and all English extant mystery cycles except Chester. On the connection with Cant. 5:2 see Bruno, *Expositio in Cantica Canticorum*, PL 164, 1263.

[33] Grigson 413.

symmetrical loops, was a common medieval decoration, whether as a ribbon bow, an embroidery design or a jewellery piece, and associated particularly with lovers' vows.[34] The poet does not use the image of the knot itself but concentrates on motifs of linking, symmetry, quadruplicity, and associations with courtship, which the knot and flower share. The knot is, of course, a frequent image in mystical writing for union with God.[35] In both religious and secular literature the associations of the Truelove knot and flower had become intertwined. Some religious lyrics use the image of the Truelove in both senses in the same poem, and in other passages it is uncertain which sense is intended.[36] The *Quatrefoil*-poet uses the image in multiple senses: in the opening scene 'trewe-lufe' refers indefinitely to a sweetheart, a flower, and a state of stable affection, and as the work continues it also gains many of the associations of the Truelove knot.

The poem's structure forms a Truelove knot: the knot has four equal bows and no visible ends; the poem begins and ends with the same words and has forty stanzas which form four equal sections. Stanzas 1–10 take us to the Annunciation; 11–21 deal with Christ's incarnate life and go up to the Harrowing of Hell; 21–30 take us to the Second Coming, and that dominates the last section, 31–40. Each transition coincides with a descent by the divine to reclaim humanity. This quadripartite design probably reflects the tradition of the Leaps of Christ.[37] (This tradition derives from Canticles 2:8 *Vox dilecti mei . . . venit saltiens in montibus*, so the Leaps are those of the divine Lover, the *trewe-lufe* in sense (2)). Thomas D. Hill has shown that the Leaps are also the organising principle in 'Mary the Rose-Bush', which, like the *Quatrefoil*, presents a series of episodes in the history of Redemption which are linked to the image of a multi-sectioned flower, here a rose with five branches.[38] Another lyric inspired by Canticles 2:8, 'In a vaile of restles mynd', employs the conceit of someone seeking for a Truelove 'in mownteyn and in mede', and finding – as the *Quatrefoil* dove urges the maiden to find – the divine Lover rather than the flower.[39]

It is probably significant that in medieval number symbolism 4 represents the

---

[34] John Brand, *Observations on the Popular Superstitions of Great Britain* 2 (London 1900), 108–12; *Scottish Alliterative Poems in Rhyming Verse*, ed. F.J.Amours, STS 65 (1918) 323 (n. on *Rauf Coilȝear* l.473); 389 (n. on *The Awntyrs off Arthure*, l.354); OED 'True-love' 3: will AD 1509; see also *The Court of Love*, l.1440; Gower, *Mirour d'omme*, ll.17892–8.

[35] Riehle 50–2.

[36] E.g. 'Loue that god loueth', *Twenty-Six Political and other Poems*, ed. J.Kail, EETS OS 124, 73–9, stanzas 16–17 (knot), 24 (flower); sense uncertain: *Rauf Coilȝear*, l.473; *Sir Gawain and the Green Knight*, l.612; *Awntyrs off Arthur*, ll.354, 510; *The English Poems of Charles of Orleans*, ed. Robert Steele and Mabel Day, EETS OS 215, 229; Appendix 3, 221; Chaucer, *Miller's Tale*, l.3692, usually assumed to be a leaf, but perhaps a sweet of the type, with a motto, still called 'Lovehearts'.

[37] Gregory, *Homilia in Evangelia*, 29.10, col. 1219.

[38] Thomas D.Hill, ' "Mary the Rose Bush" and the Leaps of Christ', *English Studies* 67 no. 6 (1986) 478–82.

[39] *A Selection of Religious Lyrics*, ed. Douglas Gray (Oxford 1975) 41–5.

created world, while 3 represents God. In the poem the full four-leaved plant, the extension from three to four, occurs when God 'lighte' down and 'Be-come man', 128–9: 'Now has þer iij leues a fourte fela tan / For lufe in oure lady es oure lorde lyghte', 144–5 (Bodleian text). Augustine in *De Doctrina Christiana* defined 40 symbolically as a life lived 'chastely and continently, away from the delights of the things of time'; it combines 4 (= the temporal world) with 10, which consists of 3 (= knowledge of God) and 7 (= knowledge of his creatures).[40]

Although the image of the knot is never used directly, the theme of linking constantly occurs, in lexical sets like *wedde, gadir, joyne, sam(en), mett, grett, message(re), tythynges, bodworde, sente, fere, companye*, etc. This theme must also underlie the choice of a dove as the expositor. Its primary role is as a go-between, which is its pre-eminent role in the Bible and Apocrypha.[41] It is appropriately Mary's messenger: she herself is often presented as a dove in poetry.[42] The poem is full of go-betweens: the Dove, Gabriel (107–10), Herod's messages (157–9), Mary Magdalene, and the Virgin (511–12). The dove is also a lover, a 'foulle full of lufe': a characterisation derived ultimately from the Bestiaries, where it remains ever true to one mate.[43] In courtly literature, too, in *chansons d'aventure*, love debates and bird parliaments, the dove comes second only to the nightingale as a spokesman for love.[44]

The dove's allegorical inheritance makes it a medial figure in the narrative, representing several of its themes, and an alter ego of its main characters. Like the divine Lover it is 'full of lufe' and 'trewe'; typologically it represents the Queen of Heaven (*Surge . . . columba mea*, Cant. 2:10, prefigures the Assumption[45]), and the human soul seeking God (*columba . . . in foraminibus petrae*, Cant. 6:18[46]), or

[40] *The Book of Enoch*, chs 76, 82, ed. R.H.Charles, 2nd edn (Oxford 1911) 163–5, 173–8; Hugh of St Victor, *Didascalion*, vol. 2. 4–5, trans. Jerome Taylor (New York 1961) 64–7; *De Doctrina Christiana* 2.16 (25), ed. Joseph Martin, CCEL 32. 56 (Turnhold 1962) 50–1. See Vincent F.Hopper, *Medieval Number Symbolism* (New York 1969) 82–6, 95–6, 99, 171.

[41] Genesis 8:8–12; Matt. 3:16; Mark 1:10; *The Gospel of Pseudo-Matthew*, ch. 8, *The Apocryphal New Testament*, ed. and trans. M.R.James (Oxford 1924) 73. See under 'Taube' in Engelbert Kirschbaum, *Lexikon der christlichen Ikonographie*, vol. 4 (Rome 1972) 244–7.

[42] E.g. Peter Damian, *In Nativitate*, 738, ll.141–3; Mone vol. 2, 292 (no. 512); Brown, *XIVth C.*, 47, ll.13–16; *The Minor Poems of the Vernon Manuscript*, vol. 2, ed. Carl Horstmann, EETS OS 98, 135, ll.43–4, etc.

[43] E.g. Hugh of St Victor, *De Bestiis et aliis rebus*, 1.3, 20–5, PL 175, 16–17, 23–6. See Beryl Rowland, *Birds with Human Souls: A Guide to Bird Symbolism* (Knoxville 1978) 41–8.

[44] E.g. 'A Parliament of Birds', ed. Eleanor Prescott Hammond, *Journal of English and Germanic Philology* 7 no. 1 (1908) 105–9; 'On a dere day, by a dale so depe', *Songs, Carols, and Other Miscellaneous Poems*, ed. Roman Dyboski, EETS ES 101 (1908) 84–5; 'The Court of Love', ed. W.W.Skeat, *Complete Works of Chaucer*, vol. 7 (Oxford 1897) 234, ll.1387–1400, etc.

[45] Carleton Brown, *Religious Lyrics of the XVth Century* (Oxford 1911) 65–7, 305 n., points out that Cant. 2:10 appears in the antiphon for Vespers on the Feast of the Assumption (*York Breviary*, ed. S.A.Lawley, Surtees Society 75 (Durham 1883) 476).

[46] Bruno, *In Cantica* ch. 5, 1203; Bernard, sermons 61, 62, *In Cantica* 1070–4.

the Church (una est columba mea, Cant. 6:18).[47] 'Socour' (20), 'comforth' (28), and its wisdom (47) link it also with the Spirit – aptly because the themes of the Trinity and the dual nature of Christ, which the dove of the Spirit revealed at Christ's Baptism, run through the Quatrefoil dove's sermon. Moreover the Spirit, from Augustine onwards, was identified particularly with the connecting love of the Godhead: Thierry of Chartres calls the Spirit amor et connexio of the Creator.[48] The dove's role as expositor may reflect Bernard's 59th sermon on Canticles, where vox turturis, 2:12, signifies the preacher, aware of earthly transience and languishing in the absence of the divine Lover, who teaches (like the Quatrefoil dove) chastity and repentence.[49] The anonymous Treatise of the Three Estates, which says that the literary 'foulis of love', nightingale, lark and dove, teach men to love God, makes the dove a symbol of the priest.[50] So the dove may also be an alter ego for the poem's narrator.

The maiden's search for a trewe-lufe is based on a tradition of the mystic marriage so widespread in medieval literature that for most features of the poem it would be pointless to look for specific sources. A few do, however, recall two major sources: Canticles and the Parable of the Bridegroom. The parable explains something that Magdalene Weale considered a blunder: the poet's mingling of the themes of love and Doomsday,[51] for the Bridegroom of Matthew 25:1–9 becomes in 10–13 the Doomsday Judge. The poem's setting, a springtime orchard where the turtle's voice is heard, summoning a maiden to love, recall the setting of Canticles 2:10–14, and her lament 'A trewe-lufe hafe I soughte be waye and be strete, . . . Als fere als I hafe soughte I fande nane 3itt', echoes Canticles 3:1–2, Quaesivi illum et non inveni . . . Per vicos et plateas quaeram quem diligit anima mea, quaesivi et non inveni.

Is the poet here also playing with popular traditions? One hesitates to use 'popular' or 'folk' of anything medieval, but the girl searching paths and flowery orchards for a four-leaved flower that will bring her 'lufe trewe' seems to be following the superstition that finding a four-leaved clover (or an even ash: the common factor is the symmetry) presages finding a lover.[52] Perhaps the poem also draws on a dancing-game rhyme like 'O Mary, what are you weeping for?', where a

---

[47] Bruno, In Cantica ch. 6, 1213–14; Aquinas, ST 3a 39 art. 6, 2060–1.

[48] Nikolaus M.Häring, 'A Commentary on Boethius' De Trinitate by Thierry de Chartes', Achives d'histoire doctrinal et littéraire du moyen âge 27 (1960) 65–135, p.102; the idea goes back to Augustine, De Doctrina Christiana 1.5, and is found in several twelfth century theologians: see Wilhelm Jansen, Der Kommentär des Clarenbaldus von Arras zu Boethius 'De Trinitate', Breslauer Studien zur historischen Theologie 8 (Breslau 1926) 8.

[49] Bernard, In Cantica 1062–6.

[50] A.I.Doyle, 'A Treatise of the Three Estates', Dominican Studies 3 (1950) 351–8; English Wycliffite Sermons, vol. 1, ed. Anne Hudson (Oxford 1938) 122.

[51] Gollancz and Weale xxiii.

[52] Four-leaved clovers have several magical properties, but they are especially associated with finding a husband: Angelo de Gubernatis, Mythologie des plantes ou les legendes de règne végétal, vol. 2 (Paris 1878) 360–2; Lady Eveline C.Gurden and C.B.Bullen, County Folk-

girl is 'weeping for a truelove'.[53] One might tentatively associate also with this the carol 'My Dancing Day', which appears to go back at least to the sixteenth century.[54] This resembles the dancing-game in that the speaker hopes that his 'truelove' will come and see his dance, and it resembles the *Quatrefoil*, in that it uses 'truelove' for Christ's wooing of humanity and its narrative consists of a series of short episodes representing God's love towards mankind.

If the *Quatrefoil*-poet is employing games and popular superstitions in conjunction with theological images to explore serious themes, then he is using a technique we find also in *Gawain and the Green Knight*. Both works, too, have as their central emblem – the Truelove and the Pentangle – an endless knot, which signifies the principle of 'treuthe' in contrast to the values of the mutable world. To compare the two works is certainly to compare the sublime and the minor – but the *Quatrefoil* is not so *ignominiously* minor a work as has usually been supposed. And the similarities at least support what we know from other areas of late medieval art: the readiness of artists to exploit the world of games as a treasury of symbols.[55]

There are interesting parallels between the poem and medieval drama.[56] Some parallels are obvious: the sequence of discrete episodes from Creation to Doom, representing the scheme of salvation, resembles a cycle play (though similar sequences do also appear in nondramatic art), and the Parable of the Bridegroom, the basis of the poem's combination of the themes of the divine Lover and Judgment, was itself the subject of Latin drama. More intriguingly, the narrative of the sermon gives the impression that it has been written from the point of view of a stage-manager or director.

The brief biblical episodes, where they are not exchanges of direct speech, tend to present events in terms of physically precise actions, like actors' gestures:

He wroghte heuen *with* his hande . . .	70
He toke þᵉ crose in his hande *and* forthe gon he ga	280
Wrange scho hir handis . . .	210

Lore, vol. 1 (London 1895) 94–5 (see Mrs Gutch, *County Folk-Lore*, vol. 2 (1899) on praying to Mary for a husband).
[53] See Iona and Peter Opie, *The Singing Game* (Oxford 1985) 325–9.
[54] William Sandys, *Christmas Carols Ancient and Modern* (London 1833) 110–12; William E.Studwell, *Christmas Carols: A Reference Guide* (New York 1985) 205; Gray 250 n. 25; Opie 3–21. The long association of carols and ring dances with courtship and flowers is perhaps relevant to the *Quatrefoil*.
[55] E.g. child with ball paralleling Fortune: *Awntyrs off Arthure*, ll.270–312; chess: *The Book of the Duchess*, ll.618–19, 650–84; cf. *Roman de la Rose*, vol. 1, ed. F.Lacoy (Paris 1976) ll.6527–30, 6619–6710; *Charles of Orleans*, ed. Steele and Day, ll.1629–57; dice: Josquin des Prés, *Missa di dadi* (I am grateful to Andrew Wathey for this reference); various: *The Wakefield Second Shepherds Play*.
[56] Bennett 50 noted a similarity with drama.

He tuk an harpe in his hande *and* weldide it . . .   264
He schall schew his wondis blody *and* bare . . .   443

Action is often presented as spectacle, in phrases like 'grete dole for to see', 'Scho sawe hire dere son dy', 'For sighte of þat selcouth he wexe al vn-fayne', etc. The poet tends to specify the location of characters when they speak: 'þan spak þat noble kynge was naylede on þat tre' (222), 'Pilate was Justice and satt appon hey' (182), etc. The cumulative effect of references to characters' movements and positioning, as in the five lines from 107–11 where they occur frequently, can create the impression that the poet visualizes events rather like a series of stage-directions: God summons Gabriel, Gabriel 'Forthe come', he kneels 'hym bi-forne', God tells him to go to Mary, and sends the Son 'owt of his heghe haulle'.

The beginnings and ends of scenes are marked particularly by references to characters moving from one place to another, in a fashion reminiscent of actors coming onto a stage from the side or above, or walking to or from an acting place. Alexandra Johnston has remarked on the practice of linking scenes by journeys in the York plays,[57] and it is almost as common in N-Town.

The details that the poet picks out in the short episodes are often those which we know in performance involved special stage effects or stage business: the star that 'rasse . . . hastily' and 'schynede and schane', 150, might recall the effect at performances where, as records of many Magi plays show, an artificial star suddenly appeared or was hoisted up, and where massed candles or a corona might create considerable effect.[58] The repertoire of theatrical special effects also included rocks that split, 214, separable souls, 241–2, 271–2, and blood flowing down a spear or oozing from wounds, 200–1, 213, 228–9, 443. Many of the narrative details refer to moments which in the mystery plays were the occasion for noisy or tumultuous activity: the barring and breaking of Hell's gates, Judas' kiss, the Jews shouting at Jesus' trial, and the resurrection of the dead at Doomsday (the poet describes them as 'on a Rawe': in performance they might rise from a trench).[59] Incidents are often described in terms of their props: David 'tuk an harpe in his hande *and* weldide it', 264; the soldiers pierce Christ: 'A bygg spere till his hert brathely was borne', 201, etc.

What is interesting about these analogies with medieval biblical drama is not

---

[57] Alexandra F.Johnston, 'The York Corpus Christi Play: A Dramatic Structure based on Performance Practice', *The Theatre in the Middle Ages*, ed. Herman Braet *et al.*, Mediaevalia Lovaniensia Series I / Studia 13 (Louvain 1985) 368–9.

[58] Young 91, 103; William Tydeman, *The Theatre in the Middle Ages: Western European Stage Conditions c.800–1576* (Cambridge 1978) 167–8; *The Staging of Religious Drama in Europe in the Later Middle Ages: Texts and Documents in English Translation*, ed. Peter Meredith and John E.Tailby (Kalamazoo 1983) 148, 250.

[59] Meredith and Tailby, rocks and souls: 90–1, 102, 113, 149, 167; blood: 87, 103, 105, 108–10, 113, 132, 136, 138, 143–4, 279; noise: e.g. N-Town, Harrowing of Hell, Betrayal, Trial, and Doomsday plays (*Ludus Coventriae*, ed. K.S.Block, EETS ES 120 (1922); trenches: N-Town, Doomsday 1.26; Tydeman 163–4.

that there are parallels in subject-matter but that there are parallels in manner: the poet's style of narrative recalls to the mind's eye the practicalities of theatrical staging. The theatrical approach helps to make the narrative, despite its essentially theological construction, light, vivid and fast-moving.

Turning back to the theology of the four leaves, if we reject the idea that the poet wanted to promote a heretical Quaternity or feminise the Godhead, what else might have inspired his structural image of the Quatrefoil? One motive must be his concern with mercy: Mary is linked theologically to Christ because they are the channels of divine mercy, and therefore she constitutes one part of the emblem that signifies the redemptive love of God, the Truelove. The poet's very visual style of narrative and the diagrammatic nature of this theological thinking also prompt one to assume that he must have been influenced by visual art. There are many precedents for using flowers to symbolize the Trinity (and other sacred configurations like the five wounds and the seven words from the Cross),[60] although, sadly, St Patrick's shamrock cannot be traced back earlier than the seventeenth century.[61] Trefoil and quatrefoil ornaments and frames are common in medieval designs. There are also the mysterious, possibly ancient, emblems of circles containing petals and curves, which Patrick Rentersward has suggested might signify the omnipresence of God in Creation.[62] Further quadripartite designs include the Cross, consecration crosses, the Chi-rho monogram and the tetragram.

Veneration for the Queen of Heaven sometimes produced art where Mary is visually equated with the Trinity. It may be an exaggeration for Alfred Hackel to say that the late Gothic Trinity began to become a Quaternity, but at least two pictures of the heavenly court add Mary to the Trinity.[63] Increasingly, Coronation scenes showed Mary on the same throne, or on the same level, as Christ, and in the fifteenth century it is often the Trinity who crown her. There are parallels in design between Coronation scenes, with Mary and Christ enthroned side by side, and scenes of the Trinity enthroned. Réau suggested, furthermore, that pictures of the Holy Family as a Trinité terrestre contributed to 'l'introduction de la Vierge

---

[60] Bonaventure, Vitis Mystica chs 6–13, 15–23, Additamentum 32 PL 184, 652–6, 665–81, 705–8; Lignum Vitae (Quaracchi ed. vol. 8) 68–87; 'The Lily with Five Leaves', Carleton Brown, English Lyrics of the XIIIth Century (Oxford 1932) 29–30, 180 n.; Elisabeth Wolff-hardt, 'Beiträge zur Pflanzensymbolik: Über die Pflanzen des Frankfurter Paradiesgärtleins', Zeitschrift für Kunstwissenschaft 8 (1954) 177–96. On the Trinity as a knot see e.g. Greene 175 (no. 282).

[61] James Forestall, 'The Shamrock Tradition', The Irish Ecclesiastical Record 36 (1930) 63–7; Ludwig Bieler, The Life and Legend of St Patrick: Problems of Modern Scholarship (Dublin 1949) 26, 128 n. 10.

[62] Patrick Rentersward, The Forgotten Symbols of God, Stockholm Studies in the History of Art 35 (Uppsala 1986).

[63] Alfred Hackel, Die Trinität in der Kunst (Berlin 1931) 79; Louis Réau, Iconographie de l'art chrétien, 2:1 (Paris 1956) 27–9.

the fifteenth century it is often the Trinity who crown her. There are parallels in design between Coronation scenes, with Mary and Christ enthroned side by side, and scenes of the Trinity enthroned. Réau suggested, furthermore, that pictures of the Holy Family as a *Trinité terrestre* contributed to 'l'introduction de la Vierge dans la *Trinité celeste*'.[64] Generally, analogies between groups containing Mary and depictions of the Trinity might have encouraged hybrid groups. An early hybrid is the so-called Winchester Quinity: the Virgin and Child enthroned beside the Trinity.[65] The Throne of Grace design, where the Father holds the dead Christ, with the Dove between them, resembles designs where Mary holds Christ: the Virgin and Child, the *Pietà, Vesperbild*, or the Man of Sorrows scheme where Christ's body is held by Mary, John, angels, or a combination of these. We can see cross-fertilisation of such schemes in a Pierpont Morgan breviary, c.1402, where the Father holds the Man of Sorrows, or a Louvre roundel, c.1400, where the Father and Mary hold the Son, with the Dove between them and John and angels at the side.[66] A *Belles Heures* illustration, c.1405–8, and several related illustrations, show the Father, and the Virgin and Child, in two rings with the Dove between them.[67] The closest parallel in art to the Quatrefoil plant with its four figures, extended through history, is the Jesse Tree, and a particularly interesting elaboration of this is the widely-known *Speculum Virginum* (which Derek Pearsall has suggested might have influenced Langland's Tree of 'Trewe-lufe'[68]). It includes allegories of the virtues and vices, and chastity, using the images of flowers, fruit, and leaves – growing, fading and falling – and numerical symbolism which includes particular play on 4.

Thus iconographical configurations, traditional and hybrid, show how readily a late medieval artist might envisage a quartet of actors in the drama of Redemption. In liturgy and prayers, too, Mary's name often follows that of God or the Trinity, and sometimes poets shift from the orthodox position, formulated by Bonaventure, that Mary ranks next after the Trinity, above all other creatures, to more heterodox statements, like a fifteenth-century carol writer's 'moder in mageste, / Yknytte in the blessed Trinity'.[69]

Although it may have been inspired by an artistic and literary ambiance full of Quaternitarian tendencies, the poem, as we have seen, used the Quatrefoil as a

[64] Réau 28.
[65] Ernst H. Kantorowicz, 'The Quinity of Winchester', *The Art Bulletin* 29 (1947) 73–85.
[66] Millard Meiss, *French Painting in the Time of Jean de Berry: The Late Fourteenth Century and the Patronage of the Duke* (London 1967) figs 823, 832; Meiss, *The Limbourgs and their Contemporaries* (New York 1974) fig. 380 (see also figs 829, 830).
[67] Meiss, *Limbourgs*, figs 388–91.
[68] Arthur Watson, 'The *Speculum Virginum*, with Special Reference to the Tree of Jesse', *Speculum* 3 (1928) 445–69; Watson, *The Early Iconography of The Tree of Jesse* (London 1934) 102, 128–4; on the Dove and the Father with the Jesse Tree: 98–7, 167–9; Langland, *Piers Plowman: An Edition of The C-Text*, ed. Derek Pearsall (London 1978) 296–7, n. 81.
[69] Greene no. 185b stanza 2, 122.
[70] 'At a sprynge-wel vnder a þorn', Brown, *XIVth C* 229; 'Vpon a lady fayre and bright',

symbol of redemptive love. For this there was a literary precedent. 'True love' is a common term in Middle English devotional literature. It was sometimes a synonym for the divine Lover, like 'lemman' and 'derelyng', and occasionally used of Mary too.[70] More often and more specifically, however, it is employed with reference to a typically medieval distinction between different levels of love: trewe [= 'stable', and 'reliable'] lufe in contrast to lower, delusory loves. The deep and perennial medieval concern with defining and differentiating love is common, of course, to both secular and religious literature. David Burnley has traced links between the fine amour and vraie amour of love literature and the moral philosophers' discussions of amicitia, the noblest and purest type of human affection.[71] In religious literature there is a rich vein of Truelove poetry, which exploits the poetic potentialities of the term true love and/or the images of the love-knot and the four-leaved flower. There are three main aspects of this tradition, more than one of which may appear in a work. Firstly, the Truelove flower may be associated with the search for the divine Lover in Canticles 3:2, per vicos et plateas; secondly, true love may be used to define an ideal of a love which is reciprocal and entirely without thought of profit: 'love for love' alone; thirdly, the Truelove may be visualised as an emblem, sign or love-token of some kind, sometimes with an inscription or with different significations assigned to each leaf.[72] The Truelove image is often associated with the wound(s) of Christ.

There is only space here to outline two Truelove poems. Both link the term Truelove to the notion of a commercium of love between God and man. The first is the Long Version of the Charter of Christ (the earliest extant text of which is mid fourteenth-century). Christ offers man his love on the parchment of his skin, asking in payment only a Truelove flower whose leaves represent shrift, penitence, amendment, and penance (or, in the Vernon MS, fear of God).[73] In the second example, 'Loue that god loueth' (perhaps early fifteenth-century), the Truelove herb is the seal on the parchment, its leaves and its central berry symbolising the five wounds. The poem begins with an extended Definition of Love, constrasting 'worldis loue' with 'trewe loue': one is transient, motivated by profit or fear, and the other is heavenly, asking for love alone as repayment: 'Loue for loue is euenest bou3te' (44, 124).[74] By the late fourteenth century, and probably earlier, a distinct cluster of ideas had become associated with the term true

Greene 121, no. 183; 'Hayle lovely lady', Dybosky 57–8, where Mary is 'trulove to the Trinite'.

[71] J.D.Burnley, 'Fine Amor: Its meaning and Context', Review of English Studies NS 31 (1980) 129–48.

[72] For the first aspect see 'In a vaile of restles mynd', Gray 41; the second: 'þey loue be stro[n]g', Political, Religious, and Love Poems, ed. F.J.Furnivall, EETS 15 (1866) 262; the third: Siegfried Wenzel, Verses in Sermons: The 'Fasciculus Morum' and its Middle English Poems (Cambridge, Mass. 1978) 59.

[73] The Minor Poems of the Vernon MS 2, ed. F.J.Furnivall, EETS OS 117 (1901) 637–57.

[74] Political and other Poems, ed. Kail 73–9.

loue: ideas of virtuous love, permanence in contrast with earthly transience, the mystic marriage of the life dedicated to chastity, Christ's wounds and desire for man's love, and repentence. This meant that poets could, on the one hand, use the term almost as shorthand, and, on the other, that in poems that refer to *true love* we may find a whole string of associated ideas running through the work even though their association with *true love* is not made explicit. The latter situation can be seen in 'Of a trewe loue pure and clene', which has many of the themes and images associated with the Truelove interwoven within it.[75]

It is hard to date the *Quatrefoil* and hard to guess where lines of influence (if there are any) run, among these poems. Siegfried Wenzel, who cites some instances of the image of the Truelove in late fourteenth-century sermons, points to wordplay on *quadrifolium . . . amoris veri* in the *Fasciculus Morum*, which may be very early fourteenth-century.[76] Since this pun only works in English, the conceit must predate the *Fasciculus* or have been invented by its author while thinking about preaching in English. The motif of the Truelove is also used in several early Tudor secular poems, including a lyric in Oxford, Bodleian Library, MS Rawlinson C. 813, where the four leaves represent four virtues, and Christopher Goodwyn's *Chance of the Dolorous Lover* (printed by de Worde, 1520) where the Truelove is a bunch of four flowers, whose initial letters represent the name Avis: like the *Quatrefoil*, this is a *chanson d'aventure* with a bird-counseller, but wholly secular.[77] The Tudor Truelove poems indicate the evergreen popularity of the tradition or, perhaps, the influence of de Worde's *Quatrefoil*. It seems wise to regard the Truelove as a widely known, widely used, and versatile motif with no simple line of descent or influence. It is a major element in several minor works, and the term Truelove is also used with easy familiarity by some of the great religious writers, including Julian of Norwich and Langland: Langland's Tree of Charity is actually the tree of *trewe-loue*.[78] Even single, brief or unelaborated uses of the term often seem genuinely to gain from being read in the light of what we may call the Truelove tradition: it could, for example, shed light on why Langland associates *trewe-loue* with a tree or 'plonte', why this represents 'Ymago-dei' – the union of human and divine – and why its best fruit is virginity and 'lyf of contemplacioun'. The *Quatrefoil of Love* is not a sublime work, but it is a sophisticated one, and it surpasses all other Truelove poems in the theological extravaganza it weaves from this most felicitously named flower.

---

[75] Vernon 2, 464–8.

[76] Wenzel 59.

[77] F.M.Padelford and A.R.Benham, 'Liedersammlungen des XVI. Jahrhunderts, besonders aus der Zeit Heinrichs VIII, no. 4', *Anglia* NS 31 (1908) 381–2; Goodwyn, *The Chaunce of the Dolorous Lover*, de Worde 1520 (STC 12046); I am grateful to Martine Braekman for information about the Goodwyn poem.

[78] Julian, vol. 2, eds Colledge and Walsh (revelation 77), 694; *Piers Plowman* C, Passus 18, ll.1–107.

Carthusian Drama
in Bodleian MS E. Museo 160?

James Hogg

To date no detailed study of Oxford, Bodleian Library, MS E. Museo 160 has been printed,[1] although it has attracted the passing attention of a number of scholars.[2] The manuscript has 176 folios, measuring 8½ x 5¾ inches, but originally it must have been slightly larger, as the pages were trimmed for binding, whereby the marginal annotations were either partially or, in a few cases, totally lost. None of the available descriptions of the volume is entirely satisfactory.[3]

---

[1] Laviece C. Ward did produce a dissertation on the manuscript in 1987 and has since delivered three papers on the Chronicle contained in it. Cf. for details, James Hogg, 'The Ways of God to Man: The Carthusian Chronicle of Universal History in Oxford Bodleian Library MS E. Museo 160', in *Kartäuserliturgie und Kartäuserschrifttum*, Analecta Cartusiana 116:4 (1989), (in the press).

[2] Carol B. Rowntree devoted a chapter to it in her York doctoral dissertation, *Studies in Carthusian History in Later Medieval England with Special Reference to the Order's Relations with Secular Society*, presented in March 1981, Chapter V being entitled: 'A Carthusian World View: Bodleian E Museo 160', pp.236–84. James Hogg printed passages from the manuscript dealing with the foundation of the Carthusian Order and the catalogue of priors of the Grande Chartreuse in 'A Middle English Carthusian Verse Chronicle on the Foundation and Progess of the Carthusian Order', in *Kartäuserliturgie und Kartäuserschrifttum*, Analecta Cartusiana 116:2 (1988), 108–18.

[3] The manuscript is not listed in N.R. Ker, *Medieval Libraries of Great Britain: A List of Surviving Books* (London 1941). The description in *A Summary Catalogue of Western Manuscripts in the Bodleian Library at Oxford*, II, part ii (Oxford 1937), 732, omits all mention of 'The Fifteen Articles of the Passion' on ff. 136v–139r. Somewhat more detailed are the descriptions by D.C. Baker and J.L. Murphy, *The Digby Plays*, Leeds Texts and Monographs 1976, pp.xiv–xv, and in their article, 'The Bodleian MS. E. Mus. 160 Burial and Resurrection and the Digby Plays', *RES* NS 19 (1968) 290–3. Even they are not infallible, however, as they declare that ff. 106–15 show damage from being nibbled by mice, when, in fact, the folios in question are 103–8 and 113–14, which constitute the concluding five folios of the Chronicle, plus two pages of its continuation and the opening page of the stanzaic fragment on Mandeville and Marco Polo. The damage clearly occured before the gathering in question fell out of the book, which was rebound in the seventeenth century, these folios being then reinserted in a confused order – a fact which has led a number of scholars astray. J.O. Wright and T. Halliwell transcribed some of the material in this gathering, including

The contents of the manuscript are: ff.1r–108r: a verse Chronicle, dealing with the progress of universal history from the creation of the world until 1518. The intentions of the author are clearly indicated on f.1r, and the reader is, in fact, presented with a theological view of human history. As contained in the Bodleian

part of the romance on Mandeville and Marco Polo, in their *Reliquiae Antiquae* (London 1841) pp.113–18. They were not, however, on particularly good form, as they transcribed the last line on f. 108v: 'In ser places out of com se did flowe' - the text refers to the flood. The passage should read: '[In se]r placis out of course did flowe'. On f. 112r the correct reading of ll.27–28 would seem to be: 'Depyst in hell in paynes grise / Salbee our set in payn endless', but Wright and Halliwell read 'Hawee' instead of 'Salbee'. On the same folio the editors misplace the line at the foot of the page, 'That when passit is a thowsand 3ere', although there is a sign marking its appropriate place in the text two lines earlier, and the rhyme scheme dictates its insertion there. On f. 112v, instead of transcribing that Mahommet was buried 'With a whit mere to gyf hym mylke', they have 'to gyf hym in ylke'. A significant contribution to the study of this manuscript was made by M.C. Seymour, 'Mandeville and Marco Polo: A Stanzaic Fragment', in *Journal of the Australasian Universities Language and Literature Association* 21 (1964), 39–52, who finally succeeded in reestablishing the correct order of the folios as 113v, 109r–v, 110r–v, 111r–v, 112r–v, 115r. Even Seymour's transcriptions are not, however, free from error: on p.43, l.28 the passage from f. 113v should read 'the chesynge of the pope of Rome' and not 'at Rome', and on p.48 l.247 from f. 112r should read 'Now it semys lowsit is sathanesse' not 'in Sathanesse', whilst on p.49, l.260 from f. 112v 'loy' is mis-transcribed as 'þy' in the phrase 'most loy in paradise salle wyn'. Seymour rather surprisingly holds that the section on Mandeville and Marco Polo did not form part of the original manuscript – 'it is certain that it did not form part of the original book' (p.37) – though the evidence of the damage by mice on the concluding folios of the Chronicle and on this item offer conclusive evidence that it was always part of this manuscript. Furthermore, the paper used for this fragment bears the same watermark, Heawood 134, a gloved hand marked with an alpha, surmounted by a star, as the bulk of the manuscript. (Cf. E. Heawood, 'Sources of Early English Paper Supply. II: The Sixteenth Century', in *The Library*, 4th series, 10 (1930), 427–54). It is true that this section reveals slight discrepancies in the hand as against the Chronicle, but nothing that could not be attributed to a change of pen and a different date of writing. Seymour himself admits that Mandeville interested the compiler of the manuscript, as there is a prayer to Sir John Mandeville on f. 88v, whilst sultans and 'caans' appear quite often both in the concluding section of the Chronicle and in the romance section. Baker and Murphy, art. cit. 292, conclude over-cautiously: 'The romance is soberly Christian in tone, and would not be out of place in this manuscript, which is a collection of helps to devotion and examples of Christian piety. We prefer to conclude that, although the leaves of the romance may well not have been part of the original manuscript, the likelihood is that they were'. (Cf. also Baker and Murphy, *The Digby Plays*, Introduction, p.xv.) It is not improbable that the compiler of the Chronicle was also responsible for the composition of the romance as well, as there are similarities in the use of sources, as also in the general – and rather wooden – rhyme scheme, ABABCDCD, which characterizes the Chronicle, its continuation, and the romance. Oddly, however, slight inconsistencies in form can be detected between these three items. Thus in the Chronicle and the romance the rhyming is indicated with a rough terminal square bracket, though this is not to be found in the continuation of the Chronicle, whilst this continuation and also the romance display the sign 3 in the inner margin to indicate the commencement of the eight-line stanzas, though this was not employed in the Chronicle itself.

MS, the Chronicle is clearly not an autograph, and it cannot be determined how many copies lay between it and the original. The Middle English compilation is also largely a condensation and adaptation of the *Fasciculus Temporum* of the prolific German Carthusian Werner Rolevinck,[4] though the English version does present some additional – particularly local – material. It should have been illustrated. Picture frames were actually drawn, but only five were utilised for pen and ink drawings. F.1r depicts Adam and Eve in the garden of Eden, with an angel guarding the gate of Paradise; f. 2r Cain clubbing his brother Abel to death; f.19v Daniel; f. 20r Ose and Amos; f. 21v Habucuck and Sophomas. A number of empty picture frames were subsequently used for sketches of Tudor gentlemen, dressed in fine attire (ff. 2v, 3r, 22r, 24v, 26r), – possibly the work of a child artist. No information either on the author or the scribe can be discovered in the manuscript, and the history and provenance of the volume are also unclear. On f. 25r there is an embroidery design, above which stands the date 'Anno domini 1568'. Below this the alphabet has been inserted, and at the bottom the letters 'AMEN IMET / FAVETD / SOPR' are spread over three lines. Their significance has not been ascertained, nor has the entry at the foot of f.171v: 'written by me W . . . ns' been resolved – the folio is damaged, causing the loss of several letters. There is a certain amount of scribbling on the manuscript, where someone has clearly tried to roughly imitate the Carthusian's writing. On a scrap of paper obtruding between ff. 60v–61r the name 'William Benson Dewlly' appears. Someone went to the trouble after the Reformation to systematically delete all references to the pope. That he (or she) was not entirely successful is, no doubt, due to the frequency of such allusions.

From a literary point of view the Chronicle can only be described as barbarous. Though the style is often quite vivid, bringing events on occasion alive before the reader's eyes, the verse is of low standard and sometimes even the sense is sacrificed to the necessities of the rhyme scheme. The spelling is also highly erratic.

Given the substantial amount of source material adapted from the German Carthusian, it is also difficult to assess how much credit should really be given to his English confrère. That there is nothing quite like it in English,[5] and no parallel among surviving manuscripts from the English Carthusian province, renders it

---

[4] For Rolevinck, cf. Hubertus Maria Blüm, 'Rolevinck, Werner', in 'Die Kartäuser-Schriftsteller im deutschsprachigen Raum', in Marijan Zadnikar (ed.), *Die Kartäuser: Der Orden der schweigenden Mönche* (Cologne 1983) p.369.

[5] Many medieval chroniclers in England and elsewhere compiled their works, of course, from a theological perspective, and numerous authors were, in fact, members of religious orders. None, however, is so exclusively theocentric as this Carthusian compiler. (Cf. for a survey of such works A. Gransden, *Historical Writing in England c. 550 to c. 1307* (London 1974).) Even Ranulf Hidgen's *Polychronicon*, which is closest to it, on detailed examination proves to be very different in style, content, and orientation, though it may not be without significance that one of the extant manuscripts of the *Polychronicon* was donated to Sheen Charterhouse by William Mede, a noted Carthusian scribe, who became vicar of Sheen. He was ordained in 1417 and died in 1475. This MS is now Bodleian Library, MS Hatton 14. It

unique. The Chronicle does show how an English Carthusian viewed national and world events beyond his monastery walls, but we cannot be certain whether it represents the personal opinion of the author, in so far as his work is independent of the *Fasciculus Temporum*, or the official attitude of the Order in England; nor can we ascertain whether it was compiled in an urban charterhouse, such as London, Coventry, or Hull, or in a Carthusian desert, though linguistic evidence, particularly in connection with the two plays contained in the manuscript, might suggest the remote charterhouse of Axholme in Lincolnshire. Obviously, a certain amount of information about world events did circulate even in isolated foundations, as the *cartae* of the Carthusian General Chapter and the regular inspections carried through by the provincial visitors would provide a minimum of such material, which must have increased during the uncertain years of the Reformation period. The urban houses and Sheen had, in any event, fairly close links with the society of their time.

The Chronicle clearly ends on f. 108r, but on f. 108v a supplement was added, dealing with such events as the Field of the Cloth of Gold in 1520. Thereafter, the folios are currently bound in incorrect sequence[6] until the continuation of the Chronicle and a romance on Marco Polo and Mandeville give way on f. 116r to a group of a hundred meditations that were often copied in connection with Henry Suso's *Horologium Sapientiae*,[7] which are concluded on f. 136r. The scribe is, however, clearly the same as for the Chronicle, although curiously the paper used for this item differs from that employed in the previous section, bearing a hand and star like Heawood 134, but the alpha is missing.

On f. 136v, though f. 136r still displays the hand of the scribe who very probably copied all the items up to this point, the writing clearly changes. The ink had previously varied from time to time but the rough cursiva currens hand is almost certainly the same. The secretary 'g' and the kidney-shaped final 's' appear consistently, as does an unusually shaped 'r'. The writing on f. 136v becomes more cursive and shows a close affinity to Tudor secretary hand. A two-stroke 'e' appears, which the main scribe never employed. Ff. 136v–139r contain 'The Fifteen Articles on the Passion', an item which is omitted in the Bodleian catalogue description of the manuscript. F. 139v is blank, and then the main scribe takes over again to conclude the book with copies of two plays, *Christ's Burial* and *Resurrection*.[8] *Christ's Burial* occupies ff. 140r–156v and *Christ's Resurrection*

dates from the fourteenth century and is described in *A Summary Catalogue of Western Manuscripts in the Bodleian Library at Oxford* II, part ii (Oxford 1937) 842.

[6]   Cf. for the correct order the indications of Seymour in fn. 3 *supra*.

[7]   Cf. e.g. Oxford, Bodleian Library, Bodley MS 88, ff. 79v–86r. These meditations are therefore manifestly not the original work of the compiler of the Chronicle.

[8]   These two plays were first printed by F.J. Furnivall in his New Shakespeare Society edition of *The Digby Mysteries* in 1882. The texts were reprinted by the Early English Text Society in 1896 along with the plays from Bodleian Library, MS Digby 133 as ES 70, pp.169–228. In his 1882 edition Furnivall wrote: '. . . I have been able to add to the old set

ff. 156v–172r. The paper is once more the same as that utilised for the Chronicle, Heawood 134, showing the hand and star together with the alpha sign.

The manuscript is thus again unique among surviving manuscripts from English charterhouses in presenting the texts of two plays, and, to judge by a linguistic examination of the dialect, plays which were most probably copied at Axholme charterhouse, though the possibility of a Beauvale or Hull copyist cannot be entirely eliminated. Conceivably, the plays might also have been transcribed elsewhere by a monk who retained these dialectical forms.[9]

The plays pose a number of problems that cannot be solved with absolute certainty. As far as we know at present, they are only extant in this Carthusian manuscript, and their literary quality is higher than the other items in the manuscript. They must therefore have been written by someone other than the compiler of the Chronicle, and probably, indeed, not by a Carthusian. Derek Pearsall finds them to possess considerable literary merit,[10] as does Hardin Craig,[11] though

one more Mystery in 2 parts – that of the "Burial and Resurrection of Christ", which evidently once belonged to the Digby MS 133, ...' (p.vii – information which he repeated at the end of 'Wisdom', taken from the Digby MS.: cf. p.166). Furnivall's rash assertion was only refuted in recent times, though E.K. Chambers, *The Mediaeval Stage* II (Oxford 1903) 431, already sounded a note of warning in commenting that Furnivall 'offers no proof'. Nevertheless, the plays were thereafter regularly referred to as the 'Digby Burial and Resurrection' (e.g. in G.C. Taylor, 'The English *Planctus Mariae*', MP 4 (1907), 605–37). Hardin Craig, *English Religious Drama of the Middle Ages* (Oxford 1955) was sceptical, but it was left to Baker and Murphy art. cit. 290, to assert: 'We have examined carefully both manuscripts in the process of editing both groups of plays and conclude that, not only is there no evidence to support the linking of the *e Mus. 160* plays to those of Digby 133, but there is convincing evidence that they could never have formed a part of the same manuscript. That evidence does not lie in the Digby MS., for it is a hotch-potch containing materials from three centuries, and almost anything might have been in it at one time or another. The three and a half Digby plays are themselves in a variety of hands. The case of MS *e Mus.* 160, however, is entirely different. It is a remarkably homogeneous manuscript, the great bulk of it clearly in one hand'. They conclude, 292–93: 'Given the homogeneous nature of *e Mus.* 160, it should not be necessary to remark the ancillary evidence against any association of its plays with those of Digby 133: no overlapping of scribal hands, totally different kinds (the *e Museo* 160 plays remain essentially liturgical drama), in short, the absolute lack of any evidence supporting Furnivall's remarkable assertion'.

9   Baker and Murphy art. cit. 292, state: 'The dialect, though marked by some admixture due to a different dialect of the plays' original sources, is the same basically north-eastern dialect of the whole manuscript'. The dialect can be localised to north-east Nottinghamshire or North-west Lincolnshire. The whole question of precise localisation of manuscripts in identifiable dialect forms is, however, hazardous, as Richard Methley's extant Middle English letter of spiritual counsel, 'To Hew Heremyte: A Pystyl of Solytary Lyfe Nowadayes', edited by James Hogg in *Analecta Cartusiana* 31 (1977), 91–119, does not reveal those Northern forms one would have expected from a monk writing at Mount Grace Charterhouse.

10   *Old English and Middle English Poetry* (London 1977) p.257. He writes that they were 'touched with grace from the start'.

11   Craig gives a fairly detailed examination of the play on pp.317–19.

both would seem to wish to date them considerably earlier than the composition of the manuscript. The plays are, however, in the vernacular, whilst most of the earlier pieces of a similar nature[12] were in Latin. The only comparable vernacular productions are to be found in the *Shrewsbury Fragments*. The *Burial* and *Resurrection* plays were, in fact, subsequently offered in a Latin version, prepared by Nicholas Grimald (1519?–62?).[13]

Though both the style and the content of the plays[14] would seem to point to an earlier date, it is disconcerting to find that the words *tender, suspiration* and *tediose*, which all appear in these texts, are not recorded before the early sixteenth century, nor would specific rhymes have functioned before that date, when changes of pronunciation took place.[15]

The two plays do not appear to have constituted part of a larger cycle.[16] Hardin Craig states:

> Plays of the Resurrection proper almost certainly continued to be played in Great Britain, France, and Germany as separate dramas throughout the period of the mystery plays. No doubt they always combined a considerable group of scenes associated with the central event of Christ's rising, and were not always united with plays of the Passion and certainly not combined with great cycles. Such plays are referred to in the records at Bath (1482), Leicester (1504–7), Morbath (1520–74), Reading (1507, 1533–5), and Kingston (1513–65). Chambers[17] expresses the opinion that we cannot be sure in these cases that the Resurrection was not played in connexion with the Passion, and some of them, if more information becomes available, may turn out to have been so combined. The

---

[12] For the background that gave birth to these plays, cf. Karl Young, *The Drama of the Medieval Church* (Oxford 1933) Vol. 1, pp.201–450; Vol. 2, pp.507–13.

[13] Cf. Craig p.375.

[14] Craig p.319, observes: 'neither metre nor language is elaborate in the Burial and Resurrection, which is pious and modest in tone. The action is recorded mainly in a simple, ancient metre, *rime couée*, aabccb. This gives way in places to the eight-line ballad stanza employed in the Chester plays, aaabaaab or aaabcccb. If the play were a recent composition, a literary exercise, a mere meditation, it would hardly have employed these ancient metres or stick so closely to the ancient traditional events. The lamentations, of which there are many, tend to appear in double quartrains, ababbcbc, and the number of accents to the line varies usually according to pattern from three to five. In general the metres are not late, and there is little of that breaking down of the line that characterizes late mystery plays, particularly in homiletic parts. The metres of the traditional parts are simple and early, the greatest amplification being the extended *planctus* of complaints. The play shows none of that forgetfulness of religious purpose that appears so frequently in the mystery plays of the fifteenth and sixteenth centuries. Indeed, in its own reverent piety it is very fine.'

[15] e.g. on f. 143v: *Shee, hee*; on f. 144v: *see, meklee*; on f. 146r: *hevylee, free, bitterlee*; on f. 152v: *see, tree, strytlee, me*.

[16] Craig pp.144–45, writes: '*Burial* and *Resurrection* from Bodleian MS e Museo 160 is apparently an independent Resurrection play'.

[17] *The Mediaeval Stage* II, 129.

joining of these subjects was customary, but, when they were united, they usually took the name of the Passion, which was the more commanding subject. The fact of the existence of the Bodleian Burial and Resurrection indicates that there were resurrection plays entirely independent of the Passion.[18]

The question immediately arises, whether we are concerned with real plays or merely meditative material, roughly cast in dramatic form. The Bodleian MS E. Museo 160 is surely a compilation primarily intended for devotional purposes in a charterhouse, just as the British Library, London, MS Add. 37049, a Northern Carthusian Miscellany, was.[19] Whether *Burial* and *Resurrection* were, however, originally plays has been disputed, and one of the authorities on the point, Rosemary Woolf, even changed her opinion over the years. Thus in *The English Mystery Plays* she maintained:

> . . . the plays of the Burial and Resurrection are preserved in a manuscript designed for private, devotional reading. A rubric nevertheless makes plain that these works could be acted instead of read, and that performance was to be on the correct liturgical occasions, the Burial on Good Friday and the Resurrection on Easter Sunday.[20]

In her earlier study, *The English Religious Lyric in the Middle Ages*,[21] she had, however, maintained that they were purely designed for meditation.[22]

---

[18] Craig pp.317–18.

[19] Interestingly, this MS also contains a passage concerning Sir John Mandeville (ff. 3v–9r). In awaiting the critical edition, which should appear as *Analecta Cartusiana* 95 in 1991, the reader may consult: James Hogg, 'Selected Texts on Heaven and Hell from the Carthusian Miscellany, British Library Additional MS. 37049', in *Zeit, Tod und Ewigkeit in der Renaissance Literatur, Analecta Cartusiana* 117:1 (1987), 63–89; James Hogg, 'A Morbid preoccupation with Mortality? The Carthusian London British Library MS Add. 37049', *Analecta Cartusiana* 117:2 (1986), 139–89; James Hogg, 'Unpublished Texts in the Carthusian Northern Middle English Religious Miscellany British Library MS Add. 37049', in James Hogg (ed.), *Essays in Honour of Erwin Stürzl on his Sixtieth Birthday, Salzburger Studien zur Anglistik und Amerikanistik* 10, Vol. 1 (1980), 241–84. Almost all the illustrations in the MS were reproduced in James Hogg, *An Illustrated Yorkshire Carthusian Religious Miscellany: British Library Additional MS 37049, Analecta Cartusiana* 95:3 (1981): *The Illustrations.*

[20] pp.331–32.

[21] (Oxford 1968) p.263.

[22] In a note on p.422 of her *The English Mystery Plays* she recants the opinion expressed in her earlier book: 'I there assumed that the Burial had been written as a meditation and that an adaptor had excised the narrative lines in order to make it suitable for acting. The possibility, however, remains that the corrector was not adapting but restoring the text to its original form. It may be noted that the Resurrection was either written as a play with a rubric specifying liturgical singing or it has been indetectably adapted for performance. The presence of vernacular rubrics in the Burial and of Latin rubrics in the Resurrection suggests a slightly different textual history, though they are surely two parts of a single work. The more plausible theory now seems to me that the works were written for performance in

A close study of the actual text in the manuscript reveals, nevertheless, with virtual certainty that the plays were conceived for presentation, even if they prove to be far more literary than other comparable pieces. An examination of the opening folios will suffice for demonstration. A note precedes the prologue, declaring:

> This play is to be playede on part on gudfriday after-none, & þe other part opon Esterday after the resurrectione. In the morowe, but at begynnynge ar certene lynes which [must] not be saide if it be plaiede, . . .[23]

This is scarcely invalidated by the following statement: 'The prologe of this treyte or meditatione off the buryalle of Criste & mowrnynge therat'. The actual prologue commences:

> A Soule that list to singe of loue
> Of crist that com till vs so lawe
> Rede this treyte, it may hymm moue
> And may hym teche lightly with awe   (f. 140r)

church, but that their meditative character . . . made them highly suitable for devotional reading and that they were subsequently copied for this purpose.'

[23] *The Digby Mysteries*, p.171. In the MS at the bottom of F. 140v the passage actually runs: 'This is a play to be played on part on Gud fri[day] afternone & þe other part opon Esterday after the resurrection In the morowe but [at the] begynnynge ar certen lynes whic[h must] not be said if it be plaied which' – the following phrase was cut off, when the MS was trimmed. Woolf, *The English Mystery Plays*, p.335, remains, however, cautious: 'The long monologues and the lack of dramatic action show that the Burial and Resurrection were either not written for performance, or, if for performance, not in a situation that demanded that the author should have observed the primary obligation of the dramatist, namely to write in such a way as to hold his audience's attention. The plays are thus supremely liturgical in the sense that the devotion of the pious and the solemnity of the liturgical occasion are essential to their capacity to move. Despite the extravagant emotion expressed within the plays, only an audience which brought to them an alert devotional receptiveness could find them moving and unwearisome. It is reasonable therefore to suppose that, when the plays were performed, it was in the church of a convent, and that some of the nuns themselves acted. One would hesitate to assume that the men's parts were also played by women, as Gustave Cohen cautiously suggested in regard to the French Nativity plays in the Chantilly manuscript, which were also acted in a convent. [The reference is to *Nativités et moralités liègeoises* (Brussels 1953) p.135.] It would be sufficient that the nuns should have played the parts of the three Marys and the Virgin, since, in a large convent at least, the priests who would necessarily form part of the community could have taken the four male parts, Joseph, Nicodemus, St John and the risen Christ. The supposition that these plays belong to a convent is likely to remain incapable of either proof or disproof, but it is worth bearing in mind, since it alone seems to make sense of an actual performance of the plays'. Furnivall, *The Digby Mysteries*, p.xii, and Chambers, *The Mediaeval Stage* II, 432, both stress that some parts of the text read more like a narrative than a drama, even though conceding that the content is wholly traditional both as regards matter and form.

This might indeed appear to be the introduction to a meditation, but after the conclusion:

> Fyrst lay vs mynde how gud Iosephe
> On this wise wepite Cristis dethe

Joseph of Arimathea begins to speak, and then the following comment is offered:

> Off the wepinge of the iij maries

The next lines:

> Man harkyn how maudleyn with þe maris ij
> Wepis & wringes thair handis os thay go   (f. 140v)

have been deleted. The stage direction 'thre mariye sais all togider in a voce' appears at the top of f. 141r. Futher deletions follow on f. 141r. First 'saide mawdleyn', then 'This hard holy Iosephe standinge ryght gayn / Saide' and

> The maries in that statione
> Then saide on this fascione

are all cancelled. Near the bottom of the folio 'said Ioseph' is, however, left standing. On f. 142r 'The secund Mary began to saye' and later 'The thrid mary saide' on f. 142v are also deleted, as are 'Than saide Iosephe right peteoslee' and 'Mawdleyn saide' on f. 143v. An identical pattern can be seen up to f. 147v, when the narrative links suddenly disappear completely and are entirely absent in the remaining sections of the texts. The indications of the speaker are henceforth inserted above the actual speech and not in the margin. Rather strangely, the stage directions continue to appear in English up to f. 158r, terminating with 'Secund marye commy in & sais', though thereafter they are always in Latin. Thus on f. 162r the first in Latin appears: 'Tunc exeunt hee tres maria / Petrus intrat flens amare'. It would seem likely that the copyist tried to adapt the dramatic text for meditative purposes, and then either lacked the time to continue methodically and gave up, merely transcribing the rest of the text as it was, or he found the whole process too laborious. That the narrative passages were really supplementary can be demonstrated from ff. 145v–146r:

> To that word mavdlen awnswert thus   [addition]
> Who saw euer a spektacle mor pitevs
> A more lamentable sight & dolorus

> Holy Iosephe awnswerit to this same   [addition]
> What meyn 3e women in goddis name
> Moder to mych sorow 3e mak ye be to blame

267

> I pray yow compleyn not thus hevylee
> Than said mawdleyn a Iosephe free   [addition]
> Nedis must I compleyn & that most bitterlee

As the rhyme scheme is AABCCB at this point in the text, the removal of the additions clearly restores the original regularity. An examination of other insertions of narrative lines into the dramas displays the same technique. It can thus safely be assumed that we are faced with plays.

Woolf maintains:

> Whilst the plays are too long for preformance as part of the liturgy, it seems clear that the place of performance was a church and the focus of them the Easter sepulchre. For the Burial there would be needed in addition a Crucifix (possibly that used for the *Adoratio*), with the figure of Christ detachable, as it was, for instance, for the *Depositio* at Barking.[24] In addition to the Easter sepulchre a subsidiary *locus* is necessary to present the place where Peter, John and Andrew are assembled: in that they have a long stretch of dialogue among themselves, this place is more solidly established than it would be in a *Visitatio*, but a side-chapel or some other fixed point in the church would nevertheless be all that was required: it may be noted that nothing realistic is said or done by the apostles that might jar with a formal and symbolic setting.[25]

This description of the probable staging of the *Burial* play would seem to rule out production in a charterhouse church, as Carthusian churches of the period were divided by a screen into separate choirs for the monks and the lay brethren, and though some Carthusian churches did possess side-chapels, others did not. Further, whilst monks or lay brothers might have taken on the male roles, it is difficult to envisage them in the female parts. There was no Carthusian nunnery in England, thus the possibility that the plays originated in such an institution is excluded. The Carthusian liturgy, with the slow chanting that was customary in the medieval period,[26] would hardly have encouraged priors to welcome a supplementary burden, which these plays would have constituted, particularly on Good Friday and Easter Sunday, days on which the monks are obliged to observe the most rigorous solitude.

The content of the plays is, however, so closely tied into the liturgy that a performance unconnected with liturgical functions would be difficult to envisage. There is virtually no action at all in *Burial*, apart from the entrance and exit of the Blessed Virgin and St John, the beloved apostle. The deposition is depicted in mime. Joseph of Arimathea and the three Marys are static, mourning beneath the

---

[24] Cf. Young, *The Drama of the Medieval Church* I, 164–65.

[25] *The English Mystery Plays*, p.332.

[26] Cf. the evidence of Dom Maurice Chauncy, *Historia Aliquot Martyrum Anglorum Maxime Octodecim Cartusianorum Sub Rege Henrico Octavo* (Montreuil-sur-Mer 1888) p.69, where he states that on occasion 'Vigilia . . . ad minus durabat per quinque horas.'

cross – a more elaborate planctus than is found in any other mystery play – and though Nicodemus enters and is aided by Joseph to take down the body from the cross, the Blessed Virgin again engages in a lengthy lamentation before the body is placed in the sepulchre provided by Joseph of Arimathea.[27]

Resurrection is, of course, an elaboration of the *Quem Quaeritis* trope, which in its simplest form dates back to the eighth century. The three Marys, on their first visit to the sepulchre, are informed by an angel that Christ has indeed risen. Meanwhile, Peter is lamenting his betrayal of Christ. The apostles Andrew and John seek to comfort him, John prophesying the Resurrection. Then follows the *Hortulanus* episode, the encounter of Christ with Mary Magdalene in the garden, and the final proclamation that Christ has risen from the dead. The *Quem Quaeritis* passage is a faithful and pedestrian rendering of the Latin, but the announcement of the Resurrection to Peter and John is communicated in racy, vernacular dialogue, though otherwise both Peter and Mary Magdalene tend to be long-winded and repetitive.[28]

Hardin Craig remarks:

> There is some use of church music within the play,[29] and at the end there is an accumulation of ancient antiphons, responses, and hymns that accompanied the earliest forms of the Resurrection drama. They include *Victimae paschali laudes*, *Dic nobis, Maria, quid vidisti in via*, *Credendum est*

[27] Woolf, *The English Mystery Plays*, pp.332–33, comments: 'The two plays are a curious hybrid in that whilst the action is liturgically determined, the leisurely speeches are reflective and meditative in style, having their origins in some of the famous Latin meditations of the Middle Ages. The first half of the Burial is oddly anticipatory of later classically influenced Passion plays in that the violent action, namely the Crucifixion, does not take place on stage but is minutely described in the speeches of eye-witnesses. Granted his purpose, the author has quite skilfully adapted traditional material: a complaint from the Cross, for instance, has been moulded into a narrative address spoken by Joseph (ll. 274–321). While the meditative sources of the first half of the play are various, there is one clear source for the second half, the *Liber de passione Christi* attributed to St Bernard. From this come ultimately the long complaints of the Virgin, vernacular lyric complaints having served as intermediaries: this static *Pietà* scene forms almost half the work'.

[28] Cf. Woolf, *The English Mystery Plays*, pp.333–34, for a detailed discussion of the portrayal of the two great penitents, St Peter and St Mary Magdalene, with indications of the source material that built up the tradition depicted in this play. She also notes the erotic language, drawn from *The Song of Songs*, which Mary uses in depicting her love for Christ, culminating in her exclamation in the *Hortulanus* episode: 'O myn harte! wher hast thou bee? / Com hom agayn, and leve with mee'. Although this is virtually only a rendering of *Song of Songs* 66, 12: 'Revertere dilecte mi: revertere dilecte votorum meorum', it is immensely more powerful in immediacy.

[29] If this implies the use of musical accompaniment, it excludes all possibility that the plays are of Carthusian origin or were performed in a Carthusian church, as musical instruments were expressly forbidden in the Carthusian Order in 1326.

magis soli Mariae veraci quam Iudaeorum turbae fallaci, Scimus Christum surrexisse, and *Tu nobis, victor rex, miserere.*[30]

The plays are frequently characterised by a rather heavy, even aureate style, with no comic relief whatever; but it was probably this deeply religious atmosphere in *Burial* and *Resurrection* which prompted our anonymous Carthusian to copy these dramas, which furnished such appropriate material for solitary meditation in the cell. The dramas appear to be a late reworking of traditional sources, which had escaped those secular influences which can be detected in much of the drama of the later fifteenth and early sixteenth centuries, but the postulation of Carthusian authorship for the pieces is not only eliminated by the traditions of the Order, but is totally unnecessary to explain their presence in Bodleian E. Museo 160.

---

[30] *English Religious Drama of the Middle Ages*, p.319.

'With what body shall they come?':
Black and White Souls in the English Mystery Plays

Meg Twycross

There is one thing about staging medieval plays: it forces you to confront questions you had never even thought of asking. In the summer of 1987, the Joculatores Lancastrienses took their production of the York *Doomsday* to its original setting in the city's medieval streets. Almost every detail of the set and costumes had presented us with a problem to solve. This about just one of them: 'on the Day of Judgement, what should the Damned wear?'[1]

The official civic *Ordo Paginarum* of the York Mystery plays, written down in 1415, lists among the characters of the Mercers' *Doomsday* play *iiij*[or] *spiritus boni &* *iiijor spiritus maligni*.[2] The York Mercers' Indenture of 1433, a formal checklist of set, properties and costumes in the possession of the Company, and the chief source of our knowledge of how the play was actually staged in the 15th century, lists immediately after the devils' costumes,

> Array for ij euell saules þat ys to say ij Sirkes ij paire hoses ij vesenes
> [masks] & ij Chauelers [wigs] Array for ij gode saules þat is to say ij Sirkes
> ij paire hoses ij vesernes & ij Cheuelers
>
> York, Merchant Adventurers' Company: MS D63[3]

Apart from the drastic reduction in the number of Souls during the intervening 18 years, this part of the Indenture corresponds both to the *Ordo Paginarum* and to

---

I quote the Bible in English from the Authorised Version, noting where it misrepresents the Vulgate version.

[1] This is not a topic which seems to have worried the contributors to the latest book on *Homo, Memento Finis: The Iconography of Just Judgement in Medieval Art and Drama*, papers by David Bevington et al., Early Drama, Art and Music Monograph Series 6 (Kalamazoo 1985).

[2] *Records of Early English Drama: York* (2 vols) edited Alexandra F. Johnston and Margaret Rogerson (Toronto 1979) (hereafter referred to as *REED: York*), p. 24.

[3] *REED: York*, p. 55.

271

the characters (*Prima* and *Secunda Anima Bona*; *Prima* and *Secunda Anima Mala*) as they appear in the script of the play transcribed into the York Register between 1467–75.[4] So far so good.

However, here we hit a snag. The checklists of garments for both types of Soul in the Indenture appear to be identical in number and description. Good Souls and Bad alike have a *Sirk* ('top' – the word 'shirt' is probably misleading, as we shall see in a moment), a pair of tights, a mask, and a wig each. Yet they are listed separately, and were presumably immediately recognisable as Good or Bad to the pageant master ticking each item off. What were their distinguishing features? How would we expect a Good Soul to be visibly differentiated from a Bad Soul?

Nothing in the script is of immediate help. The usual proceeding here is to look round other mystery-play accounts for the same episode to see if we can find any comparative material. The obvious place is Coventry, which has the only other fullish set of accounts for a Doomsday play. Inevitably, with the kind of luck that usually operates in medieval theatre studies, the play itself has not survived. Moreover, the Coventry *Doomsday* play was the responsibility of their Drapers' Guild,[5] whose earliest surviving pageant accounts date from 1534, a century after the York Mercers' Indenture. However, with the usual caveat about the dangers of assuming that what happened in one Cycle and century was automatically what happened in another, we seem to strike lucky.

The Coventry Souls turn up regularly in the accounts between 1537 and 1573. The earliest entry is *for mendyng the white & the blake soules cots viij d* (1537). In the years that follow they are described variously as *Savyd Sowles* and *damnyd Sowles* (1563) or *whyt Soules* and *blacke Soules* (1566). There were three of each. In 1538 there appears to have been a general overhaul of their garments: the *blakke Soules* were bought *v el[n]ys of Canvas for shyrts & hose*, and 9d was paid out *for Coloryng & makyng the same cots*, which suggests that in the world of theatre costume *shyrts* and *cots* were synonymous. Presumably the *Sirkes* of the York Souls, together with the *Sirke Wounded* of Christ, were the same kind of garment. They then paid *for makyng & mendynge of the blakke Soules hose*,[6] while the *white soules* had *a payre of newe hose & mendyng of olde*. The material and the terminology suggest that the Souls (they are always called that, even though strictly speaking they are body and soul reunited) wore closefitting top and tights to represent the naked resurrected body familiar from the iconography of Doomsday. In 1543, the *whytt Sollskotts*

---

4 *The York Plays*, edited Richard Beadle (London 1982), pp. 408–9.

5 *Records of Early English Drama: Coventry*, edited R.W. Ingram (Toronto 1981) (hereafter referred to as *REED: Coventry*), p. 455. The *Coventry* volume is arranged, as with other *REED* volumes, in chronological order. The transcript of the Drapers' accounts from 1537–1560 by Daffern is not, however, dated exactly, and appears as Appendix 2, pp. 455–481. 1537, p. 464; 1563, p. 224; 1566, p. 237; 1538, p. 465; 1543, p. 469; 1555, p. 472; 1557, p. 474–5.

6 In *REED: Coventry*, *for makyng & mendyng of the blakke of Soules Coats hose*. I have deleted the second *of* and *Coats*.

were mended with two skins, which suggests that while the black souls were dressed in canvas, the white souls were dressed in tawed leather, like the Adam and Eve or Christ figures of many accounts.[7] In 1555 the Guild paid *for a dossyne of Skyns for the sollys cottys* (it does not say whether these were Black, White, or both), and *for makyng*. In 1557 they bought 19 ells of canvas *for the sollys cottys*, of which 9 ells were (it seems) dyed yellow and 10 ells black, and which was made up into *cotts*. The White Souls seem to have turned yellow, or perhaps, since the vocabulary of colour is limited, cream or offwhite, to match the skin-colour of tawed leather. Ten years later these were replaced with other yellow canvas *Cotts*. In 1557, too, there is the first appearance of what is to become a regular item, *for blakyng the Sollys fassys*. Presumably these were the Black Souls, and the face blacking was a cheaper but perhaps more expressive way of producing the effect created by the York masks. The Damned are therefore black from top to toe.

The blackness and whiteness of the Souls' costumes are usually taken as purely symbolic, representing their spiritual state and signalling their eventual destination. But it may well be that the citizens of Coventry, and very possibly of York and Chester, saw it more literally than that. In at least three late medieval English works of popular religious instruction, the *Cursor Mundi*, the *Pricke of Conscience*, and *The Mirour of Man's Salvation*, the English translation of the *Speculum Humanae Salvationis*,[8] and it may well be in others, we are told that though we will all be raised body and soul together at the Last Judgement, there will be a visible distinction between the saved and the damned.

The medieval theology of the General Resurrection and the nature of the body in which we shall be raised is far too extended and complex to go into here in detail: a sketch will have to suffice. It was based on 1 Corinthians 15: 35–54, especially verses 51–53:

> Ecce mysterium vobis dico: Omnes quidem resurgemus, sed non omnes immutabimur.
>
> In momento, in ictu oculi, in novissima tuba; canet enim tuba, et mortui resurgent incorrupti, et nos immutabimur.
>
> Oportet enim corruptibile hoc induere incorruptionem, et mortale hoc induere immortalitatem.

---

[7] For a discussion of technical terms for garments and of materials used to make them, especially for closefitting garments, see my 'Apparell comlye' in *Aspects of Early English Drama*, edited by Paula Neuss (Woodbridge 1983) pp. 30–49.

[8] *Cursor Mundi* (4 vols), edited Richard Morris EETS OS 57, 59, 62, 66 (London 1874–7); *The Pricke of Conscience*, edited Richard Morris (Berlin 1863); *The Mirour of Mans Salvacioune*, A Middle English translation of the Speculum Humanae Salvationis, edited Avril Henry (Aldershot 1986). The *Mirour* (MS post 1429) is a fairly close translation of the Latin text (c.1324). The sermon tradition stemming from the *Legenda Aurea* does not deal with the topic in the same way.

At the last trumpet, we shall all be raised, body and soul, immortal and incorruptible.

'But some man will say, How are the dead raised up? and with what body do they come?' (I Cor. 15:35). The nature and appearance of the *corpus spiritale* ('spiritual body': I Cor. 15:44) provided fascinating and fertile material for speculation. The *locus classicus* for the discussion was St Augustine's *City of God* Books 20–22, which formed the basis for later compendia such as the *Sentences* of Peter Lombard[9] (c.1100–1160) and the various works of St Thomas Aquinas (c.1225–1274), especially the *Summa Theologica*, which superseded Lombard as the standard text of Catholic theology. The *Speculum Humanae Salvationis* takes much of its resurrection theology from Aquinas, probably the *Compendium Theologiae*, and it seems that in at least one respect the *Cursor* and the *Pricke of Conscience* do too.[10]

It was agreed, following St Paul's Epistle to the Ephesians 4:13, *Donec occuramus omnes in unitatem fidei, et agnitionis Filii Dei, in virum perfectum, in mensuram aetatis plenitudinis Christi* ('Till we all come in the unity of the faith and of the knowledge of the Son of God, unto a perfect man, unto the measure of the stature of the fullness of Christ') that the dead are to arise *in virum perfectum*,

> id est in virilem perfectionem, quasi scilicet in statu aetatis 30. circiter annorum, in qua Christus habuit annorum & corporis plentitudinem. Igitur vniusquisque mensurae corporis plentitudinem sui recipiet, quam in aetate 30. annorum habuit, etiam si senex obijt, vel quam illa habiturus esset si vsque ad eam peruenisset.

> 'that is, to the perfected state of man, as it were to the condition of around 30 years of age, in which Christ reached the fullness of years and [growth] of body. Therefore each person will receive the fullness of the measure of his body which he had at the age of 30, even if he died an old man, or which he would have had if he had lived to that age.'
>
> Vincent of Beauvais, *Speculum Historiale* cap CXIII[11]

or, as *Cursor Mundi* adapts it,

> All at þat mikel up-rising
> Sal be of eld als þai suld here   *age*
> Haf deied in eild o thritte yere,
> Þat eild þat crist had at his ded   *death* 22821

---

[9] *Petri Lombardi Libri IV Sententiarum* (2 vols), edited by the Franciscans of the College of S. Bonaventura (Quarracchi 1916).

[10] See *Mirour* p. 254, notes to 4331ff and 4345–46.

[11] Vincent of Beauvais, *Speculum Historiale* (Graz 1965: facsimile of 1624 Douai edition by Balthazar Bellerus) p. 1326.

and Resurrection. Strictly speaking, as *The Pricke of Conscience* points out,[12] this should be 32 years and 3 months:

> . . . sal alle ryse in þe same eld þan
> Þat God had fully here als man,
> Namly, whan he uprayse thurgh myght
> Fra dede, als says Saynt Austyn ryght;
> Þan was he of threty yhere elde and twa,
> And of thre monethes þar-with alswa   4988

Even infants and aborted children will be raised *in virum perfectum*.

The exact wording of Ephesians 4:13 gave rise to a host of further problems, some provoked by what St Augustine described as frivolous queries from the pagans, some by serious over–literalness from the believers. Were we all to be raised the same size as Christ (in which case, those taller than him would suffer an unfair diminution in substance?) Since St Paul says *in virum perfectum*, were women to be resurrected as men? No: 'Man' subsumes 'woman', and since there will be no marrying or giving in marriage, women will not provoke inconveniently lustful thoughts among the resurrected: *Non enim libido ibi erit, quae confusionis est causa*. Then since there will be no need of them, shall we be resurrected with genitalia, or, since there is no eating and drinking, with intestines? Yes, we will have them, otherwise a large part of our bodies would be lacking, but we shall not use them as they are used on earth.[13]

A good many of these queries are referred eventually to what seems at first to be purely aesthetic decorum, but which is more serious than that: the perfection of the *corpus spiritale* reflects the perfection of beatitude. This explains the insistence on one feature of the resurrected body in which they seem disproportionately interested. All congenital deformities and accidental mutilations or scars will be removed. *Cursor Mundi* reminds us quite how emotionally, rather than intellectually, satisfying this must have been to a society where congenital abnormalities

---

[12] *The Pricke of Conscience*, edited Richard Morris (Berlin 1863), following Peter Lombard *Sententiae* lib. iv dist.xliv, cap 1: *triginta enim duorum annorum et trium mensium aetas erat Christi, in qua mortuus est et resurrexit* (p. 1000). See J.A. Burrow, *The Ages of Man* (Oxford 1986) pp. 104 and 141–3 for a further development on this theme.

[13] St Augustine of Hippo, *Sancti Aurelii Augustini De Civitate Dei Libri XI–XXII*, edited B. Dombart & A. Kalb, *Corpus Christianorum Series Latina* vol. 48 (Turnholt 1955) (hereafter referred to as *DCD*). Translation from the 1610 version by John Healey *The City of God* (2 vols), edited R.V.G. Tasker (London 1945) 22, caps 12–18. St Thomas Aquinas, *Summa Theologica* in *Sancti Thomae Aquinatis Doctoris Angelici Opera Omnia* ed. iussu impensaque Leo III P.M. (Rome 1882 ff.) vol. 12 (1906) (hereafter referred to as *ST*): translation from *The 'Summa Theologica' of St. Thomas Aquinas* (22 vols) translated by the Fathers of the English Dominican Province (London 1920–22) Volume 20: Third Part (Supplement) QQ.LXIX–LXXXVI III Q.80.

could not be operated on, crippled beggars were commonplace, and the approach of age (past the perfection of 30) meant shrivelled toothlessness:

> And if þat ani her liuand
> Was wemed, or on fot or on hand,
> Or hefd, or bak, or brest, on side,
> Als we se chances oft bitide,
> On muth or nese, or elles-quar.
> Or bo[c]e apon his bodi bar,   (MS *bote*) *botch*
> Cripel, croked, or turned o baft,
> Or limes ma gain kindli craft,
> Thoru ma or less o lim haf last,
> At þis vprising þat sal be [r]ast.   (MS *last*)
> All þaa þat godd has chosin til his
> For to be broght into his blis,
> Quat-sum þai in þis luf has bene,
> It sal na wem o þam be sene,
> Ne naking thing bot all fair-hede.   22837

Even this provoked a further worry: if all our losses were to be restored to us, does this imply that we will be burdened with all the hair and nails that we have trimmed and pared during the course of our lives, since Christ had said, 'even the very hairs of your head are all numbered' (Luke 12:7)? No, they will be included in our substance, as we are not to suffer diminution, but God will redistribute them, like a potter remoulding a misthrown pot, or a sculptor melting down and recasting a defective statue.[14]

> Et si quid enormiter abundauerit in parte aliqua, per totum spargetur, ita, quod ibi nihil indecorum erit, sed omnia decentia . . . sicut statua, quando iterum funditur, quod prius erat de naso, fit de pede, vel econuerso . . .

> 'And if anything anywhere should be over-excessive, it will be dissipated throughout the whole, so that there will be nothing unbalanced, but everything in seemly proportion . . . like a statue, when it is melted and recast, what was in the nose the first time round ends up in the foot, or vice versa . . .'
>
> Vincent of Beauvais, *Speculum Historiale* cap. cxiii[15]

To our modern ears this may at first sound like purely cosmetic surgery, especially when Augustine remarks wistfully *per hoc non est macris pinguibusque metuendum, ne ibi etiam tales sint, quales si possent nec hic esse uoluissent* ('wherefore the fat or the lean need never fear to be such hereafter as, if they could choose, they would not be now'), but it is making a serious point about the decorum of proper proportions

---

14 *DCD* 22, cap. 19.
15 *Speculum Historiale* cap. 113, p. 1326.

(*congruentia*): *quae praua sunt corrigentur, et quod minus est quam decet, unde Creator nouit, inde supplebitur, et quod plus est quam decet, materiae seruata integritate detrahe-tur*[16] ('whatever is deformed will be corrected, and what is less than seemly will be made up by the Creator from his resources, and what is more than is seemly will be taken away, but preserving the integrity of its material').

Moreover, the spiritual body will have a lustre (*claritas*) like that, though not the same in nature as that of the heavenly bodies:[17] for, as Augustine quotes,[18] *Tunc justi fulgebunt sicut sol in regno Patris eorum* 'The just shall shine like the sun in the kingdom of their Father' (Mathew 13:43).

> And þus sal he do namly, to al þa
> þat sal be save and til blis ga.
> For þair bodys sal be semely and bright
> With avenand lymes til alle mennes sight.
>
> *Pricke of Conscience* 5020

However, according to the *Cursor Mundi*, there will be a striking difference between the luminous bodies of the just and the bodies into which the unjust will be resurrected:

> þaas oþer sal ha fairhed nan,
> For al welth sal þam be wan   22846

The text *Et procedent qui bona fecerunt, in resurrectionem vitae; qui vero mala egerunt, in resurrectionem judicii* ('They that have done good, unto the resurrection of life; but they that have done evil, unto the resurrection of damnation' John 5:29) suggested that there might be two different *modes* of resurrection as well as two different fates for the resurrected.[19] The plays take over this idea, probably because it emphasises their point: judgement depends on what you have done in this life (Matthew 25:31–46, the structural basis of all the *Doomsday* plays). The General Judgement is after all the sentence rather than the actual process of trial and verdict, which will be decided at each man's Particular Judgement. When the dead rise, their fates are already decided, and the plays make this visible.

But how is it to be made visible? As Aquinas argues, the Damned must, like the saved, be immortal and incorruptible (otherwise their pains would some day have an end, if only because their spiritual bodies would wear out). Therefore, like the Saved, they too must arise with their physical deformities removed:

---

[16] DCD 22 cap. 19, pp. 838–9.
[17] St Thomas Aquinas, *Summa Contra Gentiles Libri Quatuor*, issued Pope Leo III (Rome 1894), 4 cap. 86, pp. 701–2.
[18] DCD 22 cap. 19.
[19] DCD 20 cap. 6, pp. 707–8.

Unde Apostolus dicit (1. Cor. XV. 52): *Mortui resurgent incorrupti*; quod manifestum est de omnibus debere intellegi, tam bonis, quam malis, ex his quae praecedunt et sequuntur in littera.

'Whence the Apostle (Paul) says (1 Cor.15:52) "The dead shall be raised incorrupt": which it is clear is to be understood as referring to everyone, evil as well as good, from what precedes and follows in the text.'

Contra Gentiles 4: 89 p. 704.

It was of course assumed, however, that the spiritual bodies of the damned would not acquire the special characteristics of the blessed, specified by Aquinas as *subtilitas, agilitas, claritas,* and *impassibilitas:*[20]

> Claritee take for the first, the secound impassibilitee,
> Sutyltee for the thredde, the feerthe agilitee   *Mirour* 4333–4

The soul, acting as form, creates these in the bodies of the blessed:

Quamvis autem, merito Christi, defectus naturae in resurrectione tollatur ab omnibus communiter tam bonis, quam malis, remanebit tamen differentia inter bonos et malos quantum ad ea quae personaliter utrisque conveniunt. Est autem de ratione naturae quod anima humana sit corporis forma, ipsum vivicans, et in esse conservans; sed ex personalibus actibus meretur anima in gloriam divinae visionis elevari, vel ab ordine hujusmodi gloriae propter culpam excludi.

'Although, however, by the merit of Christ, the shortcomings of nature will be taken away from everyone equally, evil as well as good, nevertheless there will remain some differences between the good and the evil, as regards the things which befit each of them individually. For it is in the course of nature that the human soul is the Form [in the Platonic sense] of the body, giving life to it, and preserving it in its being: but through individual acts, the soul either deserves to be raised to the glory of the sight of God, or to be shut out from the rank of this type of glory on account of sin.'

Contra Gentiles 4: 86 p. 701

The wicked, cut off from the Beatific Vision by the misuse of their own soul, will lack the qualities that arise from participation in that Vision. Above all, they will lack *claritas:*

Erunt etiam eorum corpora opaca, et tenebrosa, sicut et eorum animae a lumine divinae cognitionis erunt alienae; et hoc est quod Apostolus dicit (1 Corinth. XV 51), quod *omnes resurgemus, sed non omnes immutabimur:*

---

[20] St Thomas Aquinas, *Compendium of Theology* translated Cyril Vollert (St Louis MO 1947), cap. 168: he quotes 1 Cor. 15:42–44 as source of these four properties.

soli enim boni immutabuntur ad gloriam; malorum vero corpora absque gloria resurgent.

'For their bodies will be opaque, and shadowed, as also their souls will be foreign to the light of divine knowledge; and this is what the Apostle says (1 Cor. 15:51), that "we shall all be raised, but we shall not all be changed": for only the good will be changed into glory: the bodies of the evil will certainly arise without glory.'[21]

Contra Gentiles 4: 89 p.704

This by itself might be enough to create the idea of White and Black Souls. The whiteness is a way of showing the *claritas* of the blessed (was the yellow canvas perhaps an attempt to match this *claritas* to the superior gilded radiance of the body of Christ?): the blackness, *opaca et tenebrosa*, is an absence of light rather than a positive quality.[22]

They will also lack *agilitas*:

Nec ipsa corpora erunt agilia, quasi sine difficultate animae obedientia; sed magis erunt ponderosa, et gravia, et quodammodo animae importabilia . . .

'Nor will their bodies be agile, as obeying the soul without difficulty: but rather they will be weighed down, and heavy, and to a certain extent unresponsive to the soul . . . '

Contra Gentiles 4:89 p.704

a feature which some commentators, notably Bede, use to explain how, at the Last Judgement, the wicked will be weighed down by their sins while the good will rise to meet their Saviour in the air,[23] thus solving the potential problem of overcrowding in the valley of Jehosaphat, by stacking the resurrected like aircraft.

By the time Aquinas comes to write the *Compendium*, he has subtly altered the tone of his description, apparently to bring it into line with the more punitive simplicity of popular eschatology:

[21] Peter Lombard *Collectanea* (*PL* 191, 1686), quoting Hrabanus Maurus (*PL* 112, 151), says also *Infidelitas enim non potest claram resurrectionem habere, quia sicut carbo cinere suo coopertus obcaecatur, ita et perfidia sua erroris tenebris circumdati luce carebunt*. ('For the infidel cannot have a luminous resurrection, because he is blinded like coal covered with its own ash, and in the same way they will lack light, surrounded by the shadows of error in their lack of faith.')
[22] Anglo-Saxon Doomsday poetry refers to the Damned as 'dark': *swearte synwyrcend* (*Christ III* line 1104) in contrast to the radiance of Christ and the blessed. See Graham Caie *The Judgement Day Theme in Old English Poetry* (Publications of the Department of English, University of Copenhagen 2, 1976) pp. 156, 180–1, 219–220. Anglo-Saxon poetry is so allusive that it is difficult to build any very firm argument for the survival of the motif from these poems.
[23] Bede, *De Tempora Ratione* cap. 70 'De Die Judicii' (*PL* 90, 575–6).

As we said above, in speaking of the saints, the beatitude of the soul will in some manner flow over to the body. In the same way the suffering of lost souls will flow over into their bodies . . . the bodies of the damned will be complete in their kind, [but] they will not have those qualities that go with the glory of the blessed. That is, they will not be subtle and impassible; instead, they will remain in their grossness and capacity for suffering, and, indeed, these defects will be heightened in them. Nor will they be agile, but will be so sluggish as scarcely to be manoeuvrable by the soul. Lastly, they will not be radiant but will be ugly in their swarthiness, so that the blackness of the soul may be mirrored in the body, as is intimated in Isaias 13:8: 'Their countenances shall be as faces burnt.'[24]

Cap. 176 (page 192)

(*Facies combustae vultus eorum*, translated in the AV as 'their faces shall be as flames'.) Here at last we have a conspicuously Black Soul.

This visible blackness has a popular feel to it. (There should be no need to state that this has nothing at all to do with racial stereotypes.) To view the state of the Damned in purely negative terms may be satisfying philosophically, but at least as far back as Augustine popular notions of poetic justice demanded that their humiliation should be visible, even vindictive. Why, for example, should their bodily deformities be removed? Peter Lombard, asking the question, points out that Augustine (*Enchiridion*) sits on the fence, saying

Utrum vero ipsi [reprobi] cum vitiis et deformitatibus suorum corporum resurgant, quaecumque in eis gestarunt, in requirendo laborare quid opus est? Non enim fatigare nos debet incerta eorum habitudo vel pulchritudo, quorum erit certa et sempiterna damnatio.[25]

'What is the point of researching to find out whether they (the Damned) will arise with blemishes and deformities in their bodies? For we ought not to exhaust ourselves on speculations about the appearance or comeliness of those we know for certain to be damned eternally.'

Aquinas deals with the question several times: his fullest exposition is in the *Summa Theologiae*. He is not in agreement with the idea that the Damned should arise with all their earthly imperfections upon them, but we learn of its details because he quotes them in order to refute them. The argument is that bodily deformity is a punishment for sin (presumably either one's own or the sins of one's fathers – to us a repellent concept), and therefore:

---

[24] This is a change from the attempt to define two different types of passibility. Hrabanus Maurus argued the same using the concept of two types of corruptibility: *illi, qui ad judicium resurrecturi sunt, non commutabuntur in illam corruptelam quae nec doloris corruptionem pati potest, illa namque fidelium est atque sanctorum: isti vero perpetua corruptione cruciabuntur, quia ignis eorum non exstinguetur, et vermis eorum non morietur* (Marc. IX).

[25] Peter Lombard, *Sententiae* 4 dis.44 cap. 4 (p. 1002). Bonaventura's *Commentary on the Sentences* apparently makes more of this: Aquinas refutes him in *ST III* Q.86.

Illud . . . quod in poenam peccati inductum est, desinere non debet. Sed membrorum defectus qui accidunt per mutilationem, in poena peccati inducti sunt; et similiter etiam omnes deformitates corporales. Ergo a damnatis, qui peccatorum remissionem non sunt consecuti, in resurrectione non removebuntur.

'. . . that which was appointed as a punishment for sin should not cease except the sin be forgiven. Now the lack of limbs that result from mutilation, as well as other bodily deformities, are appointed as punishments for sin. Therefore these deformities will not be taken away from the damned, seeing that they will not have received the forgiveness of their sins.'

III: Supplement Q.86 art.1, page 200 (trans. page 253)

Besides this, if the deformities of the just are to be removed in order to take away anything that would mar their ultimate perfection, so the damned should not be deprived of anything that might contribute to their miseries; and likewise, if the damned are not to have their *tarditas* (the opposite of the *agilitas* of the saved) removed, then neither should their deformities be removed.

In refutation, Aquinas reiterates 1 Corinthians 15:52 as evidence that all the dead shall be raised whole and incorrupt. However, there can be a further distinction. As to congenital defects (as opposed to accidental mutilations), or those which result from disease rather than accident,

Augustinus indeterminatum et sub dubio relinquit in *Enchiridio*, ut in littera Magister dicit. Sed apud doctores modernos est duplex super hoc opinio. Quidam enim dicunt quod huiusmodi deformitates et defectus in corporibus damnatorum remanebunt: considerantes eorum damnationem, qua ad summam miseriam deputantur, cui nihil incommoditas subtrahi debet.

'Augustine left this undecided and doubtful (*Enchiridion. xcii*) as the Master (Peter Lombard) remarks. Among modern masters, however, there are two opinions on this point. For some say that such-like deformities and defects will remain in the bodies of the damned, because they consider that those who are damned are sentenced to utmost unhappiness wherefrom no affliction shall be rebated.'

This, however, he says is unreasonable: *si aliquis cum defectibus vel deformitatibus resurget, hoc erit ei in poenam* ('if a person rise again with such defects and deformities, this will be for his punishment.') It would be unfair for a heavily deformed sinner to be more heavily loaded with punishment than an undeformed sinner with much graver sins. Therefore God will wipe the slate clean: and in any case, the type of punishment they will suffer in the next world will be far more severe than the kind suffered in this world. These minor earthly punishments are irrelevant.

Despite Aquinas' opposition, however, the popular tradition continued to insist on visible retribution, and even to increase it. *The Pricke of Conscience* tells how the saved will be restored whole,

> Bot God sal amend on nane wise
> Defautes of þe lyms of synful bodys,
> For þair bodys sal alle unsemely be
> And foul, and ugly, opon to se. 5024

The author here starts from the premise that the damned will continue to bear their existing defects, but he somehow manages to imply that *all* the damned will be affected in this way (or, taking *alle* as an adverb, that they will be affected *completely*, which produces the same end result): 'þair bodys sal *alle* unsemely be / And foul, and ugly, opon to se'. The *Mirour of Mans Saluacioune* draws on Aquinas (notably the *Compendium*) at this point, but interprets 'they will remain in their grossness and capacity for suffering, and indeed, these defects will be heightened in them' by adopting the arguments which Aquinas quoted in order to refute:

> At Domesday, bodyes and sawles shal be revnit certayne,
> And euermore both togidere haf joye or suffre payne.
> The wikked mens bodies shall rise vnshaply and passible,
> Bot the gude mens fulle faire without eend impassible.
> A dampnid bodie shalle rise in swilk deformitee
> Þat infinite horrour bes it the awen fote or hande to see;
> And the more þat thaire synne here haf bene abhomynable
> So mykel thaire bodyes than shalle be more defourmable.
> 4318[26]

The iconography of Doomsday never, to my knowledge, shows this distinction in this way. The saved and the damned are usually identical in bodily perfection: what distinguishes them are the gestures of despair and the rictus of terror on the faces of the damned as they are dragged or pitchforked off into Hellmouth. The only even slightly related illustration that I know is from the naive, eccentric but delightful Carthusian manuscript BL Add. MS 37049.[27]

> Here folowes a vysion of saules þat ware dampned *and* put to helle *after* þer Jugement *and* how þai ar deformed *and* myschapyn Sum of þaim was horned as bolles. *and* þai be betokyn prowd men And tothed as bares. *and* þai signyfie manslaers *and* morderers *in* wil or *in* dede. *and* ireful. And *sum* semed as þaire eene hang opon þaire chekys þe whilk ar þai þat ar inuyos lokyng apon oþer mens prosperite *and* hatyng þaire welfare *and* weleple-

---

[26] This seems to be deduced from the generally held belief in degrees of blessedness, extrapolated from 1 Cor. 15:41: *Stella enim a stella differt in claritate.*

[27] The folios with illustrations are edited by James Hogg, *An Illustrated Yorkshire Carthusian Religious Miscellany*, vol. 3 (Institut für Anglistik und Amerikanistik, Universität Salzburg, 1981).

syd of þaire ylle fare. Sum has lang hokyd nayles lyke lyons þe whilk ar
fals couetos men *and* extorciouners. Sum had bolned belys þat ar fowl
glotons *and* lyfes al in lust of þaire belys. Sum had þaire rygges al rotyn
and þaire bakkes. þat ar lycheros caytyfes þe whilk had al þair delyte *in*
lustynes of lychery. Sum had fete al to gnawyn and bun (bent) as þai wer
brokyn *and* bolned leggys. þat ar slewthly caytyfs þat wil not labour *in*
gode werkis for þe hele of þair saules. Þie[s] caytyfes ledes sathanas to
hell.   fol 74ʳ

The illustration shows a rather sprightly row of horrors looking, thanks to the
ineptitude of the artist, rather cheerful than grisly. Though the vision is organised
on the pattern of the Seven Deadly Sins, the theme is essentially the same as that
of the *Pricke* and the *Mirour*, and the premise is the same as Aquinas': that these
deformities are all the direct result of sin, a spiritual deformation made visible.

The Chester *Doomsday* play, however, suggests that there is yet another theme
underlying these hideous visions. Rex Salvatus says:

> My fowle bodye through synne blent,
> that rotten was, and all to-rent
> through thy might, lord omnipotent,
> raysed and whole yt ys.   *Chester Cycle*[28] Play 24: 125–128

Ostensibly the Saved King is pointing out how his body has been restored to him
whole and incorruptible: but what comes over is that it is not just incorruptible
but no longer corrupt, a restored corpse. In the grave it was a *fowle bodye . . .
rotten, and al to-rent*: God has now made it whole and clean. The Mercator
Damnatus, however, has been eternally reunited with his decaying, noisesome
body:

> Alas, alas, nowe woe ys mee!
> My fowle bodys, that rotten hath be,
> and soule together nowe I see.
> All stynketh, full of synne.   328

The social stratification of the Chester Saved and Damned Souls, as has often
been pointed out, echoes that of the Dance of Death,[29] or of the versions of the
Three Living and the Three Dead which are arranged to represent the Three
Estates. The Chester Damned, like Lazarus in the Towneley Play, speak as reani-
mated corpses. Mills and Lumiansky are puzzled, in the context of Augustine, at
the words of the Regina Damnata:

---

[28] *The Chester Mystery Cycle*, edited R.M. Lumiansky and David Mills (2 vols) EETS SS 3
& 9 (London 1974 & 1986) (hereafter referred to as *Chester Cycle*).
[29] Rosemary Woolf, *The English Mystery Plays* (London 1972), p. 295. She suggests that the
different ranks are recognisable by their costume: in note 96 (p. 413) she adds that this
might be just an appropriate headdress.

I, that soe seemelye was in sight,
where ys my blee that [was] so bright?   MS ys
Where ys baron, where ys knight
for mee to alledge the lawe?

Where in world ys any wight
that for my fayrenes nowe wyll fight,
And from this death I am to dight
That darre me heathen drawe?   hence 292

They comment 'the sense seems to be that the lady has lost her beauty'.[30] But the Queen's desolate lament for lost beauty belongs to a *memento mori* tradition:[31] it echoes the words of the corpse of the anonymous lady of 'The Debate between the Body and Worms', also in BL. MS Add 37049:

Now where be 3e knyghtes cum forth in place
And 3e worschipful sqwyers both hye and base
Þat sumtyme to me offerd 3our seruyse
Dayes of 3our lyfes of hertes frawnchyse   MS frawnchsyse
Saying promyttyng 3our lyfe to myne a vyse
To do me seruys cum and defende nowe me
ffro þies gret horribil wormes vgly to se
here gnawyng my flesche þus with gret cruelte
Deuowryng and etyng now as 3e may se
þat sumtyme 3e lufed so innterly
Now socour and defende here my body.   fol 33ᵛ

The worms reply that they have made short shrift of Julius Caesar, Alexander, Hector, Charlemagne, and the other Worthies, and are quite willing to take on any of her champions *à l'outrance*. Eventually they and the Body are reconciled, promising to

kys and dwell to gedyr euermore
To þat god wil þat I sal agayn vpryse
At þe day of dome before þe hye justyse
With þe body glorified to be   fol 32ʳ

It looks as if a theatrical tradition born more of a desire for an effective visual lesson than of strict theology may have crept into the mystery plays. The Towneley Lazarus, himself presented as a resurrected corpse, a *memento mori*, makes the point

Amende the, man, Whils thou may,
Let neuer no myrthe fordo thi mynde;

30 *Chester Cycle*, vol.2 p. 363.
31 See Rosemary Woolf, *English Religious Lyric in the Middle Ages* (Oxford 1968) chapter IX 'Lyrics on Death', 309–355.

> Thynke thou on the dredefull day
>> When god shall deme all mankynde . . . 117
> Amende the, man, whils thou art here,
>> Agane thou go an othere gate;
> When thou art dede and laide on bere,
>> Wyt thou well thou bees too late . . . Play 31[32] 185

This is as far as we can go in the way of proof. We do not *know* that the York Good and Bad Souls were white and black. The chain of 'evidence' illustrates the problems of this kind of research. We do not know whether the Chester *Salvati* and *Damnati* were described as White Souls and Black Souls in the accounts, because we have no accounts. We do not know what the Coventry Souls said about themselves, because we have lost the script. The N. Town Souls add a further complication: God appears to work the transformation on the bodies of the Saved in sight of the audience:

> All þo ffowle wyrmys ffrom ʒow ffalle
> With my ryght hand I blysse ʒow here
> my blyssynge burnyschith ʒow as bryght as berall
> As crystall clene it clensyth ʒow clere
> All ffylth ffrom ʒow ffade. Play 42 line 48[33]

which suggests that all the Dead were corpses, but that the Saved shed their costumes like a cocoon. All we know of the Damned from the script is that *on here fforehed*

> . . . þer is wretyn with letteris blake
> Opynly all here synne. 78

and the end of the play, which might have told us more, is missing. Conversely, the beginning of the Towneley *Doomsday* play with the opening speeches of the Good Souls is missing: though that part of the play is merely an inflated version of York.

The York Good and Bad Souls do not descant on their physical states in detail. It is only when their words are reinforced by their *array* that their lines take on a different emphasis. The First Good Soul rises with

> Loued be þou lorde, þat is so schene,
>> Þat on þis manere made vs to rise,
> Body and sawle togedir, *clene*,
>> To come before þe high justise. 100

[32] *The Towneley Plays*, edited George England EETS ES 71 (London 1897)
[33] *Ludus Coventriae or The Plaie called Corpus Christi*, edited K.S. Bloch EETS ES 120 (London 1922).

Many thanks to Dr Avril Henry for chasing up her references for me.

Even the phrase *þat is so schene* is not a casual line-filler, but refers to the infinite *claritas* of Christ. The Bad Souls seem to know from the moment of their resurrection that they are damned, but say nothing about their physical state except

> Oure wikkid werkis may we not hide,
> But on oure bakkis vs muste þem bere   155

Either they are carrying a burden of sin like a haversack, or their sins are written on rolls pinned to their backs. But we decided to dress them as black corpse-souls, and the costuming added another dimension of horror to their words. As the *Mirour* says,

> A dampnid bodie shalle rise in swilk deformite
> þat infinite horrour bes it the awen fote or hande to see   4216

Our Second Bad Soul, dressed in the blackened rags of flesh, burrowed by snakes and spiders, and wearing a mask with an eye sliding down her cheek, could draw from the depths of horror with the catalogue of

> Þe dedis þat vs schall dame bedene . . .
> Þat fote has gone or hande has wroght,
> That mouthe hath spoken or ey has sene.   166

A footnote. As the light faded, the Damned became shadows outlined against the glow of hell-mouth. But the Good Souls, dressed from top to toe in off-white, and with masked faces uncannily impassive (for which read impassible), were strangely luminous in the gathering dusk.

TABULA GRATULATORIA

Acquisitions Section, The Library, University of Lancaster, Lancaster, LA1 4YT

Valerie Adams, Dept. of English, University College London, Gower Street, London, WC1E 6BT

Rosamund Allen, English Dept., Queen Mary College, London, E1 4NS

W.R.J. Barron, Dept. of English, The University, Manchester, M13 9PL

Janet M. Bately, King's College, Strand, London, WC2R 2LS

N.F. Blake, Dept. of English Language, Sheffield, S10 2TN

Martin Blinkhorn, Dept. of History, University of Lancaster, Lancaster, LA1 4YT

Julia Boffey, Queen Mary College, University of London, Mile End Road, London, E1 4NS

Martine Braekman, Dept. of English, University of Lancaster, Lancaster, LA1 4YT

R.W. Burchfield, St Peter's College, Oxford, OX1 2DL

John Burrow, English Dept., Bristol University

Tom Burton, English Dept., University of Adelaide, South Australia

Jill Burton, English Dept., University of Adelaide, South Australia

Graham Caie, The Medieval Centre, Copenhagen University, Njalsgade 90, 2300 Copenhagen 5, Denmark

David Carroll, Dept. of English, University of Lancaster, Lancaster, LA1 4YT

James Coakley, Dept. of Religious Studies, University of Lancaster, Lancaster, LA1 4YT

Sarah Coakley, Dept. of Religious Studies, University of Lancaster, Lancaster, LA1 4YT

Janet Cowen, English Dept., King's College London, Strand, London, WC2 4LS

J.E. Cross, Dept. of English Language and Literature, The University of Liverpool, PO Box 147, Liverpool, L69 3BX

Marilyn Deegan, Dept. of English Language & Literature, University of Manchester, M13 9PL

Peter Dixon, English Dept., Westfield College, London, NW3 7ST

Rosemary Dorward, Tweedside, The Croft, St Boswell's, Melrose, Roxburghshire, TD6 0AE

A.I. Doyle, University College, The Castle, Durham, DH1 1HY

Richard Dutton, Dept. of English, University of Lancaster, LA1 4YT

Alison Easton, Dept. of English, University of Lancaster, Lancaster, LA1 4YT

Valerie Edden, Dept. of English, University of Birmingham, B15 2TT

Ralph W.V. Elliott, Humanities Research Centre, Australian National University, GPO Box 4, Canberra A.C.T. 2601, Australia

Walter Fairbairn, Dept. of Physics, University of Lancaster, Lancaster, LA1 4YT

Norman Fairclough, Dept. of Linguistics, University of Lancaster, Lancaster, LA1 4YT

Alan J. Fletcher, Dept. of English, University College, Belfield, Dublin 4

A.J. Gilbert, English Dept., University of Lancaster, Lancaster, LA1 4YT

Pamela Gradon, St Hugh's College, Oxford, OX2 6LE

Harry Hanham, Vice Chancellor, University of Lancaster, Lancaster, LA1 4YT

Keith Hanley, Dept. of English, University of Lancaster, Lancaster LA1 4YT

Joyce Hill, School of English, University of Leeds, Leeds, LS2 9JT

Victoria Hobson, Linacre College, Oxford, OX1 3JA

Phyllis Hodgson, 25, Barton Croft, Barton on Sea, New Milton, Hants, BH25 7BT

Richard Hogg, Dept. of English Language & Literature, Manchester University, Oxford Road, Manchester, M13 9PL

Sue Ellen Holbrook, Dept. of English, Southern Connecticut State University, New Haven, CT 16575, USA

D.M. Horgan, St Catherine's College, Oxford, OX1 3UJ

A.D. Horgan, St Catherine's College, Oxford, OX1 3UJ

Anne Hudson, Lady Margaret Hall, Oxford, OX2 6QA

Institute for Latin and Greek Medieval Philology, Medieval Centre, Copenhagen University, Njalsgade 90, 2300 Copenhagen 5, Denmark

Nicholas Jacobs, Jesus College, Oxford, OX1 3DW

Harold Jenkins, 22, North Crescent, Finchley, London, N3 3LL

Jesus College Library, Jesus College, Oxford OX1 3DW

George Kane, 15 Thanet Street, London, WC1

King's College Library, Strand, London, WC2R 2LS

Stephen Knight, Dept. of English, University of Melbourne, Parkville, Victoria 3052, Australia

Catherine La Farge, Birkbeck College, London University

C.A. Ladd, Elmhurst, Malt Hall, Egham, Surrey, TW20 9PB

Geoffrey Leech, Dept. of Linguistics, University of Lancaster, Lancaster, LA1 4YT

John McNeal Dodgson, English Dept., University College, London, Gower Street, London, WC1E 6BT

William Marx, English Dept., St David's University College, Lampeter, Dyfed, Wales, SA48 7ED

Stephen Medcalf, Arts Building, University of Sussex, Falmer, Brighton, Sussex, BN1 9QN

A.D. Mills, Dept. of English Language and Literature, University of Liverpool, PO Box 147, Liverpool, L69 3BX

A.J. Minnis, Dept. of English, York University

Gerald Morgan, School of English, Trinity College, Dublin 2

Margery Morgan, Theatre Studies Dept., University of Lancaster, Lancaster, LA1 4YT

John Mowat, Dept. of English, University of Lancaster, Lancaster, LA1 4YT

Marijane Osborn, University of California at Davis, Dept. of English, Davis, California 95616, USA

Gillian Overing, Wake Forest University, Winston-Salem, North Carolina 27109, USA

Oliver Pickering, Brotherton Library, The University of Leeds, Leeds, LS2 9JT

Malcolm Quainton, Modern Languages Dept., University of Lancaster, Lancaster, LA1 4YT

Jeffrey Richards, Dept. of History, University of Lancaster, Lancaster, LA1 4YT

Alan Robinson, Dept. of English, University of Lancaster, Lancaster, LA1 4YT

Salford University Library, Salford, M5 4WT

Carl Schmidt, Balliol College, Oxford, OX1 3BJ

Raman Selden, English Dept., University of Lancaster, Lancaster, LA1 4YT

M.H. Short, Linguistics Dept., University of Lancaster, Lancaster, LA1 4YT

St Edmund Hall Library, St Edmund Hall, Oxford OX1 4AR

St Martin's College Library, St Martin's College, Bowerham Road, Lancaster, LA1 3JD

Eric Stanley, Pembroke College, Oxford, OX1 1DW

Myra Stokes, English Dept., 3/5 Woodland Drive, University of Bristol, Bristol, BS8 1TB

Keith Stringer, Dept. of History, University of Lancaster, Lancaster, LA1 4YT

Keith Sturgess, Dept. of Theatre Studies, University of Lancaster, Lancaster, LA1 4YT

Patricia Thomson, 6/15 Guilford St, London, WC1N 1DX

Professer René Tixier, Université des Sciences Sociales, Toulouse I, France

J.A. Tuck, Dept. of History, Bristol University, 13 Woodland Drive, Bristol, BS8 1TB

Joan Walmsley, Rhedyn, Cilmery, Builth Wells, Powys, Wales, LD2 3LH

Ward Library, Peterhouse, Cambridge, CB2 1RD

Michael Wheeler, Dept. of English, University of Lancaster, Lancaster, LA1 4YT

Colin Wilcockson, Pembroke College, Cambridge

Franz Wöhrer, English Dept., University of Vienna, Universitätsstrasse 7/4 Stock, A-1010 Wien, Austria

Zara Zaddy, Centre for Medieval Studies, University of Lancaster, Lancaster, LA1 4YT